UNCLE
from
ANOTHER WORLD
IV

ndoshindeiru

A Man Who Survived

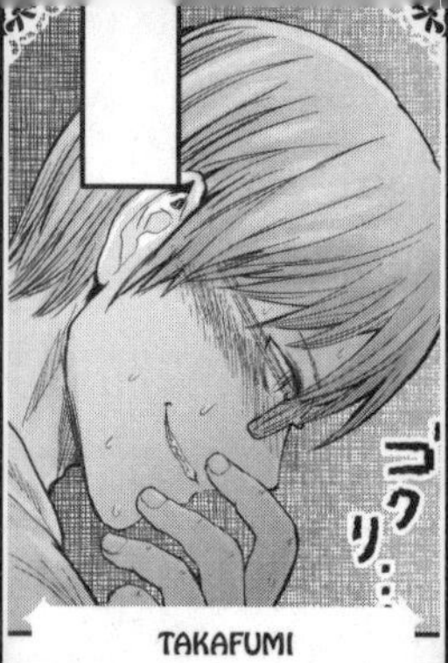
ゴクリ・・

TAKAFUMI

Uncle's nephew.
Big into isekai fantasy.

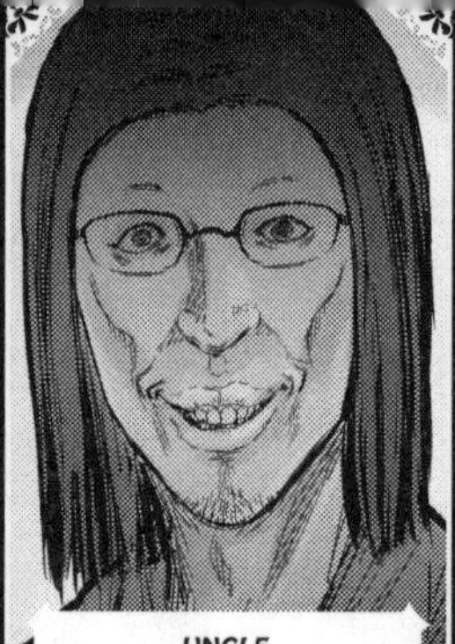

UNCLE

A repatriate from another world. Big into Se●a.

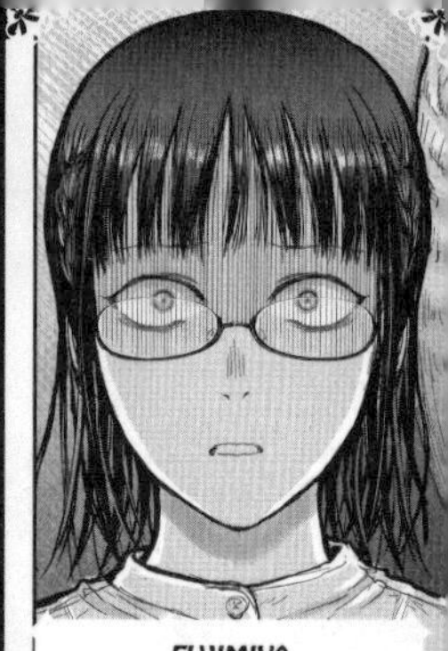

FUJIMIYA

Takafumi's childhood friend who's into him.

THE STORY SO FAR As it turns out, Uncle got a "transfer bonus" when he got sent to the other world: The Conversational Translation skill, now dubbed Wild Talker. To learn more about how the skill gets triggered, the group watches a flashback movie in which they learn who the "hero" of the realm is—Alicia, the girl from the adventuring group that Uncle once helped with goblin-slaying.

CONTENTS

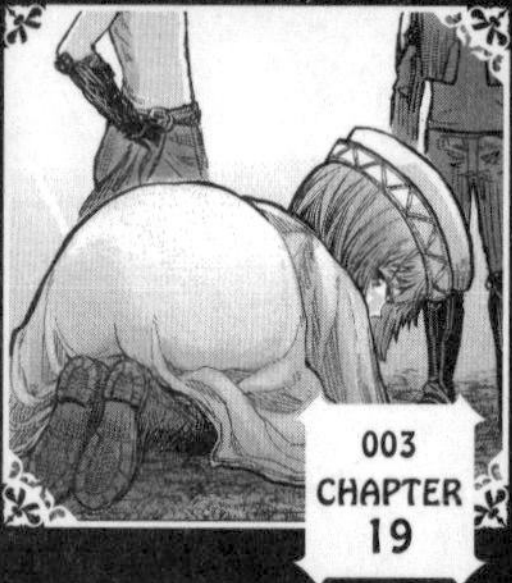

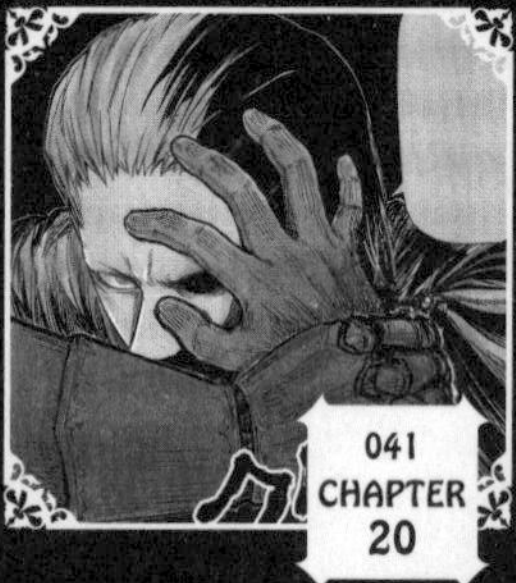

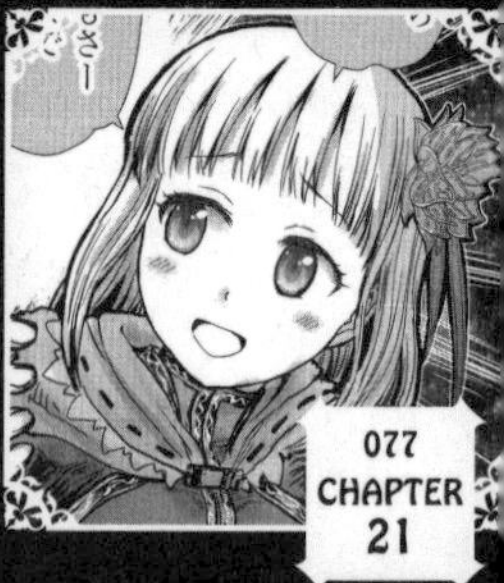

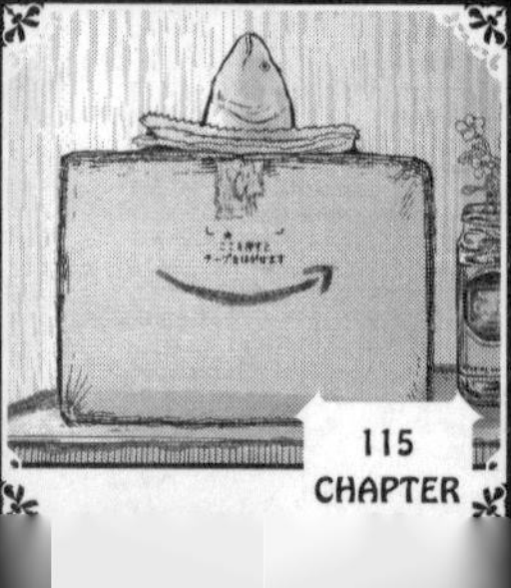

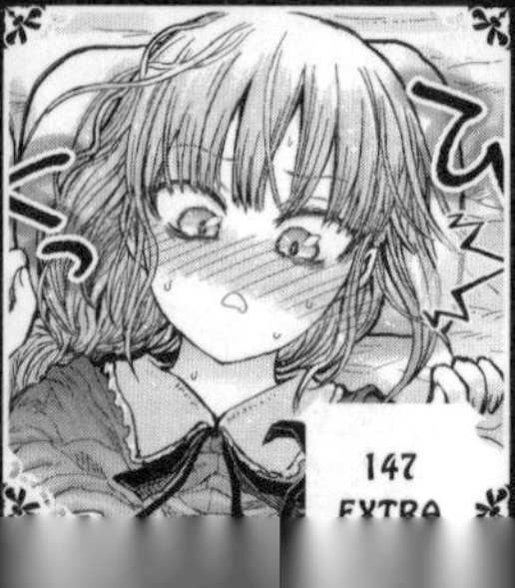

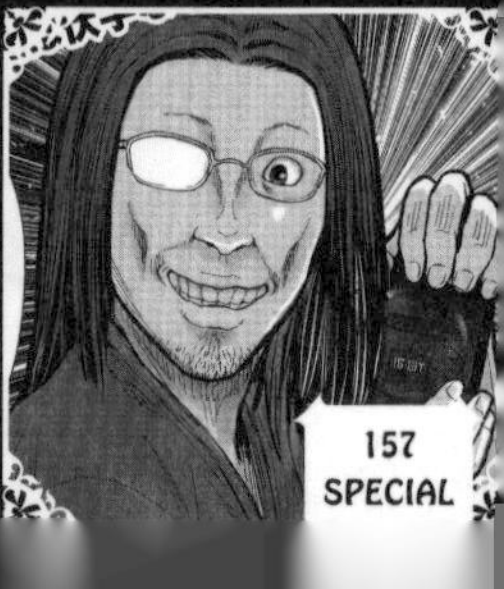

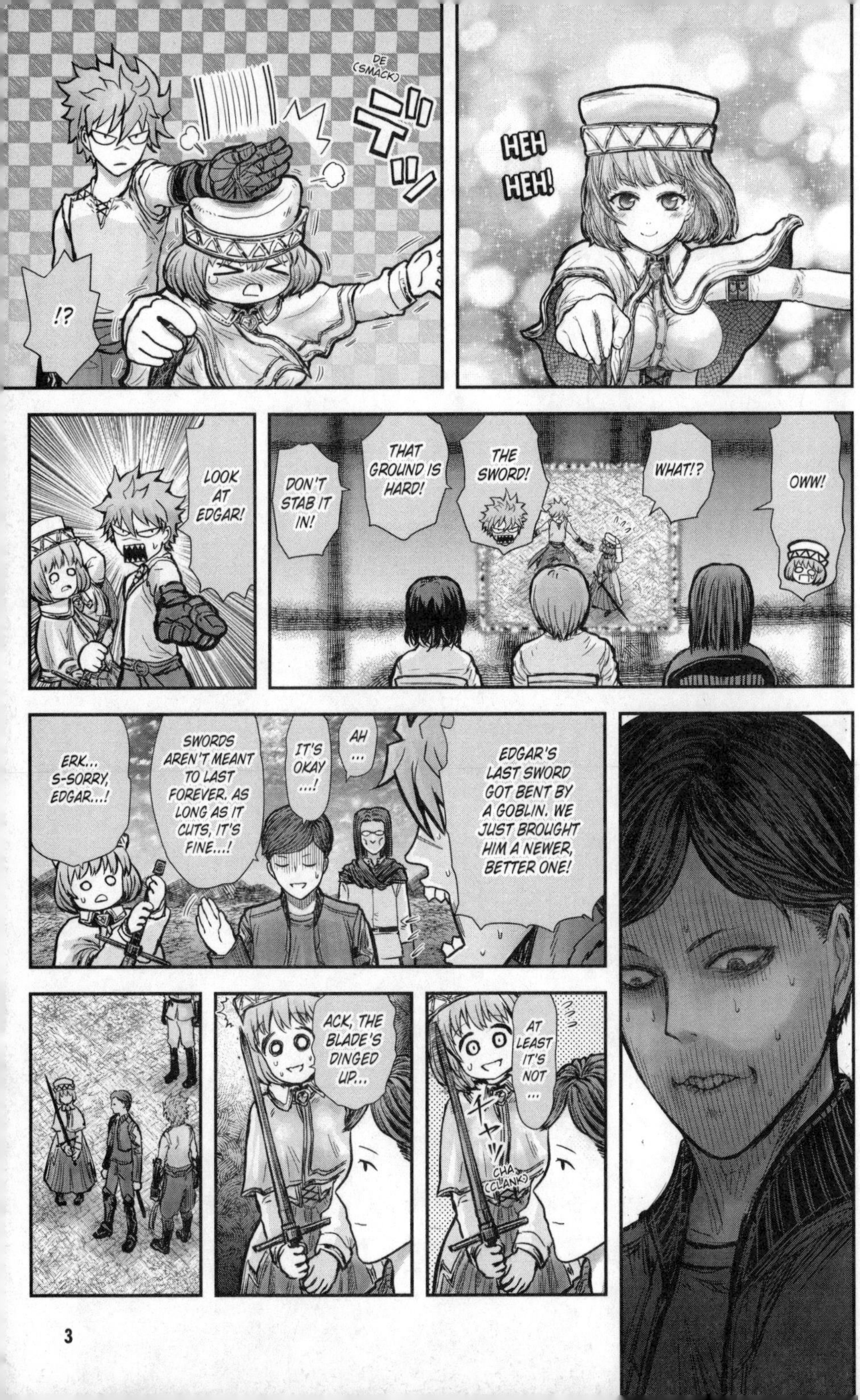
HEH HEH!
DE (SMACK)
!?
OWW!
WHAT!?
THE SWORD!
THAT GROUND IS HARD!
DON'T STAB IT IN!
LOOK AT EDGAR!
EDGAR'S LAST SWORD GOT BENT BY A GOBLIN. WE JUST BROUGHT HIM A NEWER, BETTER ONE!
AH ...
IT'S OKAY ...!
SWORDS AREN'T MEANT TO LAST FOREVER. AS LONG AS IT CUTS, IT'S FINE...!
ERK... S-SORRY, EDGAR...!
AT LEAST IT'S NOT ...
CHA (CLANK)
ACK, THE BLADE'S DINGED UP...

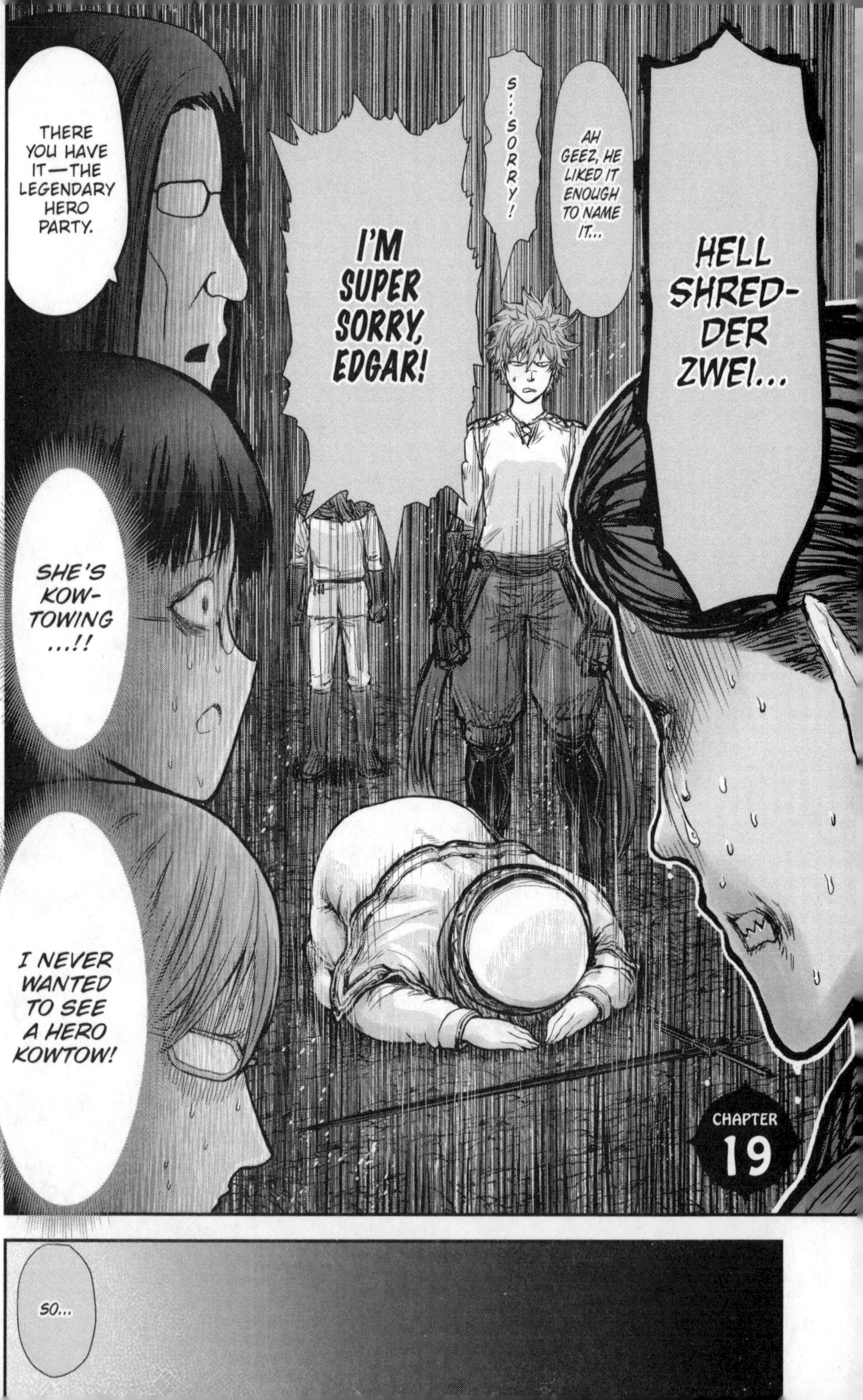
HELL SHRED-DER ZWEI...
AH GEEZ, HE LIKED IT ENOUGH TO NAME IT...
S...SORRY!
I'M SUPER SORRY, EDGAR!
THERE YOU HAVE IT—THE LEGENDARY HERO PARTY.
SHE'S KOW-TOWING...!!
I NEVER WANTED TO SEE A HERO KOWTOW!
CHAPTER 19
SO...

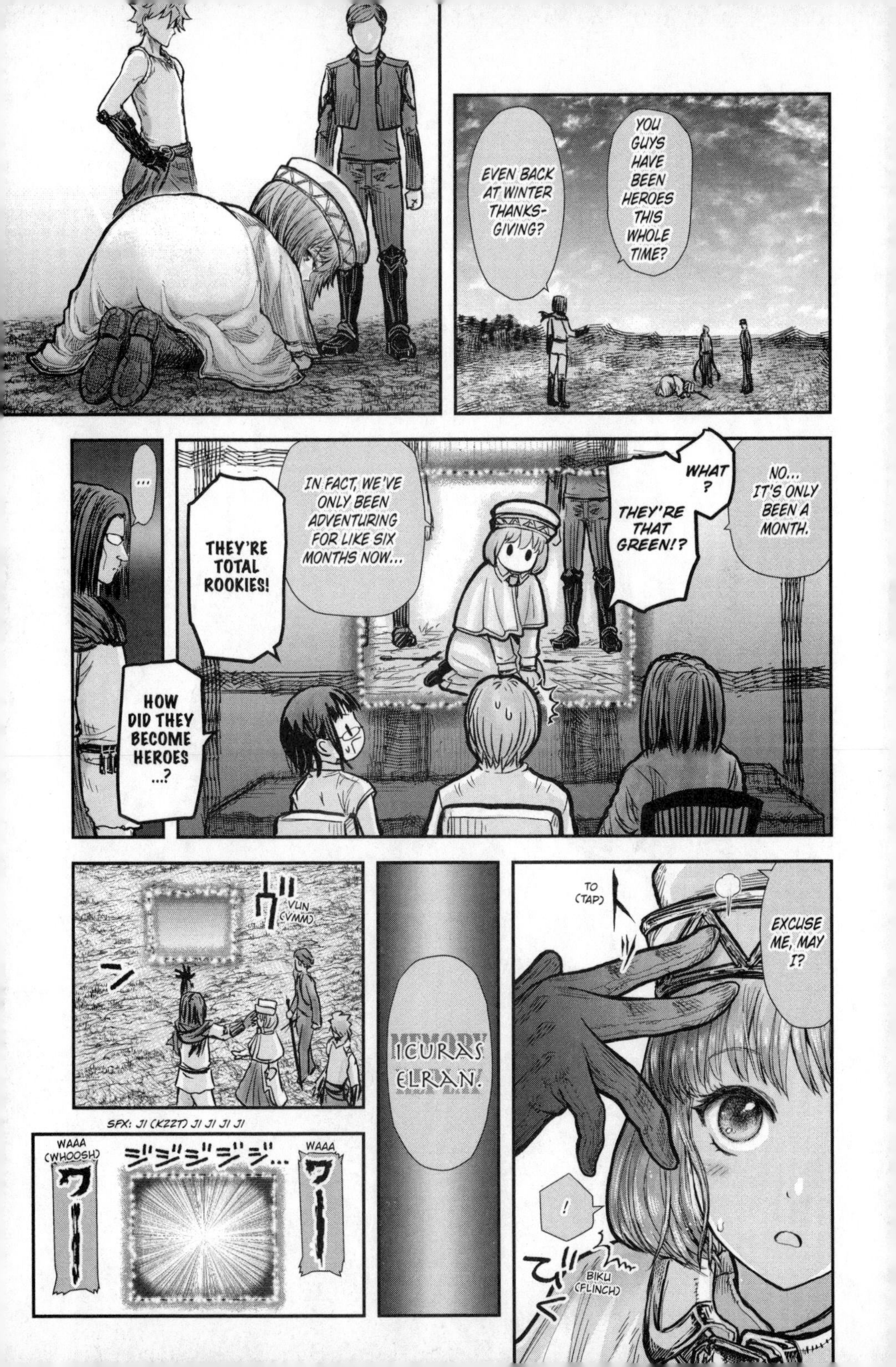
YOU GUYS HAVE BEEN HEROES THIS WHOLE TIME?
EVEN BACK AT WINTER THANKS-GIVING?
NO... IT'S ONLY BEEN A MONTH.
WHAT?
THEY'RE THAT GREEN!?
IN FACT, WE'VE ONLY BEEN ADVENTURING FOR LIKE SIX MONTHS NOW...
THEY'RE TOTAL ROOKIES!
...
HOW DID THEY BECOME HEROES ...?
EXCUSE ME, MAY I?
TO (TAP)
!
BIKU (FLINCH)
MEMORY
ICURAS ELRAN.
VUN (VMM)
SFX: JI (KZZT) JI JI JI JI
WAAA (WHOOSH)
WAAA

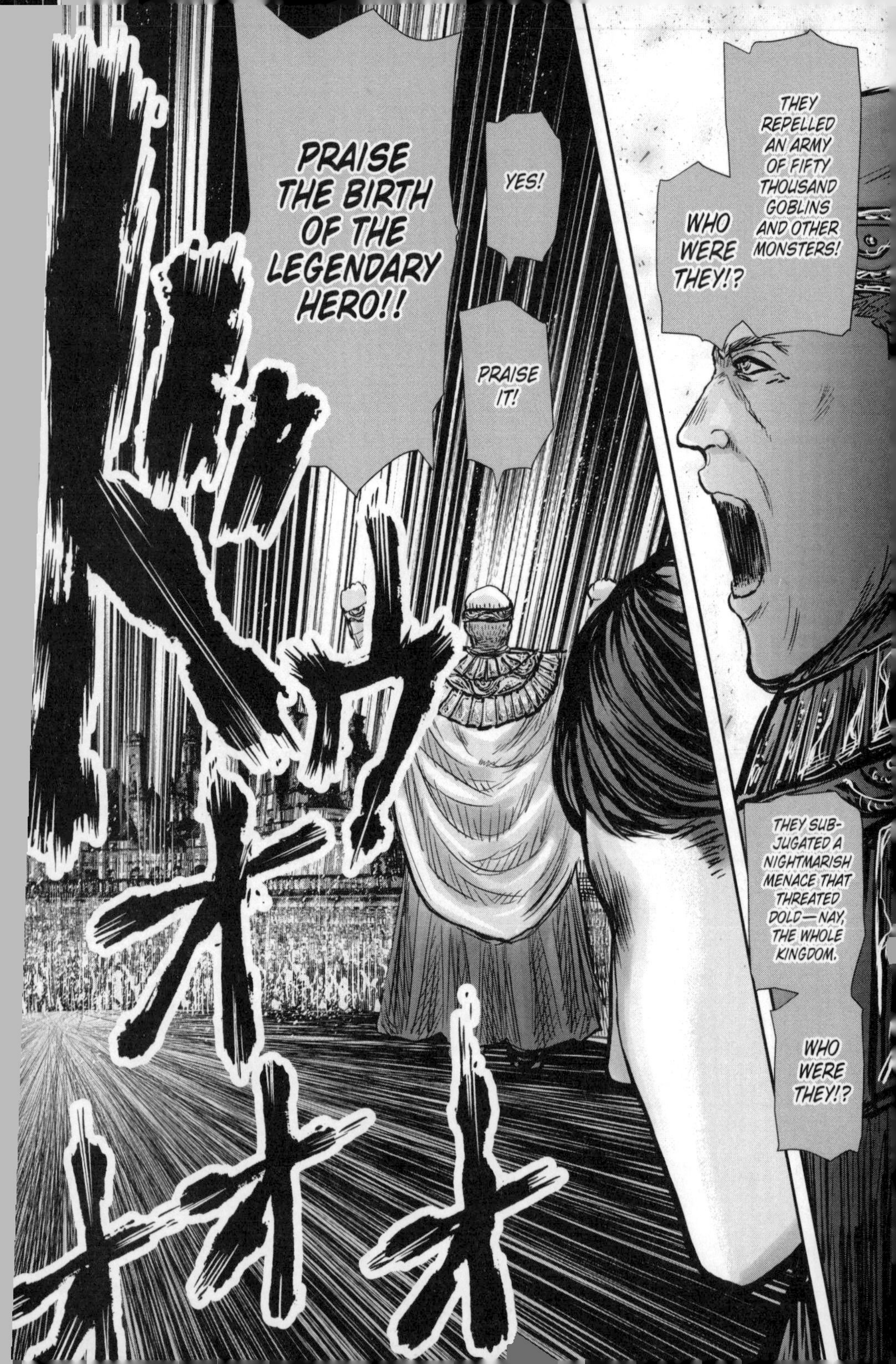
THEY REPELLED AN ARMY OF FIFTY THOUSAND GOBLINS AND OTHER MONSTERS!
WHO WERE THEY!?
THEY SUB-JUGATED A NIGHTMARISH MENACE THAT THREATED DOLD—NAY, THE WHOLE KINGDOM.
WHO WERE THEY!?
PRAISE THE BIRTH OF THE LEGENDARY HERO!!
YES!
PRAISE IT!

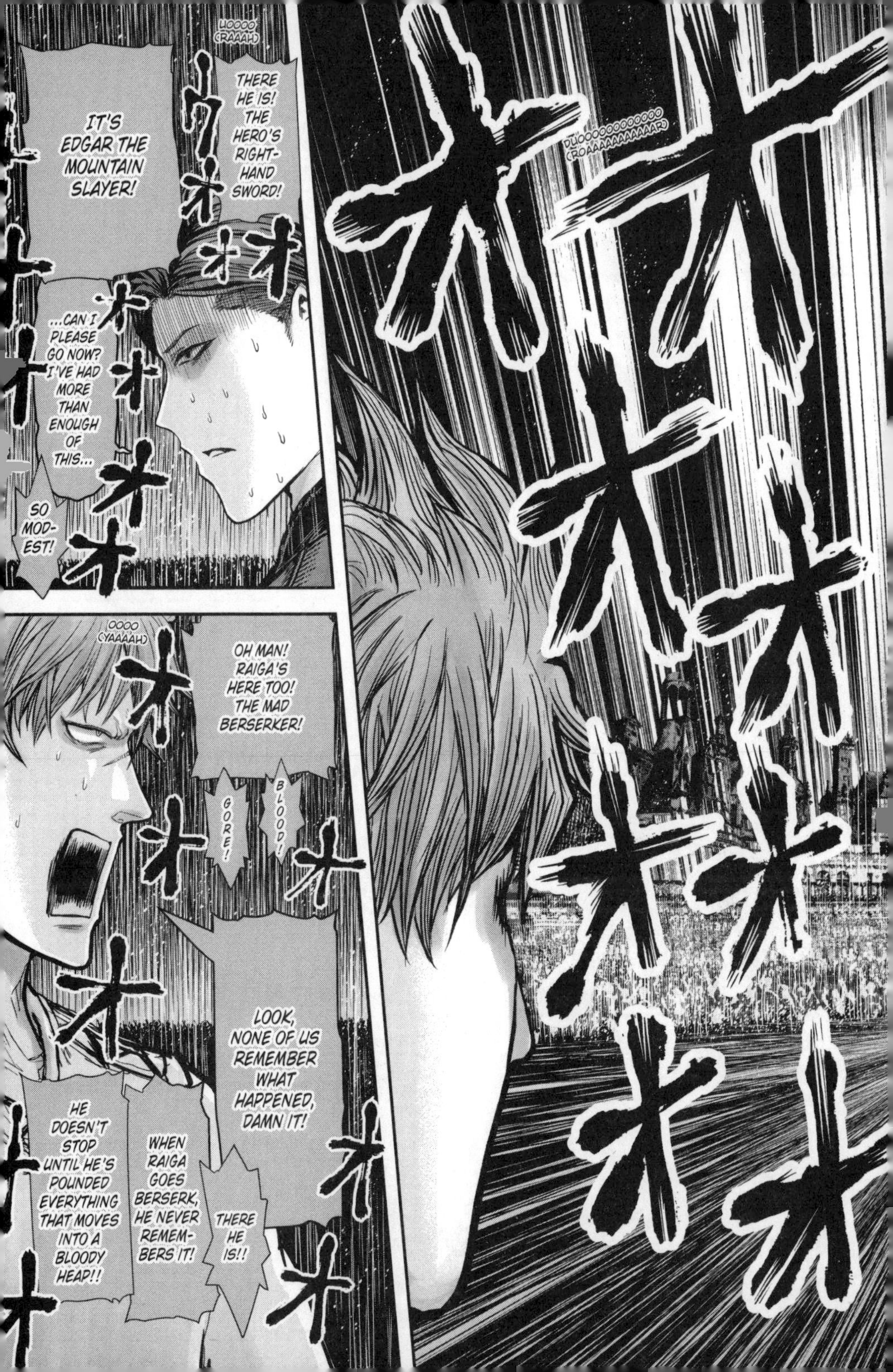
DUOOOOOOOOOOOOO (ROAAAAAAAAAAAR)
UOOOO (RAAAH)
THERE HE IS! THE HERO'S RIGHT-HAND SWORD!
IT'S EDGAR THE MOUNTAIN SLAYER!
...CAN I PLEASE GO NOW? I'VE HAD MORE THAN ENOUGH OF THIS...
SO MOD-EST!
OOOO (YAAAAH)
OH MAN! RAIGA'S HERE TOO! THE MAD BERSERKER!
BLOOD!
GORE!
LOOK, NONE OF US REMEMBER WHAT HAPPENED, DAMN IT!
THERE HE IS!!
WHEN RAIGA GOES BERSERK, HE NEVER REMEMBERS IT!
HE DOESN'T STOP UNTIL HE'S POUNDED EVERYTHING THAT MOVES INTO A BLOODY HEAP!!

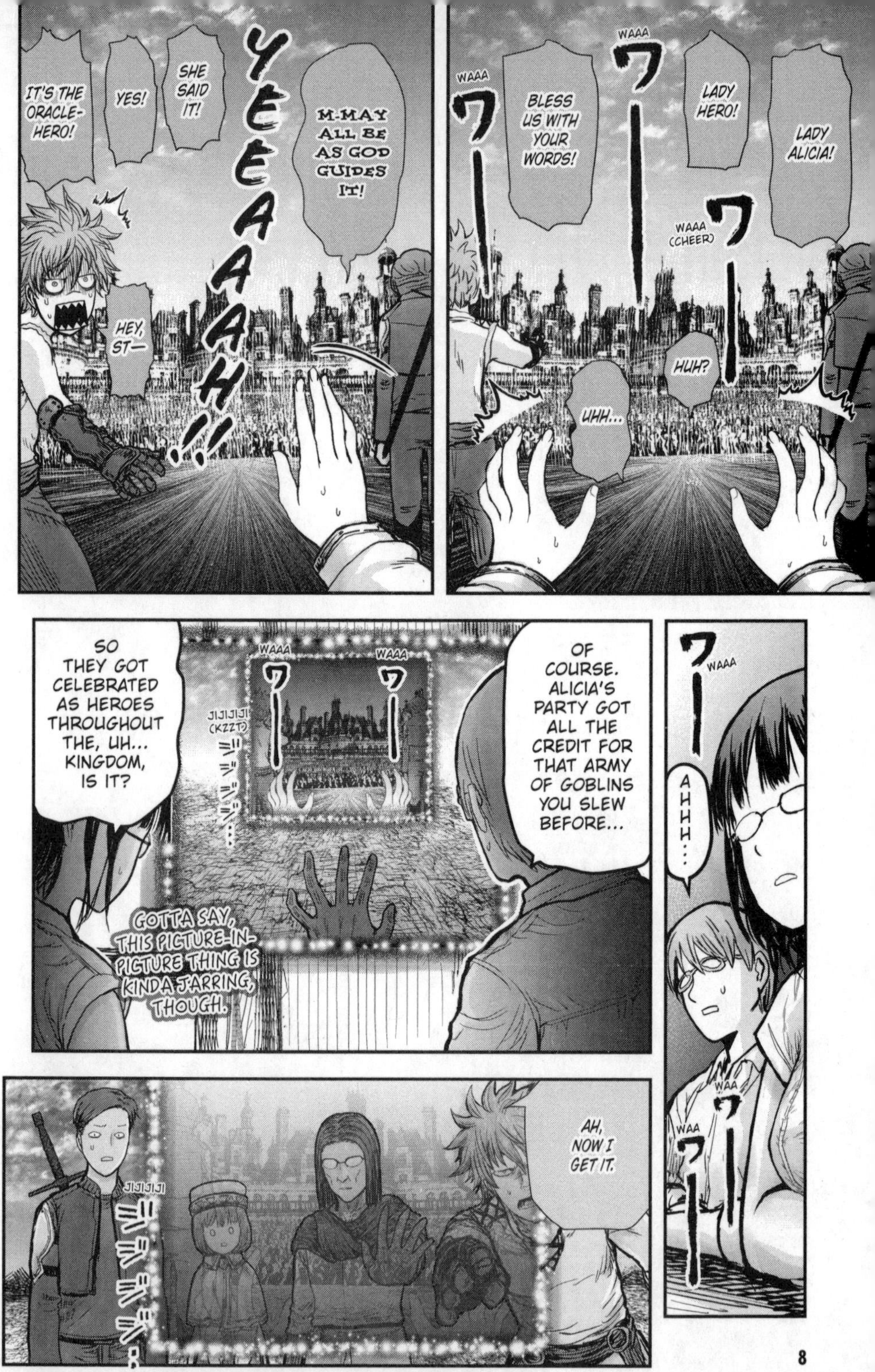
LADY ALICIA!
LADY HERO!
WAAA
ワー
BLESS US WITH YOUR WORDS!
WAAA
ワー
WAAA (CHEER)
ワー
HUH?
UHH...
M-MAY ALL BE AS GOD GUIDES IT!
YEEAAAAH!!
SHE SAID IT!
YES!
IT'S THE ORACLE-HERO!
HEY, ST—
ワー
WAAA
AHHH...
WAA
ワー
WAA
ワー
OF COURSE. ALICIA'S PARTY GOT ALL THE CREDIT FOR THAT ARMY OF GOBLINS YOU SLEW BEFORE...
WAAA
ワー
WAAA
ワー
JIJIJIJI (KZZT)
ジジジジ...
SO THEY GOT CELEBRATED AS HEROES THROUGHOUT THE, UH... KINGDOM, IS IT?
GOTTA SAY, THIS PICTURE-IN-PICTURE THING IS KINDA JARRING, THOUGH.
AH, NOW I GET IT.
JIJIJIJI
ジジジジ...

?

HEY, UM...

WH-WHAT IS THIS SPELL?

SUKA (FWIP)
ズカッ

SUKA
ズカッ

HYUUUUUUUU (WHOOSH)

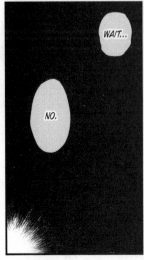

ALICIA ARC
—

THE END

WAIT...

NO.

ZAWA (MENACE)

KUROKI, YOU RECONSTRUCTED THE LUVALDRAM BARRIER BEFORE, RIGHT...?

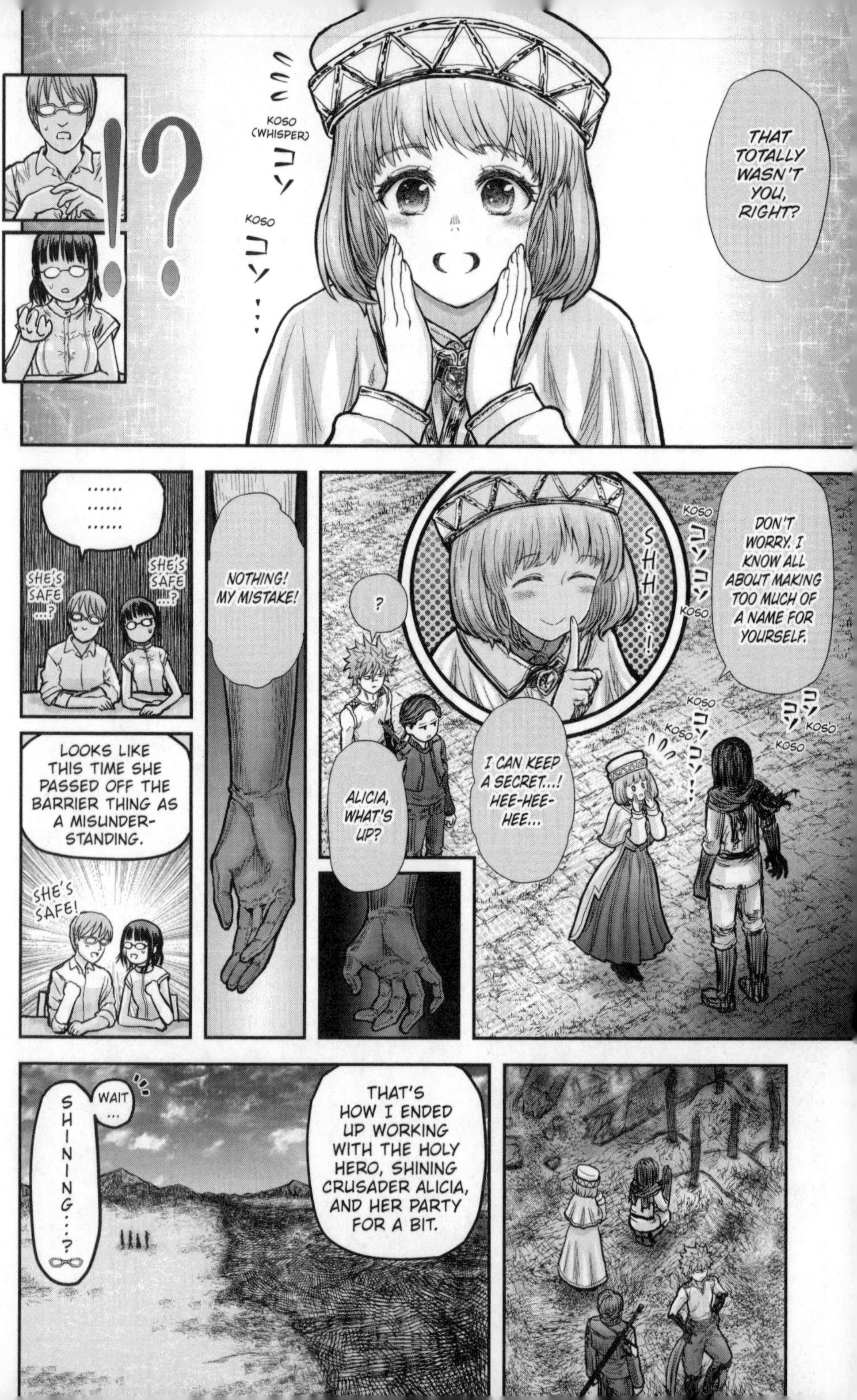
THAT TOTALLY WASN'T YOU, RIGHT?
KOSO (WHISPER)
コソ
KOSO
コソ…
!?
DON'T WORRY. I KNOW ALL ABOUT MAKING TOO MUCH OF A NAME FOR YOURSELF.
KOSO
KOSO
SHH…!
KOSO
KOSO
KOSO
KOSO
I CAN KEEP A SECRET…! HEE-HEE-HEE…
?
ALICIA, WHAT'S UP?
NOTHING! MY MISTAKE!
……
……
……
SHE'S SAFE…?
SHE'S SAFE…?
LOOKS LIKE THIS TIME SHE PASSED OFF THE BARRIER THING AS A MISUNDERSTANDING.
SHE'S SAFE!
THAT'S HOW I ENDED UP WORKING WITH THE HOLY HERO, SHINING CRUSADER ALICIA, AND HER PARTY FOR A BIT.
WAIT…
SHINING…?

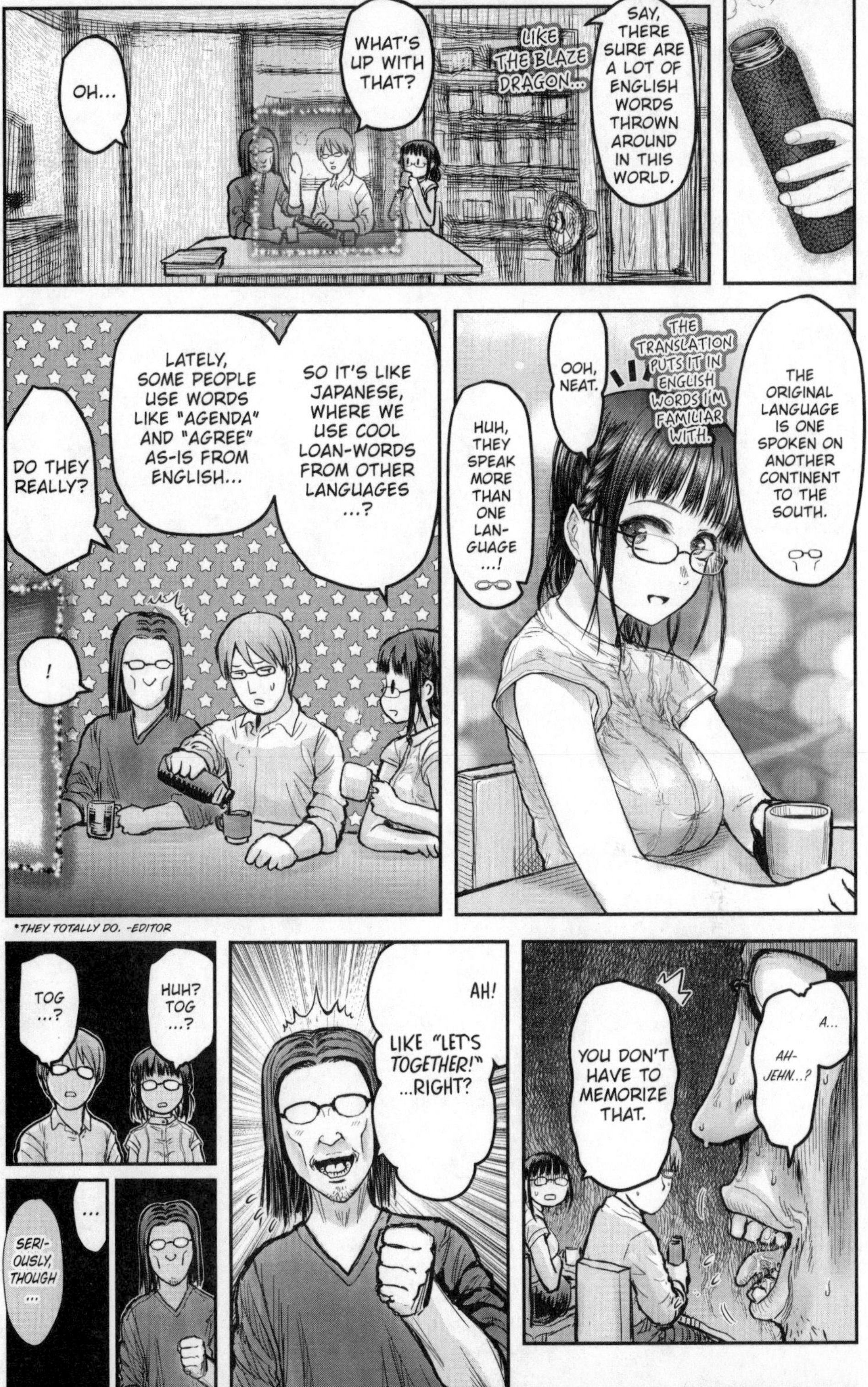
SAY, THERE SURE ARE A LOT OF ENGLISH WORDS THROWN AROUND IN THIS WORLD.
LIKE THE BLAZE DRAGON...
WHAT'S UP WITH THAT?
OH...
THE ORIGINAL LANGUAGE IS ONE SPOKEN ON ANOTHER CONTINENT TO THE SOUTH.
THE TRANSLATION PUTS IT IN ENGLISH WORDS I'M FAMILIAR WITH.
OOH, NEAT.
HUH, THEY SPEAK MORE THAN ONE LAN-GUAGE ...!
SO IT'S LIKE JAPANESE, WHERE WE USE COOL LOAN-WORDS FROM OTHER LANGUAGES ...?
LATELY, SOME PEOPLE USE WORDS LIKE "AGENDA" AND "AGREE" AS-IS FROM ENGLISH...
DO THEY REALLY?
!
*THEY TOTALLY DO. -EDITOR
A... AH-JEHN...?
YOU DON'T HAVE TO MEMORIZE THAT.
AH!
LIKE "LET'S TOGETHER!" ...RIGHT?
HUH? TOG ...?
TOG ...?
...
SERI-OUSLY, THOUGH ...

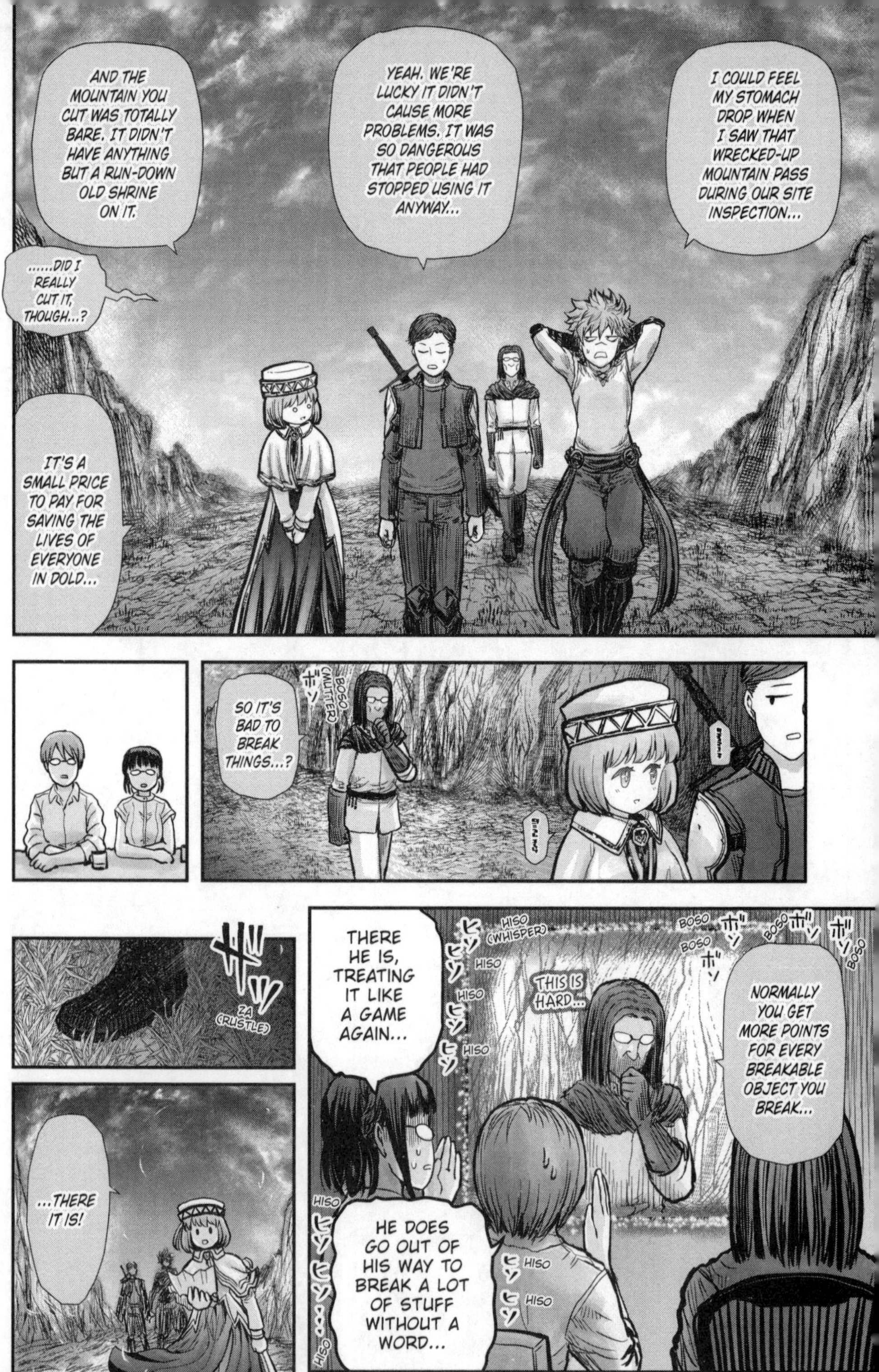
I COULD FEEL MY STOMACH DROP WHEN I SAW THAT WRECKED-UP MOUNTAIN PASS DURING OUR SITE INSPECTION...
YEAH. WE'RE LUCKY IT DIDN'T CAUSE MORE PROBLEMS. IT WAS SO DANGEROUS THAT PEOPLE HAD STOPPED USING IT ANYWAY...
AND THE MOUNTAIN YOU CUT WAS TOTALLY BARE. IT DIDN'T HAVE ANYTHING BUT A RUN-DOWN OLD SHRINE ON IT.
......DID I REALLY CUT IT, THOUGH...?
IT'S A SMALL PRICE TO PAY FOR SAVING THE LIVES OF EVERYONE IN DOLD...
BOSO (MUTTER)
SO IT'S BAD TO BREAK THINGS...?
BOSO BOSO BOSO BOSO
NORMALLY YOU GET MORE POINTS FOR EVERY BREAKABLE OBJECT YOU BREAK...
THIS IS HARD...
HISO (WHISPER) HISO HISO HISO
THERE HE IS, TREATING IT LIKE A GAME AGAIN...
HISO HISO HISO
HE DOES GO OUT OF HIS WAY TO BREAK A LOT OF STUFF WITHOUT A WORD...
ZA (RUSTLE)
...THERE IT IS!

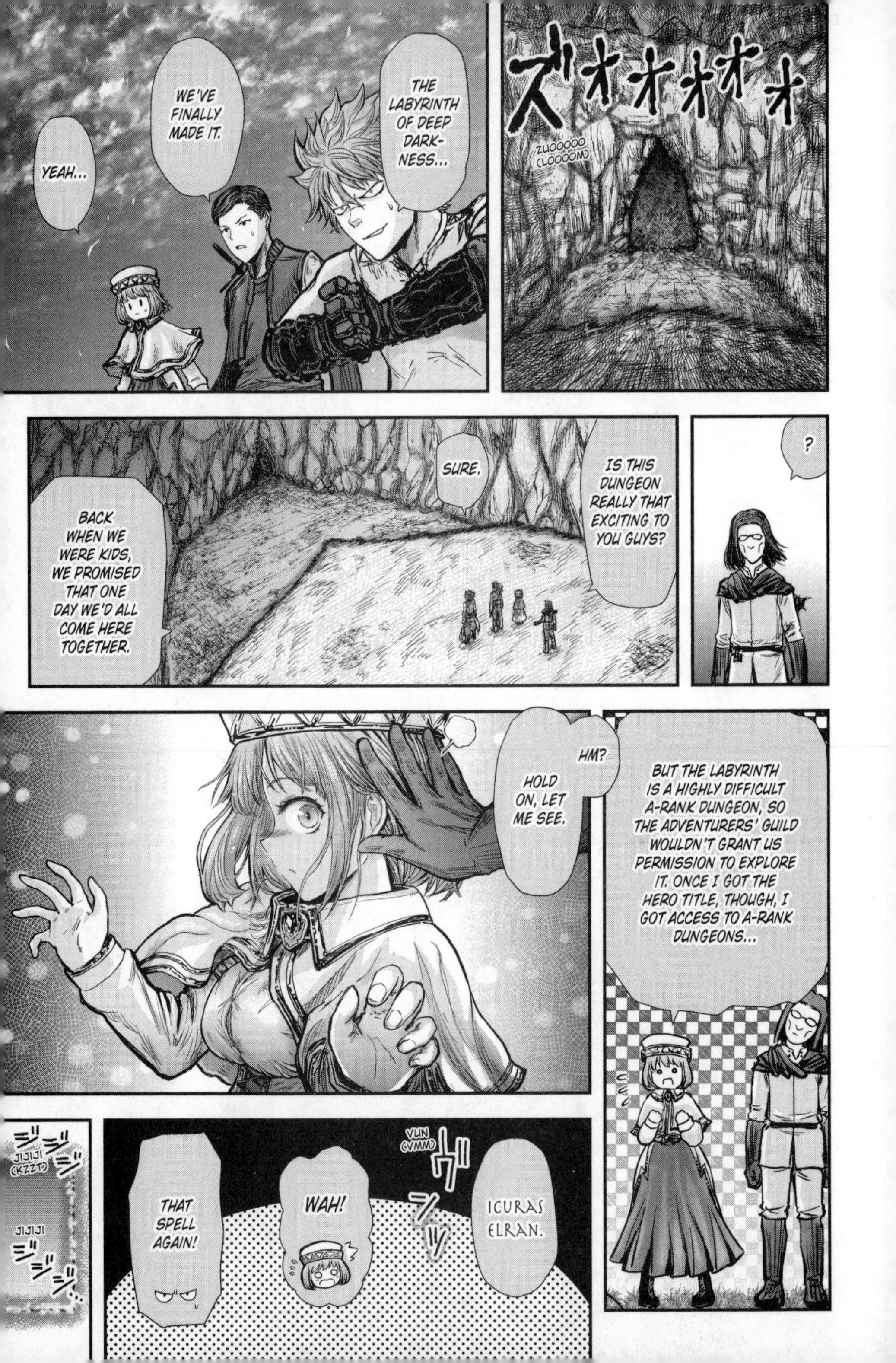
ズオオオオオ
ZUOOOOO (LOOOOM)
THE LABYRINTH OF DEEP DARKNESS...
WE'VE FINALLY MADE IT.
YEAH...
?
IS THIS DUNGEON REALLY THAT EXCITING TO YOU GUYS?
SURE.
BACK WHEN WE WERE KIDS, WE PROMISED THAT ONE DAY WE'D ALL COME HERE TOGETHER.
BUT THE LABYRINTH IS A HIGHLY DIFFICULT A-RANK DUNGEON, SO THE ADVENTURERS' GUILD WOULDN'T GRANT US PERMISSION TO EXPLORE IT. ONCE I GOT THE HERO TITLE, THOUGH, I GOT ACCESS TO A-RANK DUNGEONS...
HM?
HOLD ON, LET ME SEE.
ICURAS ELRAN.
ヴゥン
VUN (VMM)
WAH!
THAT SPELL AGAIN!
ジジジ
JIJIJI (KZZT)
JIJIJI
ジジジ...

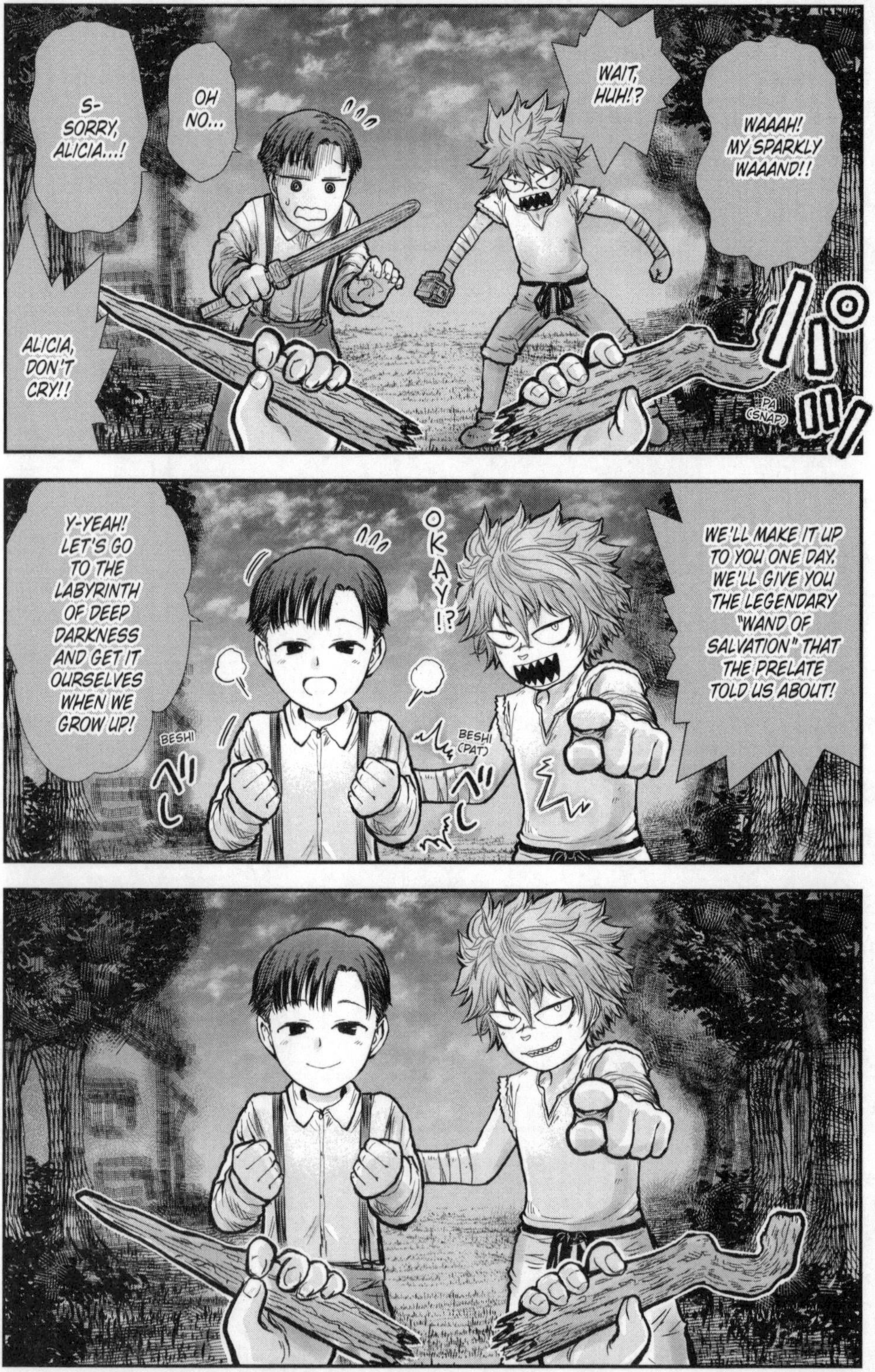
WAAAH! MY SPARKLY WAAAND!!
PA (SNAP)
WAIT, HUH!?
OH NO...
S-SORRY, ALICIA...!
ALICIA, DON'T CRY!!
WE'LL MAKE IT UP TO YOU ONE DAY. WE'LL GIVE YOU THE LEGENDARY "WAND OF SALVATION" THAT THE PRELATE TOLD US ABOUT!
OKAY!?
BESHI (PAT)
BESHI
Y-YEAH! LET'S GO TO THE LABYRINTH OF DEEP DARKNESS AND GET IT OURSELVES WHEN WE GROW UP!

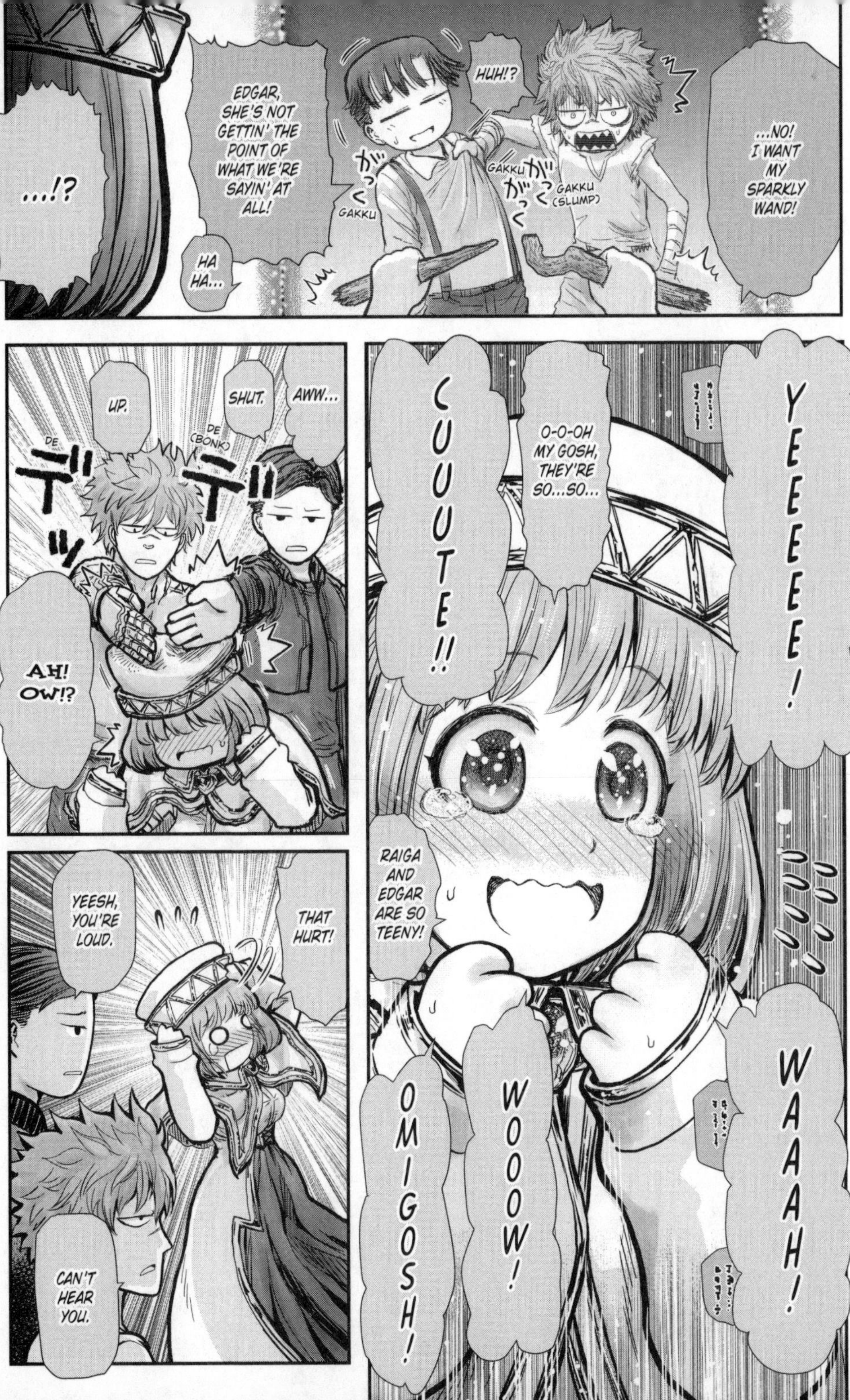
...NO! I WANT MY SPARKLY WAND!
HUH!?
GAKKU (SLUMP)
GAKKU
GAKKU
EDGAR, SHE'S NOT GETTIN' THE POINT OF WHAT WE'RE SAYIN' AT ALL!
HA HA...
...!?
YEEEEEE!
O-O-OH MY GOSH, THEY'RE SO...SO...
CUUUTE!!
RAIGA AND EDGAR ARE SO TEENY!
WAAAAH!
WOOOOW!
OMIGOSH!
AWW...
SHUT.
UP.
DE (BONK)
DE
AH! OW!?
THAT HURT!
YEESH, YOU'RE LOUD.
CAN'T HEAR YOU.

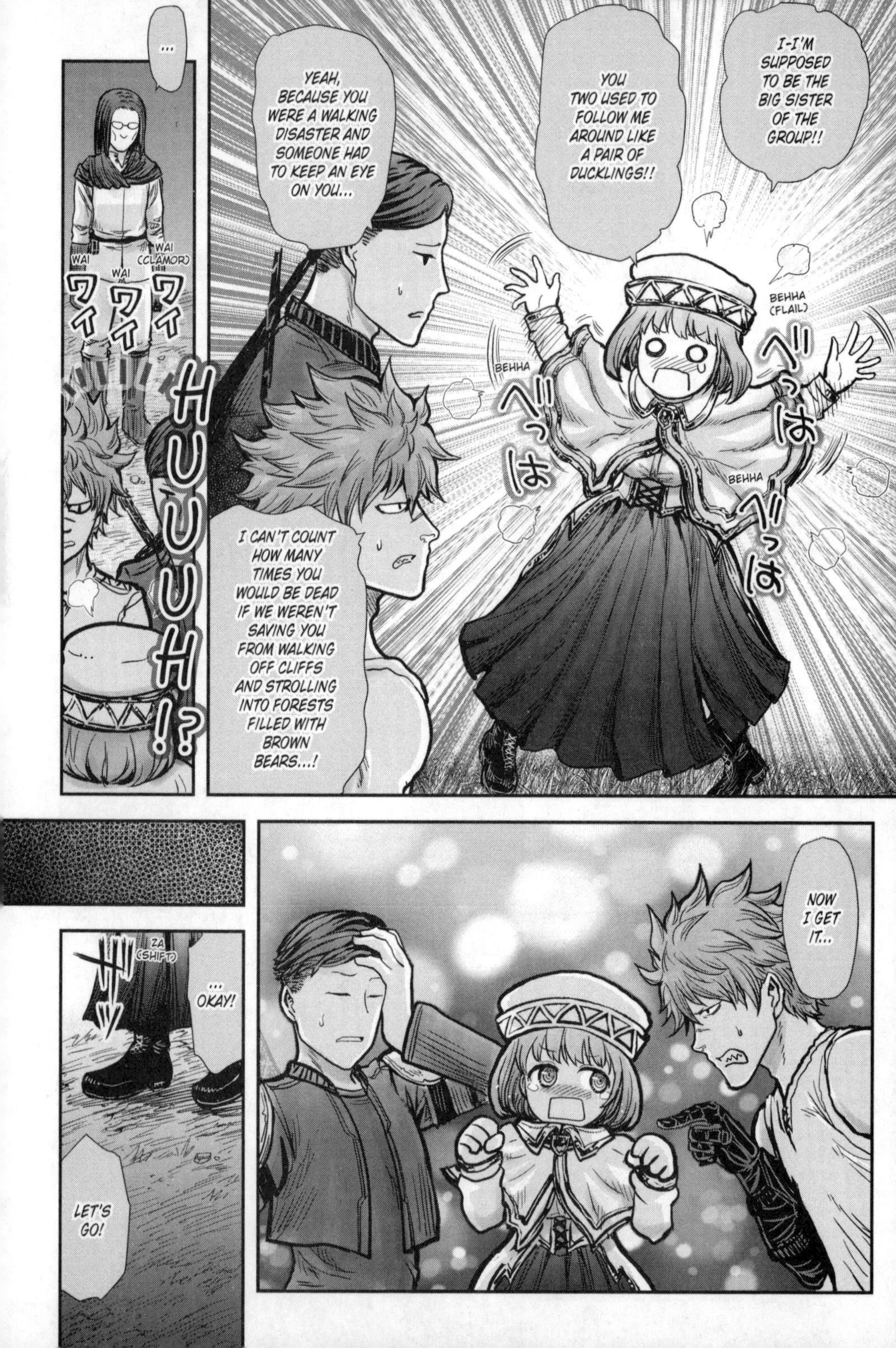

I-I'M SUPPOSED TO BE THE BIG SISTER OF THE GROUP!!
YOU TWO USED TO FOLLOW ME AROUND LIKE A PAIR OF DUCKLINGS!!
BEHHA (FLAIL)
べっは
BEHHA
べっは
BEHHA
べっは
YEAH, BECAUSE YOU WERE A WALKING DISASTER AND SOMEONE HAD TO KEEP AN EYE ON YOU...
I CAN'T COUNT HOW MANY TIMES YOU WOULD BE DEAD IF WE WEREN'T SAVING YOU FROM WALKING OFF CLIFFS AND STROLLING INTO FORESTS FILLED WITH BROWN BEARS...!
...
WAI (CLAMOR)
ワィ
WAI
ワィ
WAI
ワィ
HUUUH!?
...
NOW I GET IT...
ZA (SHIFT)
... OKAY!
LET'S GO!

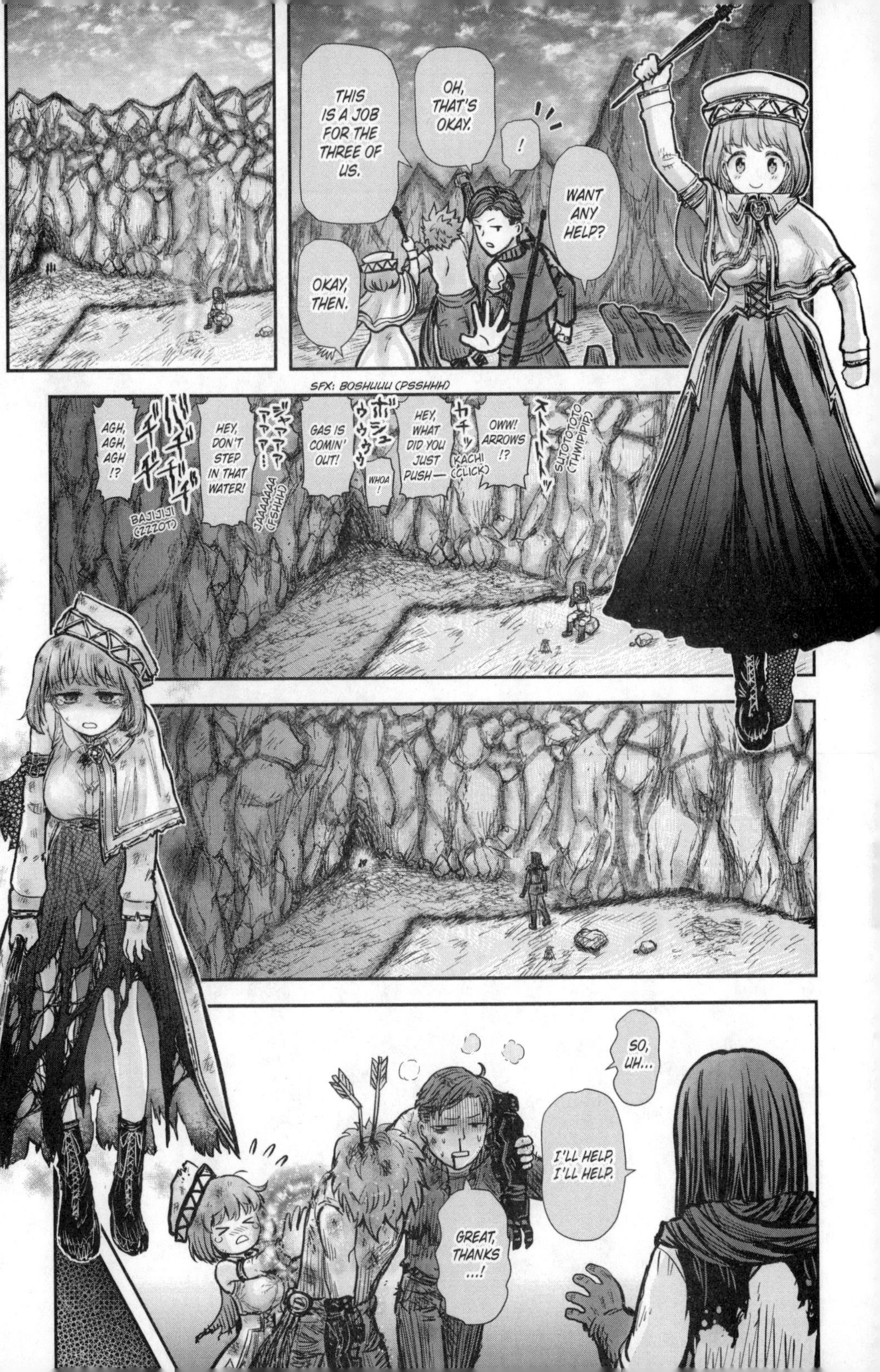
WANT ANY HELP?
!
OH, THAT'S OKAY.
THIS IS A JOB FOR THE THREE OF US.
OKAY, THEN.
SFX: BOSHUUU (PSSHHH)
SUTOTOTO (THWIPIPIP)
OWW! ARROWS!?
カチッ
KACHI (CLICK)
HEY, WHAT DID YOU JUST PUSH—
WHOA!
GAS IS COMIN' OUT!
JAAAAAAA (ESHHH)
HEY, DON'T STEP IN THAT WATER!
BAJIJIJI (ZZZOT)
AGH, AGH, AGH!?
SO, UH...
I'LL HELP, I'LL HELP.
GREAT, THANKS...!

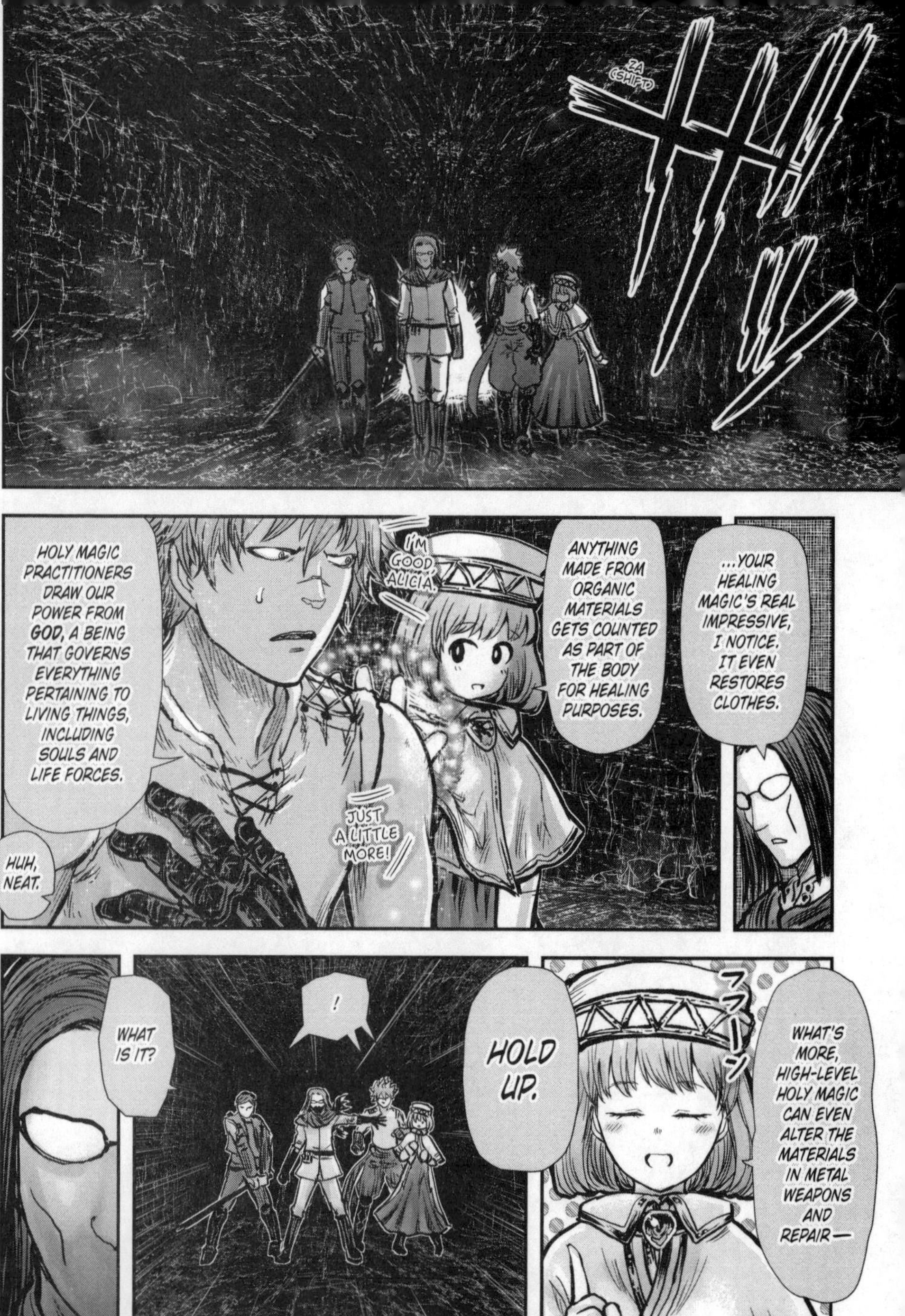
ZA (SHIFT)
...YOUR HEALING MAGIC'S REAL IMPRESSIVE, I NOTICE. IT EVEN RESTORES CLOTHES.
ANYTHING MADE FROM ORGANIC MATERIALS GETS COUNTED AS PART OF THE BODY FOR HEALING PURPOSES.
I'M GOOD, ALICIA.
HOLY MAGIC PRACTITIONERS DRAW OUR POWER FROM GOD, A BEING THAT GOVERNS EVERYTHING PERTAINING TO LIVING THINGS, INCLUDING SOULS AND LIFE FORCES.
JUST A LITTLE MORE!
HUH, NEAT.
WHAT'S MORE, HIGH-LEVEL HOLY MAGIC CAN EVEN ALTER THE MATERIALS IN METAL WEAPONS AND REPAIR—
HOLD UP.
!
WHAT IS IT?

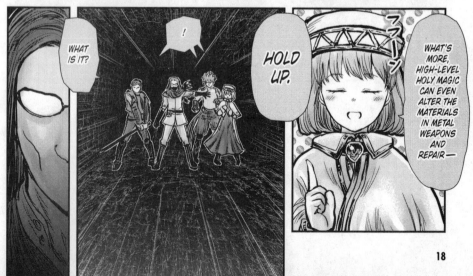

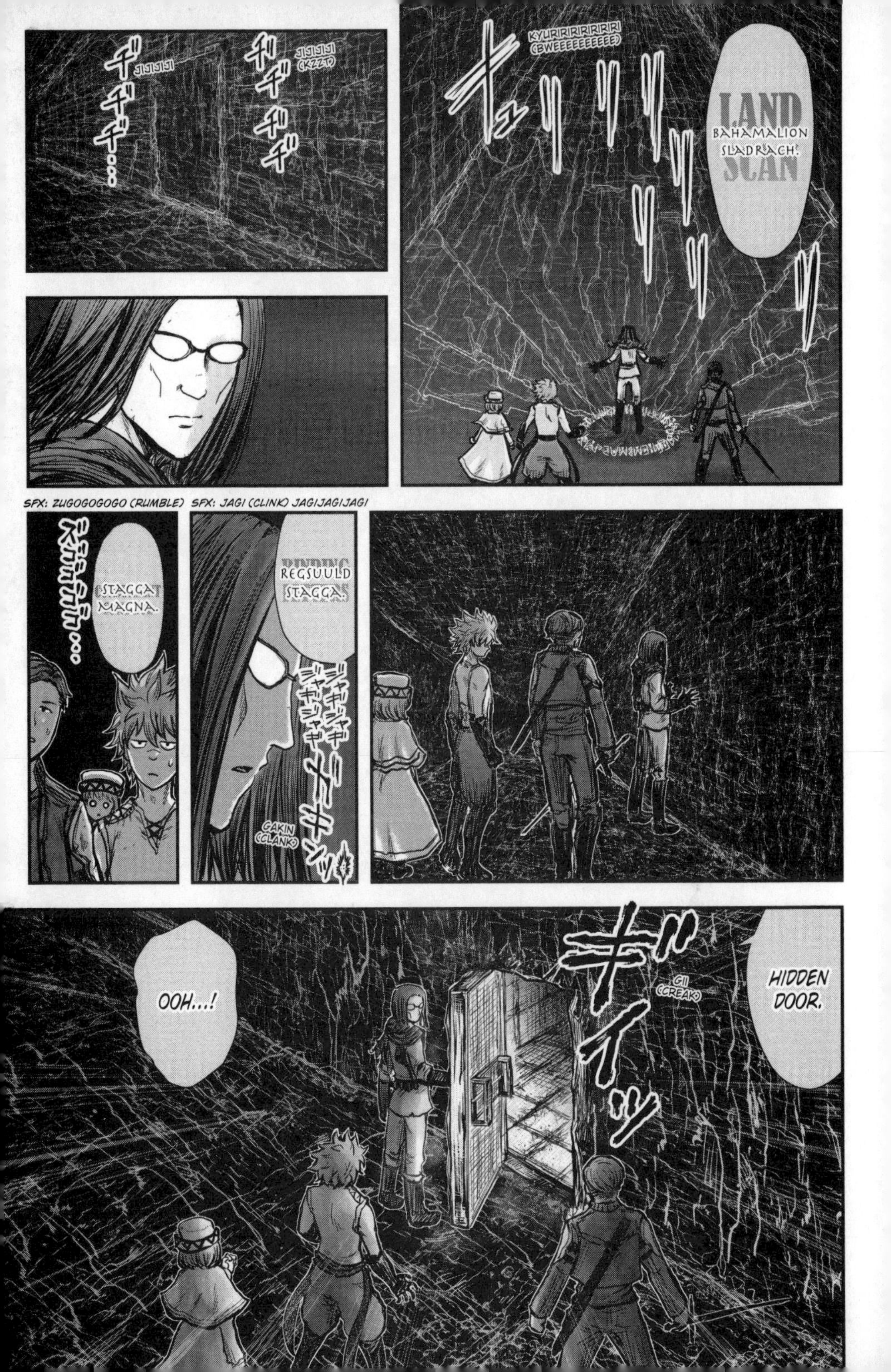
LAND SCAN
BAHAMALION SLADRACH!
KYURIRIRIRIRIRI (BWEEEEEEEEEEE)
JIJIJIJI (KZZT)
JIJIJIJI
SFX: ZUGOGOGOGO (RUMBLE) SFX: JAGI (CLINK) JAGIJAGIJAGI
REGSUULD STAGGA.
GAKIN (CLANK)
STAGGAT MAGNA.
HIDDEN DOOR.
GII (CREAK)
OOH...!

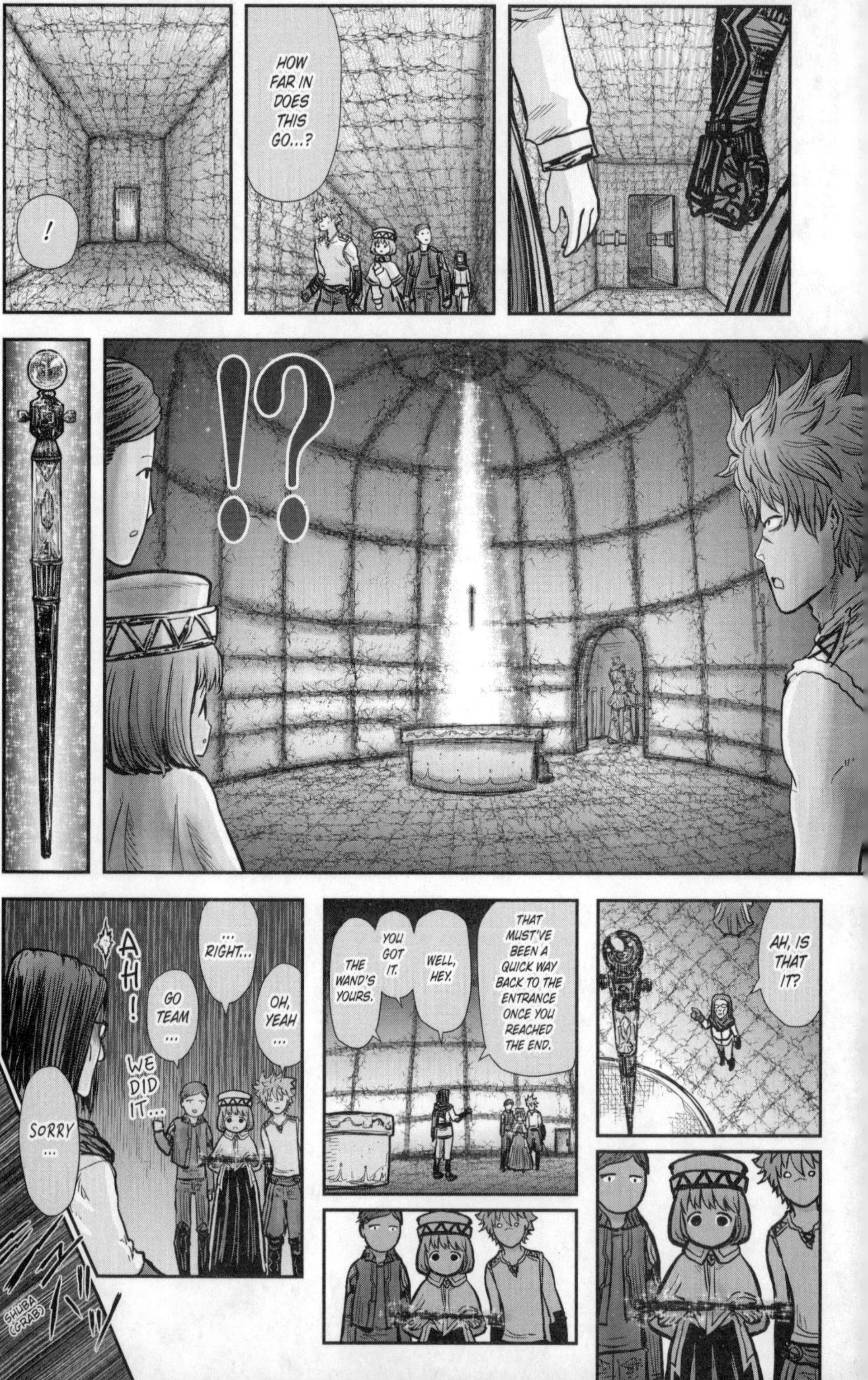
HOW FAR IN DOES THIS GO...?
!
!?
AH, IS THAT IT?
THAT MUST'VE BEEN A QUICK WAY BACK TO THE ENTRANCE ONCE YOU REACHED THE END.
WELL, HEY.
YOU GOT IT.
THE WAND'S YOURS.
...RIGHT...
OH, YEAH...
GO TEAM...
AH!
WE DID IT...
SORRY...
SHUBA (GRAB)

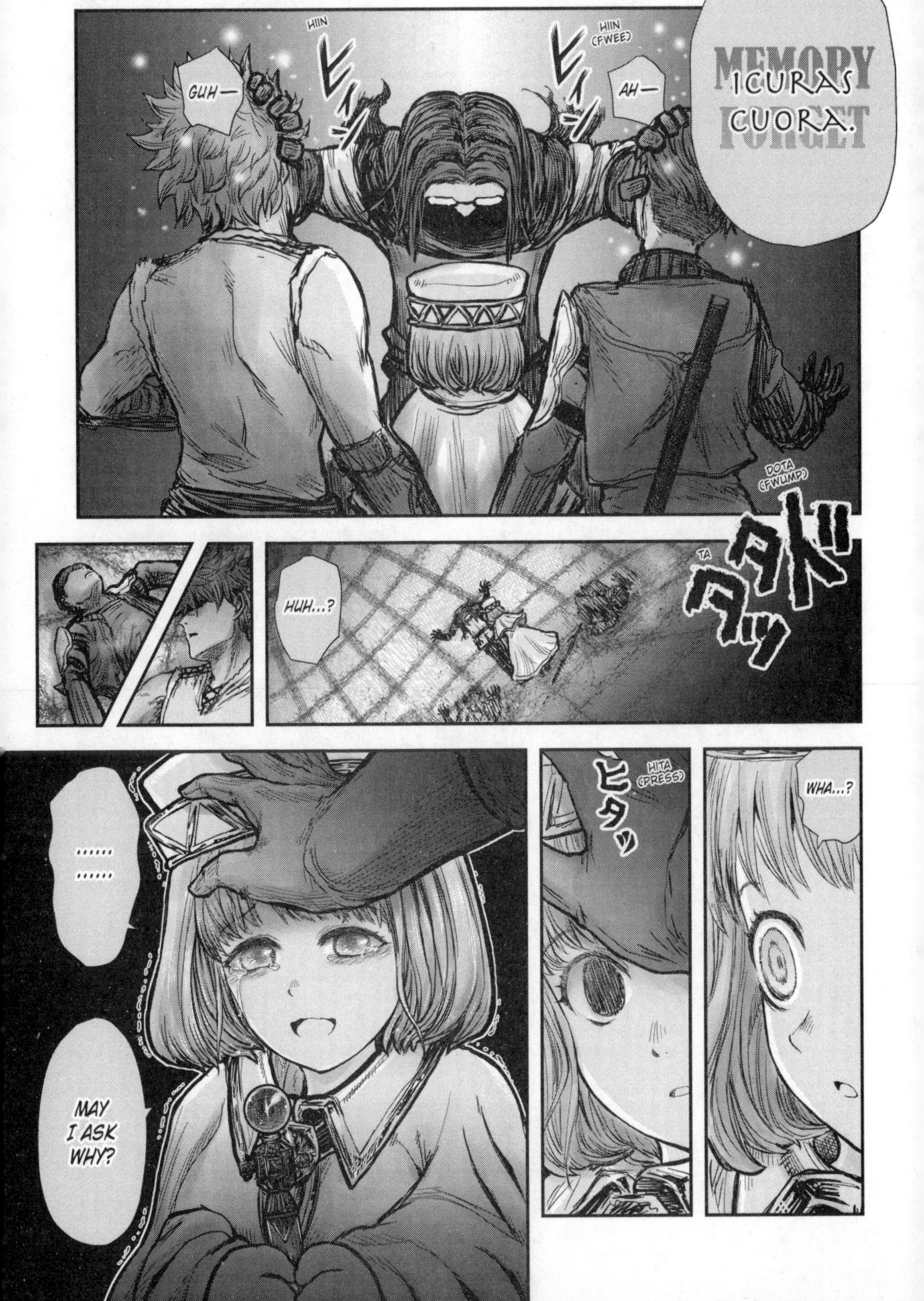
MEMORY
ICURAS CUORA.
FORGET
HIIN (FWEE)
AH—
HIIN
GUH—
DOTA (FWUMP)
ドタ
TA
タッ
HUH...?
WHA...?
HITA (PRESS)
ヒタッ
......
......
MAY I ASK WHY?

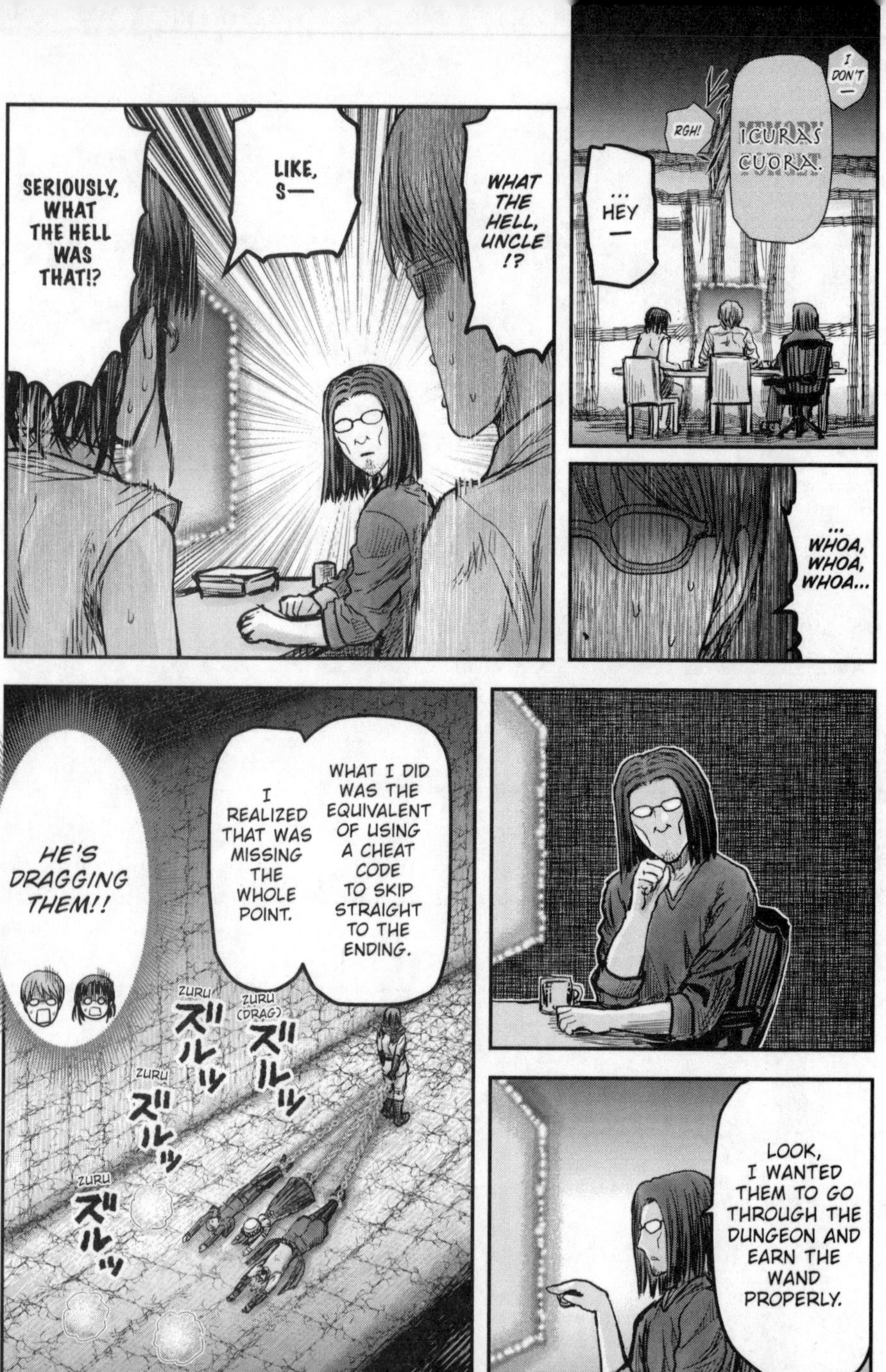
I DON'T —
ICURA'S CUORA.
RGH!
... HEY —
... WHOA, WHOA, WHOA...
WHAT THE HELL, UNCLE !?
LIKE, S—
SERIOUSLY, WHAT THE HELL WAS THAT!?
LOOK, I WANTED THEM TO GO THROUGH THE DUNGEON AND EARN THE WAND PROPERLY.
WHAT I DID WAS THE EQUIVALENT OF USING A CHEAT CODE TO SKIP STRAIGHT TO THE ENDING.
I REALIZED THAT WAS MISSING THE WHOLE POINT.
HE'S DRAGGING THEM!!
ZURU (DRAG) ズルッ
ZURU ズルッ
ZURU ズルッ
ZURU ズルッ

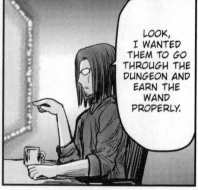

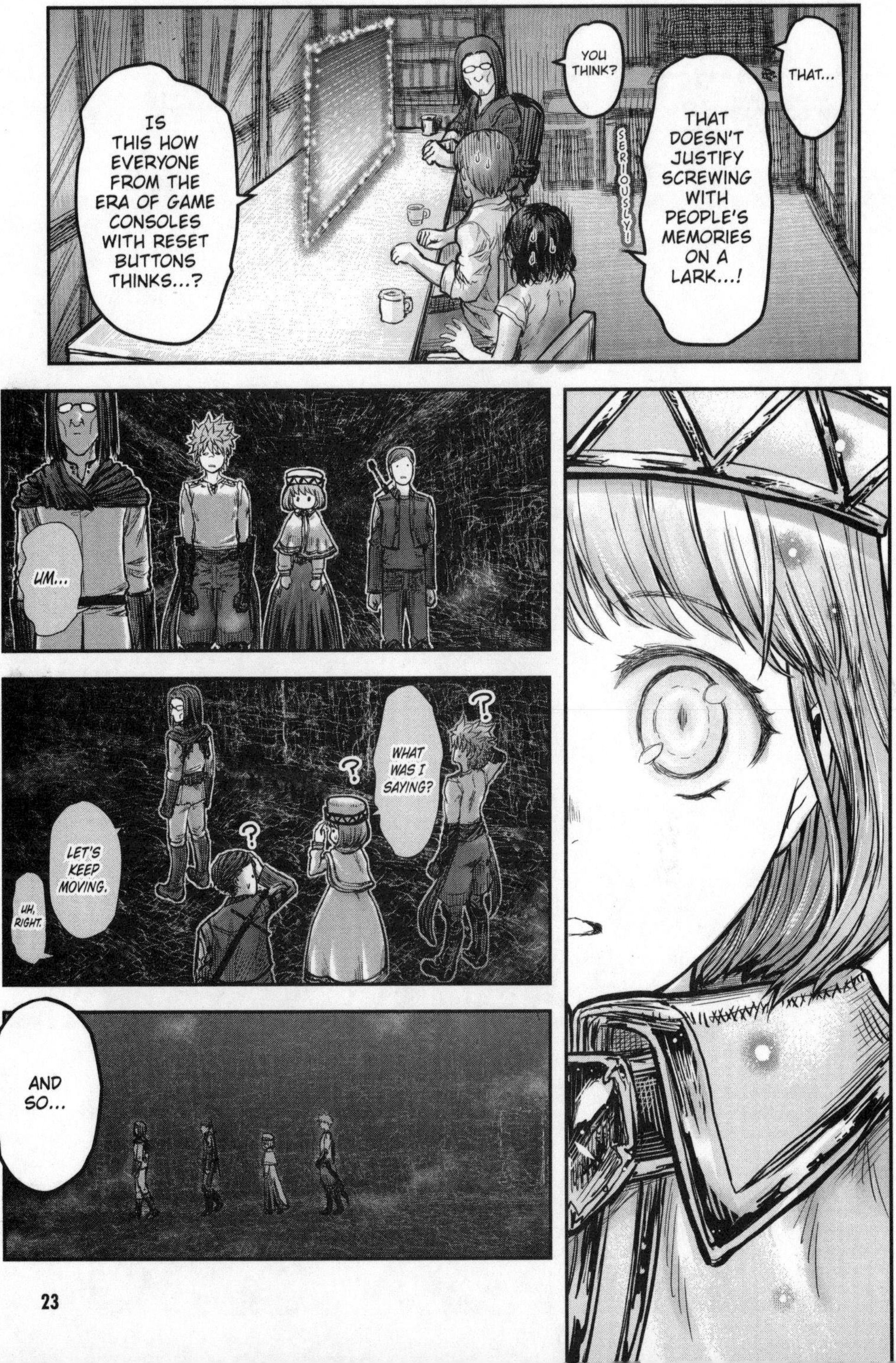
THAT...
THAT DOESN'T JUSTIFY SCREWING WITH PEOPLE'S MEMORIES ON A LARK...!
SERIOUSLY!
YOU THINK?
IS THIS HOW EVERYONE FROM THE ERA OF GAME CONSOLES WITH RESET BUTTONS THINKS...?
UM...
WHAT WAS I SAYING?
LET'S KEEP MOVING.
UH, RIGHT.
AND SO...

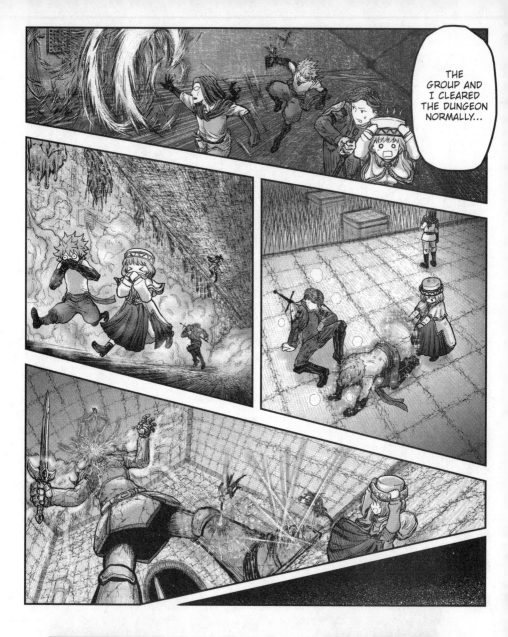

THE GROUP AND I CLEARED THE DUNGEON NORMALLY...

OH...!

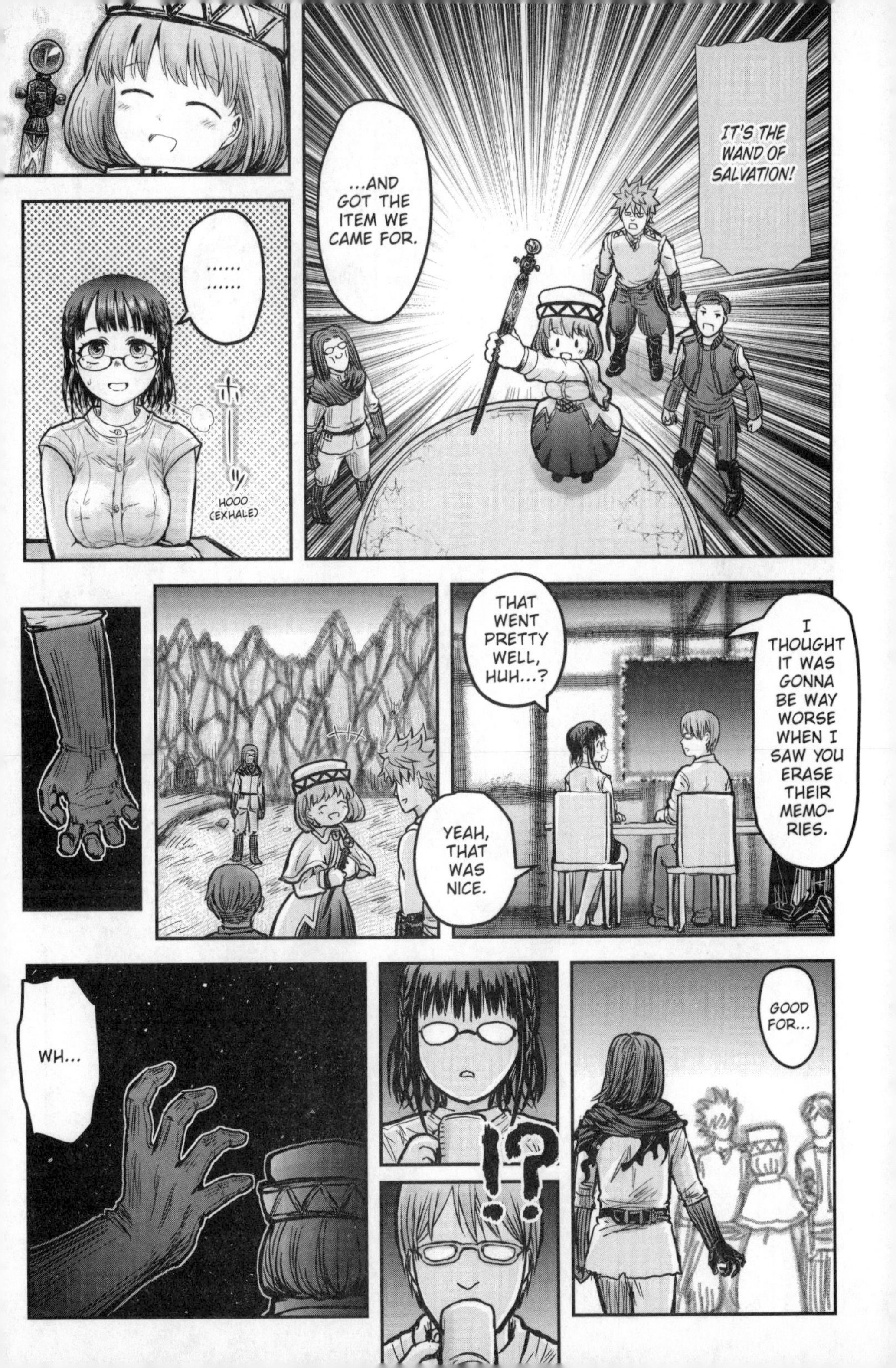
IT'S THE WAND OF SALVATION!
...AND GOT THE ITEM WE CAME FOR.
......
......
ホーーッ
HOOO (EXHALE)
I THOUGHT IT WAS GONNA BE WAY WORSE WHEN I SAW YOU ERASE THEIR MEMORIES.
THAT WENT PRETTY WELL, HUH...?
YEAH, THAT WAS NICE.
GOOD FOR...
!?
WH...

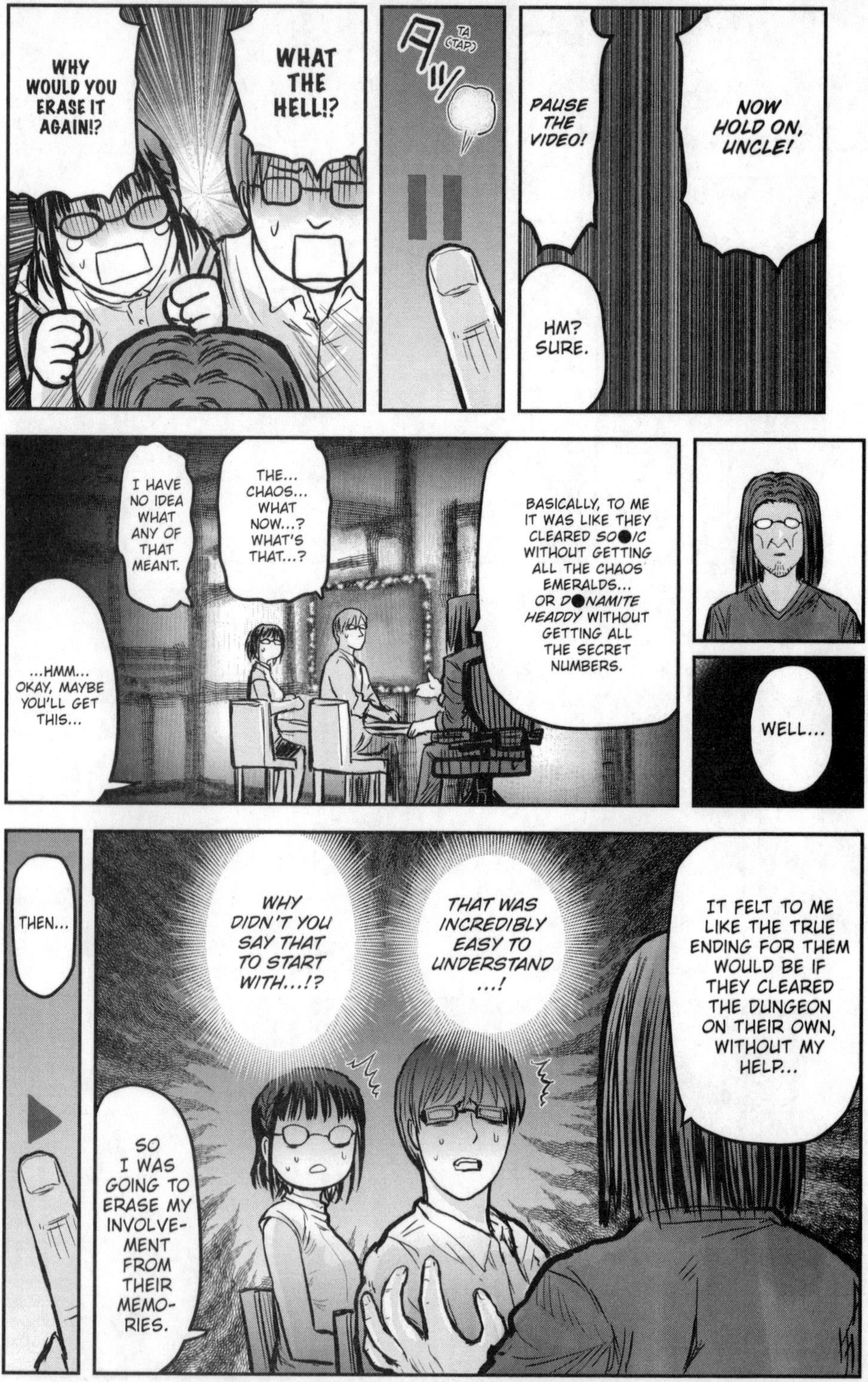
NOW HOLD ON, UNCLE!
PAUSE THE VIDEO!
HM? SURE.
TA (TAP)
WHAT THE HELL!?
WHY WOULD YOU ERASE IT AGAIN!?
WELL...
BASICALLY, TO ME IT WAS LIKE THEY CLEARED SO●IC WITHOUT GETTING ALL THE CHAOS EMERALDS... OR D●NAMITE HEADDY WITHOUT GETTING ALL THE SECRET NUMBERS.
THE... CHAOS... WHAT NOW...? WHAT'S THAT...?
I HAVE NO IDEA WHAT ANY OF THAT MEANT.
...HMM... OKAY, MAYBE YOU'LL GET THIS...
IT FELT TO ME LIKE THE TRUE ENDING FOR THEM WOULD BE IF THEY CLEARED THE DUNGEON ON THEIR OWN, WITHOUT MY HELP...
THAT WAS INCREDIBLY EASY TO UNDERSTAND...!
WHY DIDN'T YOU SAY THAT TO START WITH...!?
SO I WAS GOING TO ERASE MY INVOLVEMENT FROM THEIR MEMORIES.
THEN...

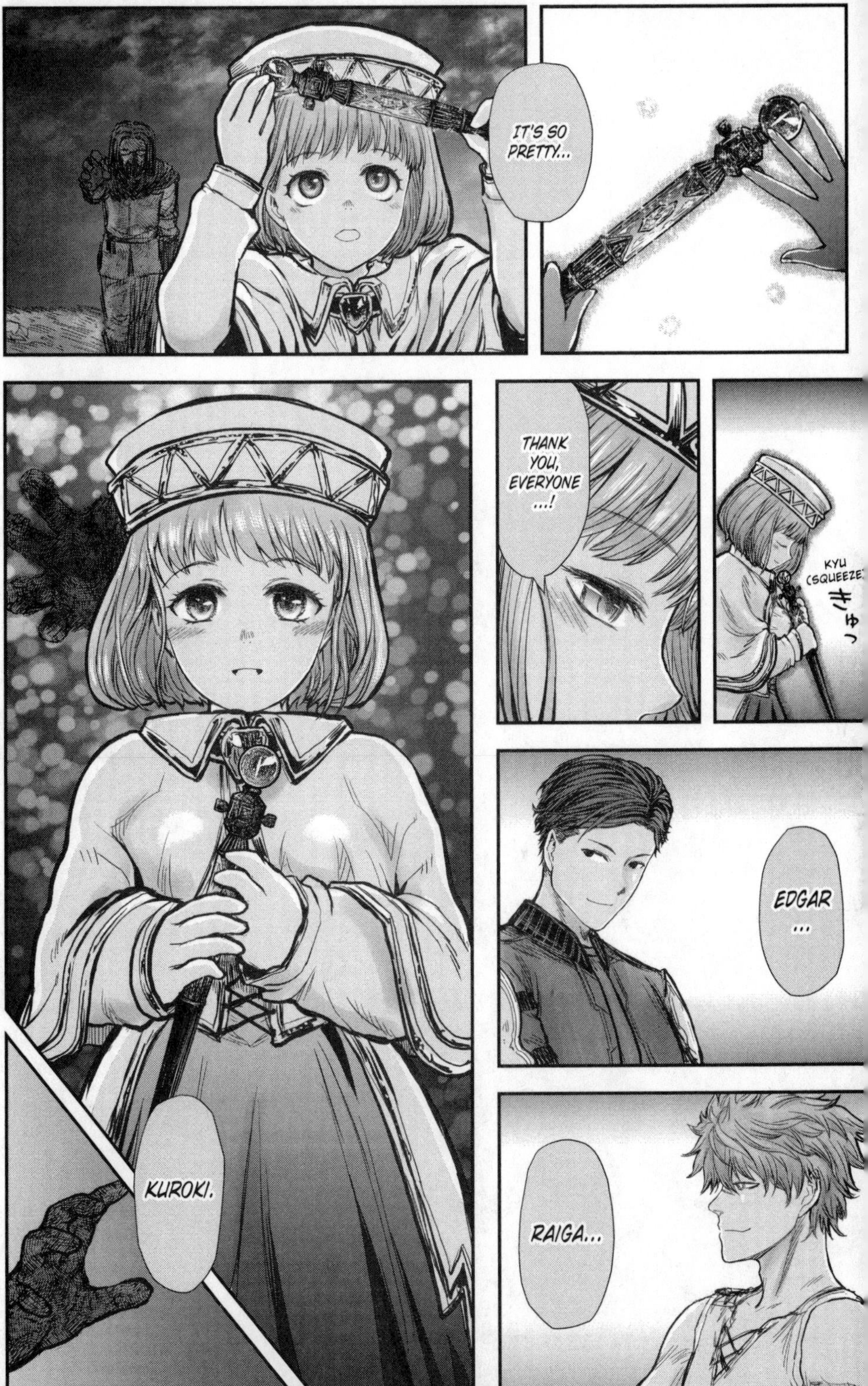
IT'S SO PRETTY...
KYU (SQUEEZE)
きゅっ
THANK YOU, EVERYONE ...!
EDGAR ...
RAIGA...
KUROKI.

THE FOUR OF US SPENT THIS DAY TOGETHER...

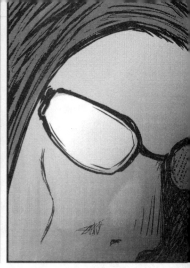

YEAH, FOR SURE.

...I'LL NEVER FORGET IT.

...AND I'M SURE...

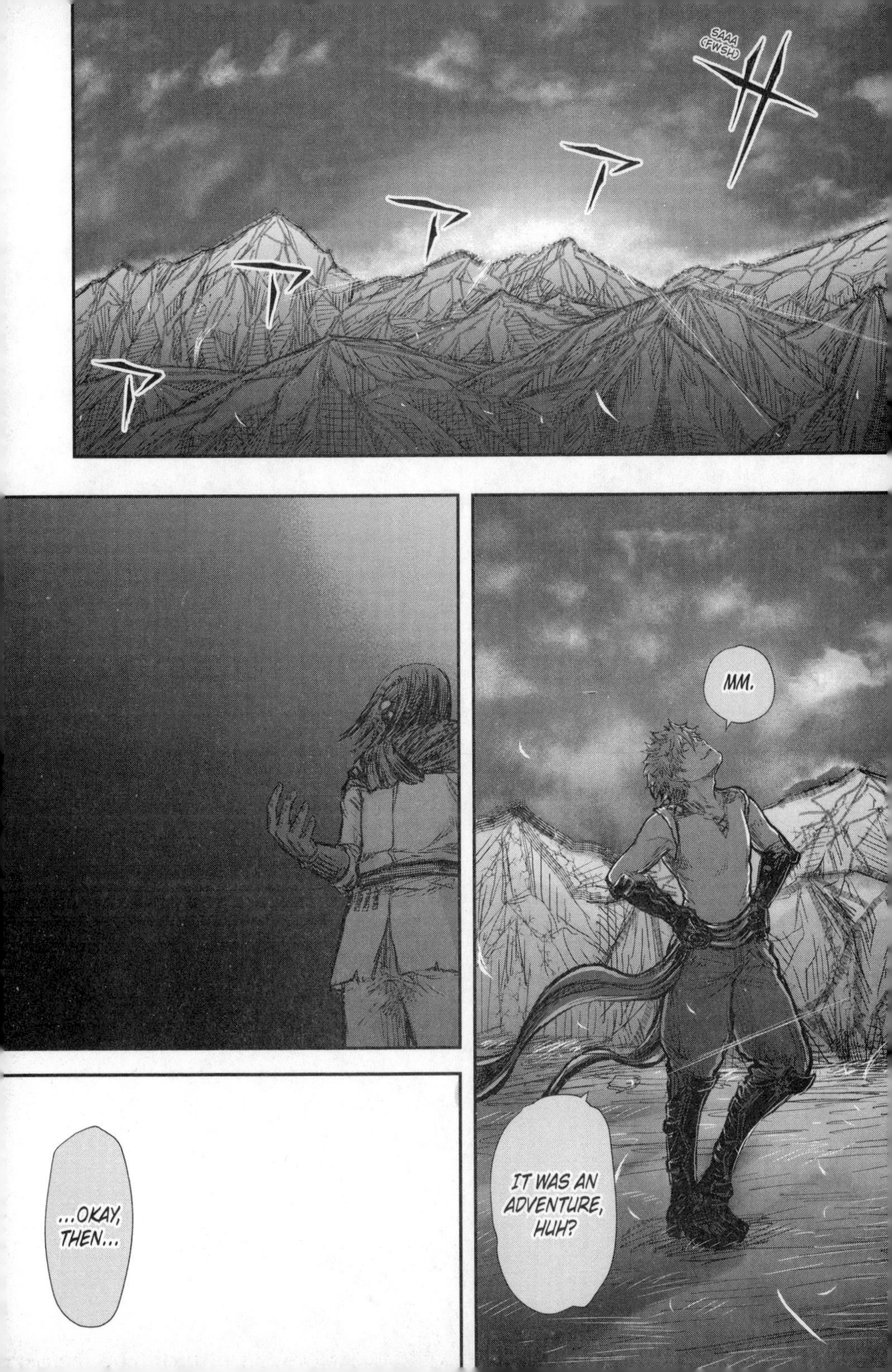
SAAA
(FWSH)
MM.
IT WAS AN ADVENTURE, HUH?
...OKAY, THEN...

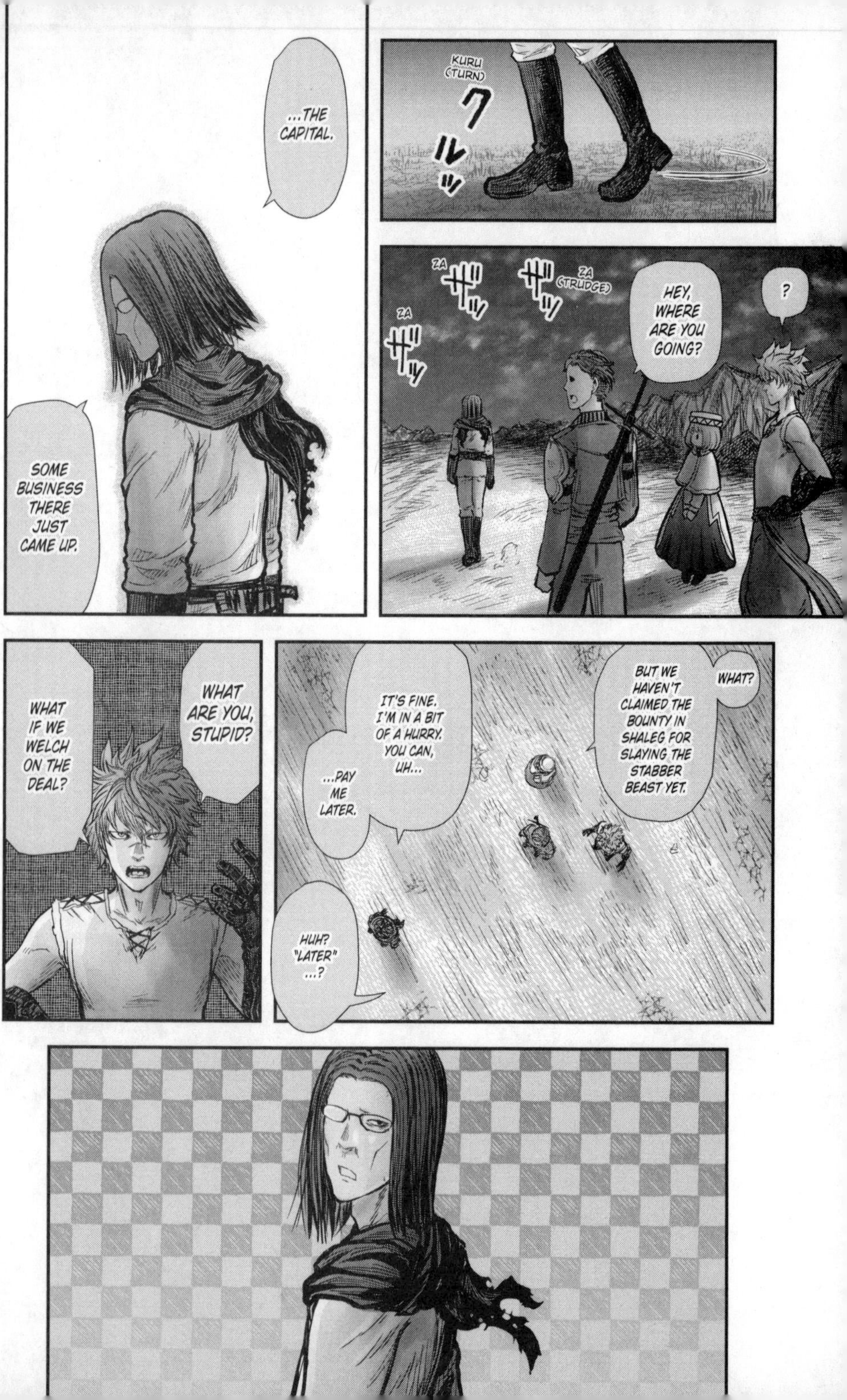
KURU (TURN)
クルッ
?
HEY, WHERE ARE YOU GOING?
ZA (TRUDGE)
ザッ
ZA
ザッ
ZA
ザッ
...THE CAPITAL.
SOME BUSINESS THERE JUST CAME UP.
WHAT?
BUT WE HAVEN'T CLAIMED THE BOUNTY IN SHALEG FOR SLAYING THE STABBER BEAST YET.
IT'S FINE. I'M IN A BIT OF A HURRY. YOU CAN, UH...
...PAY ME LATER.
HUH? "LATER" ...?
WHAT ARE YOU, STUPID?
WHAT IF WE WELCH ON THE DEAL?

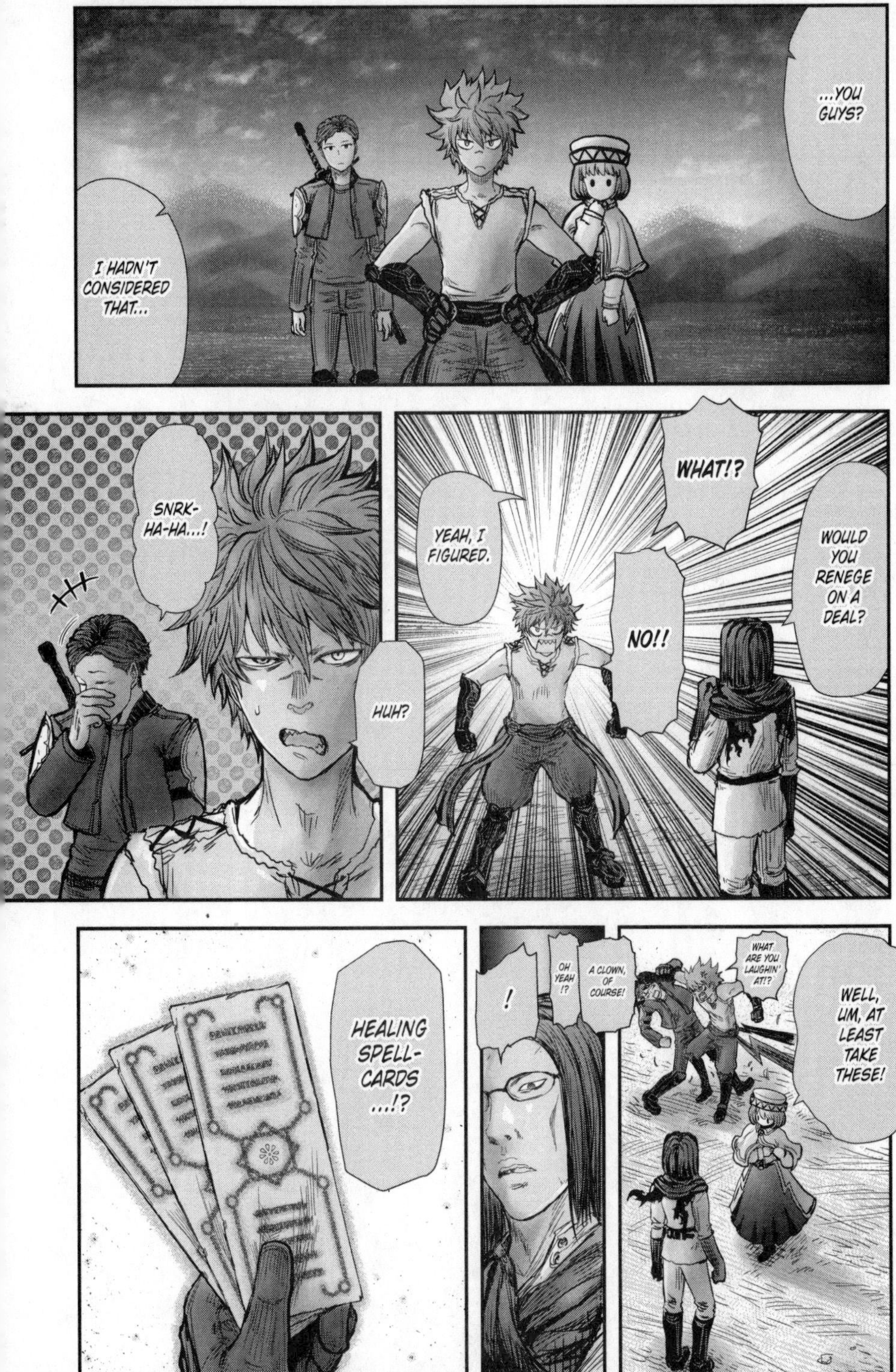
...YOU GUYS?
I HADN'T CONSIDERED THAT...
WOULD YOU RENEGE ON A DEAL?
WHAT!?
NO!!
YEAH, I FIGURED.
HUH?
SNRK-HA-HA...!
WELL, UM, AT LEAST TAKE THESE!
WHAT ARE YOU LAUGHIN' AT!?
A CLOWN, OF COURSE!
OH YEAH!?
!
HEALING SPELL-CARDS ...!?

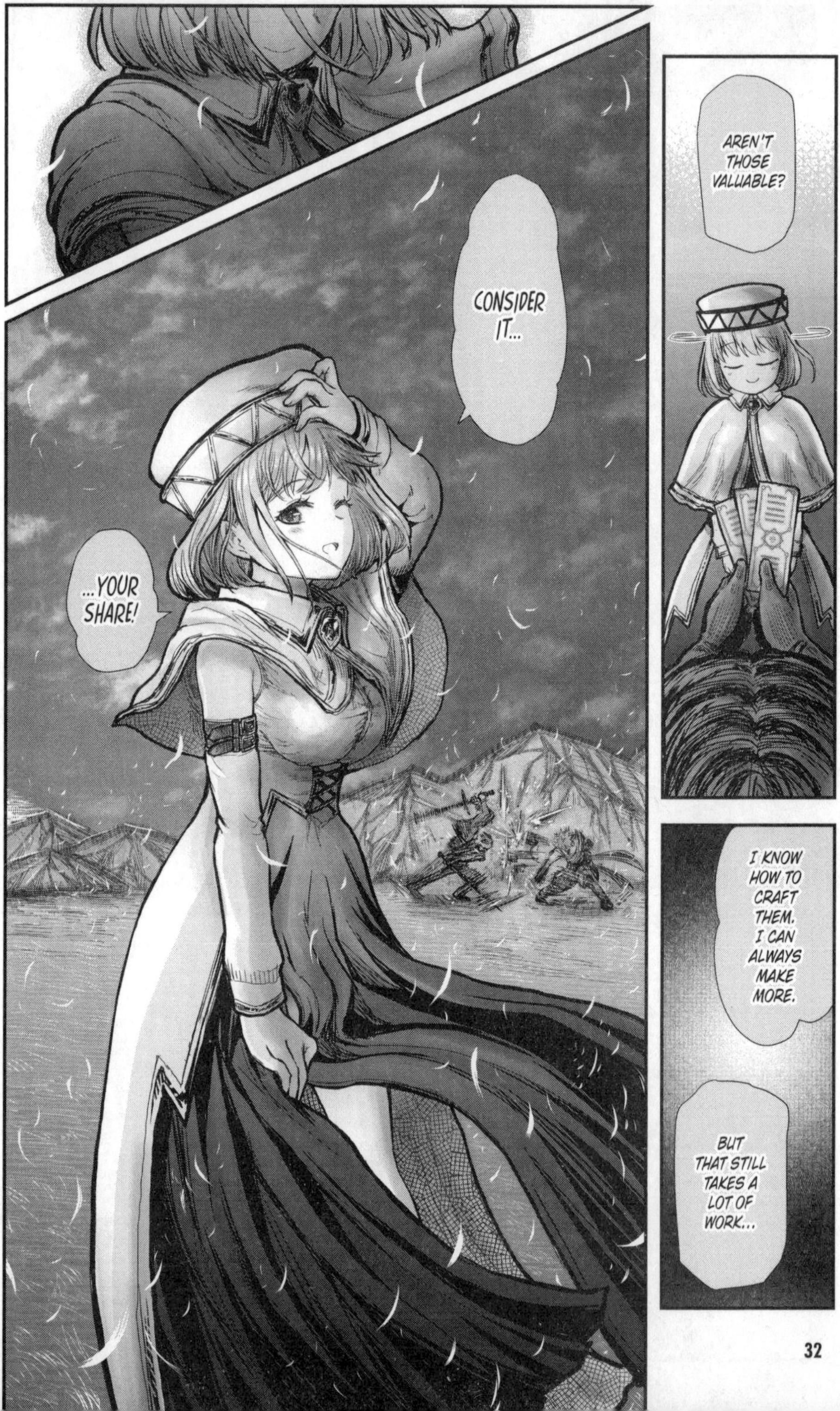
AREN'T THOSE VALUABLE?
I KNOW HOW TO CRAFT THEM. I CAN ALWAYS MAKE MORE.
BUT THAT STILL TAKES A LOT OF WORK...
CONSIDER IT...
...YOUR SHARE!

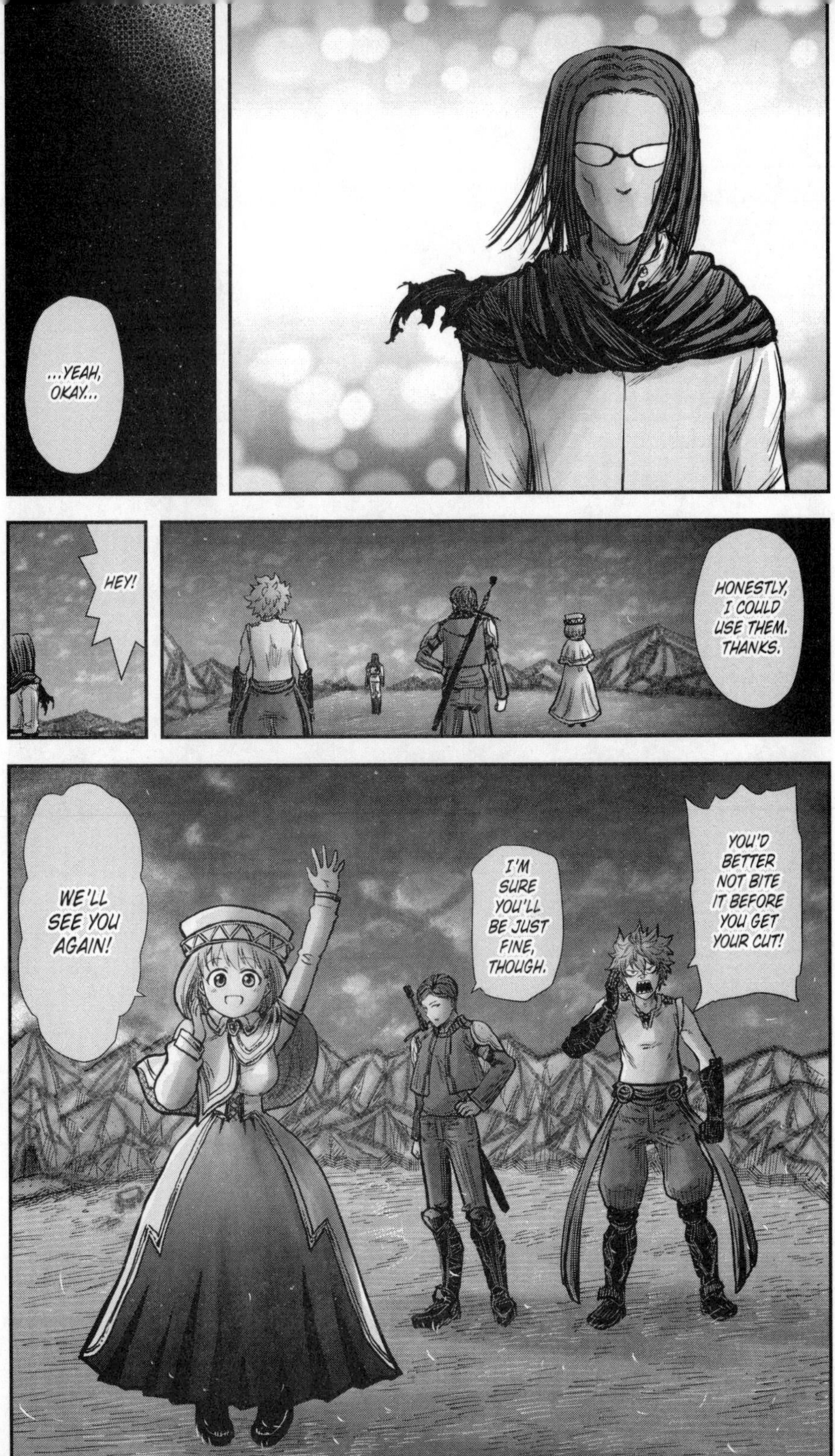
...YEAH, OKAY...
HONESTLY, I COULD USE THEM. THANKS.
HEY!
YOU'D BETTER NOT BITE IT BEFORE YOU GET YOUR CUT!
I'M SURE YOU'LL BE JUST FINE, THOUGH.
WE'LL SEE YOU AGAIN!

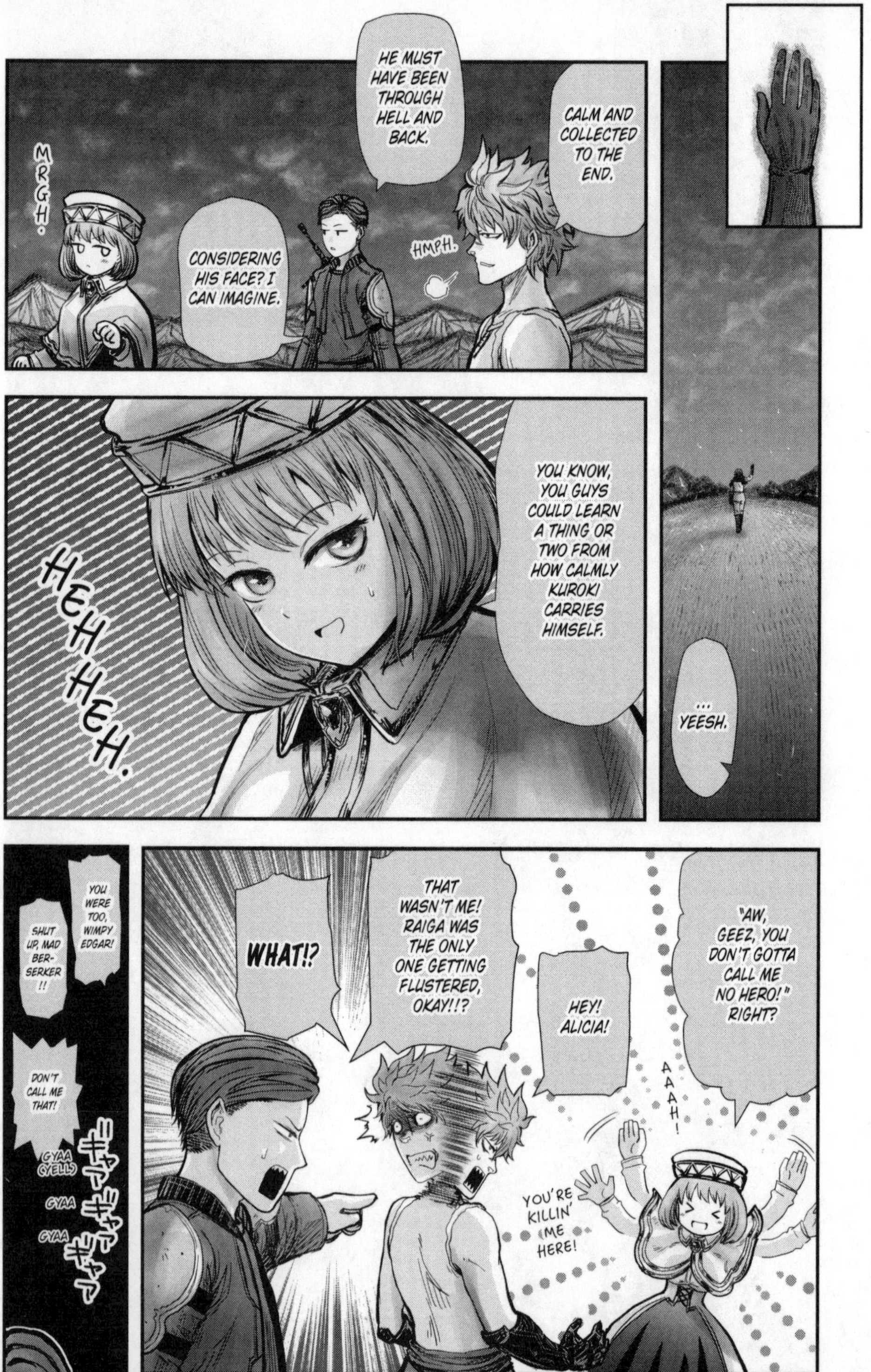
CALM AND COLLECTED TO THE END.
HE MUST HAVE BEEN THROUGH HELL AND BACK.
HMPH.
CONSIDERING HIS FACE? I CAN IMAGINE.
MRGH!
YOU KNOW, YOU GUYS COULD LEARN A THING OR TWO FROM HOW CALMLY KUROKI CARRIES HIMSELF.
HEH HEH HEH.
...YEESH.
"AW, GEEZ, YOU DON'T GOTTA CALL ME NO HERO!" RIGHT?
AAAH!
HEY! ALICIA!
THAT WASN'T ME! RAIGA WAS THE ONLY ONE GETTING FLUSTERED, OKAY!!?
WHAT!?
YOU'RE KILLIN' ME HERE!
YOU WERE TOO, WIMPY EDGAR!
SHUT UP, MAD BER-SERKER!!
DON'T CALL ME THAT!
ギャアギャアギャア
GYAA (YELL)
GYAA
GYAA

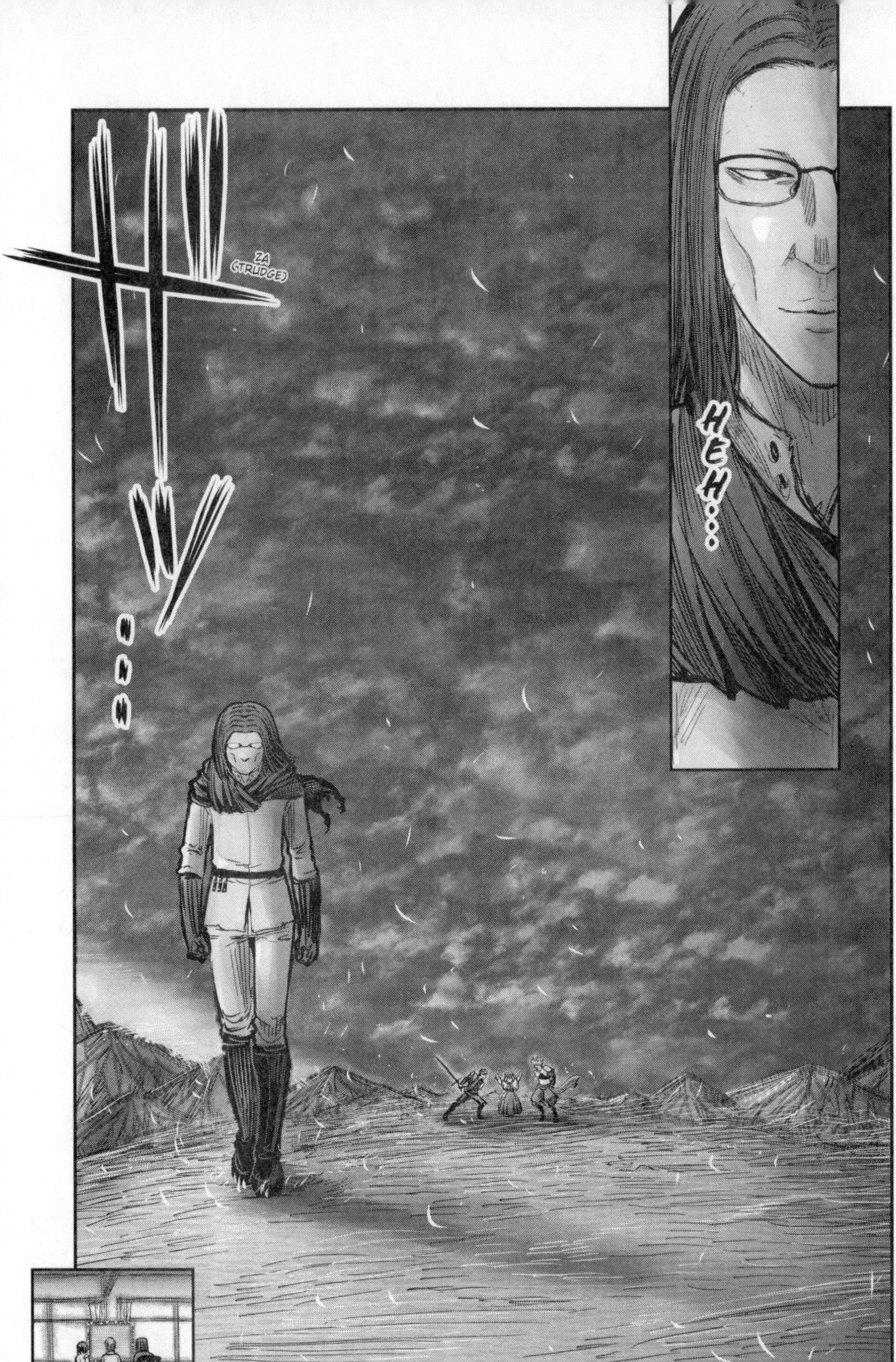
HEH...
ZA
(TRUDGE)

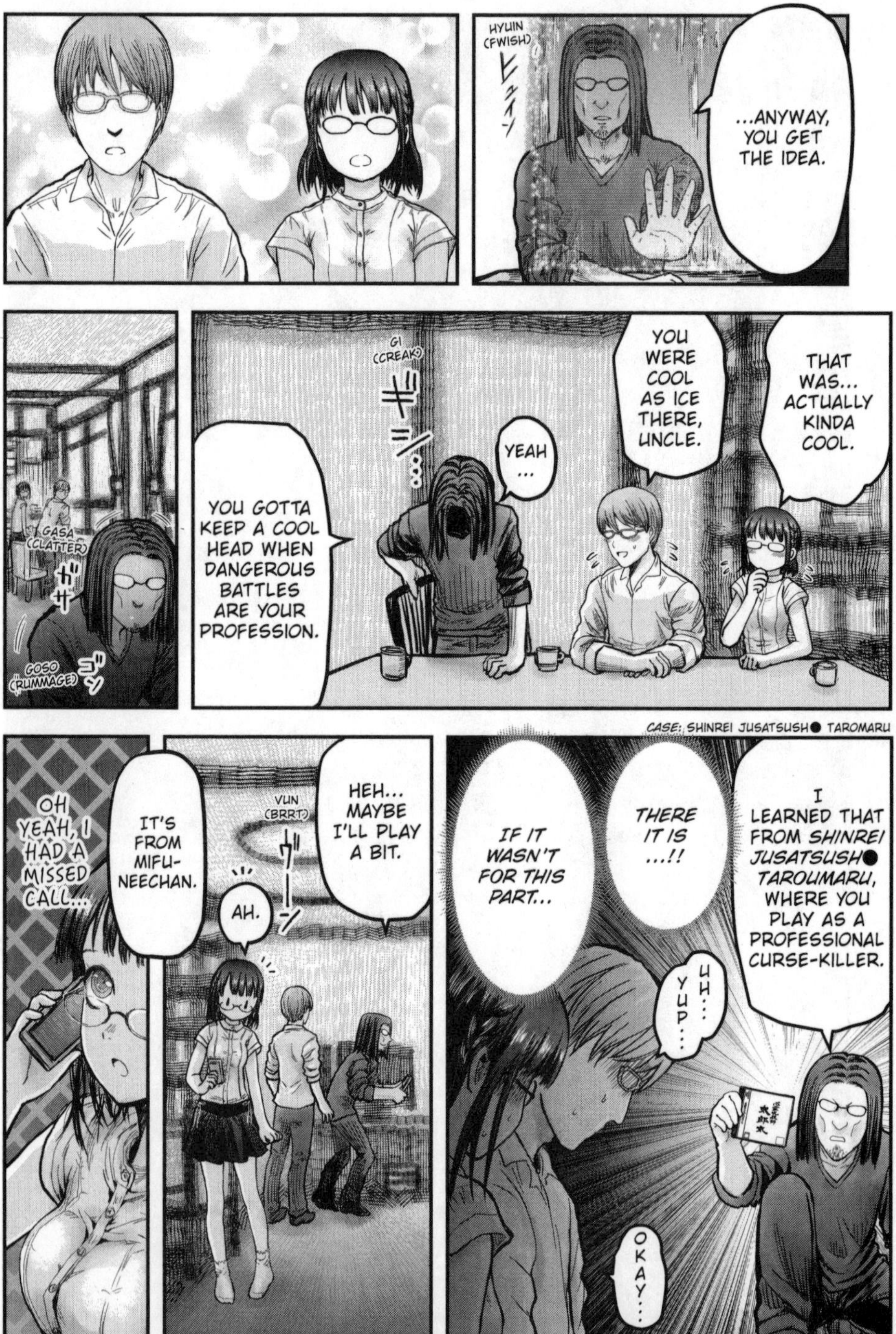
HYUIN (FWISH)
...ANYWAY, YOU GET THE IDEA.
THAT WAS... ACTUALLY KINDA COOL.
YOU WERE COOL AS ICE THERE, UNCLE.
YEAH...
GI (CREAK)
YOU GOTTA KEEP A COOL HEAD WHEN DANGEROUS BATTLES ARE YOUR PROFESSION.
GASA (CLATTER)
GOSO (RUMMAGE)
CASE: SHINREI JUSATSUSH● TAROMARU
I LEARNED THAT FROM SHINREI JUSATSUSH● TAROUMARU, WHERE YOU PLAY AS A PROFESSIONAL CURSE-KILLER.
THERE IT IS ...!!
IF IT WASN'T FOR THIS PART...
UH... YUP...
OKAY...
HEH... MAYBE I'LL PLAY A BIT.
VUN (BRRT)
AH.
IT'S FROM MIFU-NEECHAN.
OH YEAH, I HAD A MISSED CALL...

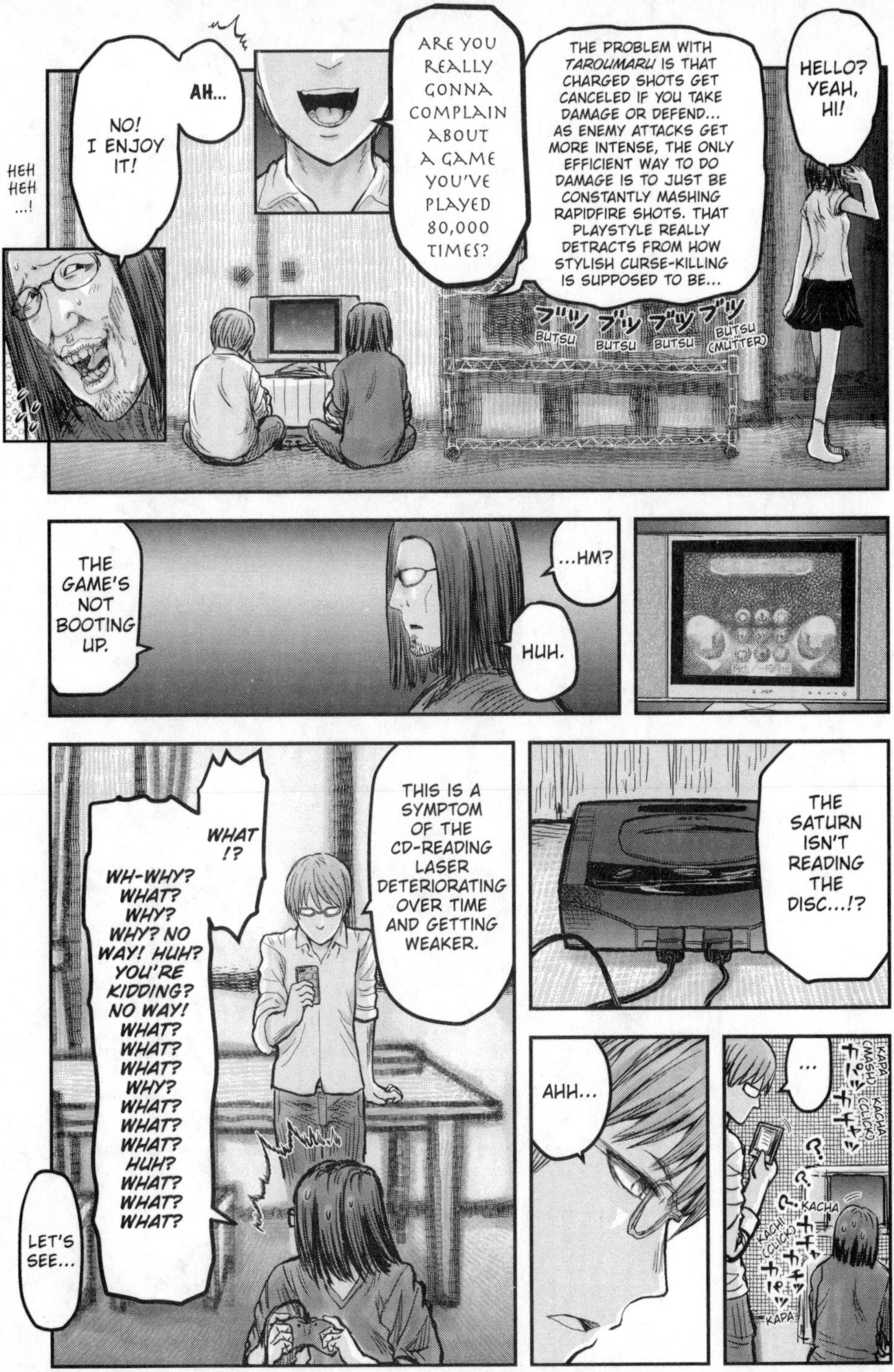
HELLO? YEAH, HI!
THE PROBLEM WITH *TAROUMARU* IS THAT CHARGED SHOTS GET CANCELED IF YOU TAKE DAMAGE OR DEFEND... AS ENEMY ATTACKS GET MORE INTENSE, THE ONLY EFFICIENT WAY TO DO DAMAGE IS TO JUST BE CONSTANTLY MASHING RAPIDFIRE SHOTS. THAT PLAYSTYLE REALLY DETRACTS FROM HOW STYLISH CURSE-KILLING IS SUPPOSED TO BE...
ブツ ブツ ブツ ブツ
BUTSU BUTSU BUTSU BUTSU (MUTTER)
ARE YOU REALLY GONNA COMPLAIN ABOUT A GAME YOU'VE PLAYED 80,000 TIMES?
AH...
NO! I ENJOY IT!
HEH HEH ...!
...HM?
HUH.
THE GAME'S NOT BOOTING UP.
THE SATURN ISN'T READING THE DISC...!?
...
カパッ カチャッ
KAPA (MASH) KACHA (CLICK)
KACHA
カチャ カチッ カパッ
KACHI (CLICK) KAPA
AHH...
THIS IS A SYMPTOM OF THE CD-READING LASER DETERIORATING OVER TIME AND GETTING WEAKER.
WHAT!?
WH-WHY? WHAT? WHY? WHY? NO WAY! HUH? YOU'RE KIDDING? NO WAY! WHAT? WHAT? WHAT? WHY? WHAT? WHAT? WHAT? HUH? WHAT? WHAT? WHAT?
LET'S SEE...

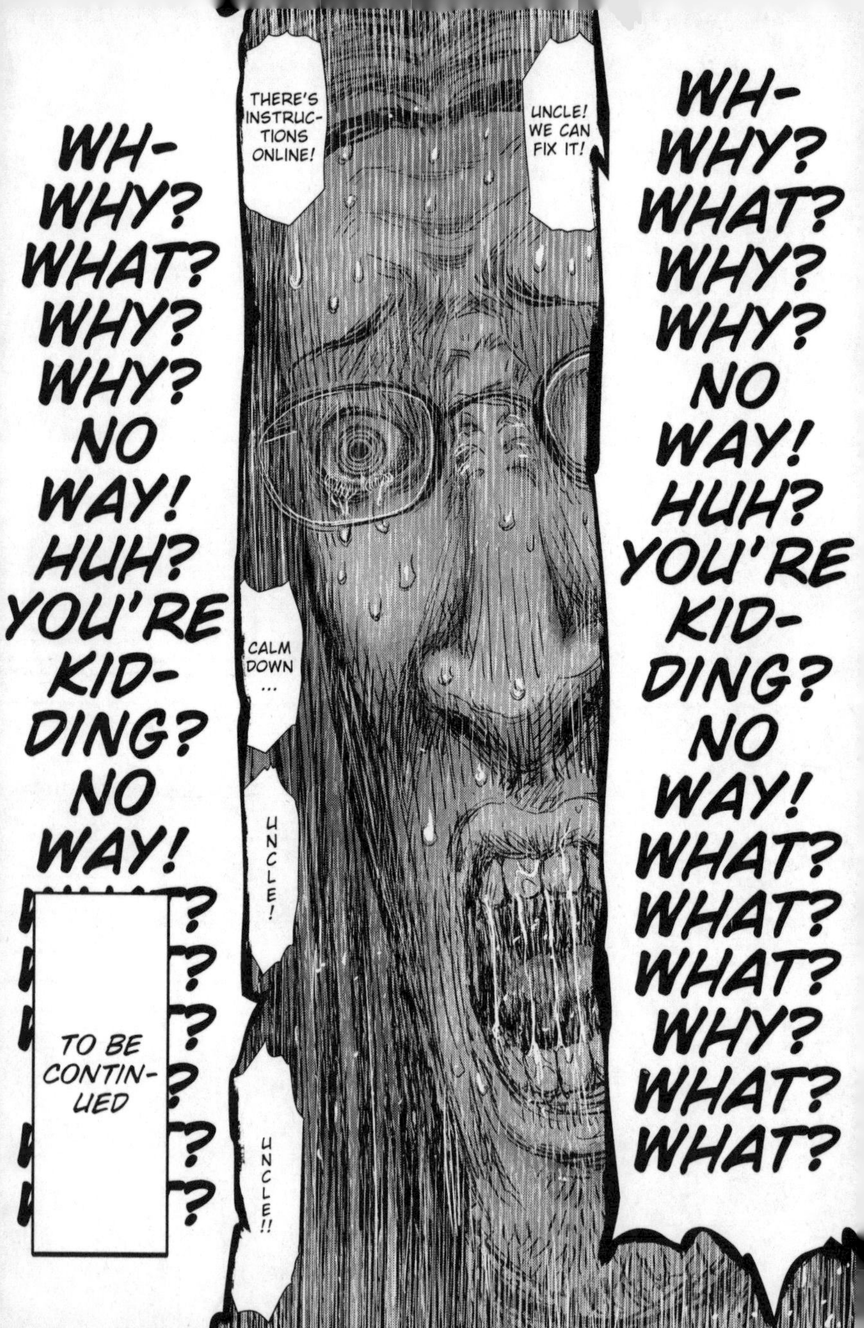
WH-WHY? WHAT? WHY? WHY? NO WAY! HUH? YOU'RE KID-DING? NO WAY! WHAT? WHAT? WHAT? WHY? WHAT? WHAT?
UNCLE! WE CAN FIX IT!
THERE'S INSTRUC-TIONS ONLINE!
CALM DOWN ...
UNCLE!
UNCLE!!
WH-WHY? WHAT? WHY? WHY? NO WAY! HUH? YOU'RE KID-DING? NO WAY!
TO BE CONTIN-UED

Business Lingo

Agenda (noun): A list of items to discuss at a meeting. An outline.
Agree (verb): To concur about something. To consent to something.
Example sentence:
"Please share the stakeholder AGENDA our company AGREED to ASAP."

TIPS

UNCLE from ANOTHER WORLD

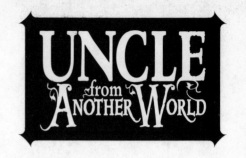

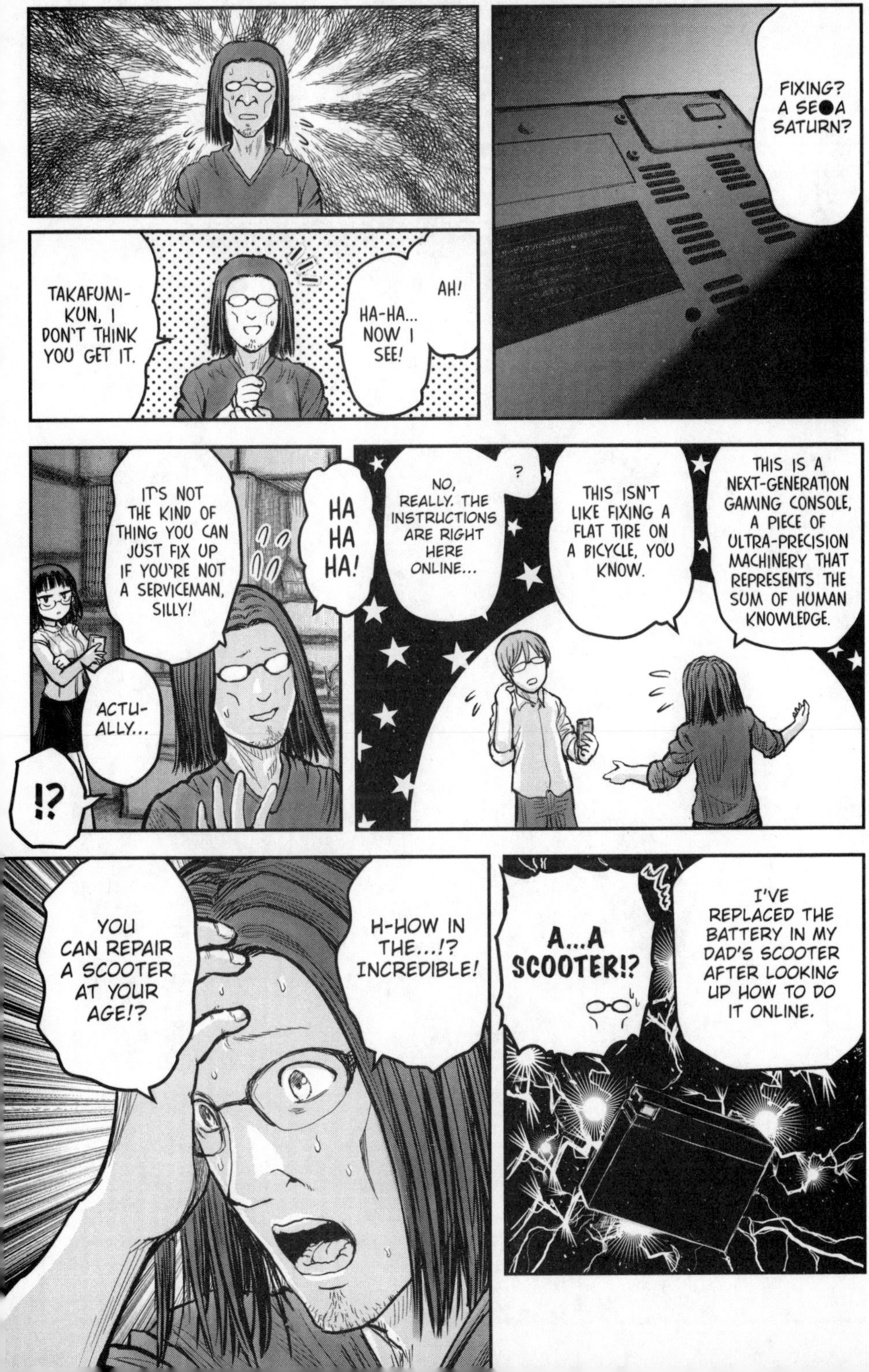
FIXING? A SE●A SATURN?
AH!
HA-HA... NOW I SEE!
TAKAFUMI-KUN, I DON'T THINK YOU GET IT.
THIS IS A NEXT-GENERATION GAMING CONSOLE, A PIECE OF ULTRA-PRECISION MACHINERY THAT REPRESENTS THE SUM OF HUMAN KNOWLEDGE.
THIS ISN'T LIKE FIXING A FLAT TIRE ON A BICYCLE, YOU KNOW.
?
NO, REALLY. THE INSTRUCTIONS ARE RIGHT HERE ONLINE...
HA HA HA!
IT'S NOT THE KIND OF THING YOU CAN JUST FIX UP IF YOU'RE NOT A SERVICEMAN, SILLY!
ACTU-ALLY...
!?
I'VE REPLACED THE BATTERY IN MY DAD'S SCOOTER AFTER LOOKING UP HOW TO DO IT ONLINE.
A...A SCOOTER!?
H-HOW IN THE...!? INCREDIBLE!
YOU CAN REPAIR A SCOOTER AT YOUR AGE!?

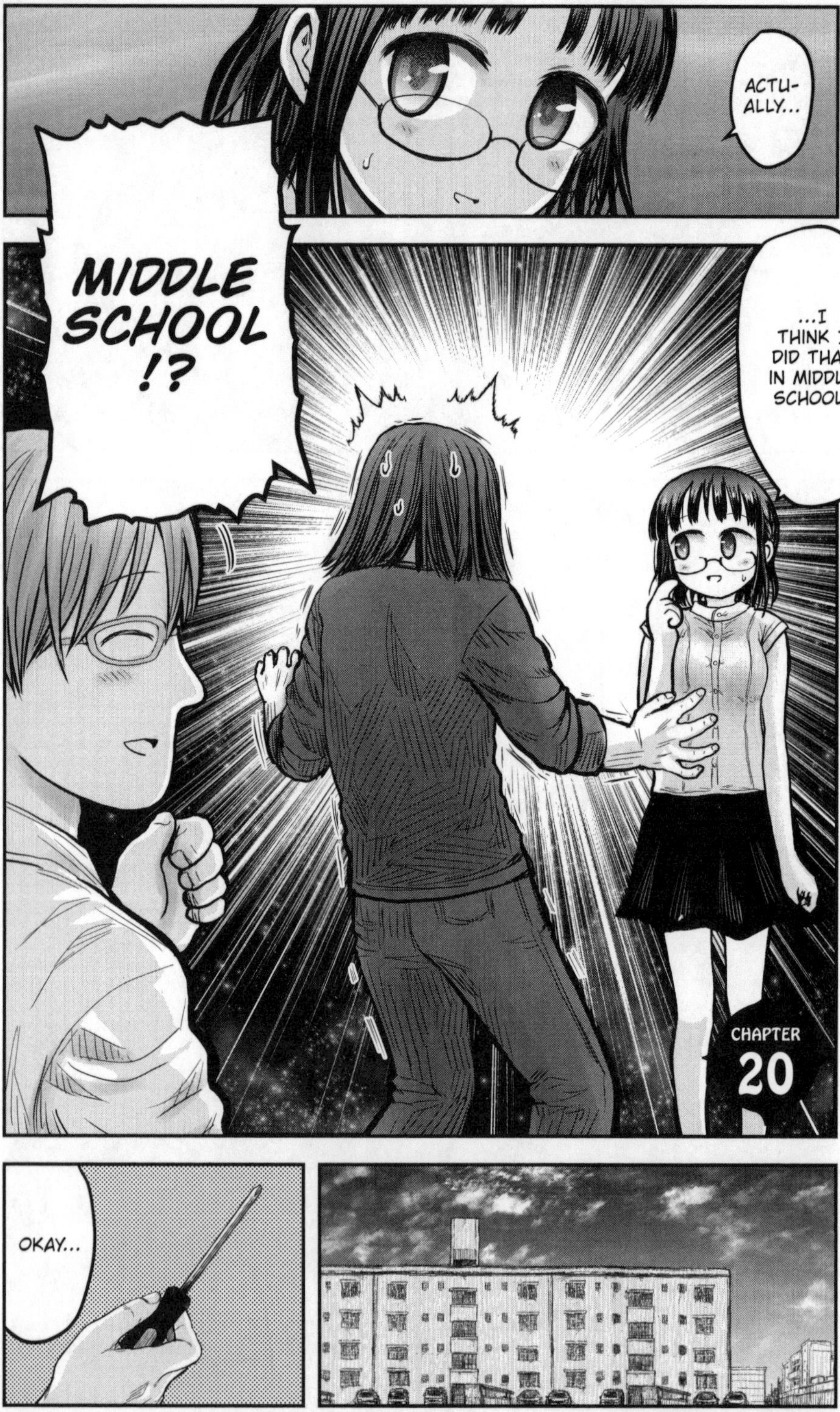
ACTU-ALLY...
...I THINK I DID THAT IN MIDDLE SCHOOL.
MIDDLE SCHOOL !?
CHAPTER 20
OKAY...

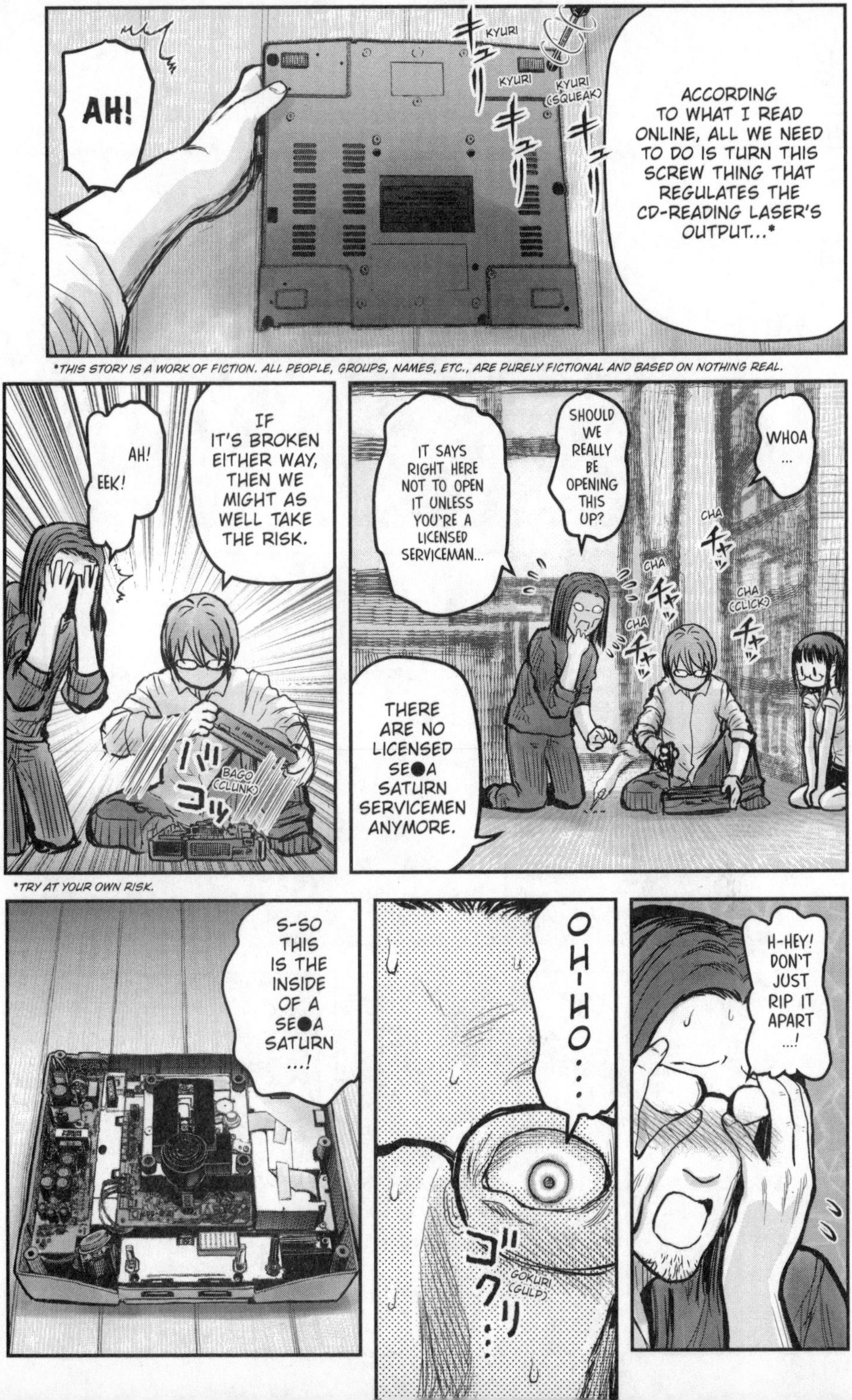
ACCORDING TO WHAT I READ ONLINE, ALL WE NEED TO DO IS TURN THIS SCREW THING THAT REGULATES THE CD-READING LASER'S OUTPUT...*
KYURI (SQUEAK)
KYURI
KYURI
AH!
WHOA...
SHOULD WE REALLY BE OPENING THIS UP?
IT SAYS RIGHT HERE NOT TO OPEN IT UNLESS YOU'RE A LICENSED SERVICEMAN...
CHA
CHA (CLICK)
CHA
CHA
THERE ARE NO LICENSED SE●A SATURN SERVICEMEN ANYMORE.
IF IT'S BROKEN EITHER WAY, THEN WE MIGHT AS WELL TAKE THE RISK.
AH!
EEK!
BAGO (CLUNK)
H-HEY! DON'T JUST RIP IT APART...!
OH-HO...
GOKURI (GULP)
S-SO THIS IS THE INSIDE OF A SE●A SATURN...!

*THIS STORY IS A WORK OF FICTION. ALL PEOPLE, GROUPS, NAMES, ETC., ARE PURELY FICTIONAL AND BASED ON NOTHING REAL.

*TRY AT YOUR OWN RISK.

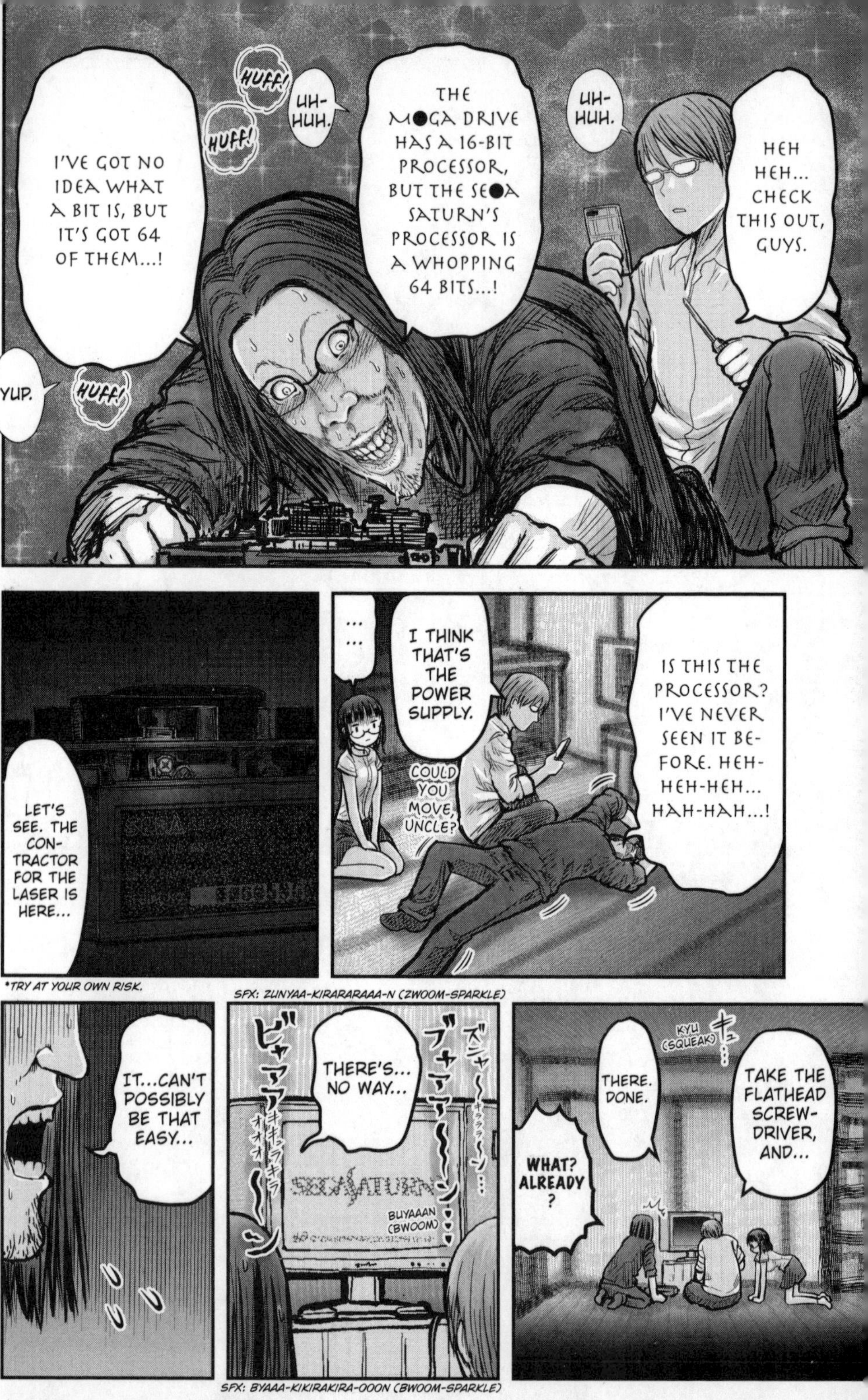
HEH HEH... CHECK THIS OUT, GUYS.
UH-HUH.
THE M●GA DRIVE HAS A 16-BIT PROCESSOR, BUT THE SE●A SATURN'S PROCESSOR IS A WHOPPING 64 BITS...!
UH-HUH.
HUFF!
HUFF!
I'VE GOT NO IDEA WHAT A BIT IS, BUT IT'S GOT 64 OF THEM...!
HUFF!
YUP.
IS THIS THE PROCESSOR? I'VE NEVER SEEN IT BEFORE. HEH-HEH-HEH... HAH-HAH...!
I THINK THAT'S THE POWER SUPPLY.
......
COULD YOU MOVE, UNCLE?
LET'S SEE. THE CONTRACTOR FOR THE LASER IS HERE...
*TRY AT YOUR OWN RISK.
キュ…
KYU (SQUEAK)
TAKE THE FLATHEAD SCREWDRIVER, AND...
THERE. DONE.
WHAT? ALREADY?
SFX: ZUNYAA-KIRARARAAA-N (ZWOOM-SPARKLE)
ズニャ～キラララ～ン…
ブヤァア～～ン…
BUYAAAN (BWOOM)
THERE'S... NO WAY...
ビャアァ～キュラキラオオオ～～ン
IT...CAN'T POSSIBLY BE THAT EASY...
SFX: BYAAA-KIKIRAKIRA-OOON (BWOOM-SPARKLE)

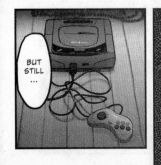

BUT
STILL
...

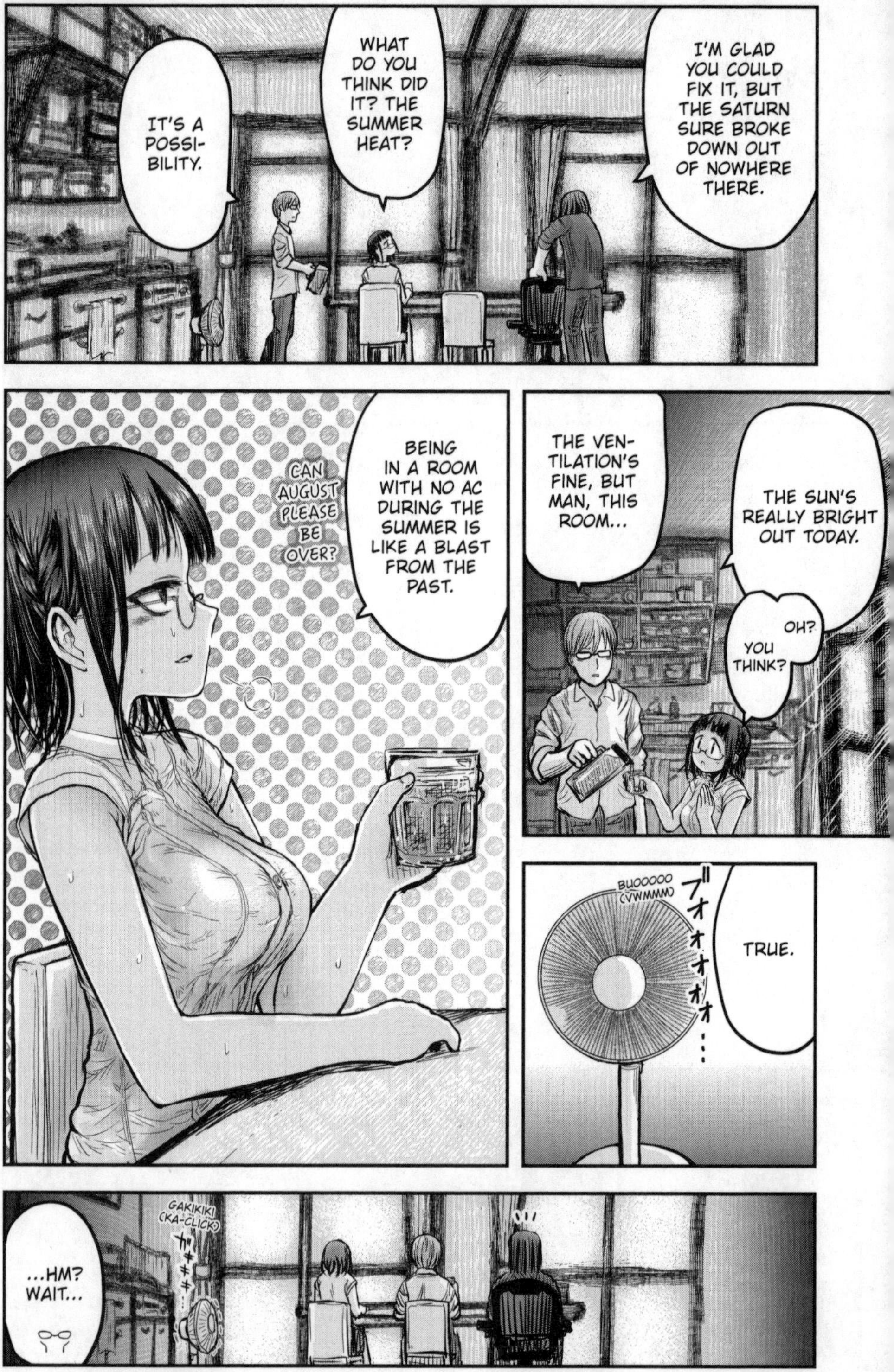
I'M GLAD YOU COULD FIX IT, BUT THE SATURN SURE BROKE DOWN OUT OF NOWHERE THERE.
WHAT DO YOU THINK DID IT? THE SUMMER HEAT?
IT'S A POSSIBILITY.
THE SUN'S REALLY BRIGHT OUT TODAY.
THE VENTILATION'S FINE, BUT MAN, THIS ROOM...
OH? YOU THINK?
BUOOOOO (VWMMM)
ブォォォォォ…
TRUE.
BEING IN A ROOM WITH NO AC DURING THE SUMMER IS LIKE A BLAST FROM THE PAST.
CAN AUGUST PLEASE BE OVER?
GAKIKIKI (KA-CLICK)
ガキキキ
...HM? WAIT...

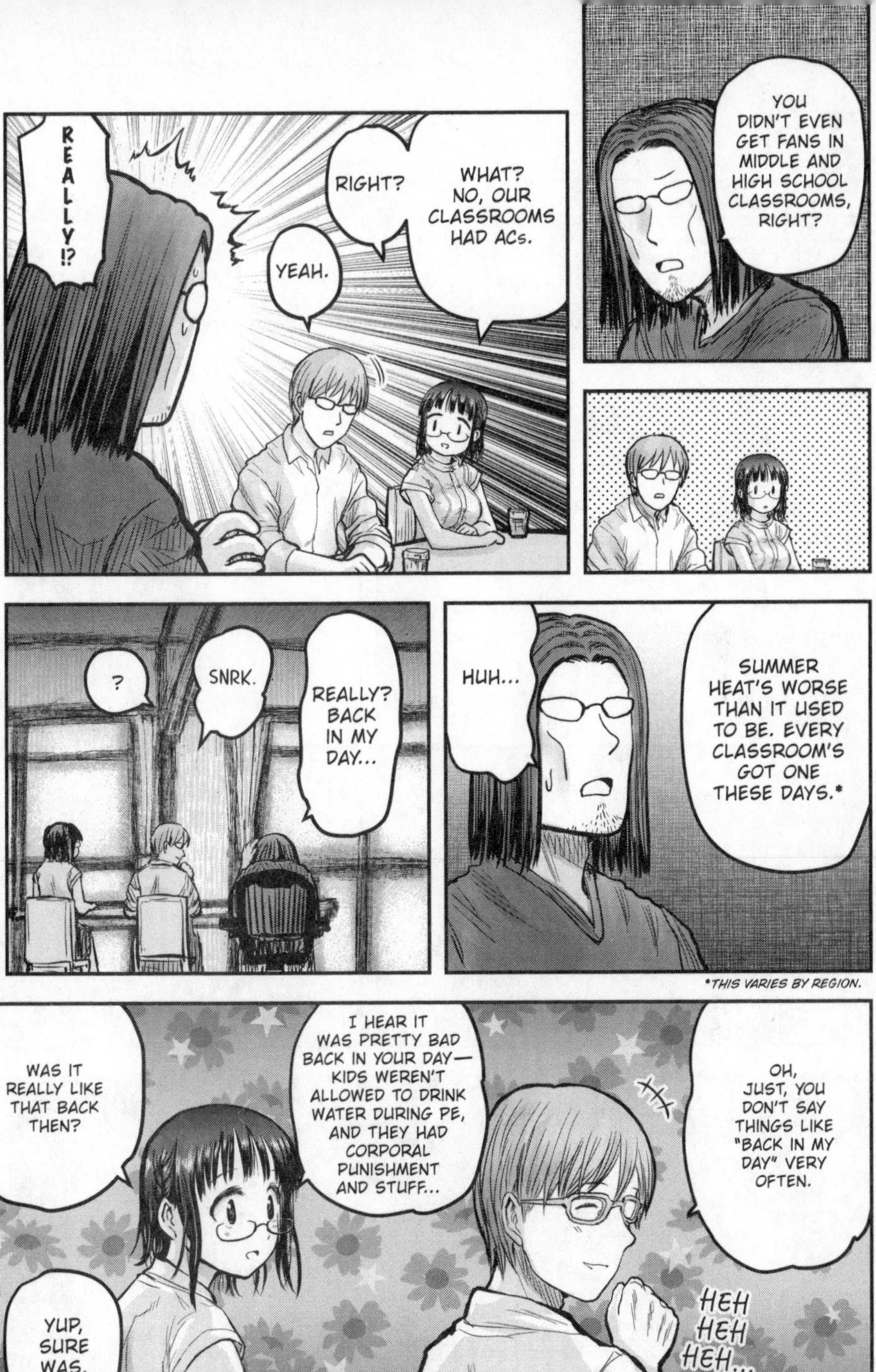
YOU DIDN'T EVEN GET FANS IN MIDDLE AND HIGH SCHOOL CLASSROOMS, RIGHT?
WHAT? NO, OUR CLASSROOMS HAD ACs.
RIGHT?
YEAH.
REALLY!?
SUMMER HEAT'S WORSE THAN IT USED TO BE. EVERY CLASSROOM'S GOT ONE THESE DAYS.*
HUH...
REALLY? BACK IN MY DAY...
SNRK.
?
*THIS VARIES BY REGION.
OH, JUST, YOU DON'T SAY THINGS LIKE "BACK IN MY DAY" VERY OFTEN.
I HEAR IT WAS PRETTY BAD BACK IN YOUR DAY—KIDS WEREN'T ALLOWED TO DRINK WATER DURING PE, AND THEY HAD CORPORAL PUNISHMENT AND STUFF...
WAS IT REALLY LIKE THAT BACK THEN?
HEH HEH HEH...
YUP, SURE WAS.

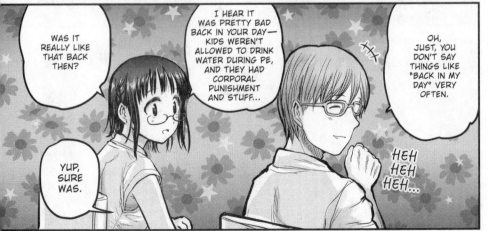

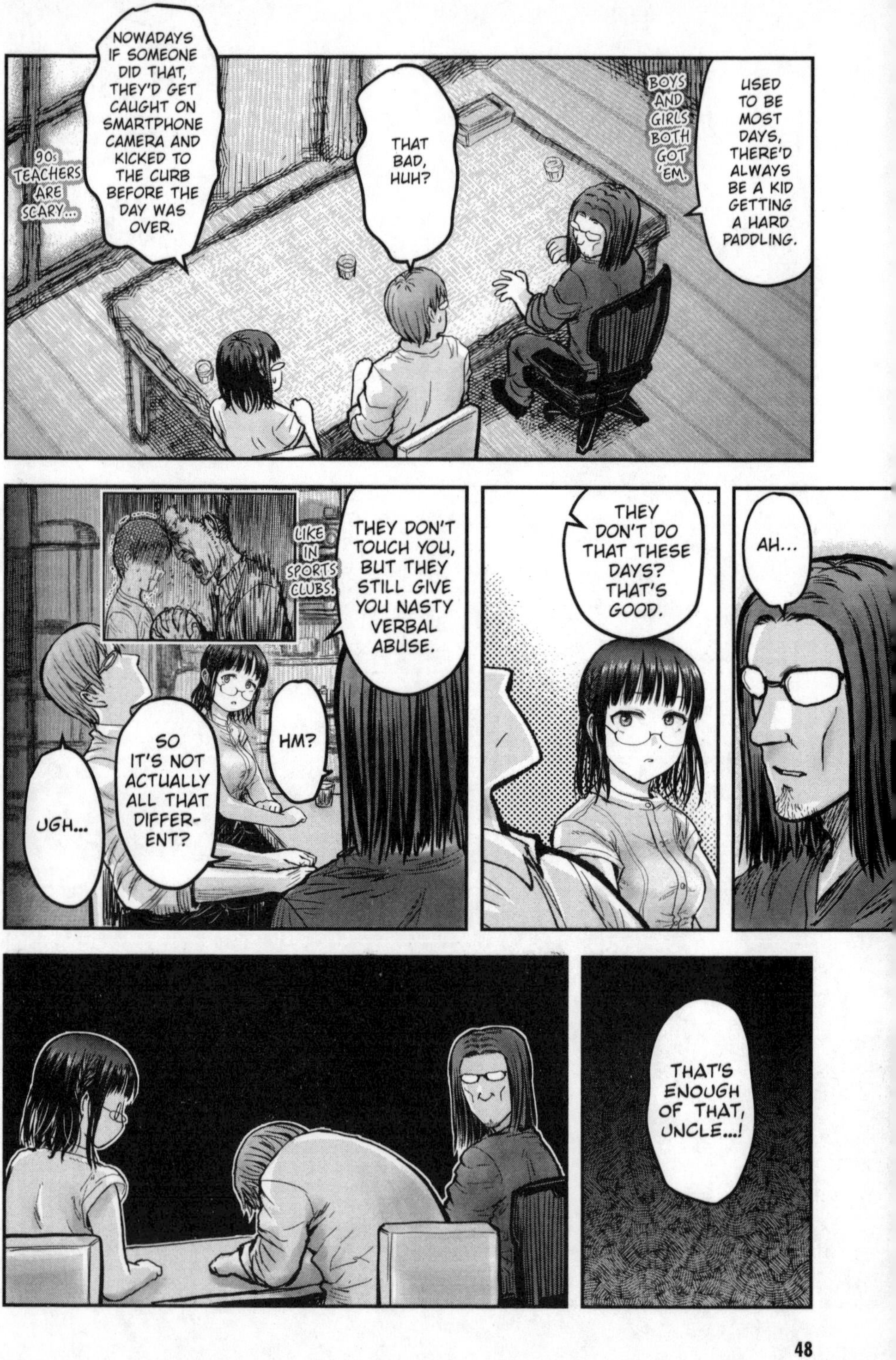
USED TO BE MOST DAYS, THERE'D ALWAYS BE A KID GETTING A HARD PADDLING.
BOYS AND GIRLS BOTH GOT 'EM.
THAT BAD, HUH?
NOWADAYS IF SOMEONE DID THAT, THEY'D GET CAUGHT ON SMARTPHONE CAMERA AND KICKED TO THE CURB BEFORE THE DAY WAS OVER.
90s TEACHERS ARE SCARY...
AH...
THEY DON'T DO THAT THESE DAYS? THAT'S GOOD.
THEY DON'T TOUCH YOU, BUT THEY STILL GIVE YOU NASTY VERBAL ABUSE.
LIKE IN SPORTS CLUBS.
HM?
SO IT'S NOT ACTUALLY ALL THAT DIFFER-ENT?
UGH...
THAT'S ENOUGH OF THAT, UNCLE...!

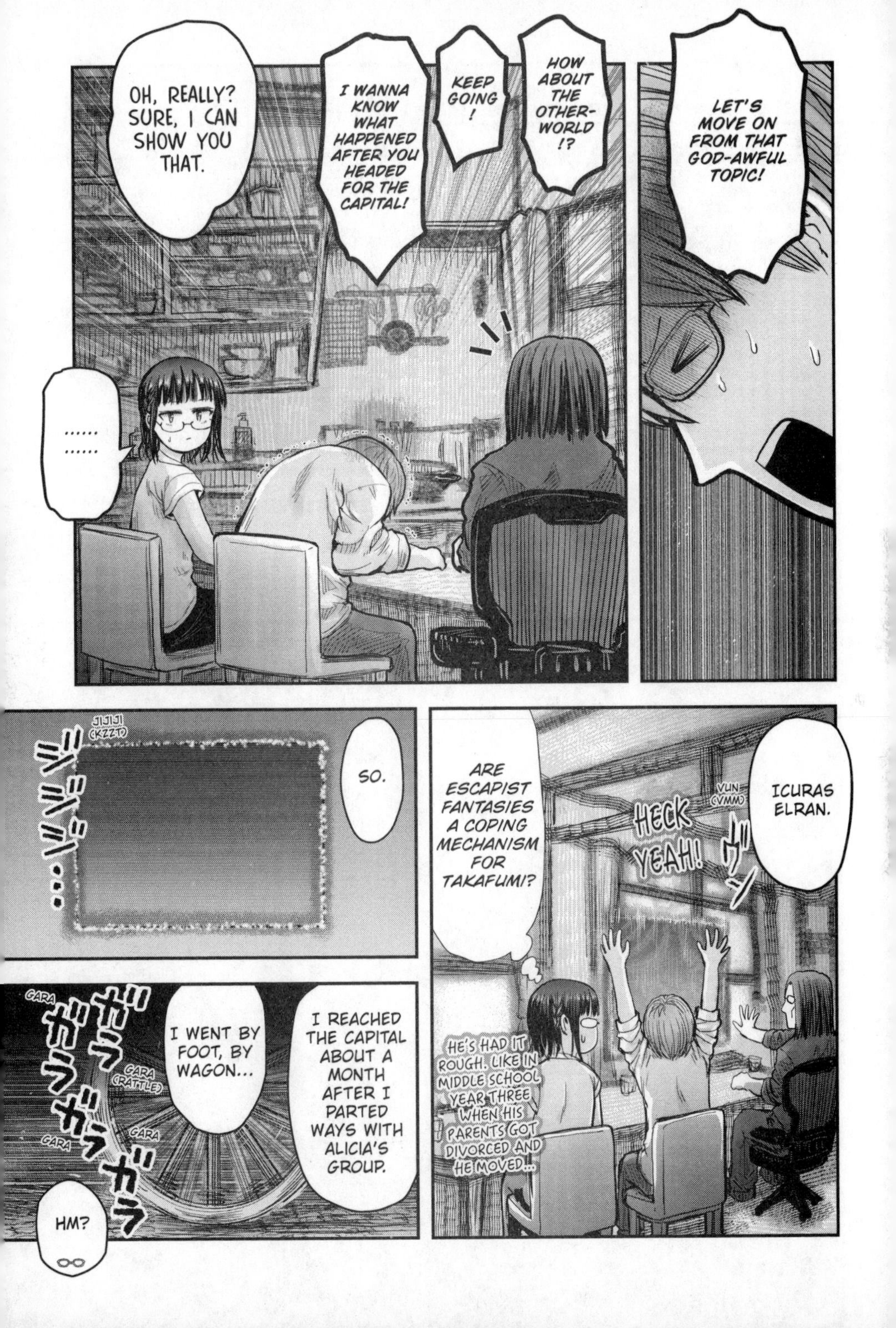

LET'S MOVE ON FROM THAT GOD-AWFUL TOPIC!
HOW ABOUT THE OTHER-WORLD!?
KEEP GOING!
I WANNA KNOW WHAT HAPPENED AFTER YOU HEADED FOR THE CAPITAL!
OH, REALLY? SURE, I CAN SHOW YOU THAT.
......
......
ICURAS ELRAN.
VUN (VMM)
HECK YEAH!
ARE ESCAPIST FANTASIES A COPING MECHANISM FOR TAKAFUMI?
HE'S HAD IT ROUGH. LIKE IN MIDDLE SCHOOL YEAR THREE WHEN HIS PARENTS GOT DIVORCED AND HE MOVED...
SO.
JIJIJI (KZZT)
I REACHED THE CAPITAL ABOUT A MONTH AFTER I PARTED WAYS WITH ALICIA'S GROUP.
I WENT BY FOOT, BY WAGON...
GARA
GARA (RATTLE)
GARA
GARA
HM?

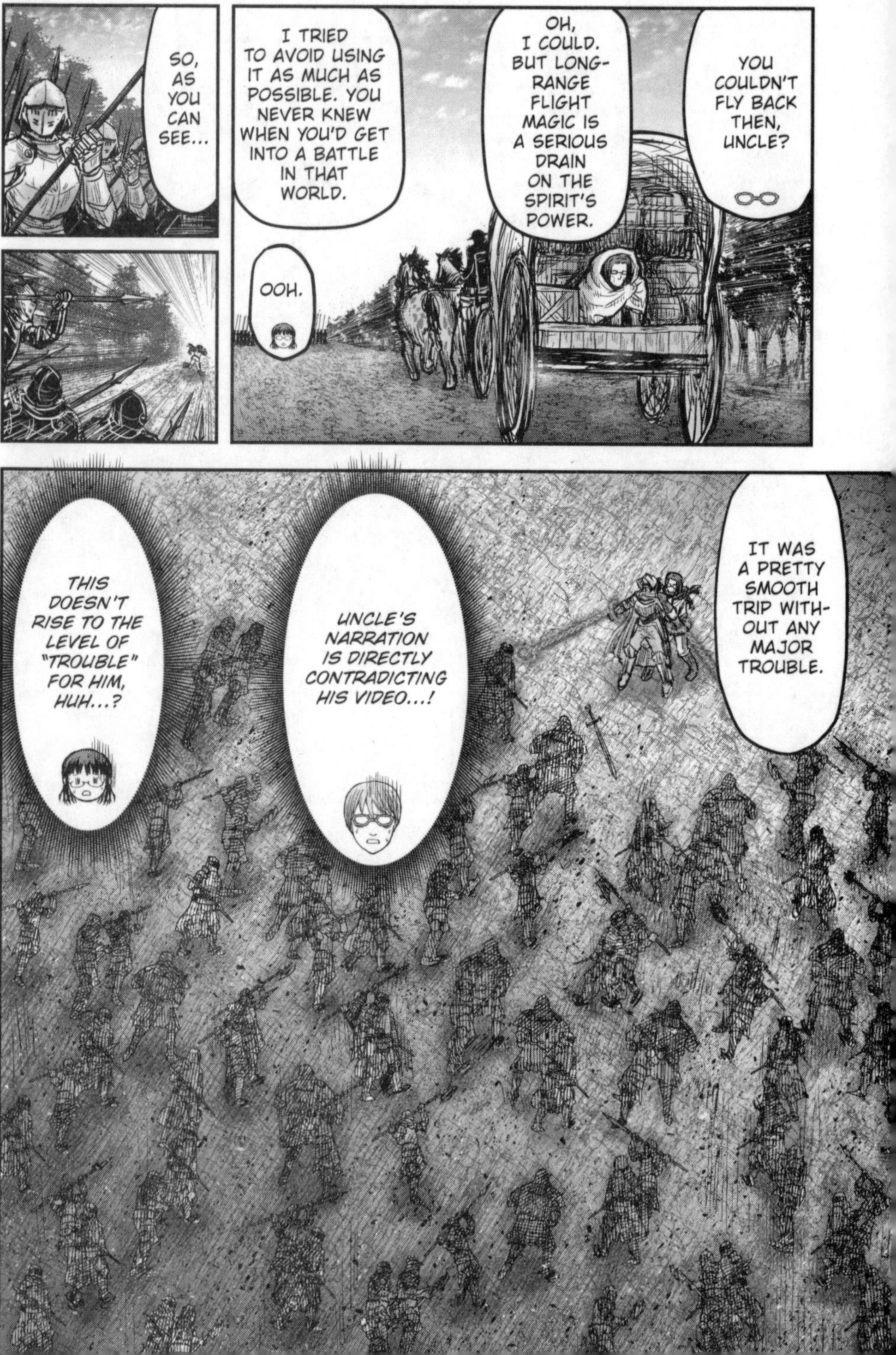
YOU COULDN'T FLY BACK THEN, UNCLE?
OH, I COULD. BUT LONG-RANGE FLIGHT MAGIC IS A SERIOUS DRAIN ON THE SPIRIT'S POWER.
I TRIED TO AVOID USING IT AS MUCH AS POSSIBLE. YOU NEVER KNEW WHEN YOU'D GET INTO A BATTLE IN THAT WORLD.
OOH.
SO, AS YOU CAN SEE...
IT WAS A PRETTY SMOOTH TRIP WITH-OUT ANY MAJOR TROUBLE.
UNCLE'S NARRATION IS DIRECTLY CONTRADICTING HIS VIDEO...!
THIS DOESN'T RISE TO THE LEVEL OF "TROUBLE" FOR HIM, HUH...?

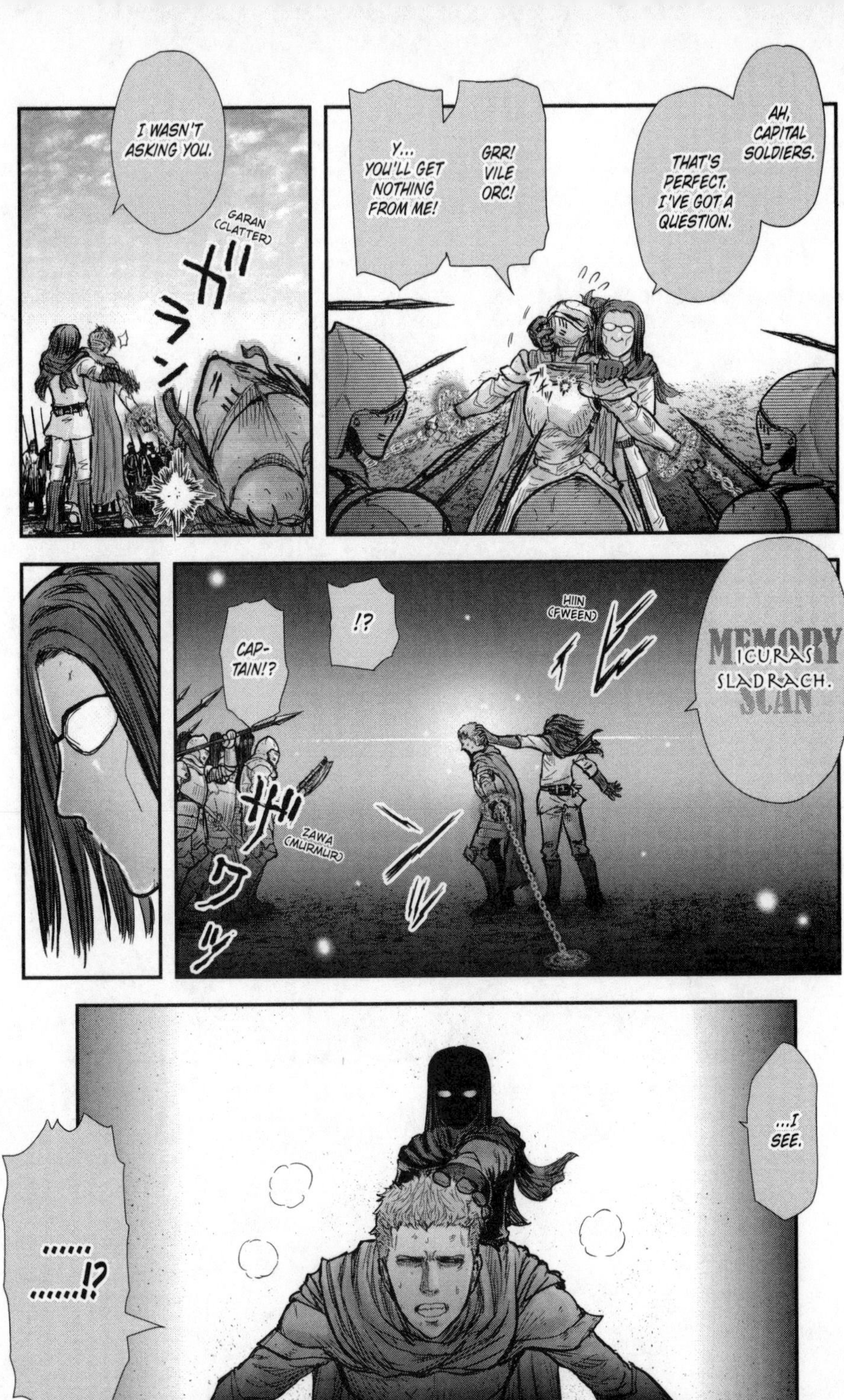
AH, CAPITAL SOLDIERS.
THAT'S PERFECT. I'VE GOT A QUESTION.
GRR! VILE ORC!
Y... YOU'LL GET NOTHING FROM ME!
I WASN'T ASKING YOU.
GARAN (CLATTER)
MEMORY SCAN
ICURAS SLADRACH.
HIIN (FWEEN)
!?
CAP-TAIN!?
ZAWA (MURMUR)
...I SEE.
......
......!?

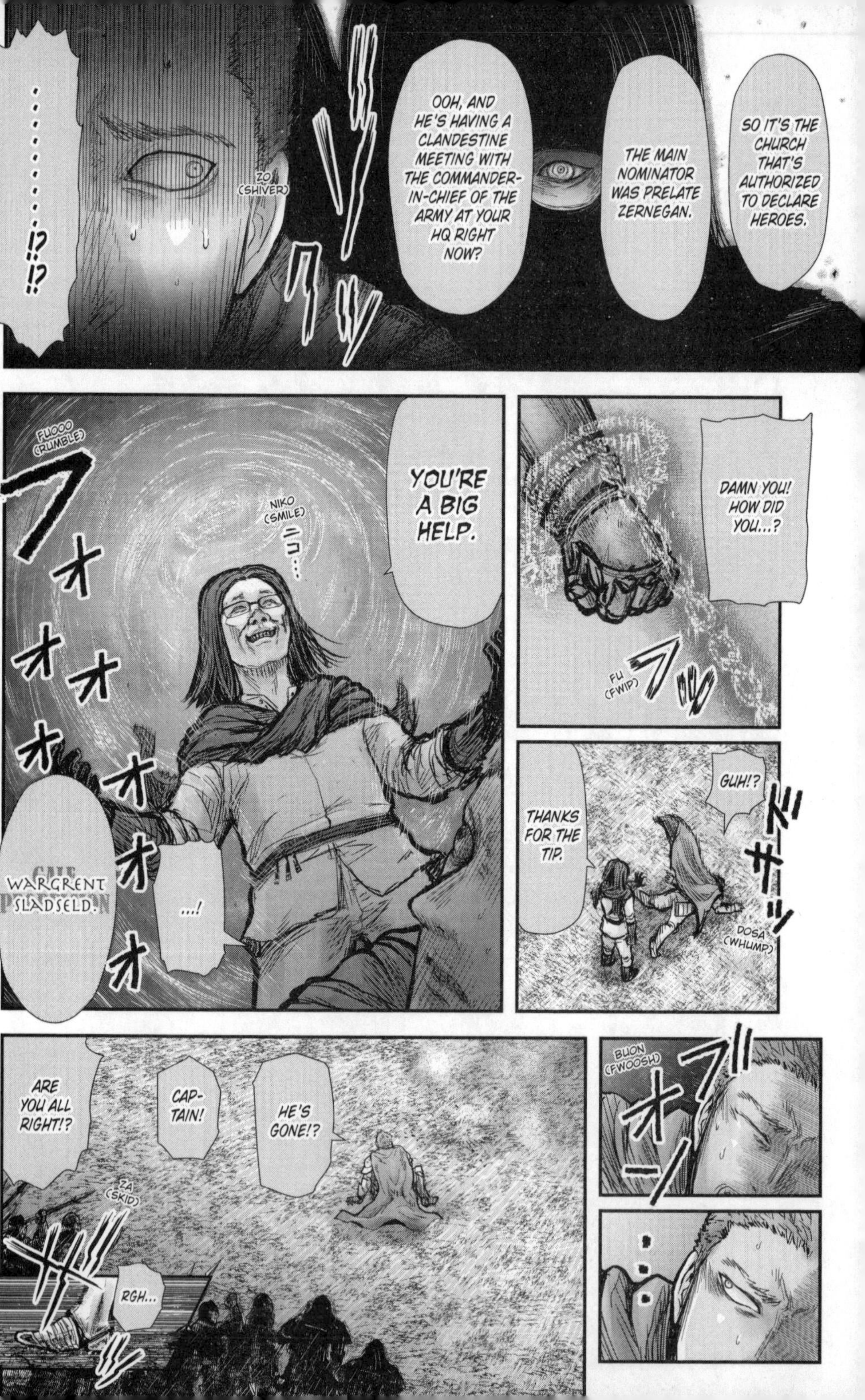
SO IT'S THE CHURCH THAT'S AUTHORIZED TO DECLARE HEROES.
THE MAIN NOMINATOR WAS PRELATE ZERNEGAN.
OOH, AND HE'S HAVING A CLANDESTINE MEETING WITH THE COMMANDER-IN-CHIEF OF THE ARMY AT YOUR HQ RIGHT NOW?
ZO (SHIVER)
.........!?!?
DAMN YOU! HOW DID YOU...?
FU (FWIP)
GUH!?
THANKS FOR THE TIP.
DOSA (WHUMP)
YOU'RE A BIG HELP.
NIKO (SMILE)
FUOOO (RUMBLE)
...!
WARGRENT SLADSELD.
BUON (FWOOSH)
...
HE'S GONE!?
CAP-TAIN!
ARE YOU ALL RIGHT!?
ZA (SKID)
RGH...

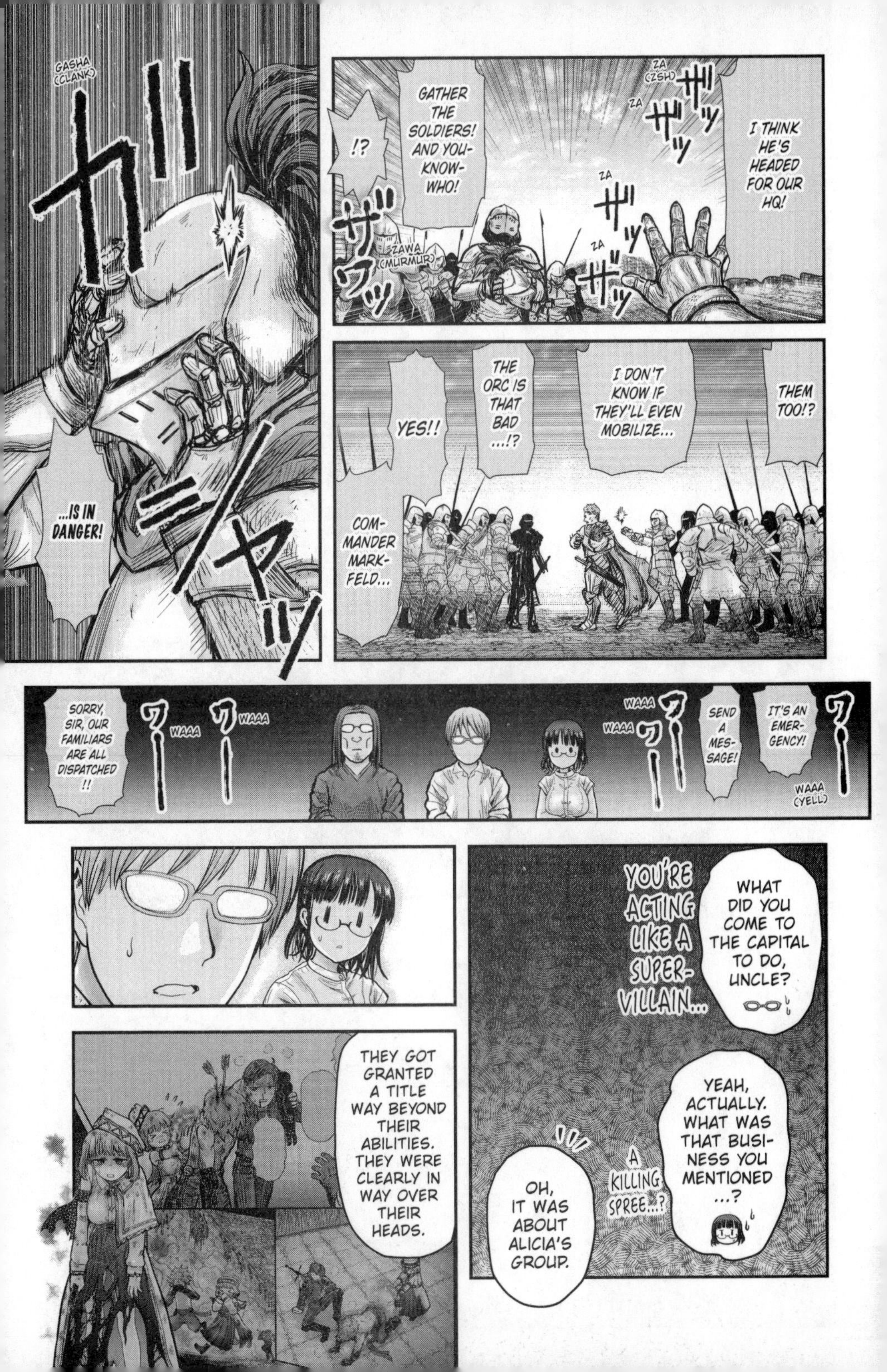
ZA (ZSH)
ZA
I THINK HE'S HEADED FOR OUR HQ!
ZA
ZA
GATHER THE SOLDIERS! AND YOU-KNOW-WHO!
!?
ZAWA (MURMUR)
THEM TOO!?
I DON'T KNOW IF THEY'LL EVEN MOBILIZE...
THE ORC IS THAT BAD ...!?
YES!!
COMMANDER MARKFELD...
GASHA (CLANK)
...IS IN DANGER!
WAAA (YELL)
IT'S AN EMERGENCY!
SEND A MESSAGE!
WAAA
WAAA
WAAA
WAAA
SORRY, SIR, OUR FAMILIARS ARE ALL DISPATCHED !!
YOU'RE ACTING LIKE A SUPER-VILLAIN...
WHAT DID YOU COME TO THE CAPITAL TO DO, UNCLE?
YEAH, ACTUALLY. WHAT WAS THAT BUSINESS YOU MENTIONED ...?
A KILLING SPREE...?
OH, IT WAS ABOUT ALICIA'S GROUP.
THEY GOT GRANTED A TITLE WAY BEYOND THEIR ABILITIES. THEY WERE CLEARLY IN WAY OVER THEIR HEADS.

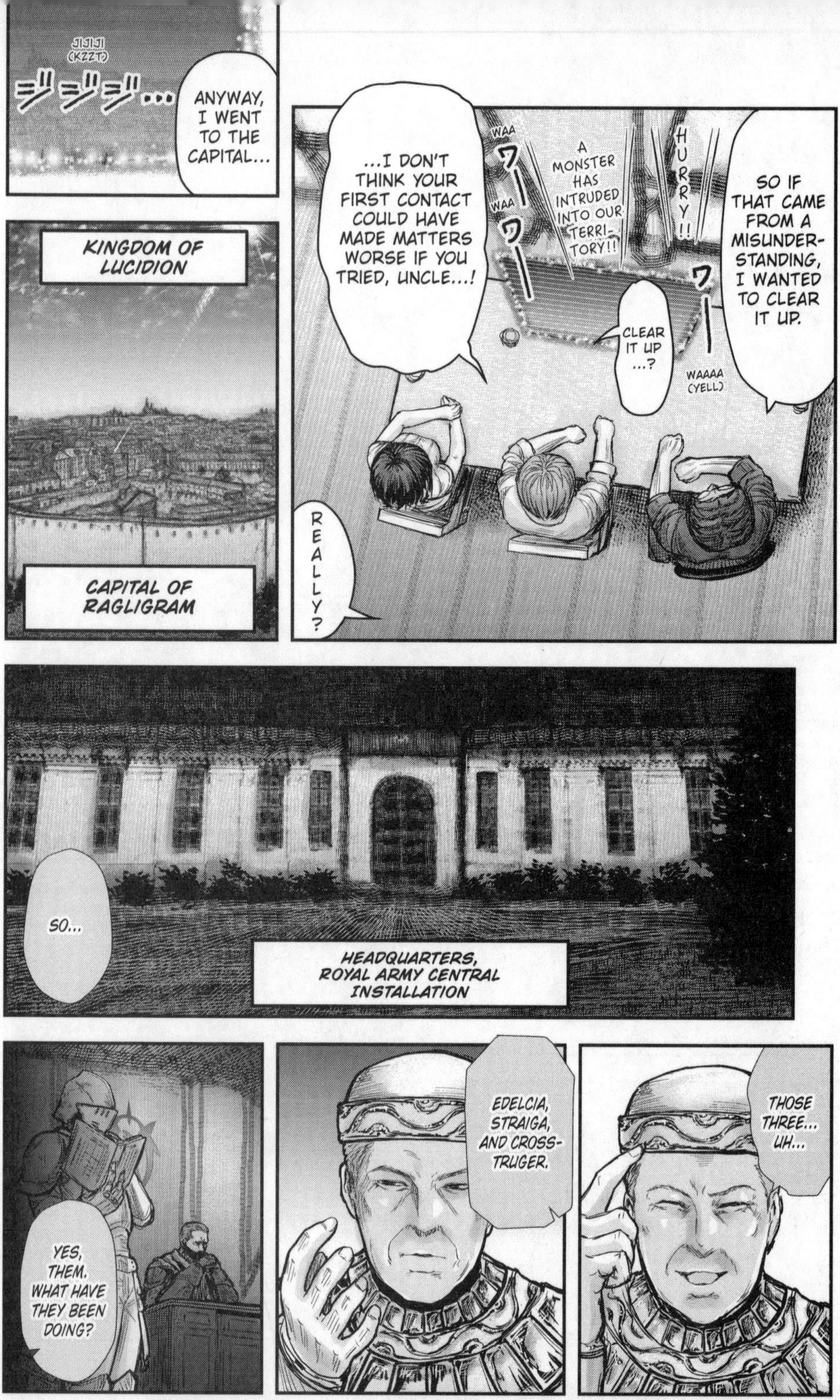
SO IF THAT CAME FROM A MISUNDERSTANDING, I WANTED TO CLEAR IT UP.
HURRY!!
ワー
WAAAA (YELL)
CLEAR IT UP ...?
A MONSTER HAS INTRUDED INTO OUR TERRITORY!!
WAA ワー
WAA ワー
...I DON'T THINK YOUR FIRST CONTACT COULD HAVE MADE MATTERS WORSE IF YOU TRIED, UNCLE...!
REALLY?
ANYWAY, I WENT TO THE CAPITAL...
JIJIJI (KZZT)
ジジジ...
KINGDOM OF LUCIDION
CAPITAL OF RAGLIGRAM
HEADQUARTERS, ROYAL ARMY CENTRAL INSTALLATION
SO...
THOSE THREE... UH...
EDELCIA, STRAIGA, AND CROSS-TRUGER.
YES, THEM. WHAT HAVE THEY BEEN DOING?

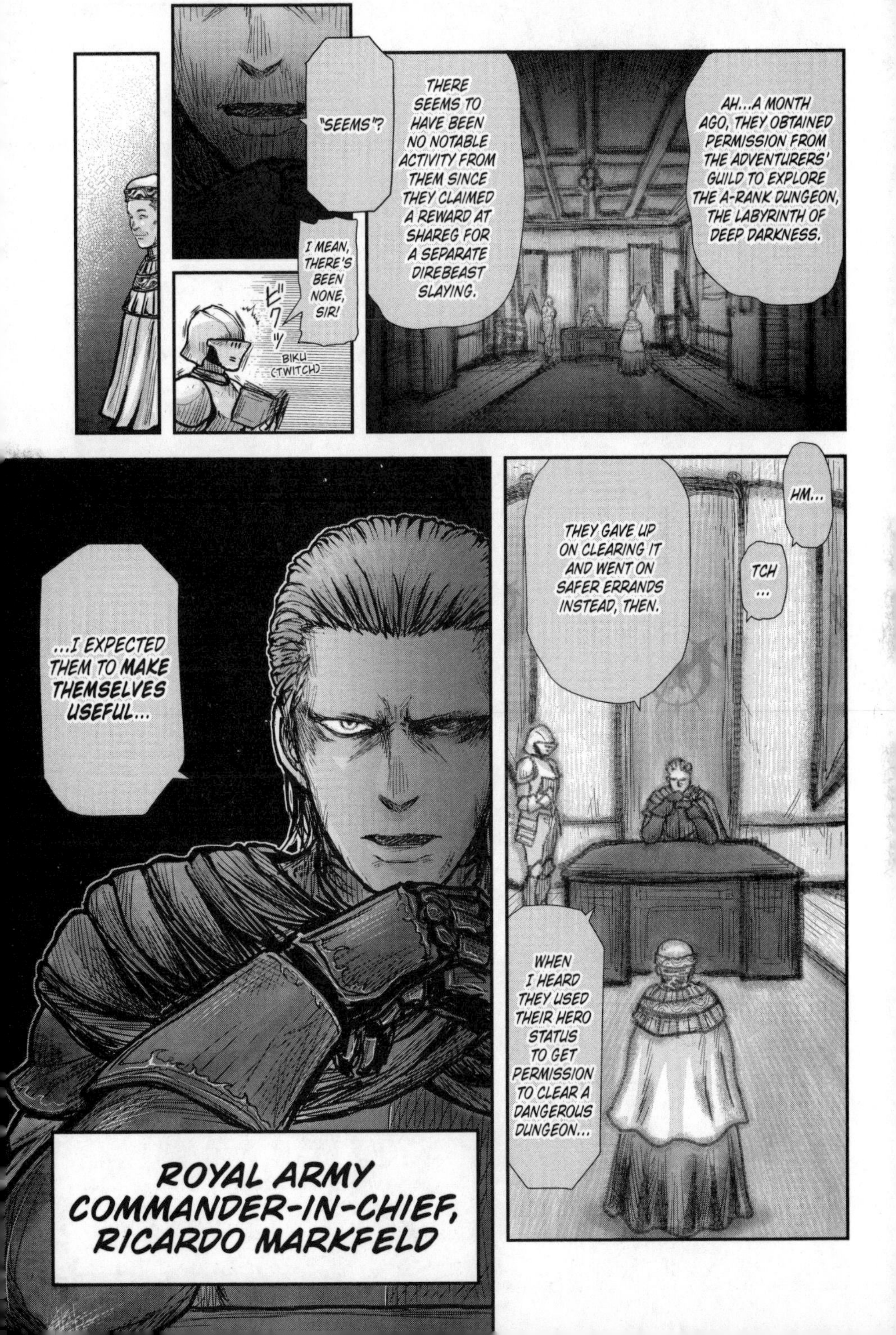
AH...A MONTH AGO, THEY OBTAINED PERMISSION FROM THE ADVENTURERS' GUILD TO EXPLORE THE A-RANK DUNGEON, THE LABYRINTH OF DEEP DARKNESS.
THERE SEEMS TO HAVE BEEN NO NOTABLE ACTIVITY FROM THEM SINCE THEY CLAIMED A REWARD AT SHAREG FOR A SEPARATE DIREBEAST SLAYING.
"SEEMS"?
I MEAN, THERE'S BEEN NONE, SIR!
BIKU (TWITCH)
HM...
TCH...
THEY GAVE UP ON CLEARING IT AND WENT ON SAFER ERRANDS INSTEAD, THEN.
WHEN I HEARD THEY USED THEIR HERO STATUS TO GET PERMISSION TO CLEAR A DANGEROUS DUNGEON...
...I EXPECTED THEM TO MAKE THEMSELVES USEFUL...
ROYAL ARMY COMMANDER-IN-CHIEF, RICARDO MARKFELD

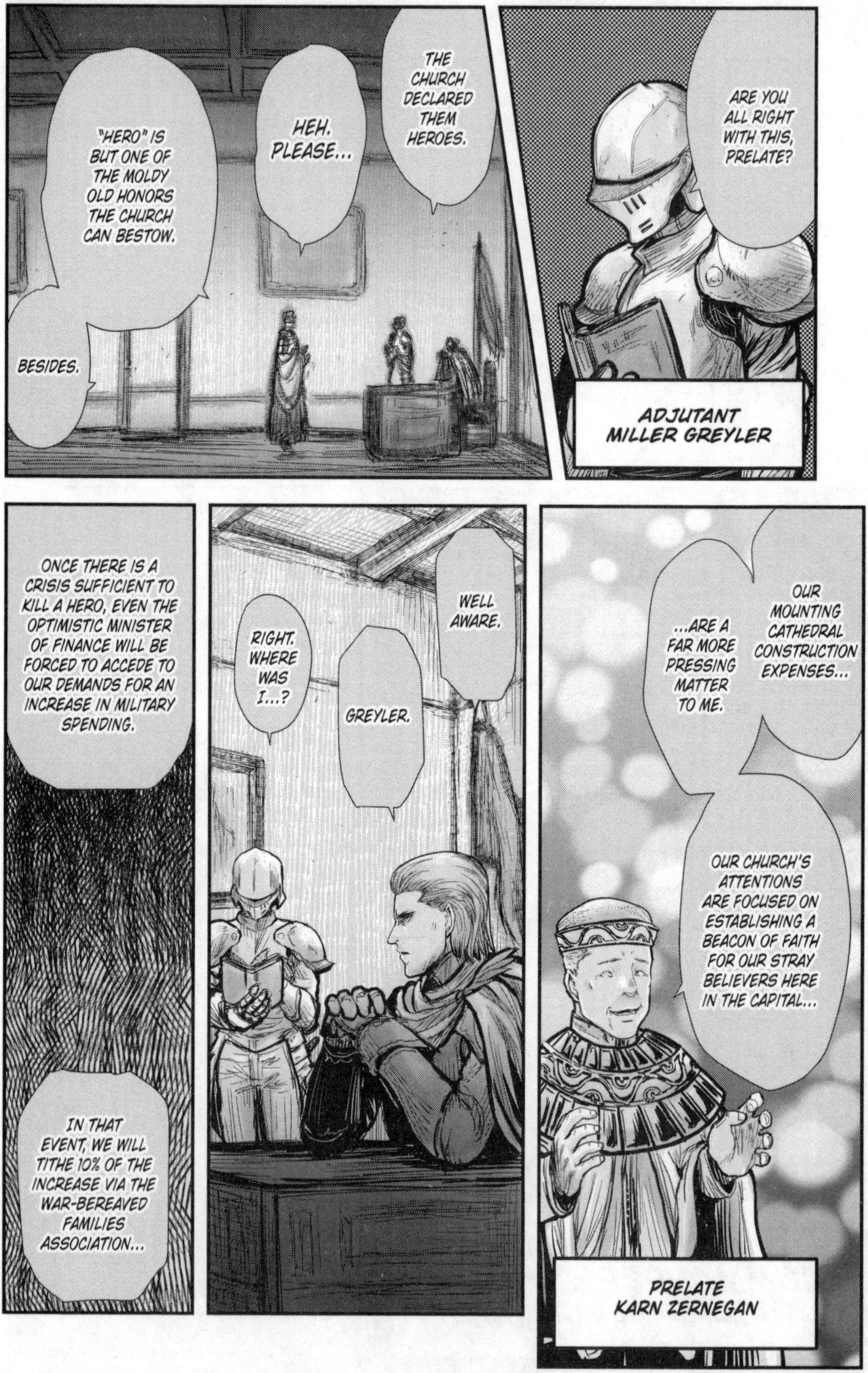
ARE YOU ALL RIGHT WITH THIS, PRELATE?
ADJUTANT MILLER GREYLER
THE CHURCH DECLARED THEM HEROES.
HEH. PLEASE...
"HERO" IS BUT ONE OF THE MOLDY OLD HONORS THE CHURCH CAN BESTOW.
BESIDES.
OUR MOUNTING CATHEDRAL CONSTRUCTION EXPENSES...
...ARE A FAR MORE PRESSING MATTER TO ME.
OUR CHURCH'S ATTENTIONS ARE FOCUSED ON ESTABLISHING A BEACON OF FAITH FOR OUR STRAY BELIEVERS HERE IN THE CAPITAL...
PRELATE KARN ZERNEGAN
WELL AWARE.
GREYLER.
RIGHT. WHERE WAS I...?
ONCE THERE IS A CRISIS SUFFICIENT TO KILL A HERO, EVEN THE OPTIMISTIC MINISTER OF FINANCE WILL BE FORCED TO ACCEDE TO OUR DEMANDS FOR AN INCREASE IN MILITARY SPENDING.
IN THAT EVENT, WE WILL TITHE 10% OF THE INCREASE VIA THE WAR-BEREAVED FAMILIES ASSOCIATION...

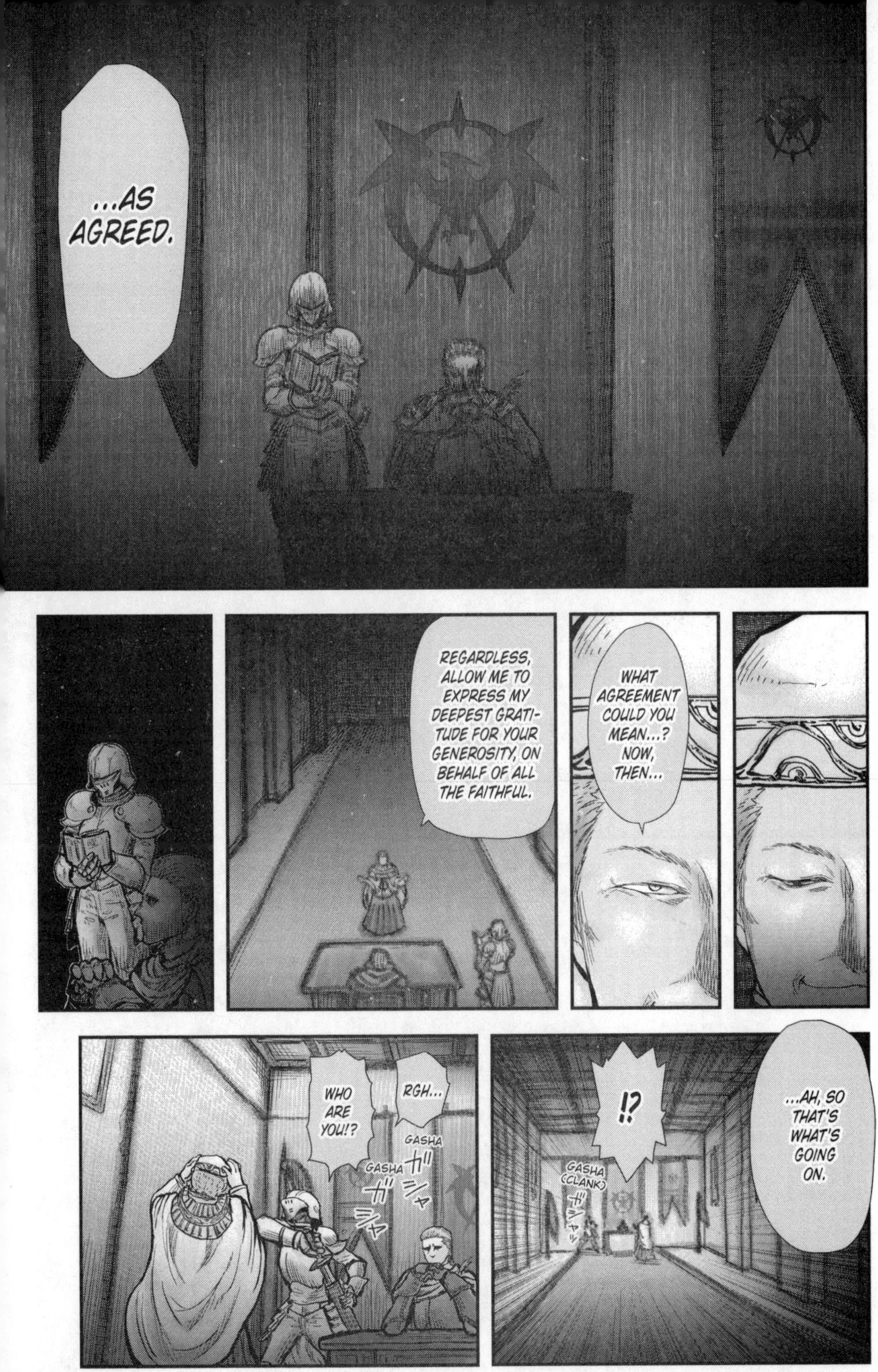
...AS AGREED.
WHAT AGREEMENT COULD YOU MEAN...? NOW, THEN...
REGARDLESS, ALLOW ME TO EXPRESS MY DEEPEST GRATI-TUDE FOR YOUR GENEROSITY, ON BEHALF OF ALL THE FAITHFUL.
...AH, SO THAT'S WHAT'S GOING ON.
!?
GASHA (CLANK)
RGH...
WHO ARE YOU!?
GASHA
GASHA

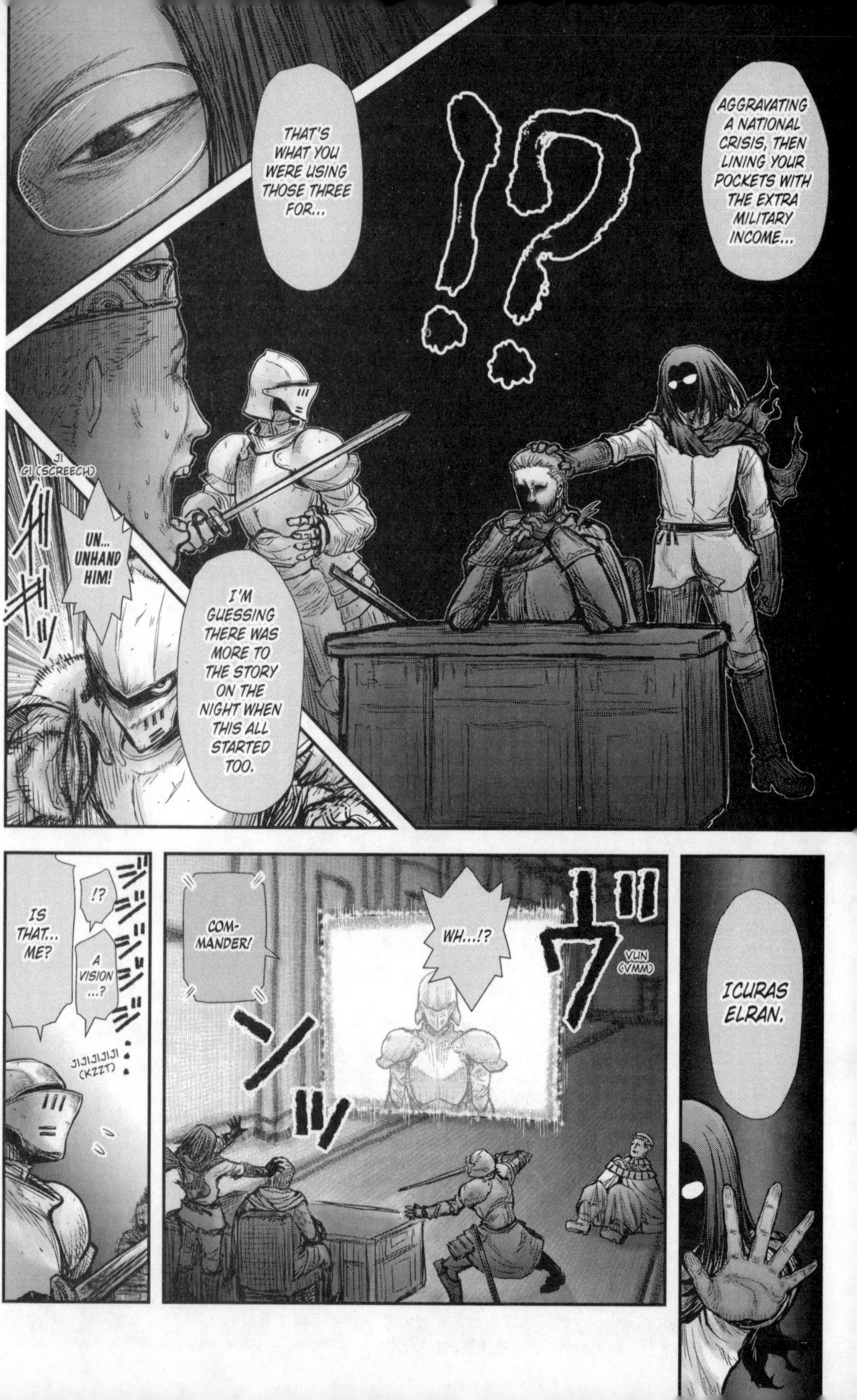
AGGRAVATING A NATIONAL CRISIS, THEN LINING YOUR POCKETS WITH THE EXTRA MILITARY INCOME...
!?
THAT'S WHAT YOU WERE USING THOSE THREE FOR...
I'M GUESSING THERE WAS MORE TO THE STORY ON THE NIGHT WHEN THIS ALL STARTED TOO.
JI GI (SCREECH)
UN... UNHAND HIM!
ICURAS ELRAN.
VUN (VMM)
WH...!?
COM-MANDER!
!?
A VISION ...?
IS THAT... ME?
JIJIJIJIJI (KZZT)

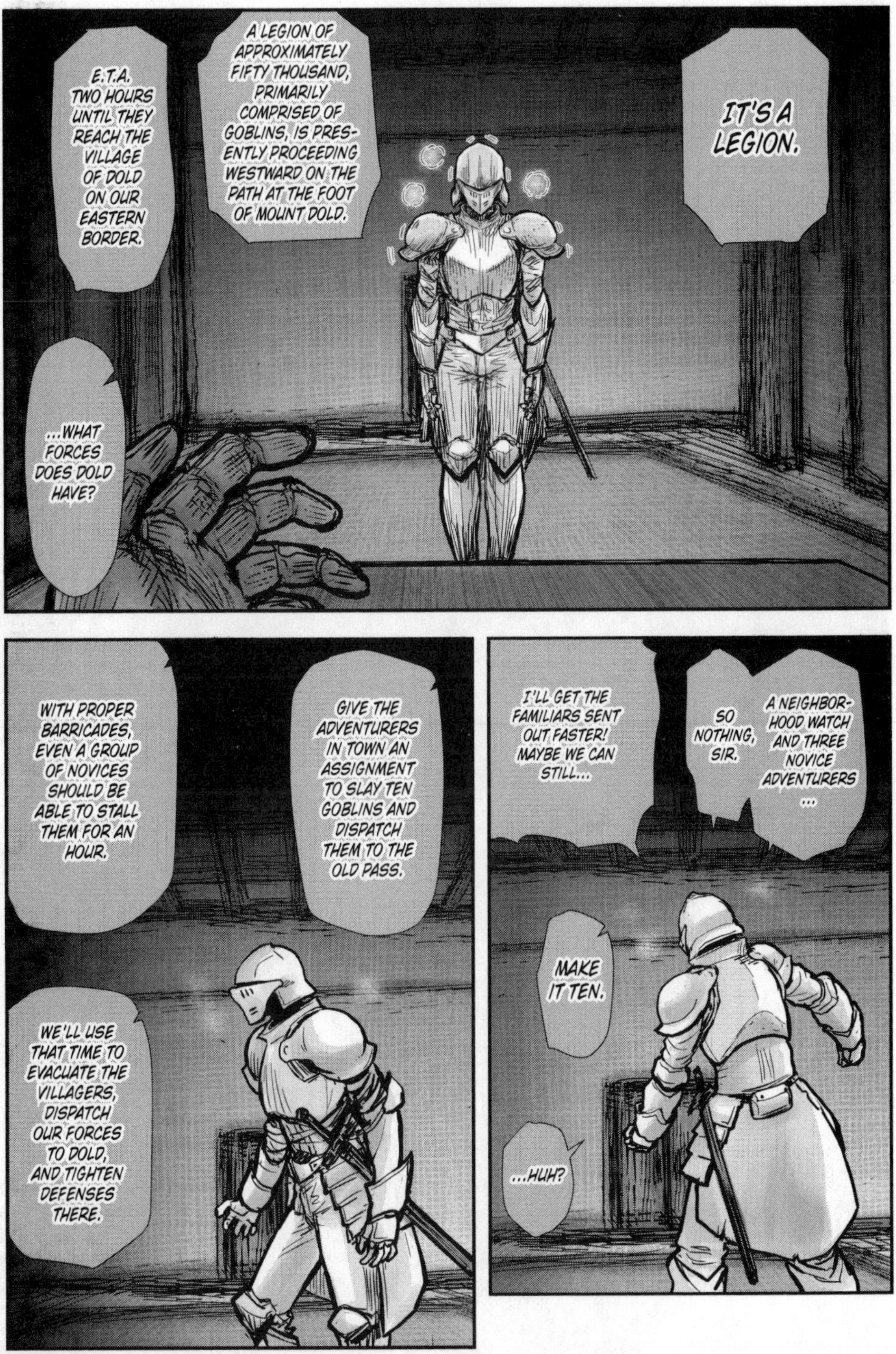
IT'S A LEGION.
A LEGION OF APPROXIMATELY FIFTY THOUSAND, PRIMARILY COMPRISED OF GOBLINS, IS PRESENTLY PROCEEDING WESTWARD ON THE PATH AT THE FOOT OF MOUNT DOLD.
E.T.A. TWO HOURS UNTIL THEY REACH THE VILLAGE OF DOLD ON OUR EASTERN BORDER.
...WHAT FORCES DOES DOLD HAVE?
A NEIGHBORHOOD WATCH AND THREE NOVICE ADVENTURERS...
SO NOTHING, SIR.
I'LL GET THE FAMILIARS SENT OUT FASTER! MAYBE WE CAN STILL...
MAKE IT TEN.
...HUH?
GIVE THE ADVENTURERS IN TOWN AN ASSIGNMENT TO SLAY TEN GOBLINS AND DISPATCH THEM TO THE OLD PASS.
WITH PROPER BARRICADES, EVEN A GROUP OF NOVICES SHOULD BE ABLE TO STALL THEM FOR AN HOUR.
WE'LL USE THAT TIME TO EVACUATE THE VILLAGERS, DISPATCH OUR FORCES TO DOLD, AND TIGHTEN DEFENSES THERE.

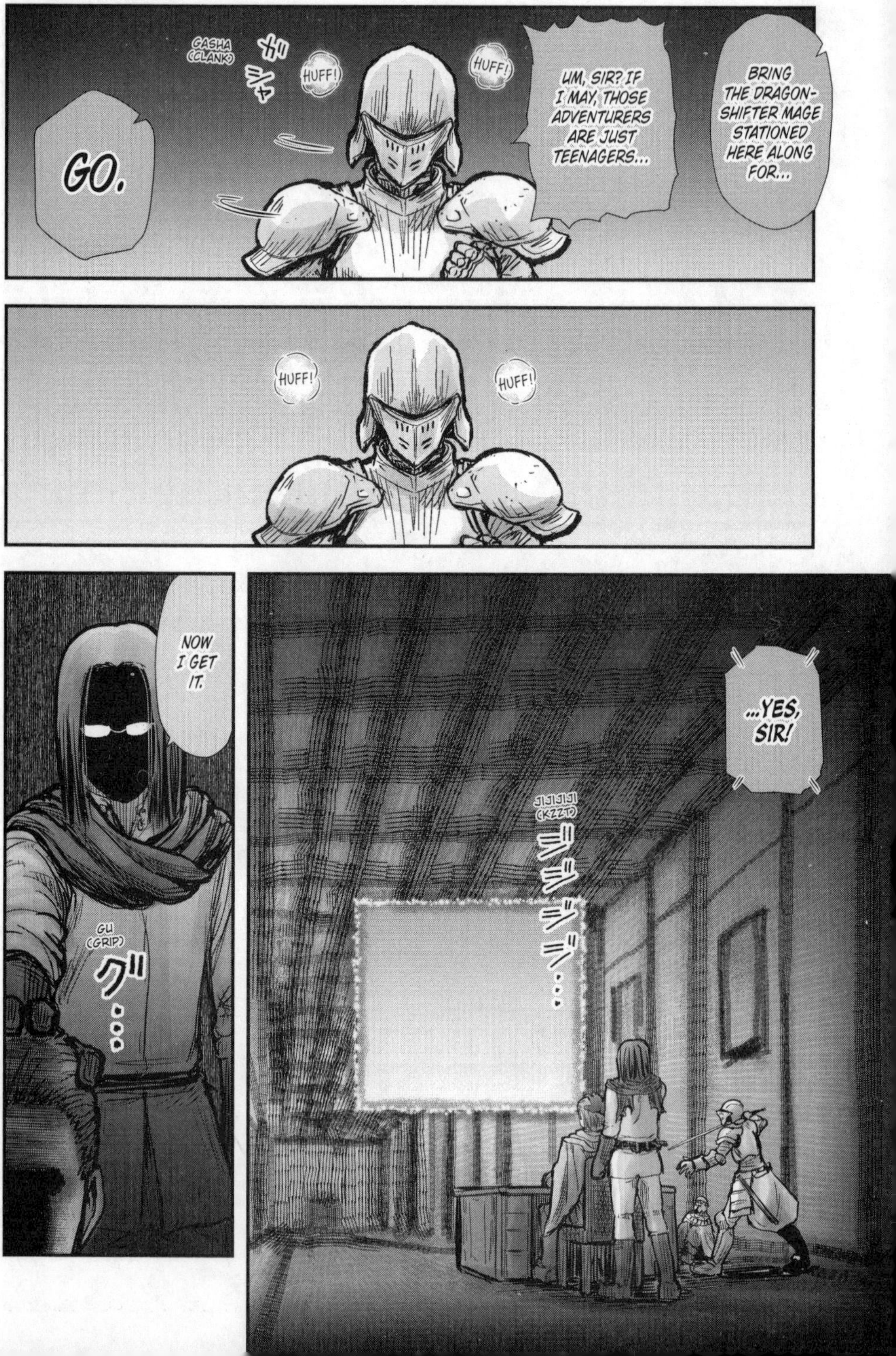
BRING THE DRAGON-SHIFTER MAGE STATIONED HERE ALONG FOR...
UM, SIR? IF I MAY, THOSE ADVENTURERS ARE JUST TEENAGERS...
HUFF!
HUFF!
GASHA (CLANK)
GO.
HUFF!
HUFF!
...YES, SIR!
JIJIJIJI (KZZT)
NOW I GET IT.
GU (GRIP)

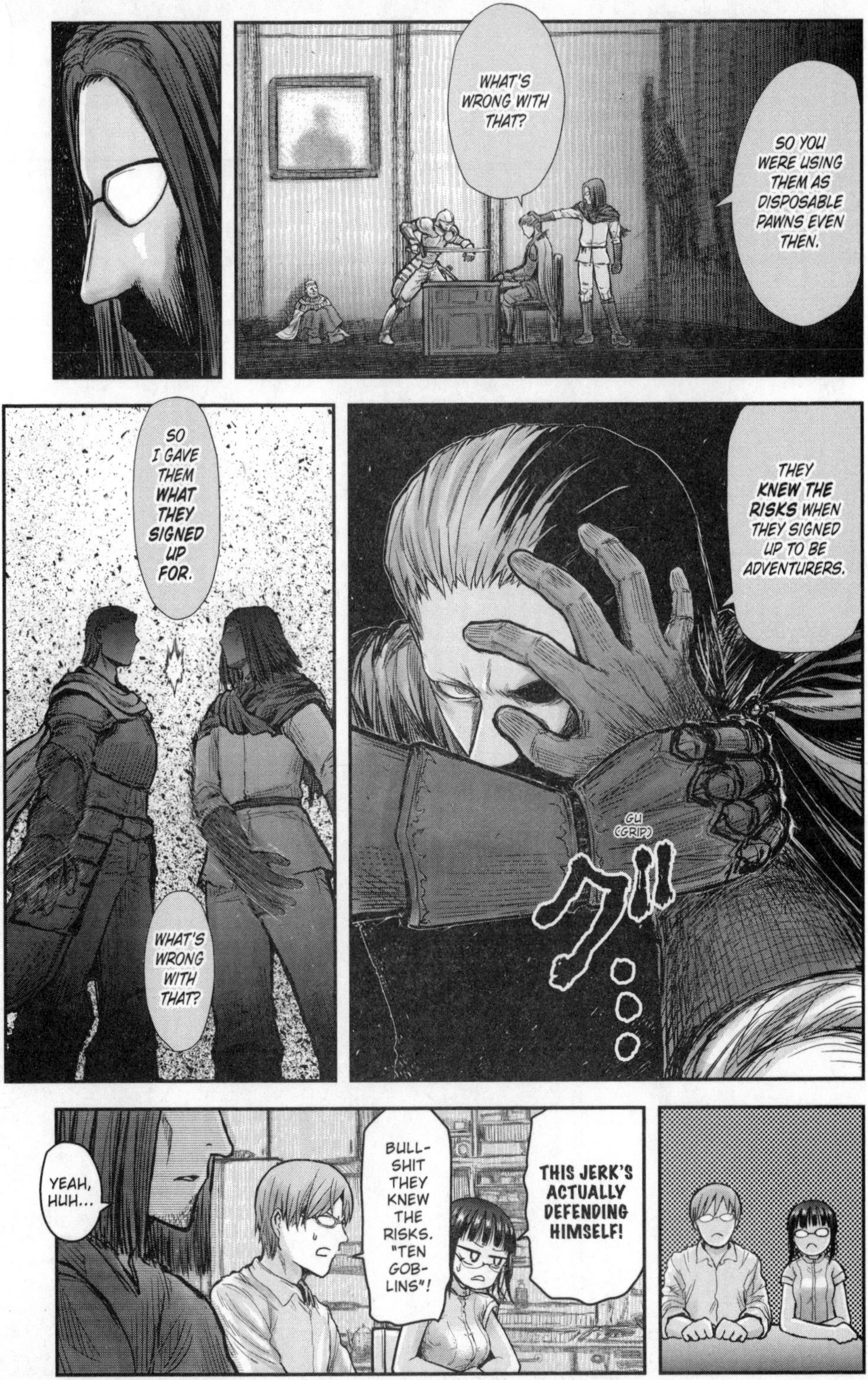
SO YOU WERE USING THEM AS DISPOSABLE PAWNS EVEN THEN.
WHAT'S WRONG WITH THAT?
THEY KNEW THE RISKS WHEN THEY SIGNED UP TO BE ADVENTURERS.
GU (GRIP)
グッ...
SO I GAVE THEM WHAT THEY SIGNED UP FOR.
WHAT'S WRONG WITH THAT?
THIS JERK'S ACTUALLY DEFENDING HIMSELF!
BULL-SHIT THEY KNEW THE RISKS. "TEN GOB-LINS"!
YEAH, HUH...

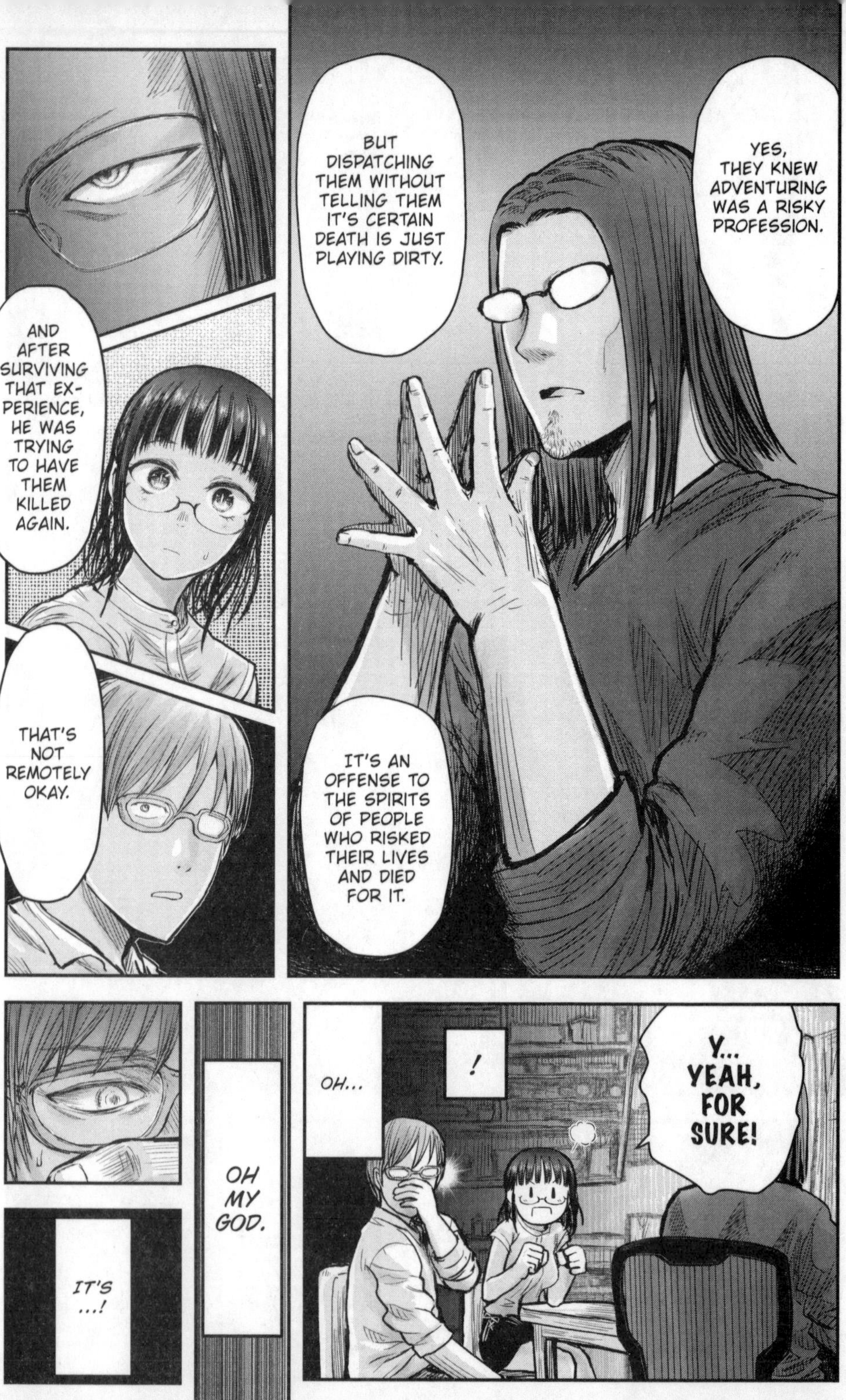

YES, THEY KNEW ADVENTURING WAS A RISKY PROFESSION.
BUT DISPATCHING THEM WITHOUT TELLING THEM IT'S CERTAIN DEATH IS JUST PLAYING DIRTY.
IT'S AN OFFENSE TO THE SPIRITS OF PEOPLE WHO RISKED THEIR LIVES AND DIED FOR IT.
AND AFTER SURVIVING THAT EX-PERIENCE, HE WAS TRYING TO HAVE THEM KILLED AGAIN.
THAT'S NOT REMOTELY OKAY.
Y... YEAH, FOR SURE!
!
OH...
OH MY GOD.
IT'S ...!

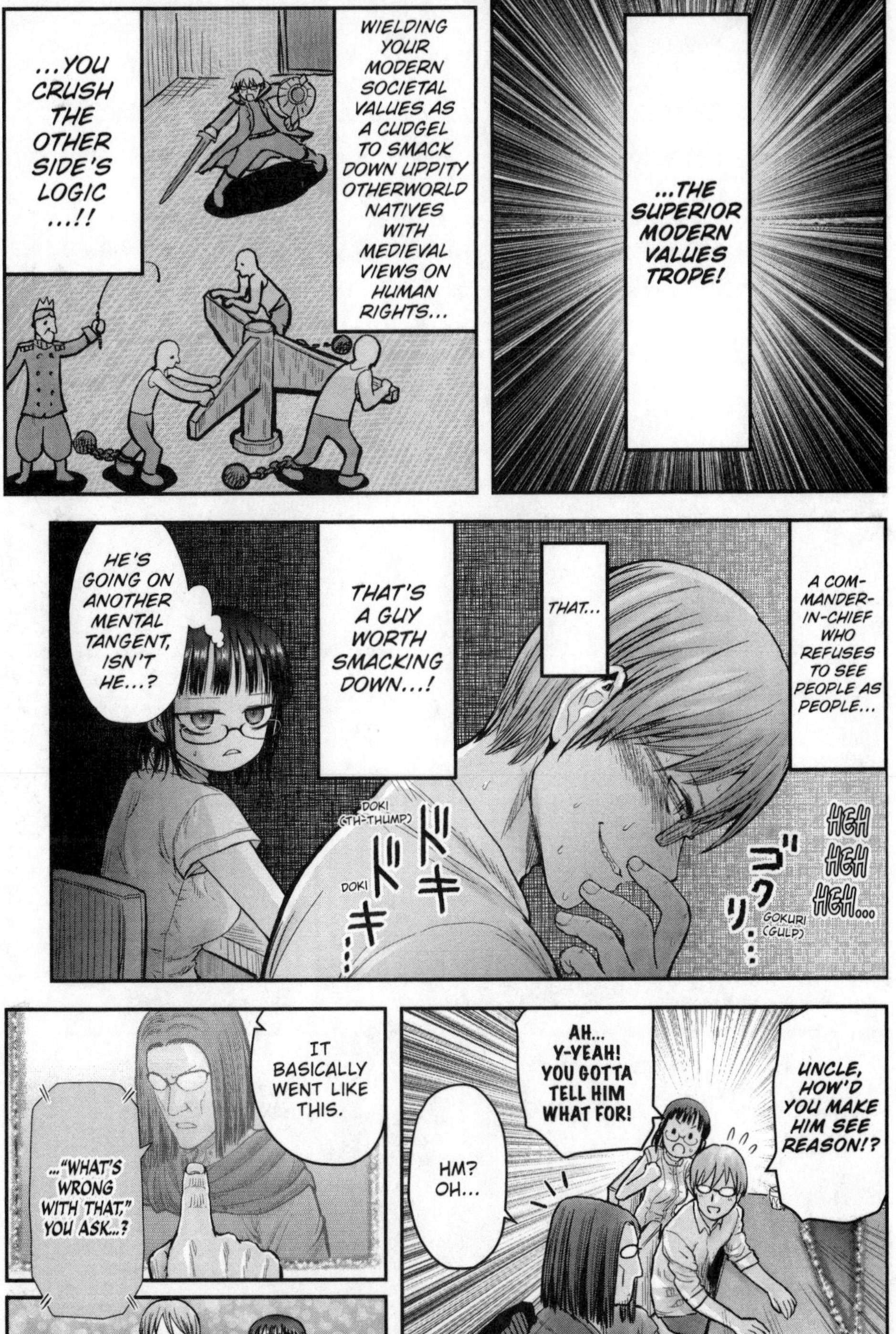
...THE SUPERIOR MODERN VALUES TROPE!
WIELDING YOUR MODERN SOCIETAL VALUES AS A CUDGEL TO SMACK DOWN UPPITY OTHERWORLD NATIVES WITH MEDIEVAL VIEWS ON HUMAN RIGHTS...
...YOU CRUSH THE OTHER SIDE'S LOGIC ...!!
A COM-MANDER-IN-CHIEF WHO REFUSES TO SEE PEOPLE AS PEOPLE...
HEH HEH HEH...
ゴクリ...
GOKURI (GULP)
THAT...
THAT'S A GUY WORTH SMACKING DOWN...!
ドキドキ...
DOKI (TH-THUMP)
DOKI
HE'S GOING ON ANOTHER MENTAL TANGENT, ISN'T HE...?
UNCLE, HOW'D YOU MAKE HIM SEE REASON!?
AH... Y-YEAH! YOU GOTTA TELL HIM WHAT FOR!
HM? OH...
IT BASICALLY WENT LIKE THIS.
..."WHAT'S WRONG WITH THAT," YOU ASK...?

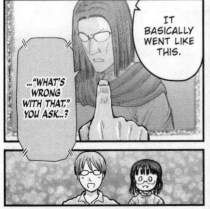

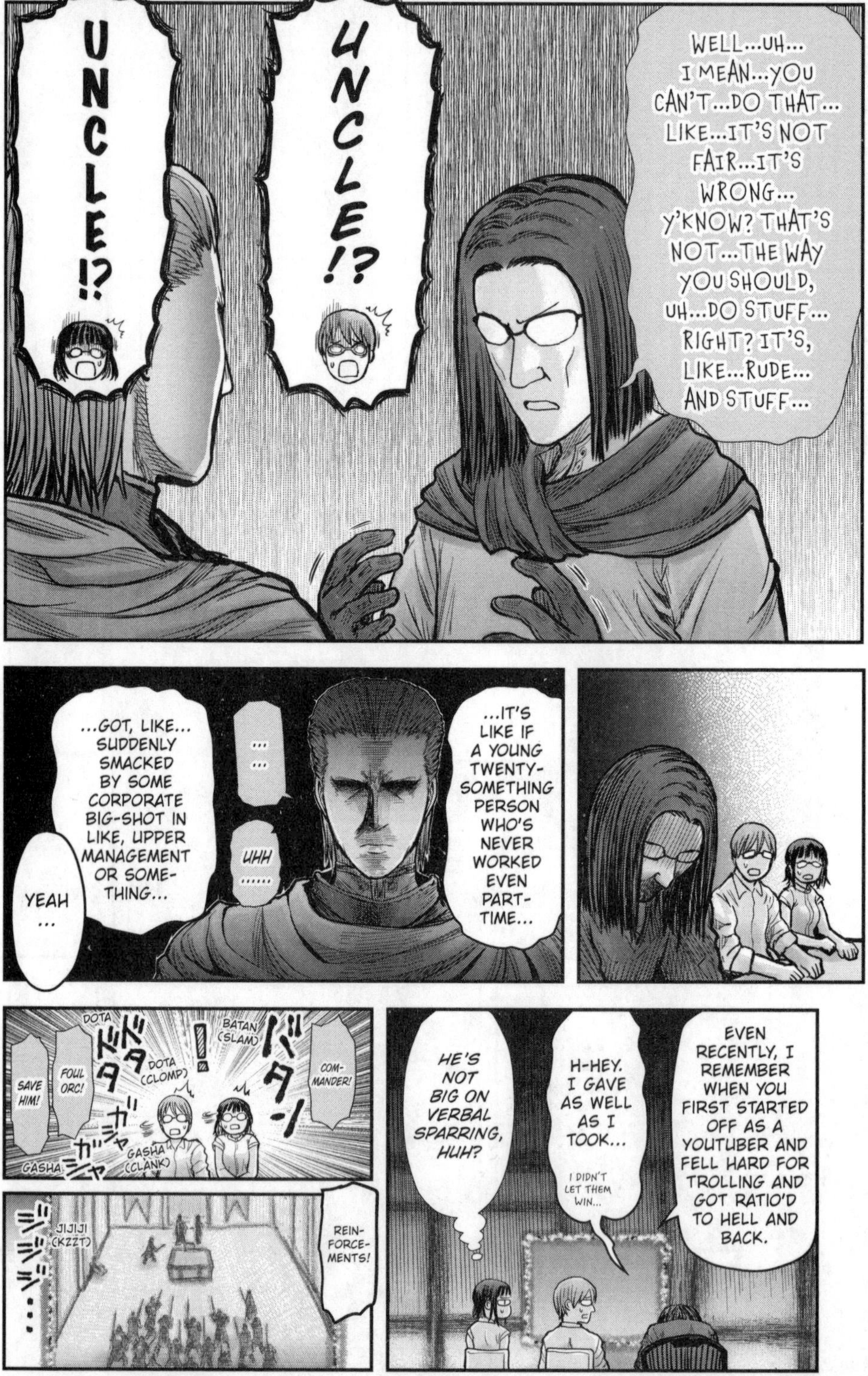
WELL...UH... I MEAN...YOU CAN'T...DO THAT... LIKE...IT'S NOT FAIR...IT'S WRONG... Y'KNOW? THAT'S NOT...THE WAY YOU SHOULD, UH...DO STUFF... RIGHT? IT'S, LIKE...RUDE... AND STUFF...
UNCLE!?
UNCLE!?
...IT'S LIKE IF A YOUNG TWENTY-SOMETHING PERSON WHO'S NEVER WORKED EVEN PART-TIME...
... ...
UHH ......
...GOT, LIKE... SUDDENLY SMACKED BY SOME CORPORATE BIG-SHOT IN LIKE, UPPER MANAGEMENT OR SOME-THING...
YEAH ...
EVEN RECENTLY, I REMEMBER WHEN YOU FIRST STARTED OFF AS A YOUTUBER AND FELL HARD FOR TROLLING AND GOT RATIO'D TO HELL AND BACK.
H-HEY. I GAVE AS WELL AS I TOOK...
I DIDN'T LET THEM WIN...
HE'S NOT BIG ON VERBAL SPARRING, HUH?
COM-MANDER!
BATAN (SLAM)
!
DOTA (CLOMP)
DOTA
FOUL ORC!
SAVE HIM!
GASHA (CLANK)
GASHA
REIN-FORCE-MENTS!
JIJIJI (KZZT)

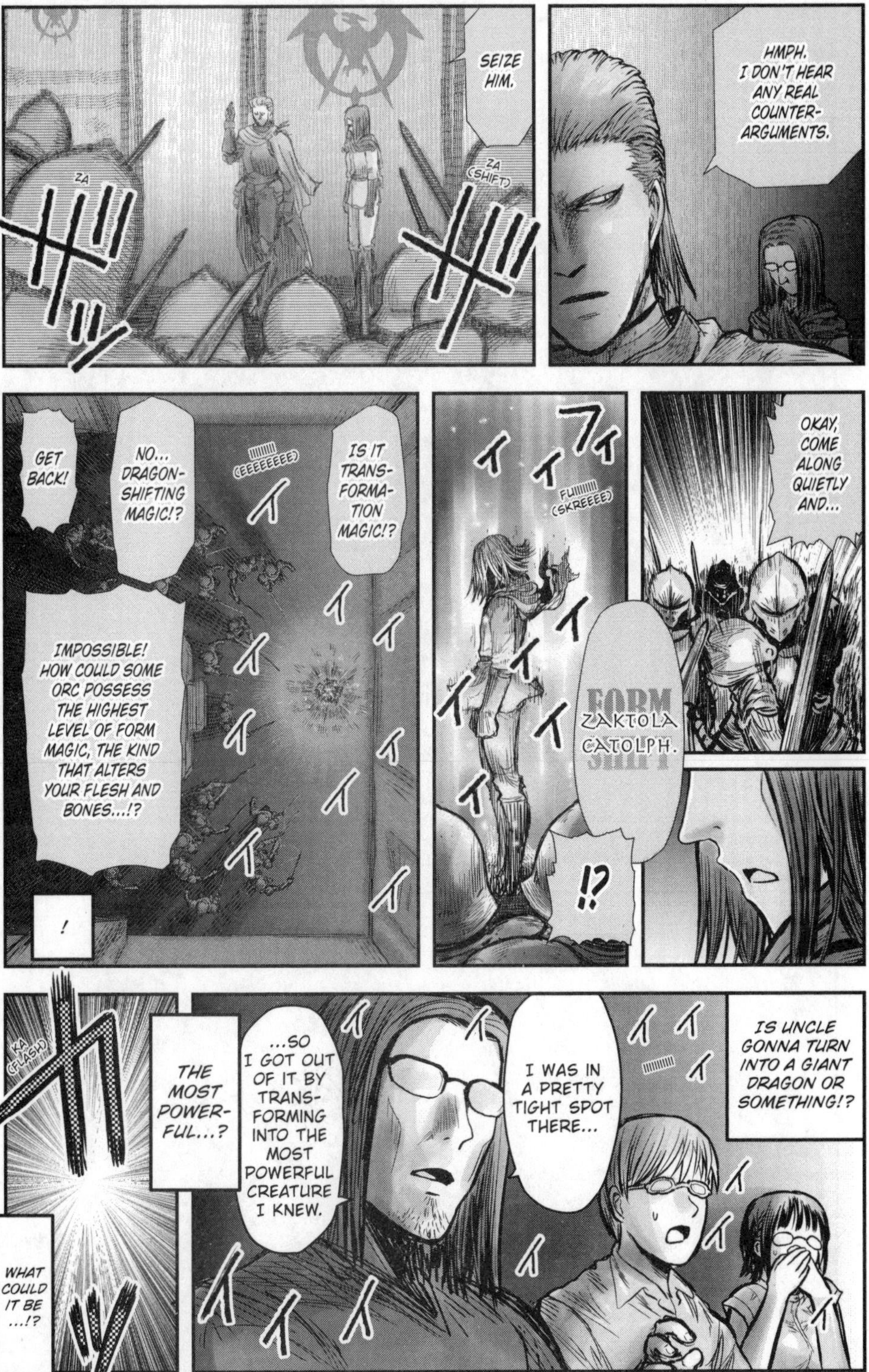
HMPH. I DON'T HEAR ANY REAL COUNTER-ARGUMENTS.
SEIZE HIM.
ZA (SHIFT)
ZA
OKAY, COME ALONG QUIETLY AND...
FUIIIIIII (SKREEEEE)
FORM SHIFT
ZAKTOLA CATOLPH.
!?
IS IT TRANSFORMATION MAGIC!?
IIIIIIII (EEEEEEEE)
NO... DRAGON-SHIFTING MAGIC!?
GET BACK!
IMPOSSIBLE! HOW COULD SOME ORC POSSESS THE HIGHEST LEVEL OF FORM MAGIC, THE KIND THAT ALTERS YOUR FLESH AND BONES...!?
!
IS UNCLE GONNA TURN INTO A GIANT DRAGON OR SOMETHING!?
IIIIIIII
I WAS IN A PRETTY TIGHT SPOT THERE...
...SO I GOT OUT OF IT BY TRANSFORMING INTO THE MOST POWERFUL CREATURE I KNEW.
THE MOST POWERFUL...?
KA (FLASH)
WHAT COULD IT BE...!?

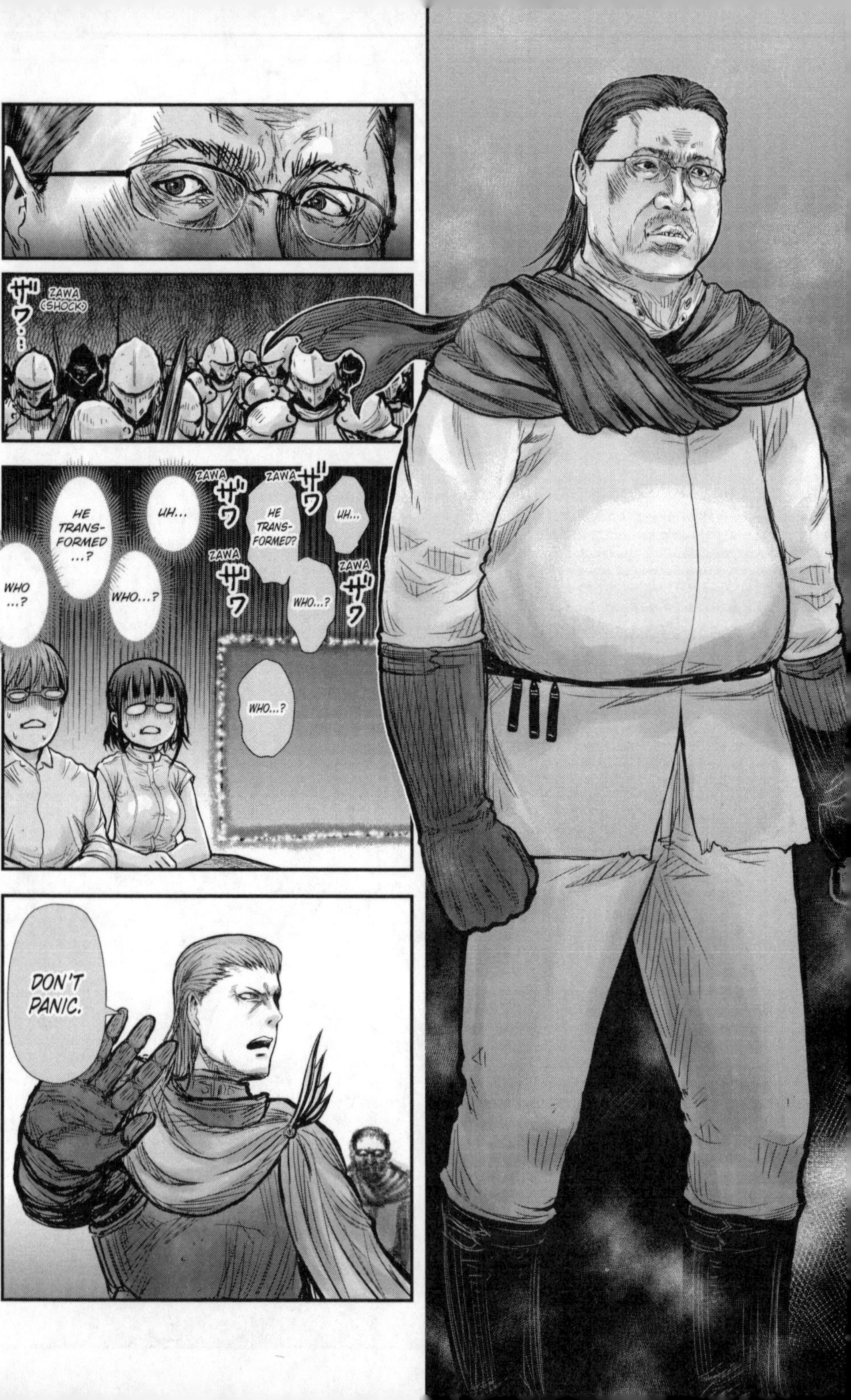
ザワ…
ZAWA (SHOCK)
ZAWA ザワ
UH...
HE TRANSFORMED?
ZAWA ザワ
WHO...?
WHO...?
ZAWA ザワ
ZAWA ザワ
UH...
HE TRANSFORMED ...?
WHO...?
WHO ...?
DON'T PANIC.

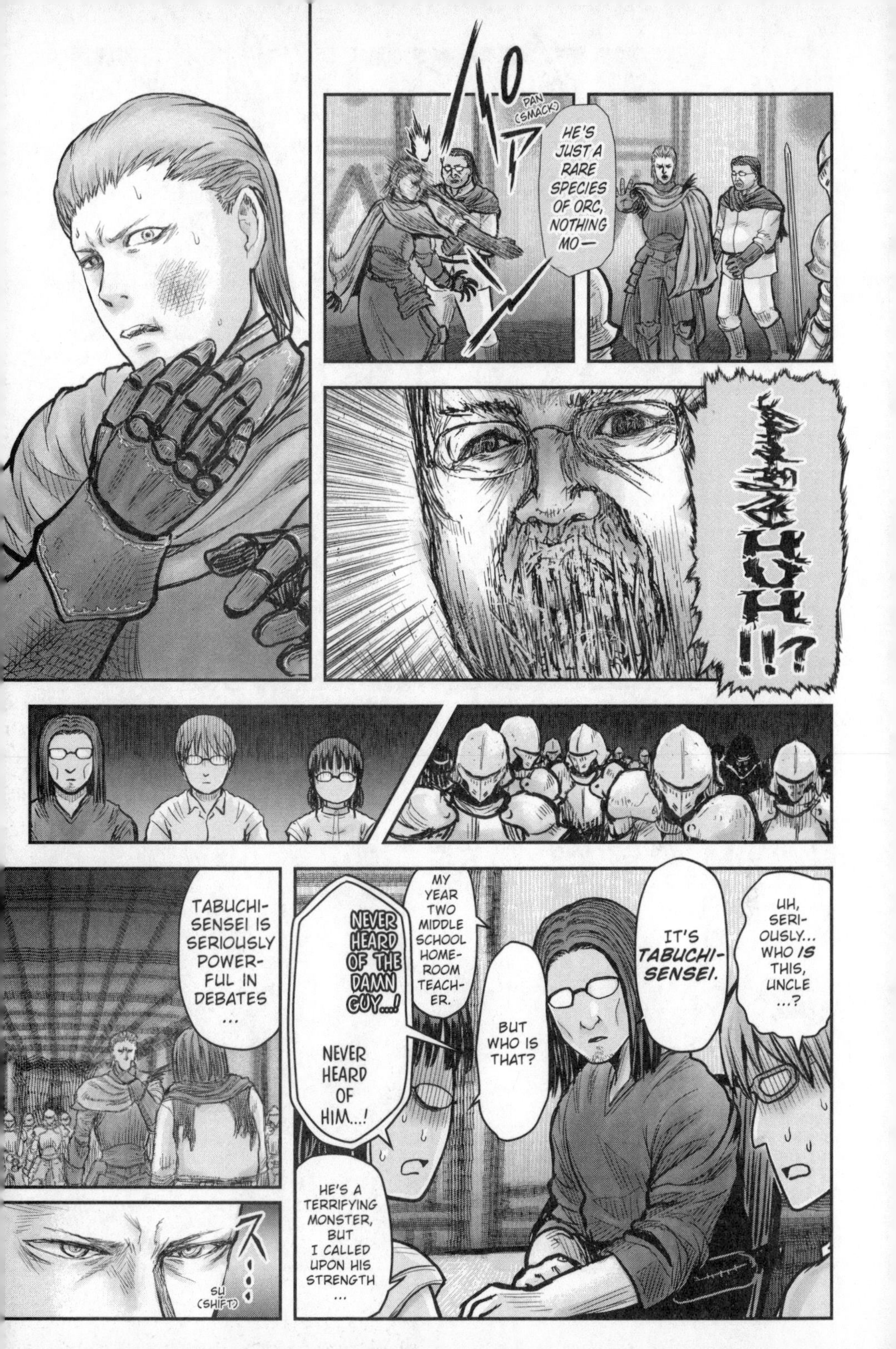
HE'S JUST A RARE SPECIES OF ORC, NOTHING MO—
PAN (SMACK)
HUH!!?
UH, SERIOUSLY... WHO *IS* THIS, UNCLE ...?
IT'S *TABUCHI-SENSEI.*
MY YEAR TWO MIDDLE SCHOOL HOMEROOM TEACHER.
BUT WHO IS THAT?
NEVER HEARD OF THE DAMN GUY...!
NEVER HEARD OF HIM...!
HE'S A TERRIFYING MONSTER, BUT I CALLED UPON HIS STRENGTH ...
TABUCHI-SENSEI IS SERIOUSLY POWERFUL IN DEBATES ...
SU (SHIFT)

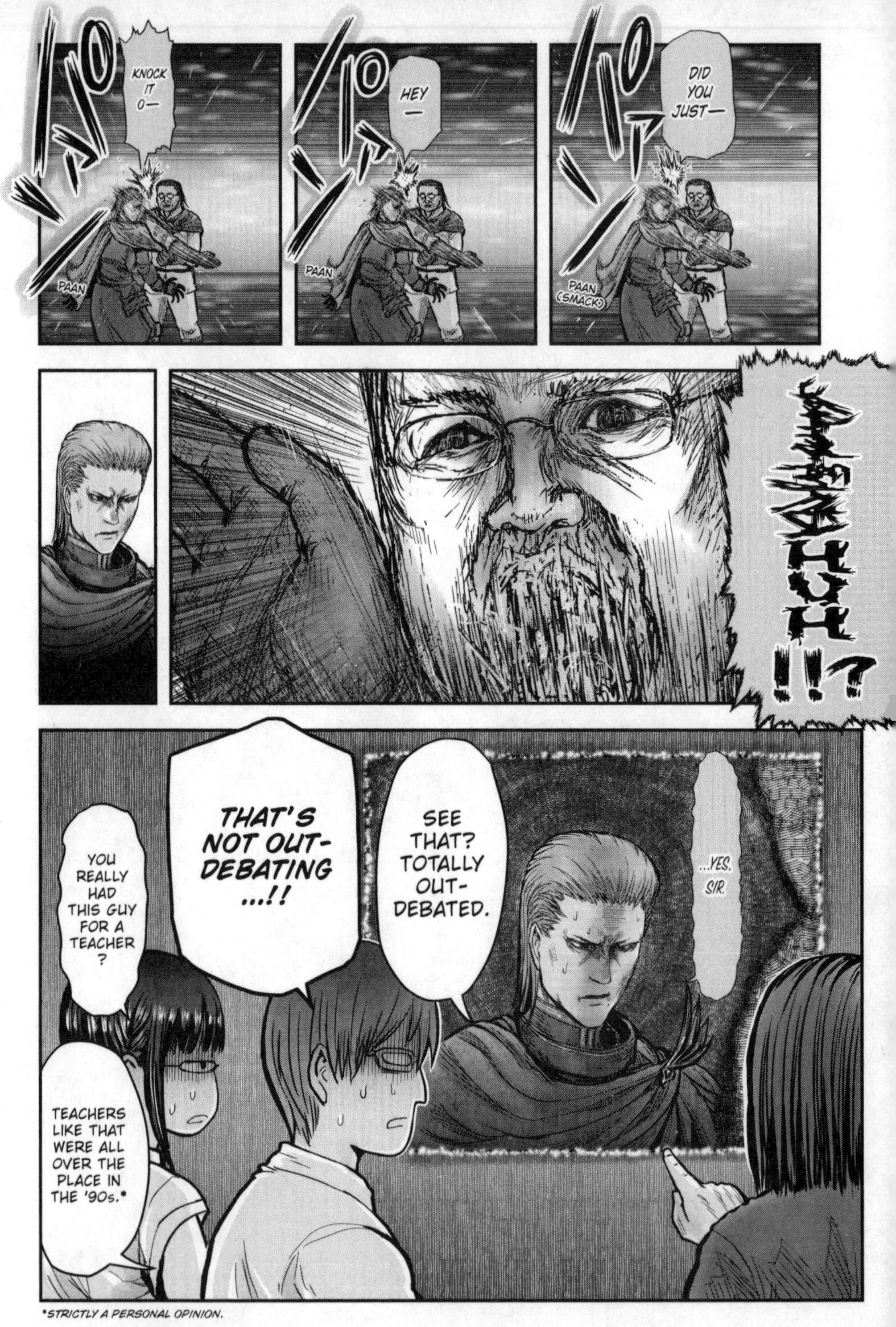
DID YOU JUST—
PAAN (SMACK)
HEY —
PAAN
KNOCK IT O—
PAAN
HUH!!?
...YES, SIR.
SEE THAT? TOTALLY OUT-DEBATED.
THAT'S NOT OUT-DEBATING ...!!
YOU REALLY HAD THIS GUY FOR A TEACHER?
TEACHERS LIKE THAT WERE ALL OVER THE PLACE IN THE '90s.*

*STRICTLY A PERSONAL OPINION.

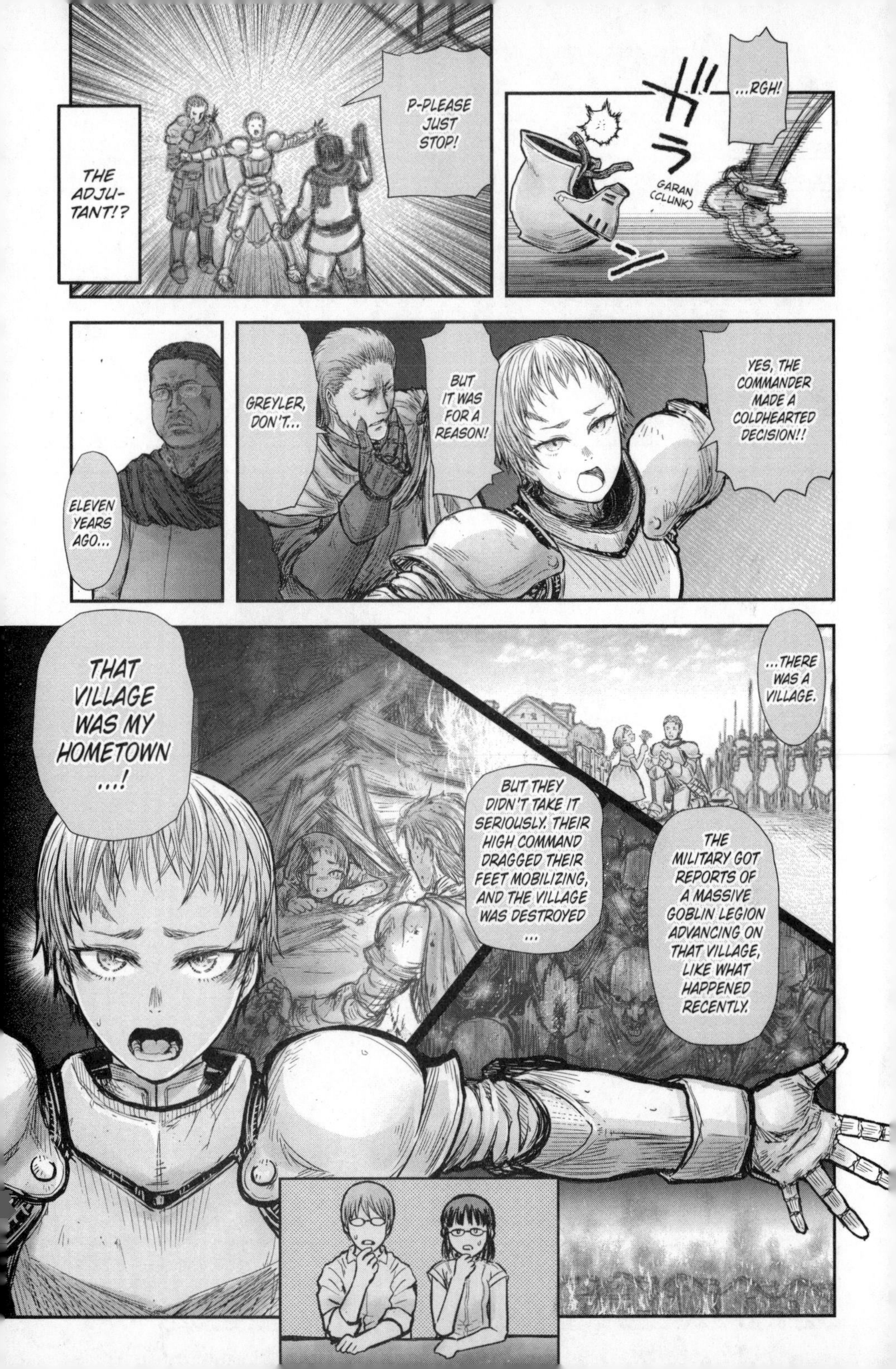
...RGH!
ガラン
GARAN (CLUNK)
P-PLEASE JUST STOP!
THE ADJUTANT!?
YES, THE COMMANDER MADE A COLDHEARTED DECISION!!
BUT IT WAS FOR A REASON!
GREYLER, DON'T...
ELEVEN YEARS AGO...
...THERE WAS A VILLAGE.
THE MILITARY GOT REPORTS OF A MASSIVE GOBLIN LEGION ADVANCING ON THAT VILLAGE, LIKE WHAT HAPPENED RECENTLY.
BUT THEY DIDN'T TAKE IT SERIOUSLY. THEIR HIGH COMMAND DRAGGED THEIR FEET MOBILIZING, AND THE VILLAGE WAS DESTROYED...
THAT VILLAGE WAS MY HOMETOWN...!

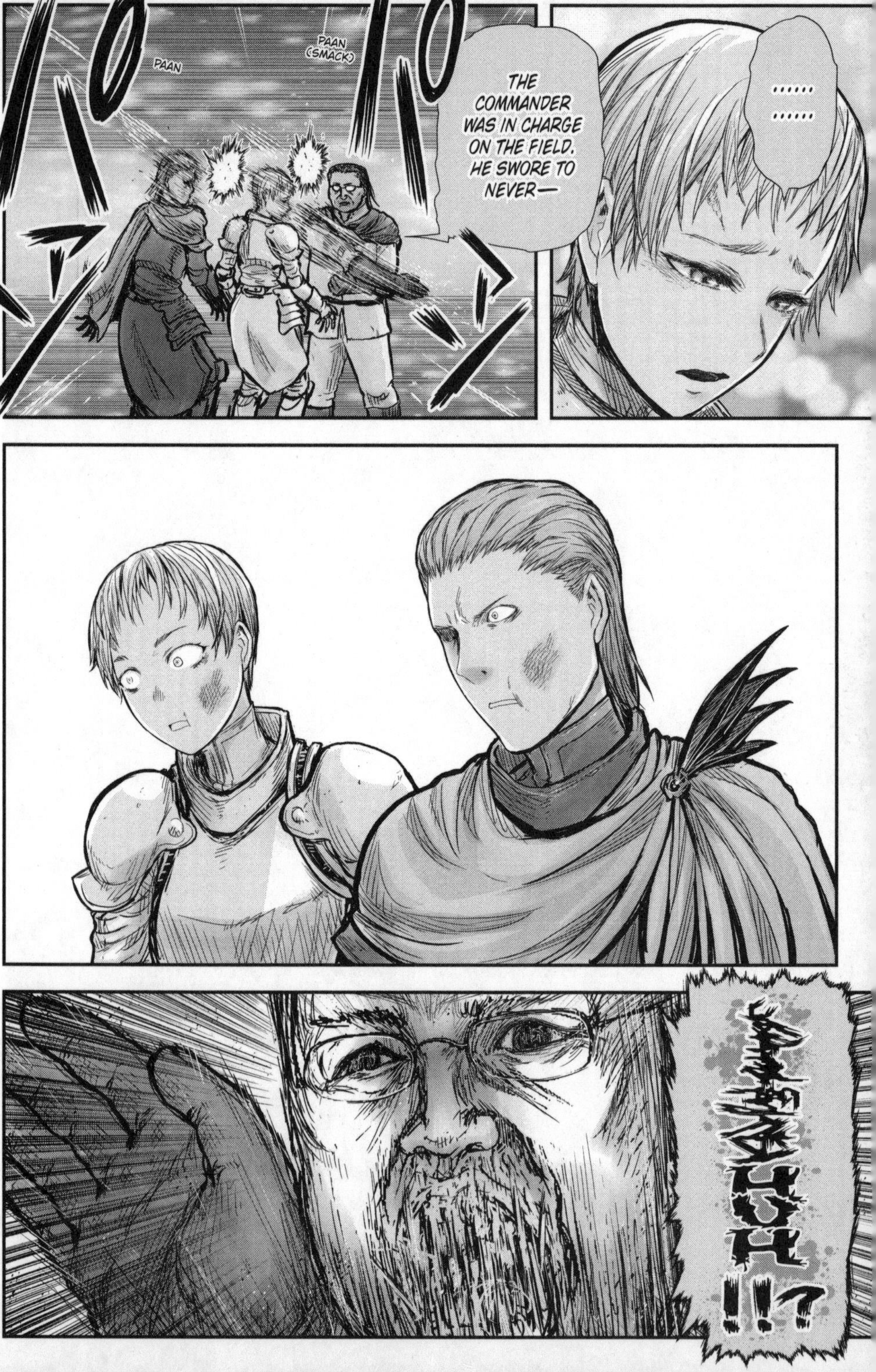
……
……
THE COMMANDER WAS IN CHARGE ON THE FIELD. HE SWORE TO NEVER—
PAAN (SMACK)
PAAN
HUH!!?

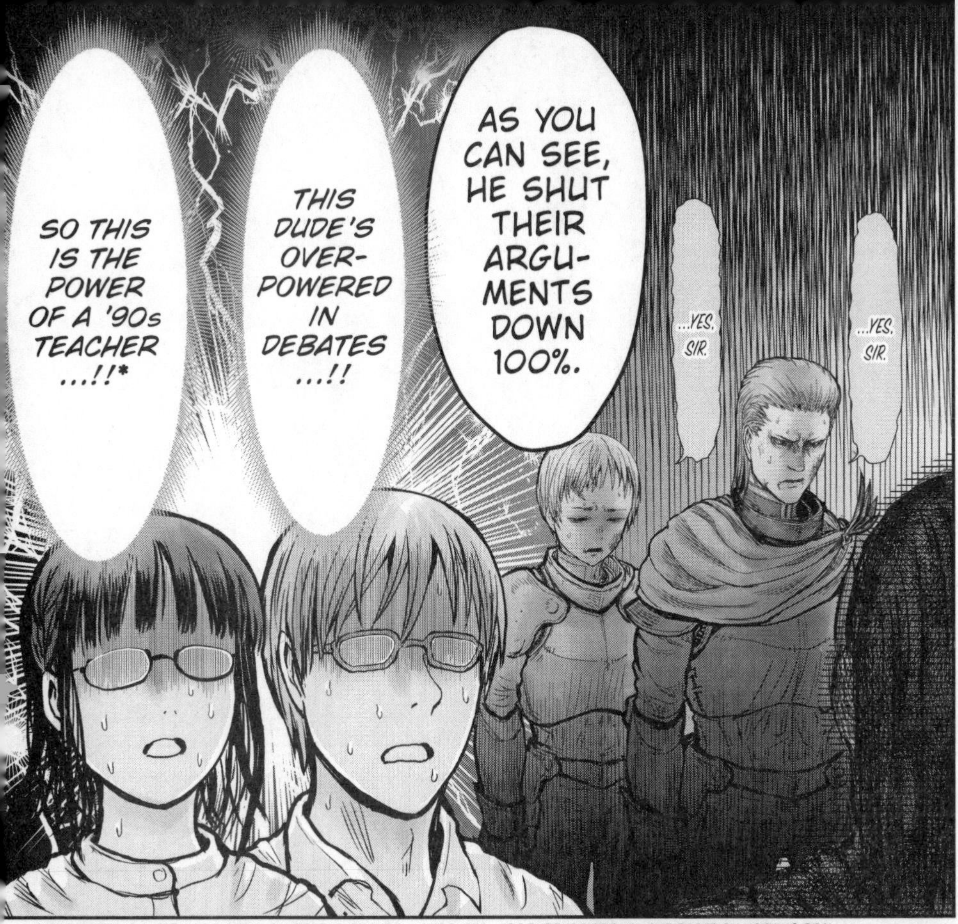
...YES, SIR.
...YES, SIR.
AS YOU CAN SEE, HE SHUT THEIR ARGU- MENTS DOWN 100%.
THIS DUDE'S OVER- POWERED IN DEBATES ...!!
SO THIS IS THE POWER OF A '90s TEACHER ...!!*

*THIS STORY IS A WORK OF FICTION. ALL PEOPLE, GROUPS, NAMES, ETC., ARE PURELY FICTIONAL AND BASED ON NOTHING REAL.

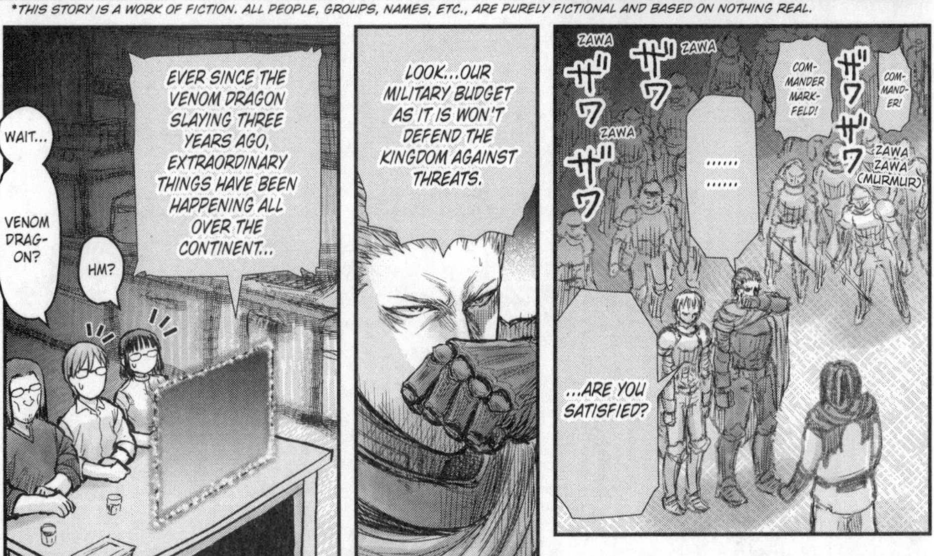
COM- MANDER!
ザワ
ザワ
ZAWA ZAWA (MURMUR)
COM- MANDER MARK- FELD!
ZAWA
ザワ
ZAWA
ザワ
ZAWA
ザワ
......
......
...ARE YOU SATISFIED?
LOOK...OUR MILITARY BUDGET AS IT IS WON'T DEFEND THE KINGDOM AGAINST THREATS.
EVER SINCE THE VENOM DRAGON SLAYING THREE YEARS AGO, EXTRAORDINARY THINGS HAVE BEEN HAPPENING ALL OVER THE CONTINENT...
WAIT...
VENOM DRAG- ON?
HM?

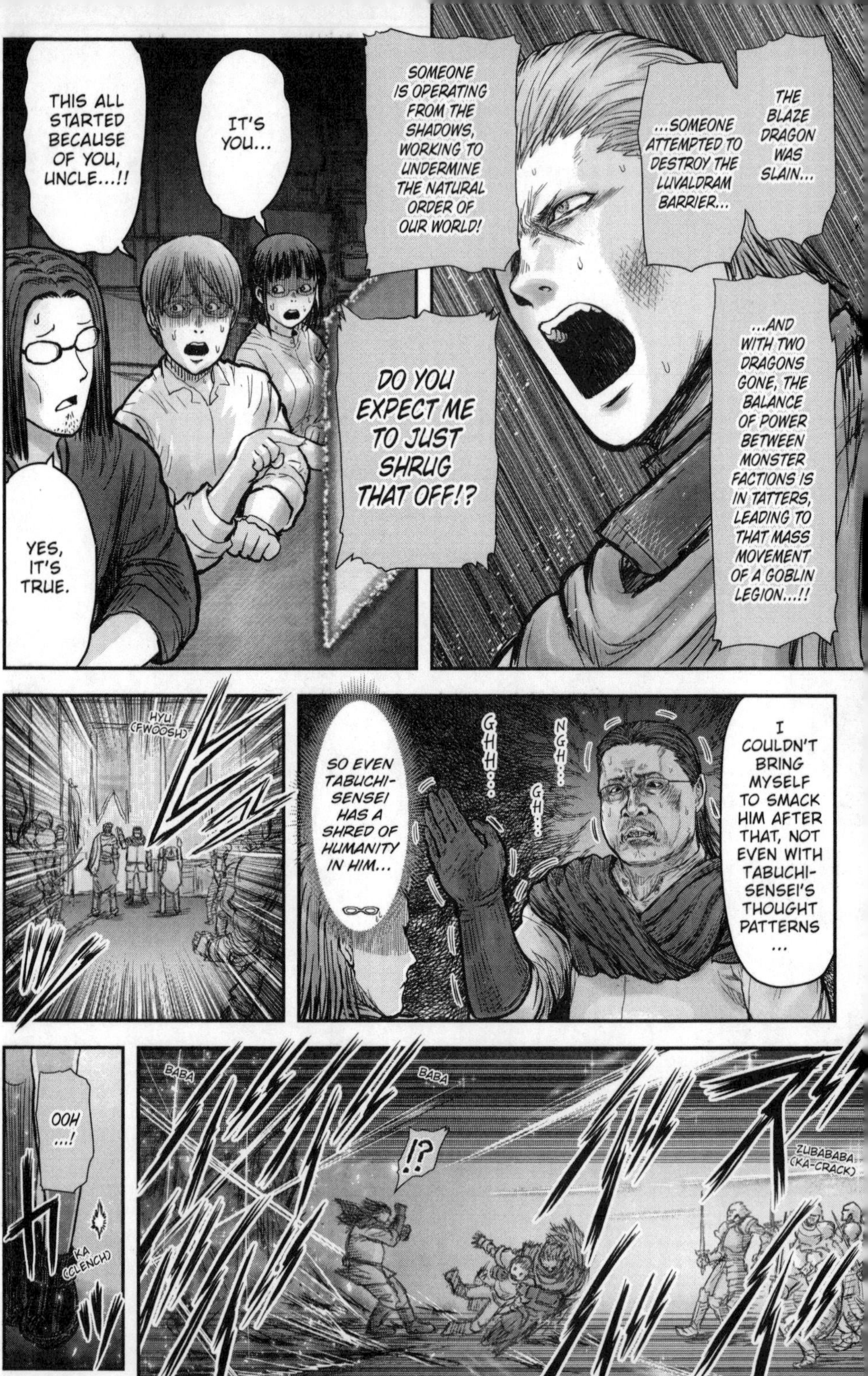
THE BLAZE DRAGON WAS SLAIN...
...SOMEONE ATTEMPTED TO DESTROY THE LUVALDRAM BARRIER...
...AND WITH TWO DRAGONS GONE, THE BALANCE OF POWER BETWEEN MONSTER FACTIONS IS IN TATTERS, LEADING TO THAT MASS MOVEMENT OF A GOBLIN LEGION...!!
SOMEONE IS OPERATING FROM THE SHADOWS, WORKING TO UNDERMINE THE NATURAL ORDER OF OUR WORLD!
DO YOU EXPECT ME TO JUST SHRUG THAT OFF!?
IT'S YOU...
THIS ALL STARTED BECAUSE OF YOU, UNCLE...!!
YES, IT'S TRUE.
I COULDN'T BRING MYSELF TO SMACK HIM AFTER THAT, NOT EVEN WITH TABUCHI-SENSEI'S THOUGHT PATTERNS...
NGH...
GH...
GHH...
SO EVEN TABUCHI-SENSEI HAS A SHRED OF HUMANITY IN HIM...
HYU (FWOOSH)
ZUBABABA (KA-CRACK)
BABA
!?
BABA
OOH...!
KA (CLENCH)

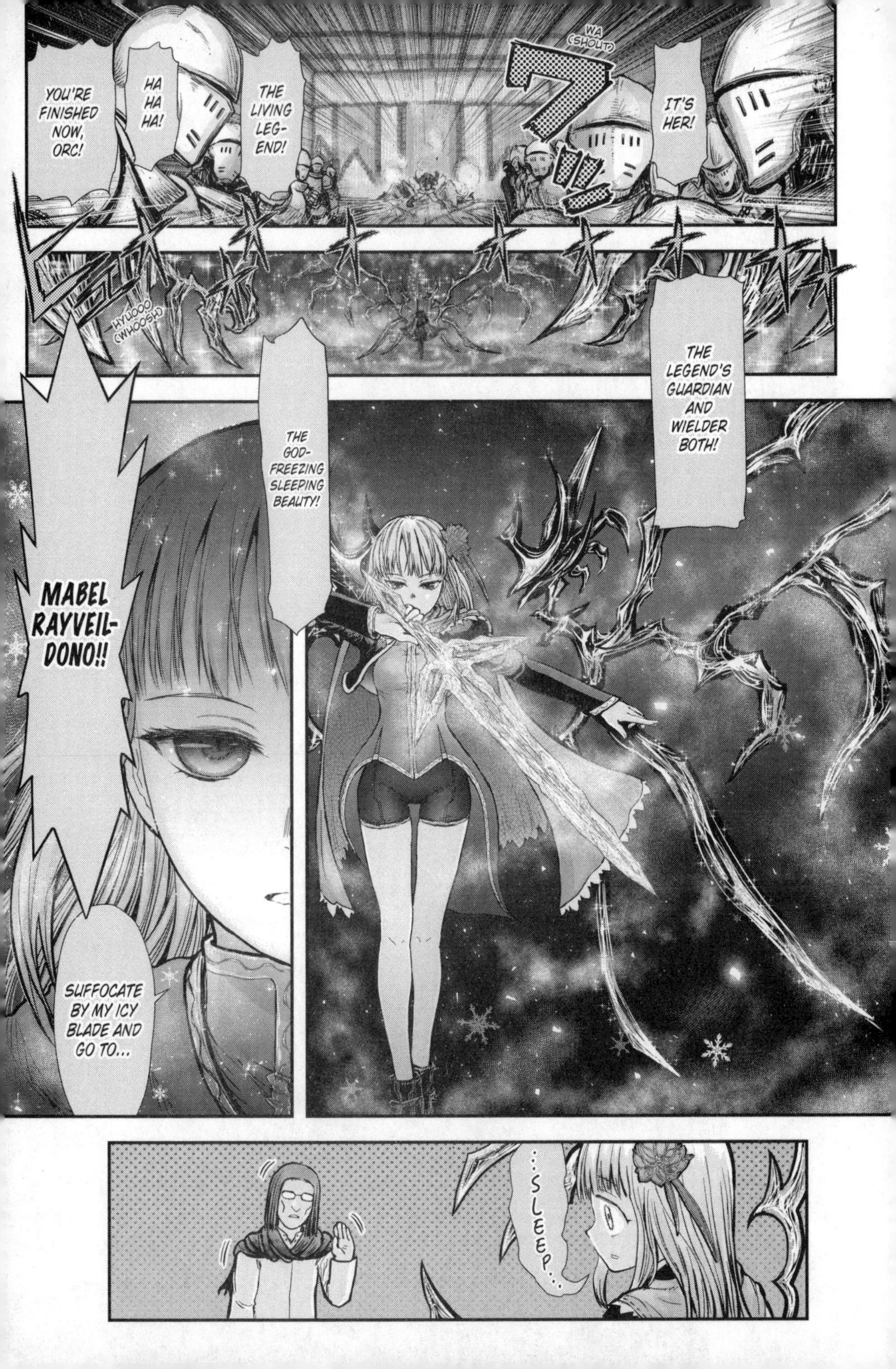
WA (SHOUT)
IT'S HER!
THE LIVING LEG-END!
HA HA HA!
YOU'RE FINISHED NOW, ORC!
HYUOOO (WHOOSH)
THE LEGEND'S GUARDIAN AND WIELDER BOTH!
THE GOD-FREEZING SLEEPING BEAUTY!
MABEL RAYVEIL-DONO!!
SUFFOCATE BY MY ICY BLADE AND GO TO...
...SLEEP...

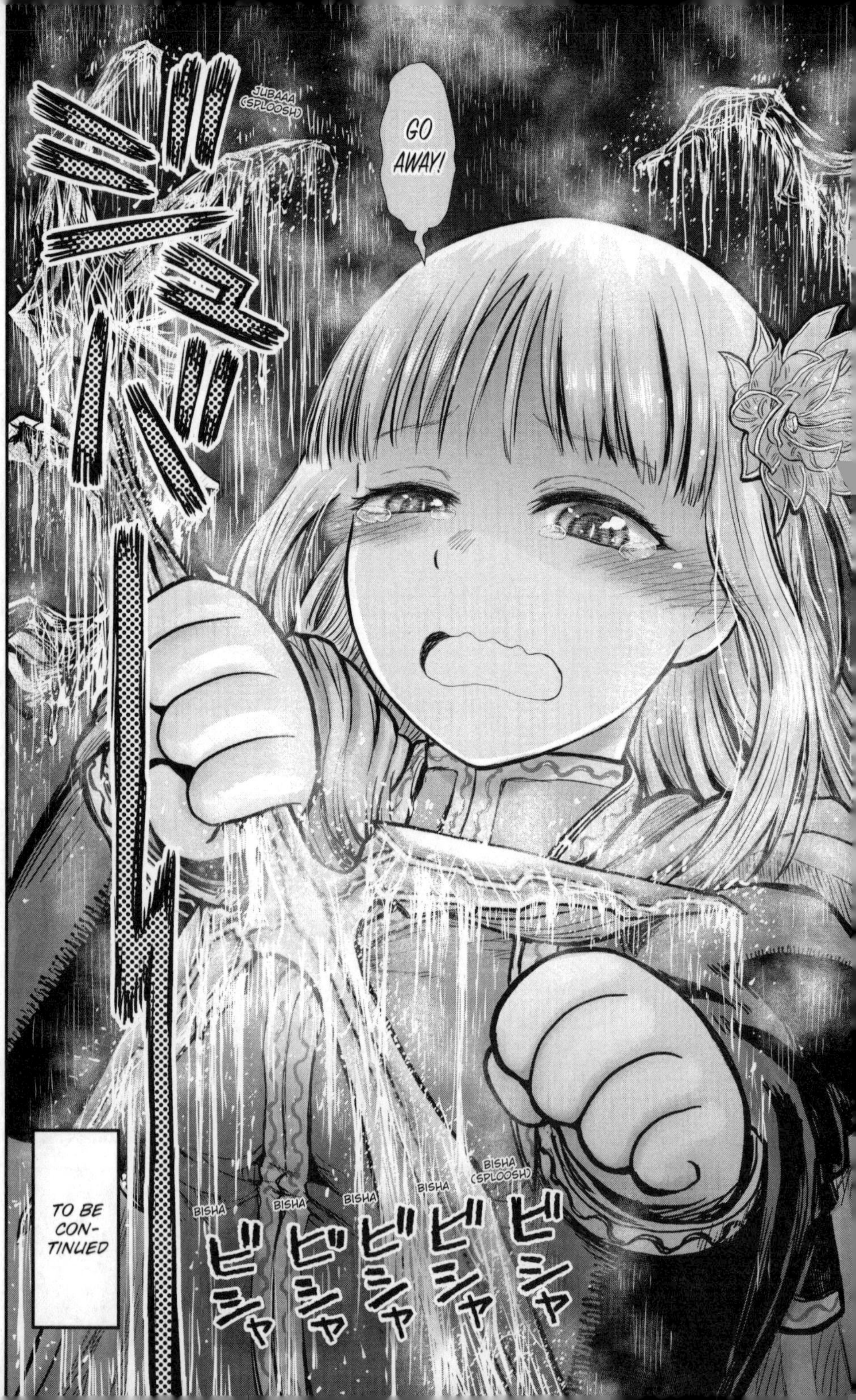
GO AWAY!
JUBAAA (SPLOOSH)
BISHA (SPLOOSH)
ビシャ
BISHA
ビシャ
BISHA
ビシャ
BISHA
ビシャ
BISHA
ビシャ
TO BE CON-TINUED

Corporal Punishment

A style of teaching often seen in Japanese school education up until the 1990s. A form of bullying categorized as power harassment. Corporal punishment has been on the decline for many years, but it is still present today.

TIPS

UNCLE from ANOTHER WORLD

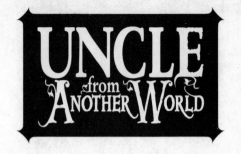

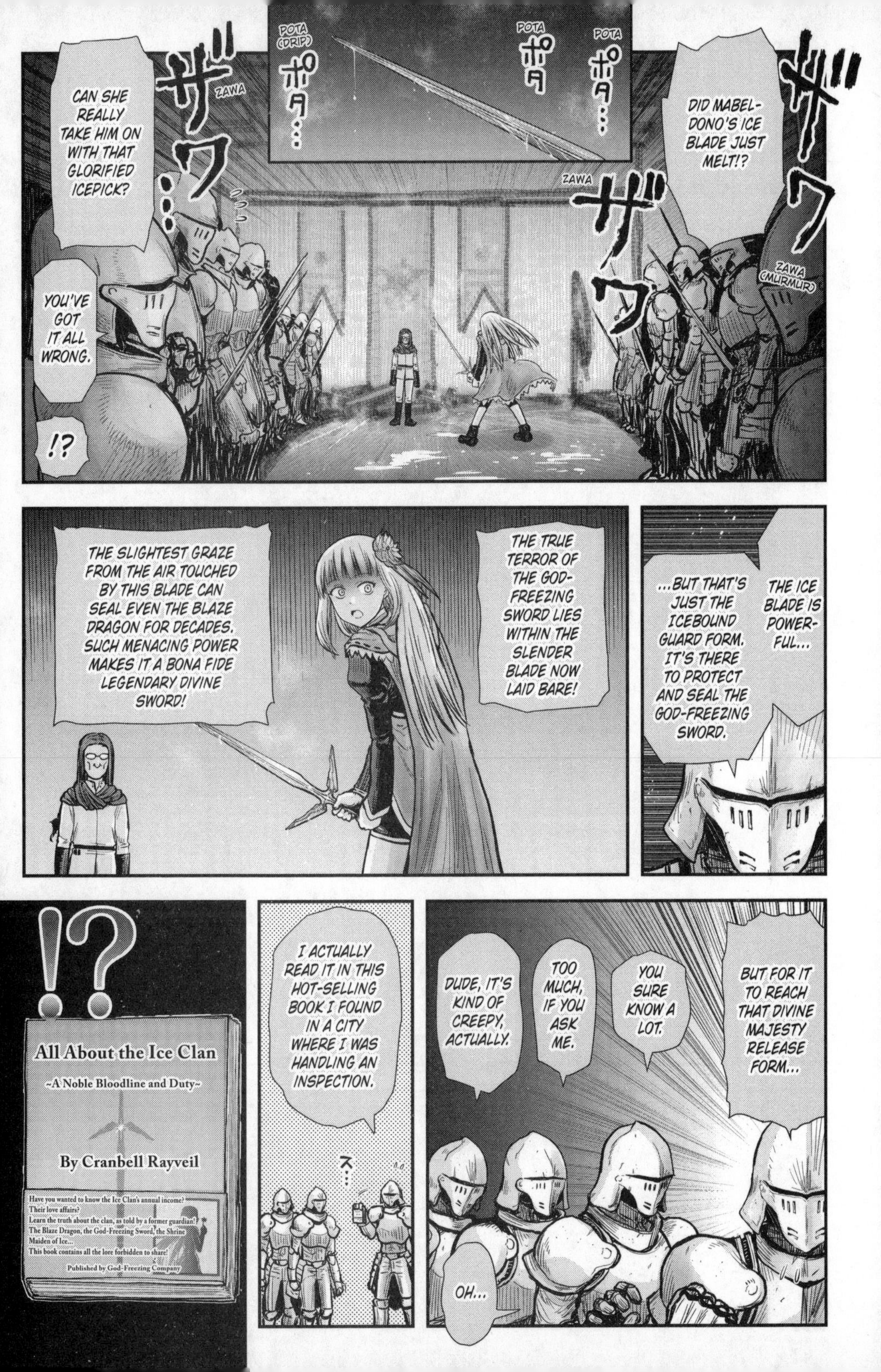

ザワ
DID MABEL-DONO'S ICE BLADE JUST MELT!?
ZAWA
ザワ
ZAWA (MURMUR)
ザワ
POTA
ポタ…
POTA
ポタ
POTA (DRIP)
ポタ…
ZAWA
ザワ…
CAN SHE REALLY TAKE HIM ON WITH THAT GLORIFIED ICEPICK?
YOU'VE GOT IT ALL WRONG.
!?
THE ICE BLADE IS POWER-FUL…
…BUT THAT'S JUST THE ICEBOUND GUARD FORM. IT'S THERE TO PROTECT AND SEAL THE GOD-FREEZING SWORD.
THE TRUE TERROR OF THE GOD-FREEZING SWORD LIES WITHIN THE SLENDER BLADE NOW LAID BARE!
THE SLIGHTEST GRAZE FROM THE AIR TOUCHED BY THIS BLADE CAN SEAL EVEN THE BLAZE DRAGON FOR DECADES. SUCH MENACING POWER MAKES IT A BONA FIDE LEGENDARY DIVINE SWORD!
BUT FOR IT TO REACH THAT DIVINE MAJESTY RELEASE FORM…
YOU SURE KNOW A LOT.
TOO MUCH, IF YOU ASK ME.
DUDE, IT'S KIND OF CREEPY, ACTUALLY.
OH…
I ACTUALLY READ IT IN THIS HOT-SELLING BOOK I FOUND IN A CITY WHERE I WAS HANDLING AN INSPECTION.
ス…
!?
All About the Ice Clan
~A Noble Bloodline and Duty~
By Cranbell Rayveil
Have you wanted to know the Ice Clan's annual income? Their love affairs? Learn the truth about the clan, as told by a former guardian! The Blaze Dragon, the God-Freezing Sword, the Shrine Maiden of Ice… This book contains all the lore forbidden to share!
Published by God-Freezing Company

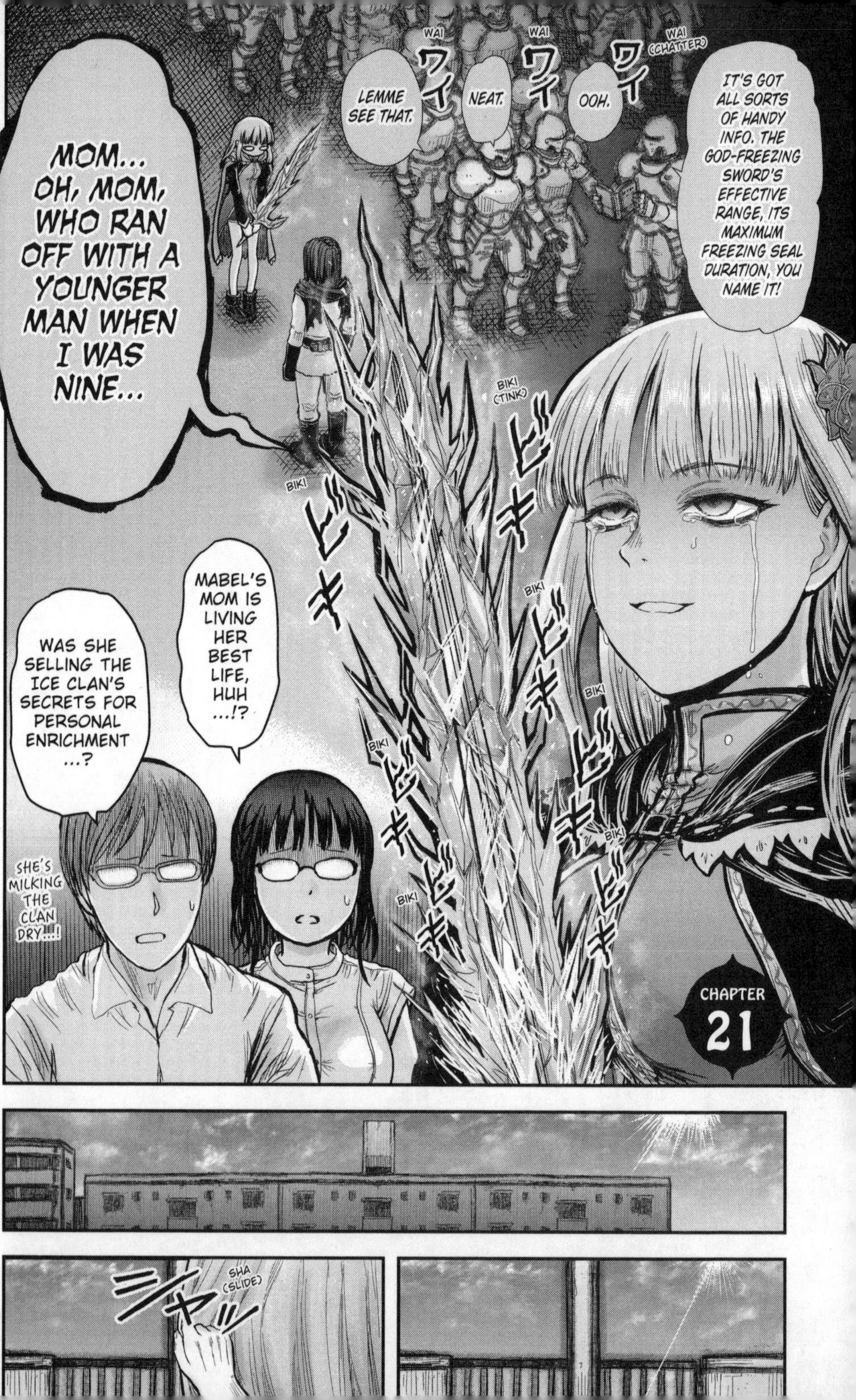
IT'S GOT ALL SORTS OF HANDY INFO. THE GOD-FREEZING SWORD'S EFFECTIVE RANGE, ITS MAXIMUM FREEZING SEAL DURATION, YOU NAME IT!
WAI (CHATTER)
ワイ
OOH.
WAI
ワイ
NEAT.
WAI
ワイ
LEMME SEE THAT.
MOM... OH, MOM, WHO RAN OFF WITH A YOUNGER MAN WHEN I WAS NINE...
BIKI (TINK)
ビキ
BIKI
ビキ
BIKI
ビキ
BIKI
ビキ
BIKI
ビキ
BIKI
ビキ
BIKI
ビキ
MABEL'S MOM IS LIVING HER BEST LIFE, HUH ...!?
WAS SHE SELLING THE ICE CLAN'S SECRETS FOR PERSONAL ENRICHMENT ...?
SHE'S MILKING THE CLAN DRY...!
CHAPTER 21
SHA (SLIDE)
シャッ

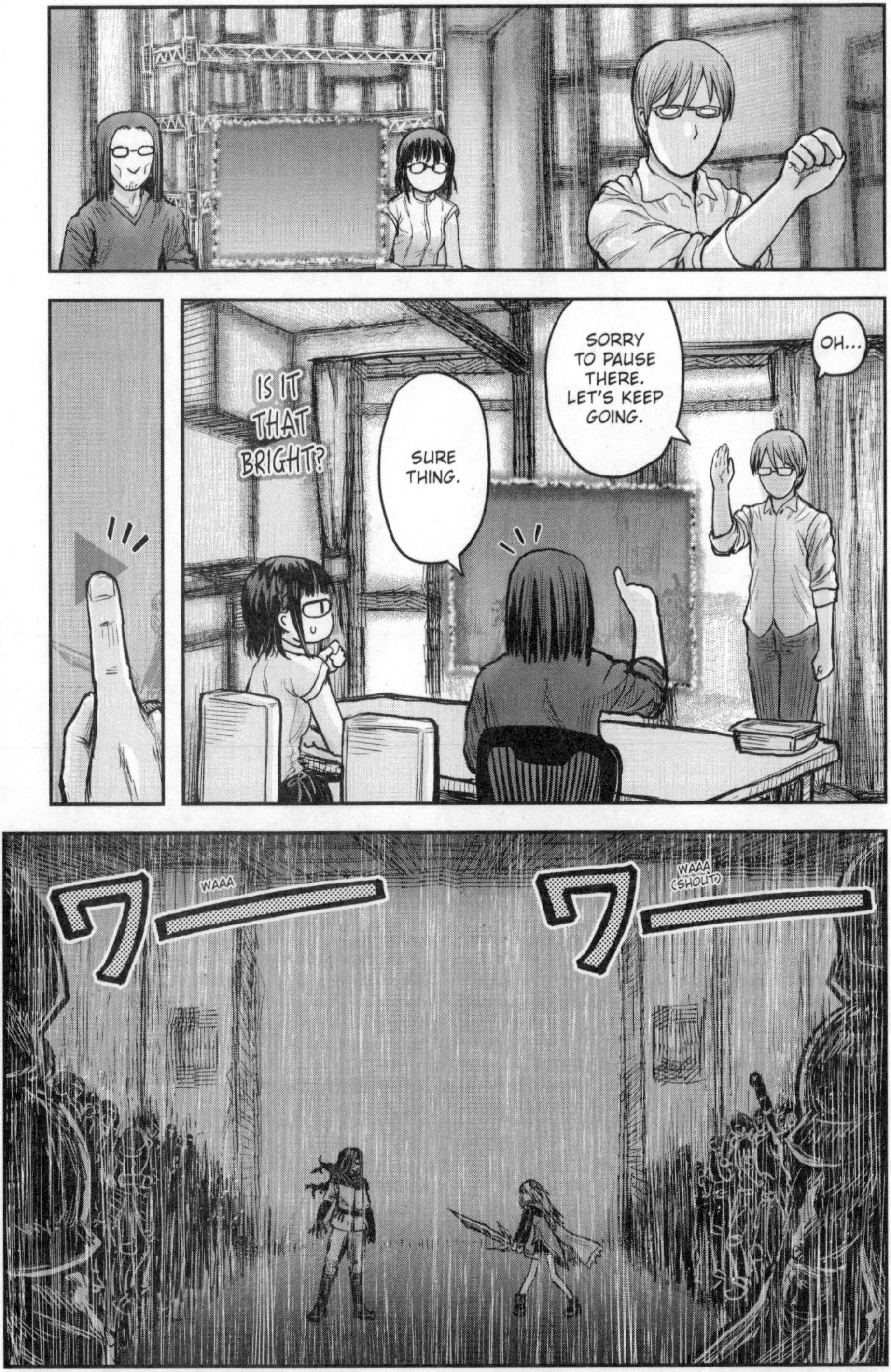
OH...
SORRY TO PAUSE THERE. LET'S KEEP GOING.
SURE THING.
IS IT THAT BRIGHT?
ワー
WAAA (SHOUT)
ワー
WAAA

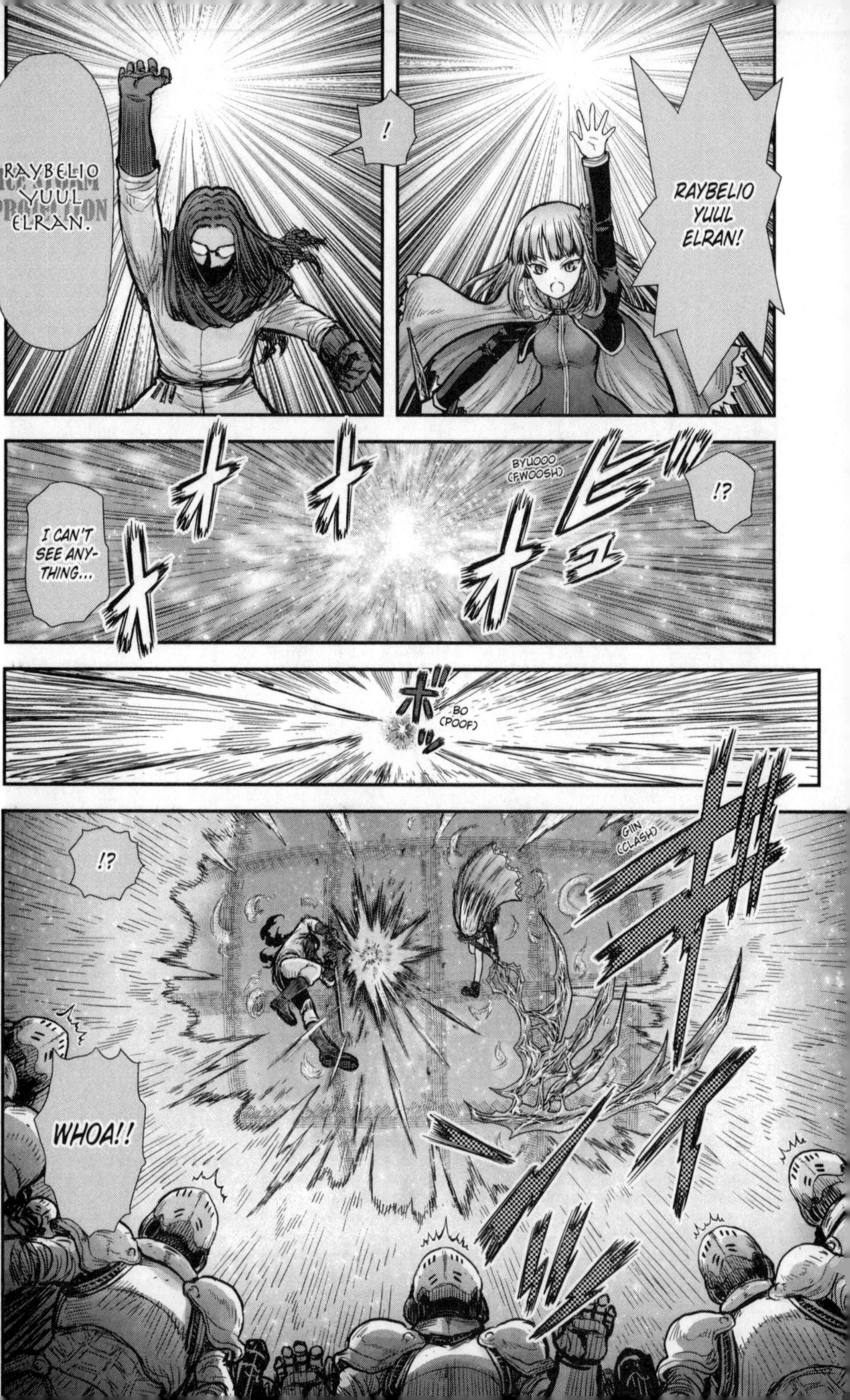
!
RAYBELIO YUUL ELRAN!
RAYBELIO YUUL ELRAN.
!?
BYUOOO (FWOOSH)
I CAN'T SEE ANYTHING...
BO (POOF)
GIIN (CLASH)
!?
WHOA!!

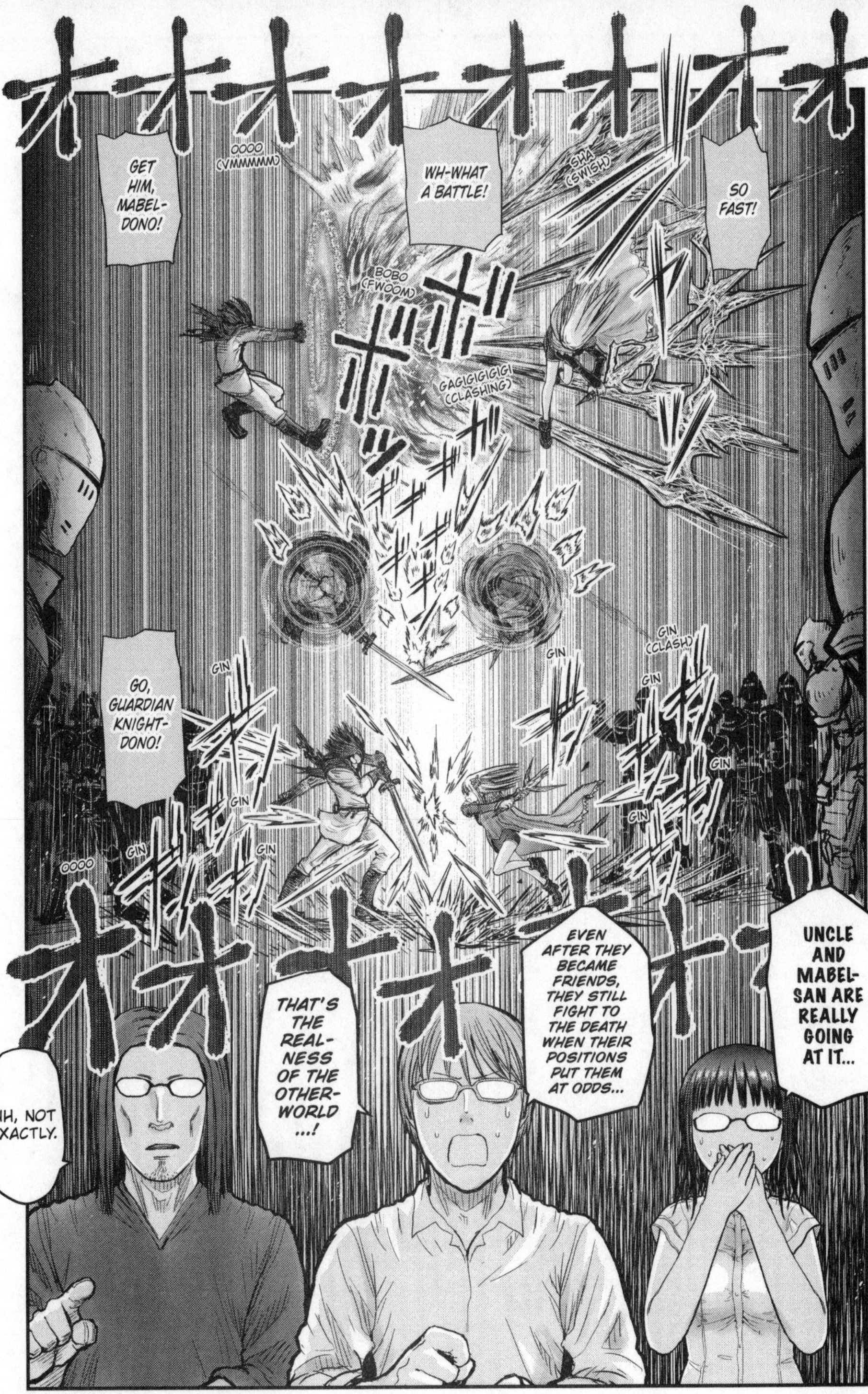
SO FAST!
SHA (SWISH)
WH-WHAT A BATTLE!
OOOO (VMMMMM)
GET HIM, MABEL-DONO!
BOBO (FWOOM)
GAGIGIGIGI (CLASHING)
GIN (CLASH)
GIN
GIN
GIN
GIN
GIN
GIN
GIN
GO, GUARDIAN KNIGHT-DONO!
OOOO
UNCLE AND MABEL-SAN ARE REALLY GOING AT IT...
EVEN AFTER THEY BECAME FRIENDS, THEY STILL FIGHT TO THE DEATH WHEN THEIR POSITIONS PUT THEM AT ODDS...
THAT'S THE REAL-NESS OF THE OTHER-WORLD ...!
UH, NOT EXACTLY.

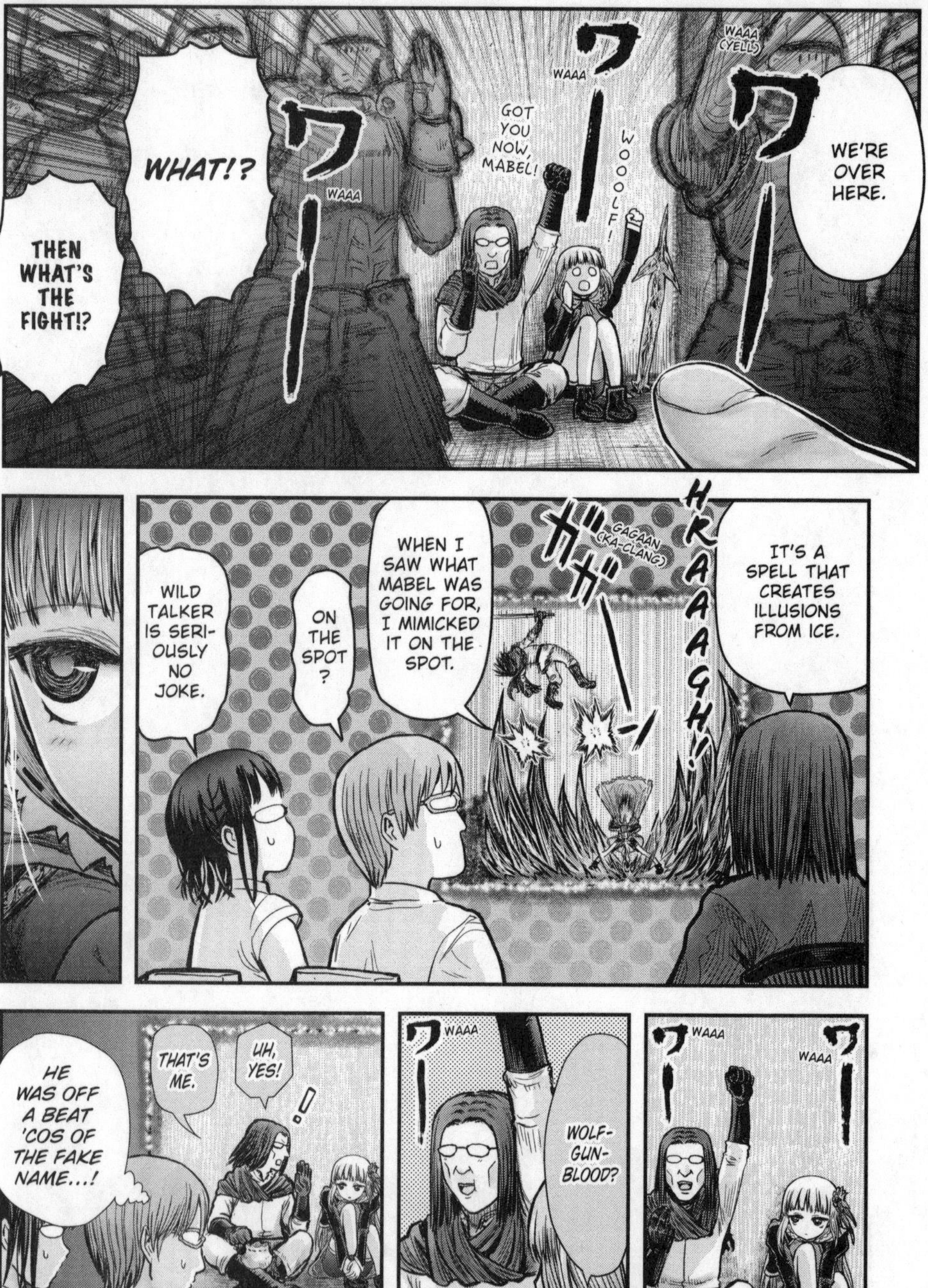
WAAA (YELL)
WE'RE OVER HERE.
WAAA
WOOOLF!
GOT YOU NOW, MABEL!
WAAA
WHAT!?
THEN WHAT'S THE FIGHT!?
IT'S A SPELL THAT CREATES ILLUSIONS FROM ICE.
HRAAAAGH!!
GAGAAN (KA-CLANG)
WHEN I SAW WHAT MABEL WAS GOING FOR, I MIMICKED IT ON THE SPOT.
ON THE SPOT?
WILD TALKER IS SERIOUSLY NO JOKE.
WAAA
WAAA
WAAA
WOLF-GUN-BLOOD?
UH, YES!
!
THAT'S ME.
HE WAS OFF A BEAT 'COS OF THE FAKE NAME...!

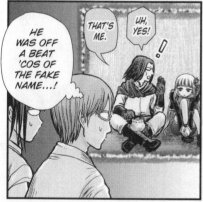

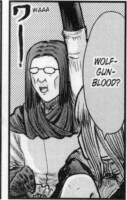

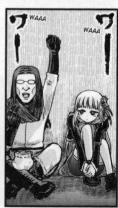

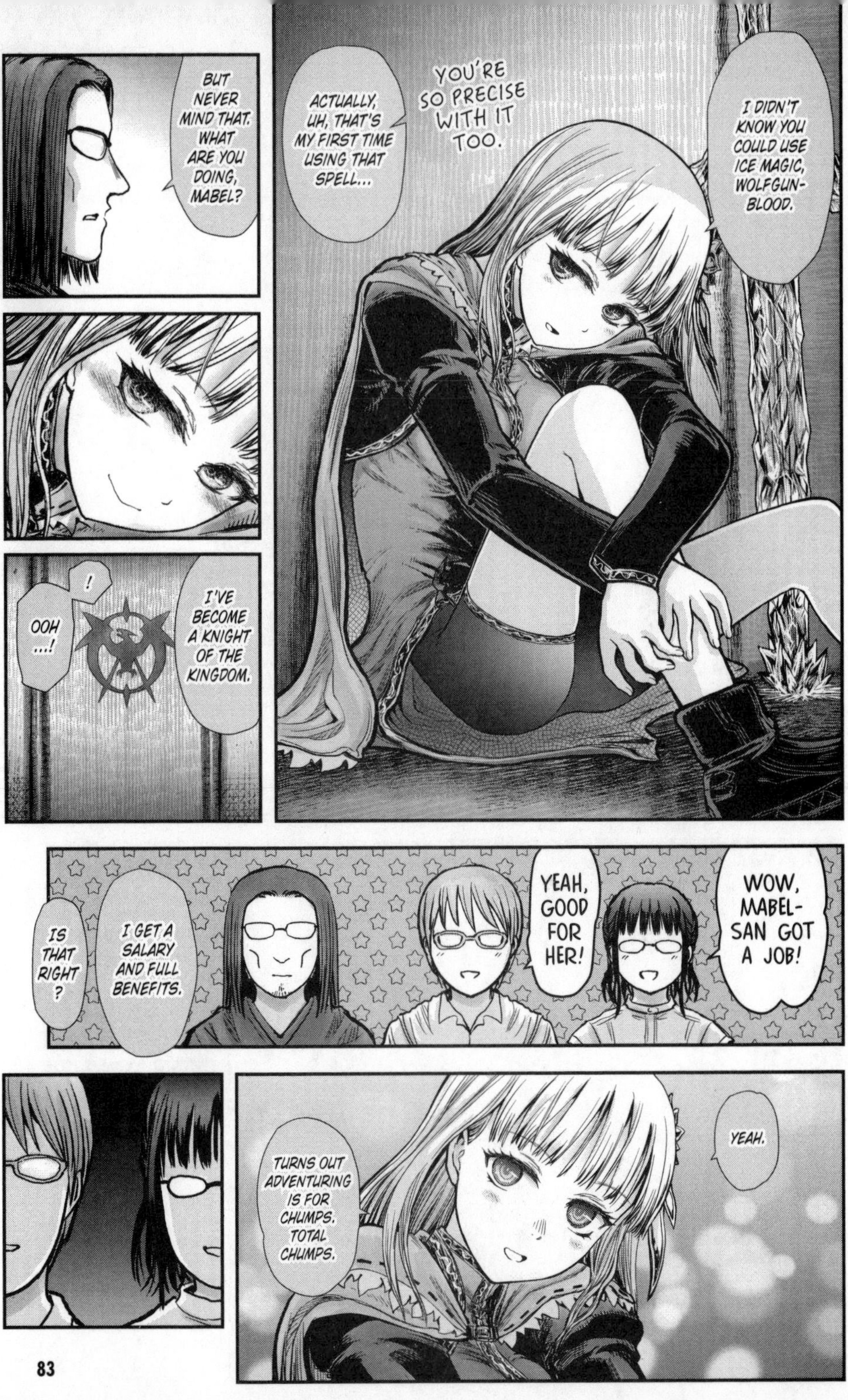
I DIDN'T KNOW YOU COULD USE ICE MAGIC, WOLFGUN-BLOOD.
YOU'RE SO PRECISE WITH IT TOO.
ACTUALLY, UH, THAT'S MY FIRST TIME USING THAT SPELL...
BUT NEVER MIND THAT. WHAT ARE YOU DOING, MABEL?
I'VE BECOME A KNIGHT OF THE KINGDOM.
!
OOH ...!
WOW, MABEL-SAN GOT A JOB!
YEAH, GOOD FOR HER!
I GET A SALARY AND FULL BENEFITS.
IS THAT RIGHT?
YEAH.
TURNS OUT ADVENTURING IS FOR CHUMPS. TOTAL CHUMPS.

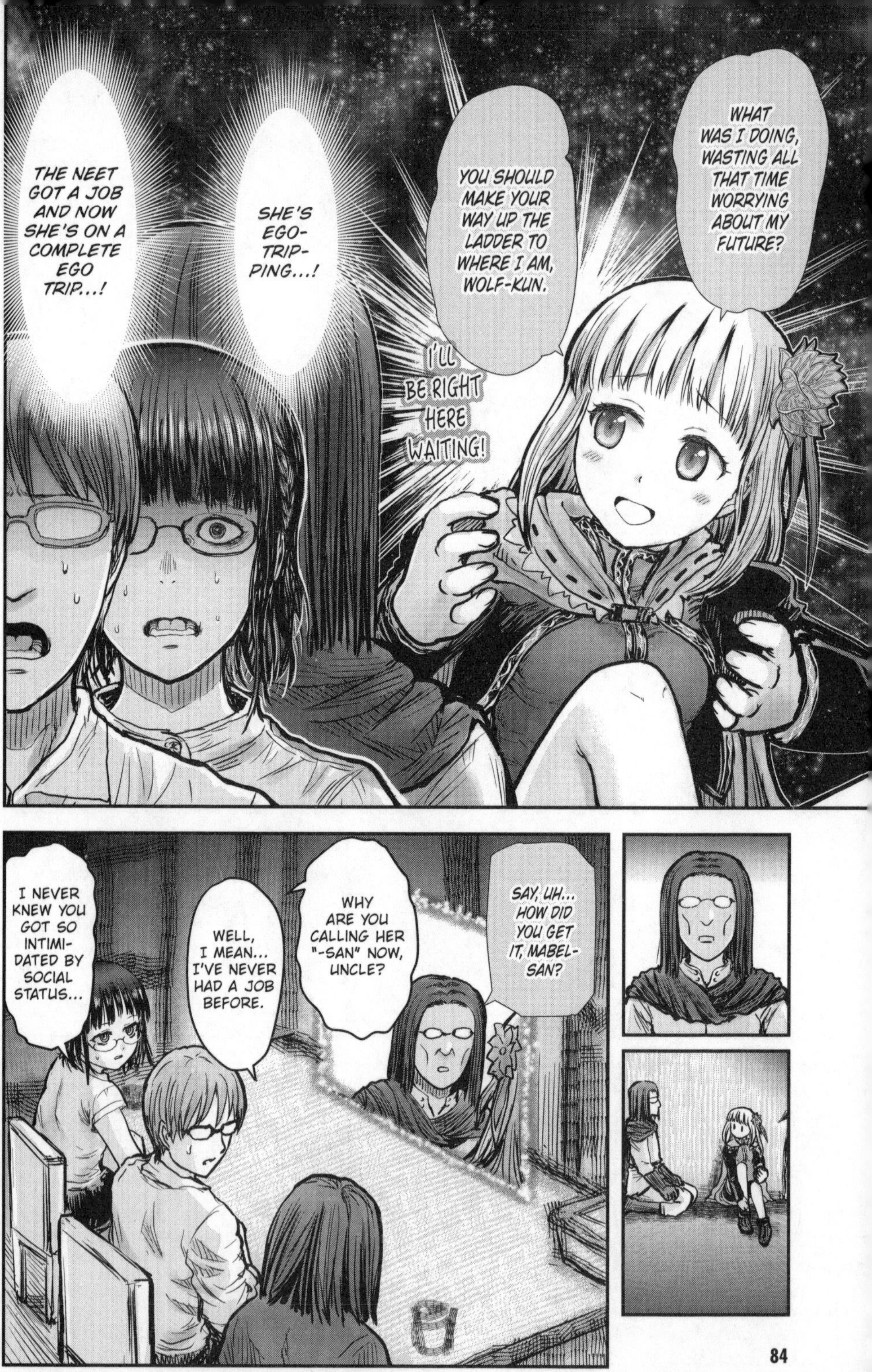
WHAT WAS I DOING, WASTING ALL THAT TIME WORRYING ABOUT MY FUTURE?
YOU SHOULD MAKE YOUR WAY UP THE LADDER TO WHERE I AM, WOLF-KUN.
I'LL BE RIGHT HERE WAITING!
SHE'S EGO-TRIP-PING...!
THE NEET GOT A JOB AND NOW SHE'S ON A COMPLETE EGO TRIP...!
SAY, UH... HOW DID YOU GET IT, MABEL-SAN?
WHY ARE YOU CALLING HER "-SAN" NOW, UNCLE?
WELL, I MEAN... I'VE NEVER HAD A JOB BEFORE.
I NEVER KNEW YOU GOT SO INTIMI-DATED BY SOCIAL STATUS...

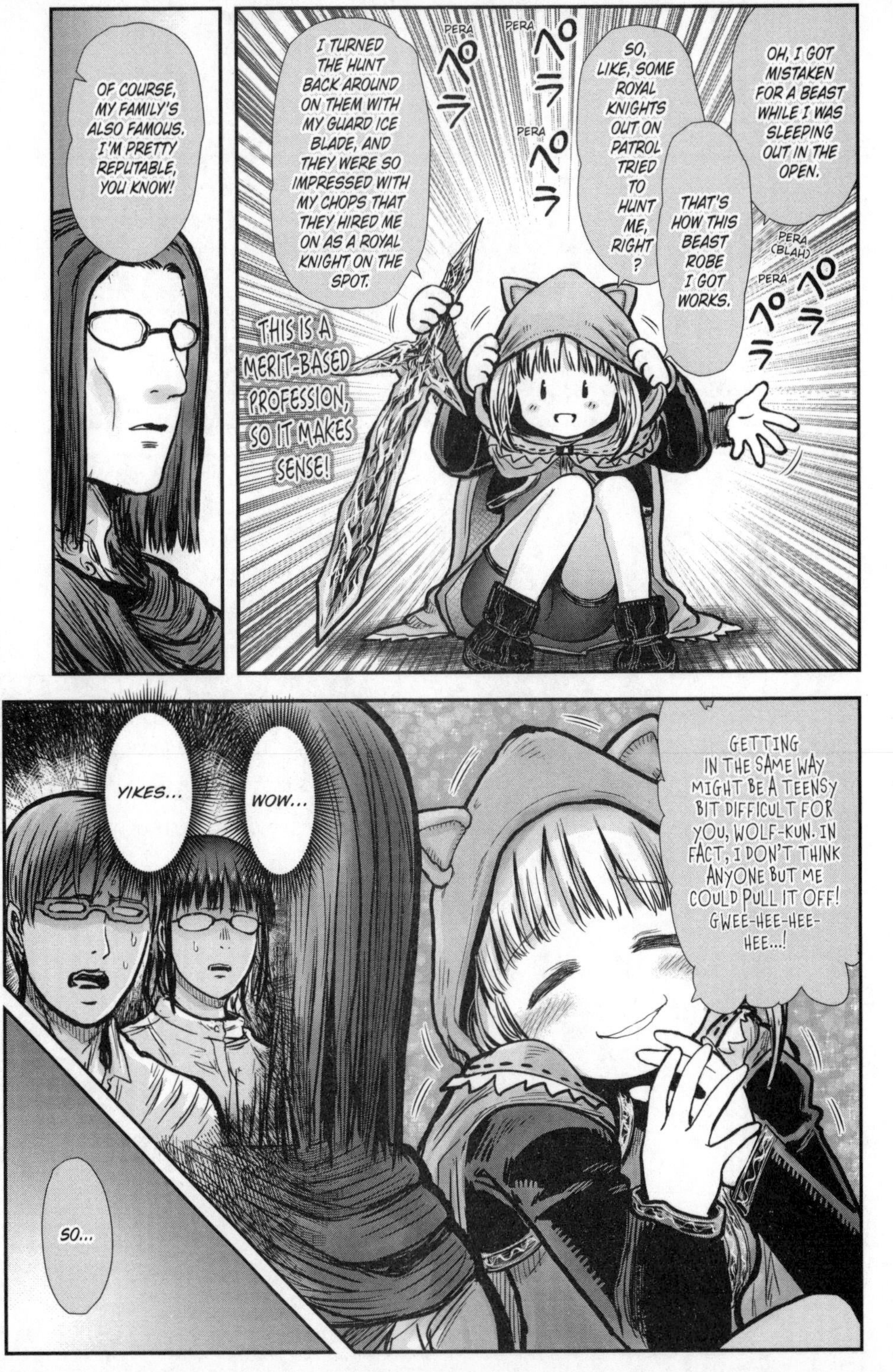
OH, I GOT MISTAKEN FOR A BEAST WHILE I WAS SLEEPING OUT IN THE OPEN.
THAT'S HOW THIS BEAST ROBE I GOT WORKS.
PERA (BLAH) ペラ
PERA ペラ
SO, LIKE, SOME ROYAL KNIGHTS OUT ON PATROL TRIED TO HUNT ME, RIGHT?
PERA ペラ
PERA ペラ
PERA ペラ
I TURNED THE HUNT BACK AROUND ON THEM WITH MY GUARD ICE BLADE, AND THEY WERE SO IMPRESSED WITH MY CHOPS THAT THEY HIRED ME ON AS A ROYAL KNIGHT ON THE SPOT.
THIS IS A MERIT-BASED PROFESSION, SO IT MAKES SENSE!
OF COURSE, MY FAMILY'S ALSO FAMOUS. I'M PRETTY REPUTABLE, YOU KNOW!
GETTING IN THE SAME WAY MIGHT BE A TEENSY BIT DIFFICULT FOR YOU, WOLF-KUN. IN FACT, I DON'T THINK ANYONE BUT ME COULD PULL IT OFF! GWEE-HEE-HEE-HEE...!
WOW...
YIKES...
SO...

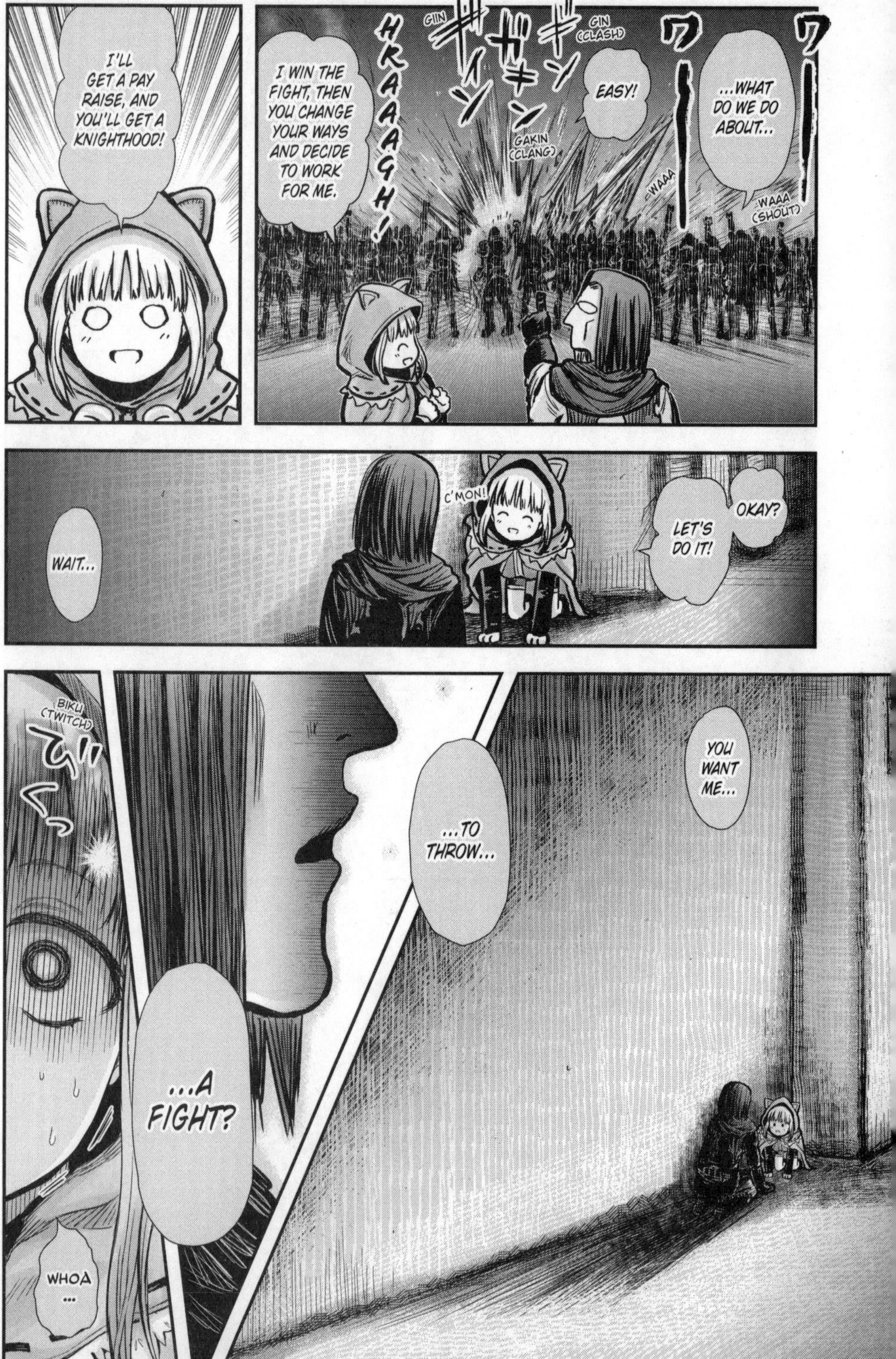
...WHAT DO WE DO ABOUT...
WAAA (SHOUT)
WAAA
EASY!
GIN (CLASH)
GAKIN (CLANG)
GIIN
HRAAAAGH!
I WIN THE FIGHT, THEN YOU CHANGE YOUR WAYS AND DECIDE TO WORK FOR ME.
I'LL GET A PAY RAISE, AND YOU'LL GET A KNIGHTHOOD!
OKAY?
LET'S DO IT!
C'MON!
WAIT...
YOU WANT ME...
...TO THROW...
...A FIGHT?
BIKU (TWITCH)
WHOA ...

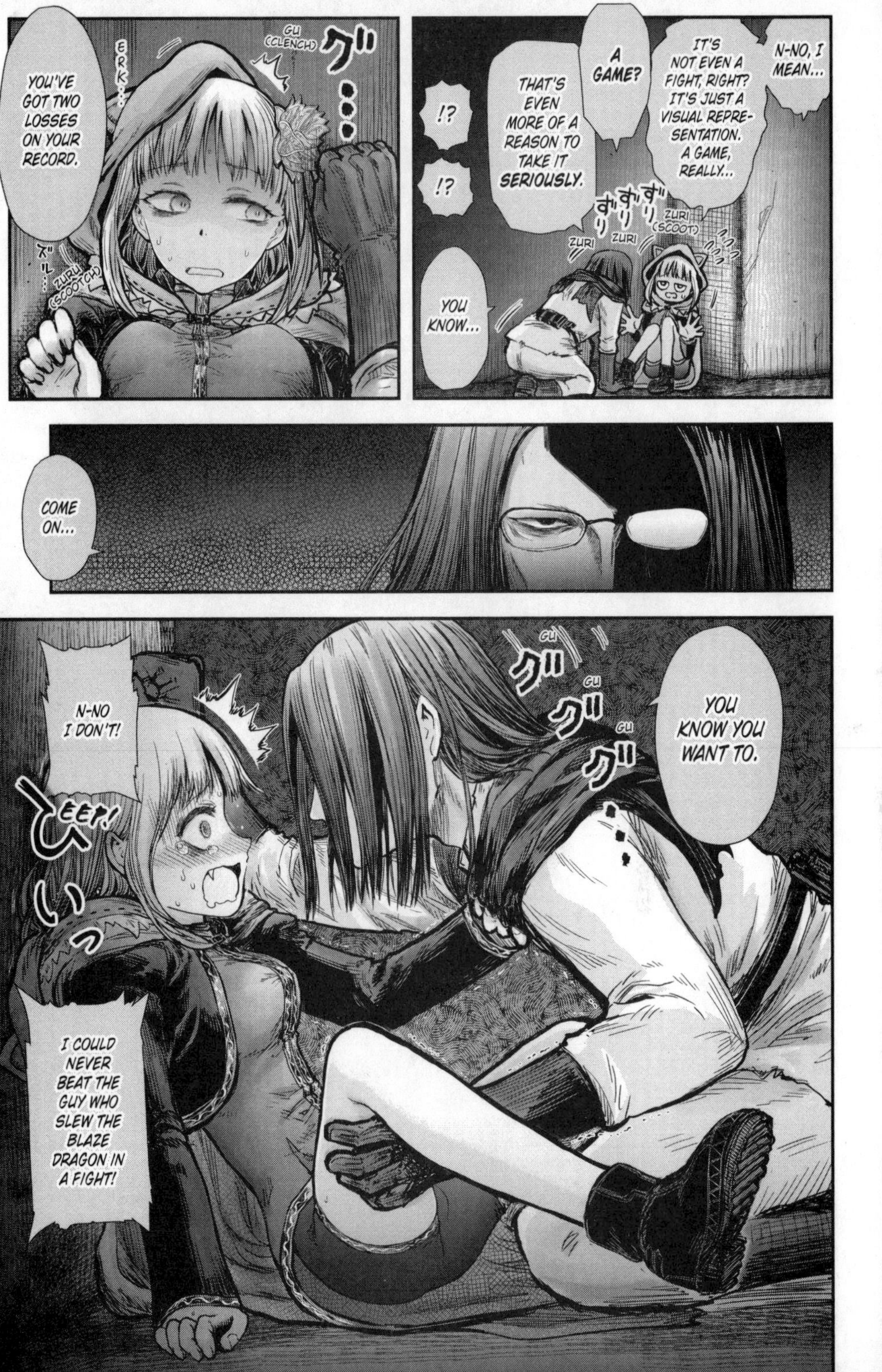
N-NO, I MEAN...
IT'S NOT EVEN A FIGHT, RIGHT? IT'S JUST A VISUAL REPRESENTATION. A GAME, REALLY...
A GAME?
THAT'S EVEN MORE OF A REASON TO TAKE IT SERIOUSLY.
!?
!?
ずりずりずり
ZURI ZURI ZURI (SCOOT)
YOU KNOW...
GU (CLENCH)
グ
ERK...
YOU'VE GOT TWO LOSSES ON YOUR RECORD.
ズル…
ZURU (SCOOTCH)
COME ON...
YOU KNOW YOU WANT TO.
GU グッ
GU グッ
GU グッ
N-NO I DON'T!
EEP!
ひぃっ
I COULD NEVER BEAT THE GUY WHO SLEW THE BLAZE DRAGON IN A FIGHT!

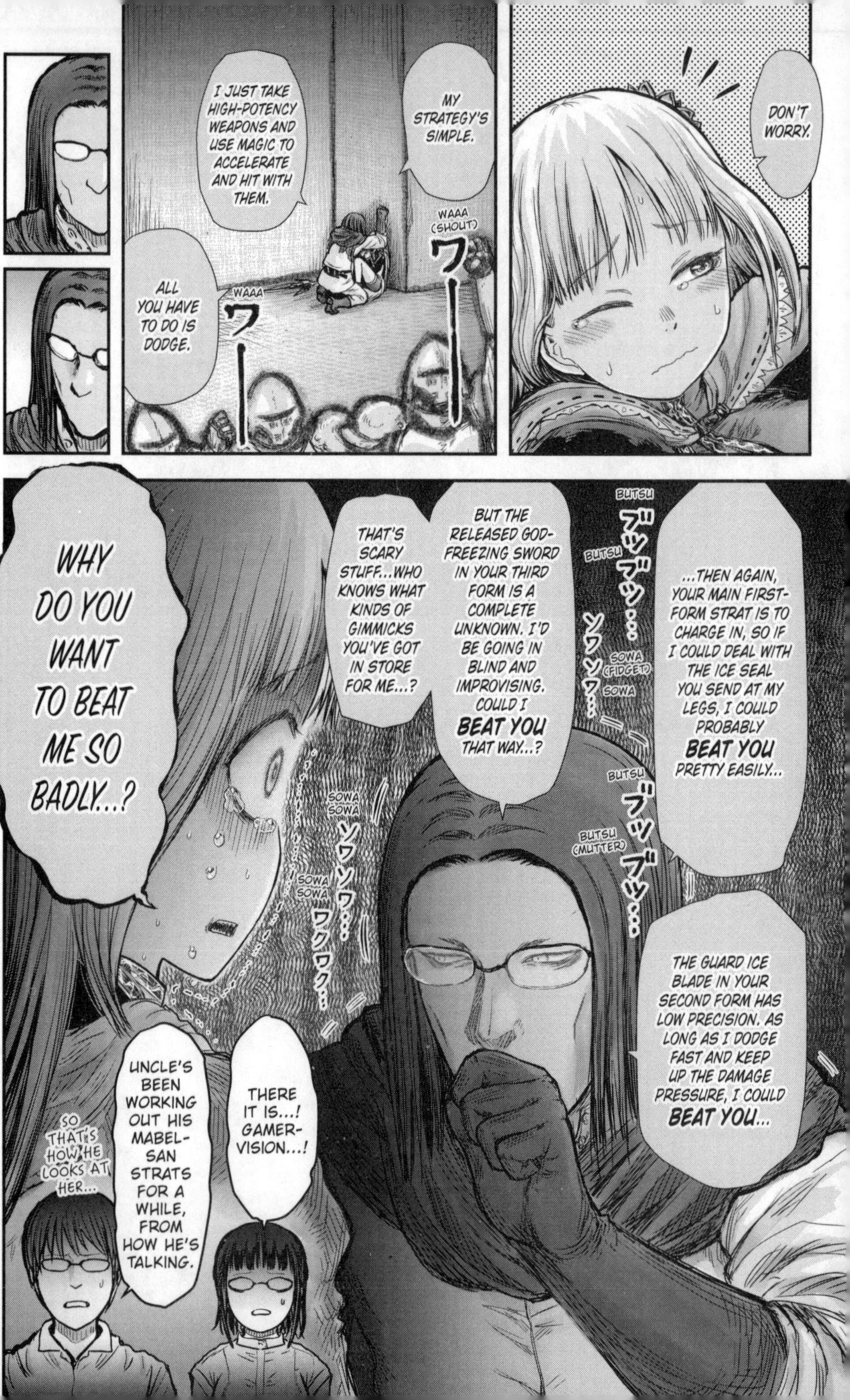
DON'T WORRY.
MY STRATEGY'S SIMPLE.
I JUST TAKE HIGH-POTENCY WEAPONS AND USE MAGIC TO ACCELERATE AND HIT WITH THEM.
WAAA (SHOUT)
ワー
WAAA
ワー
ALL YOU HAVE TO DO IS DODGE.
...THEN AGAIN, YOUR MAIN FIRST-FORM STRAT IS TO CHARGE IN, SO IF I COULD DEAL WITH THE ICE SEAL YOU SEND AT MY LEGS, I COULD PROBABLY **BEAT YOU** PRETTY EASILY...
BUTSU BUTSU
ブツブツ...
SOWA (FIDGET) SOWA
ソワソワ...
BUT THE RELEASED GOD-FREEZING SWORD IN YOUR THIRD FORM IS A COMPLETE UNKNOWN. I'D BE GOING IN BLIND AND IMPROVISING. COULD I **BEAT YOU** THAT WAY...?
THAT'S SCARY STUFF...WHO KNOWS WHAT KINDS OF GIMMICKS YOU'VE GOT IN STORE FOR ME...?
WHY DO YOU WANT TO BEAT ME SO BADLY...?
THE GUARD ICE BLADE IN YOUR SECOND FORM HAS LOW PRECISION. AS LONG AS I DODGE FAST AND KEEP UP THE DAMAGE PRESSURE, I COULD **BEAT YOU**...
BUTSU BUTSU (MUTTER)
ブツブツ...
SOWA SOWA
ソワソワ...
SOWA SOWA
ワクワク...
THERE IT IS...! GAMER-VISION...!
UNCLE'S BEEN WORKING OUT HIS MABEL-SAN STRATS FOR A WHILE, FROM HOW HE'S TALKING.
SO THAT'S HOW HE LOOKS AT HER...

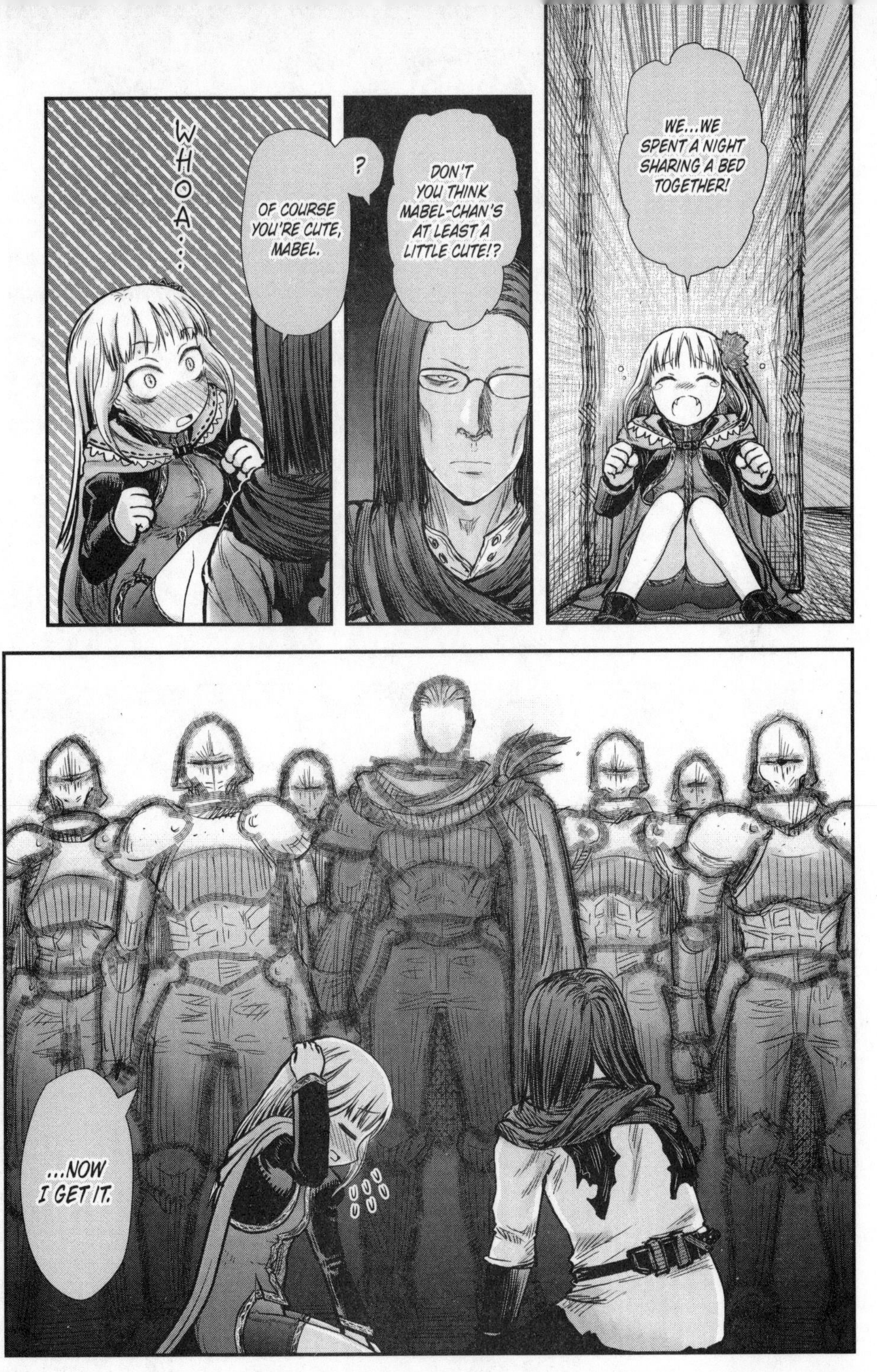
WE...WE SPENT A NIGHT SHARING A BED TOGETHER!
DON'T YOU THINK MABEL-CHAN'S AT LEAST A LITTLE CUTE!?
?
OF COURSE YOU'RE CUTE, MABEL.
WHOA...
...NOW I GET IT.

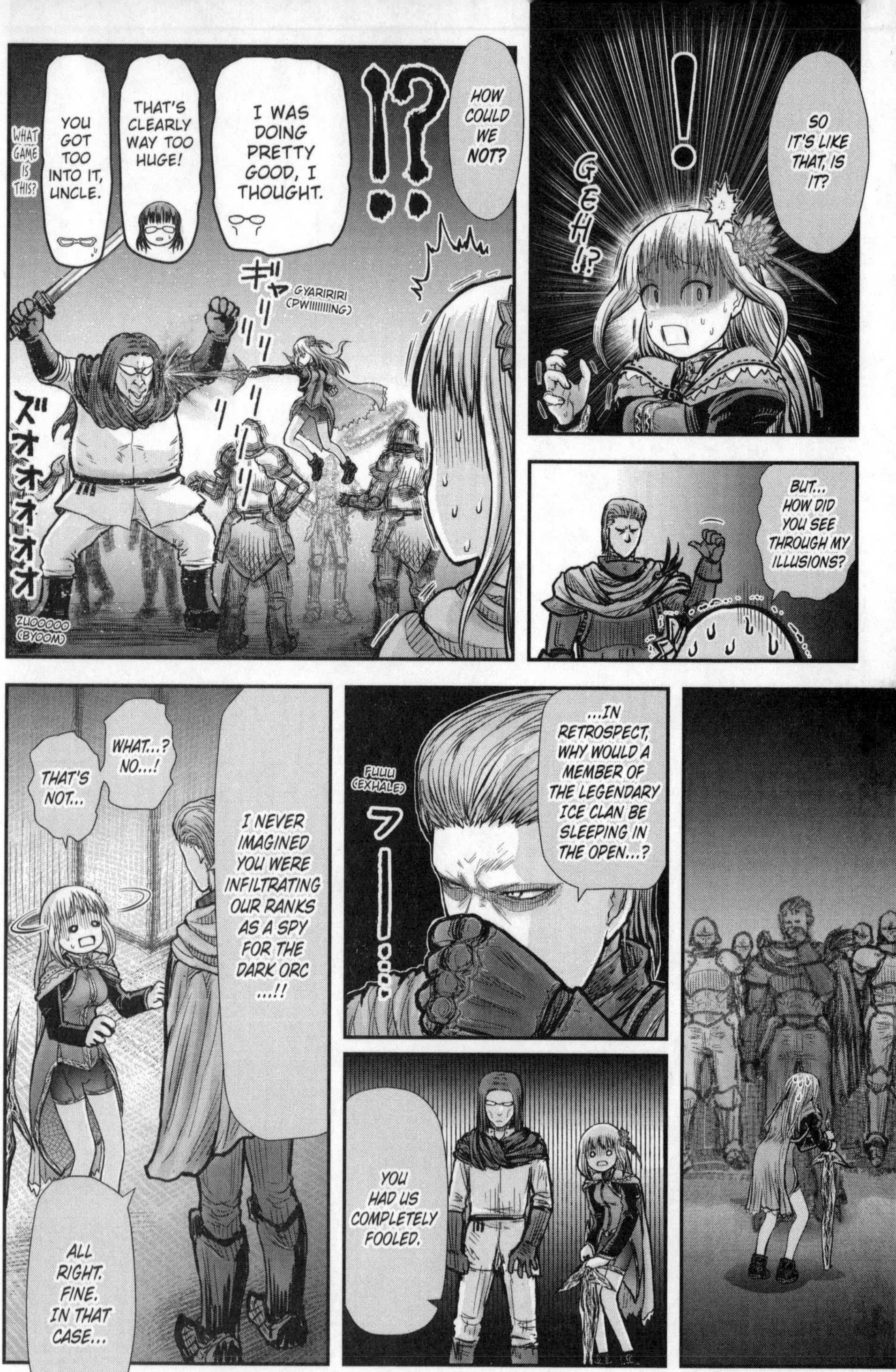
!
SO IT'S LIKE THAT, IS IT?
GEH!?
BUT... HOW DID YOU SEE THROUGH MY ILLUSIONS?
HOW COULD WE NOT?
!?
I WAS DOING PRETTY GOOD, I THOUGHT.
THAT'S CLEARLY WAY TOO HUGE!
YOU GOT TOO INTO IT, UNCLE.
WHAT GAME IS THIS?
ギャリリリリリ
GYARIRIRI (PWIIIIIIING)
ズオオオオオオ
ZUOOOOO (BYOOM)
...IN RETROSPECT, WHY WOULD A MEMBER OF THE LEGENDARY ICE CLAN BE SLEEPING IN THE OPEN...?
フーーー
FUUU (EXHALE)
YOU HAD US COMPLETELY FOOLED.
I NEVER IMAGINED YOU WERE INFILTRATING OUR RANKS AS A SPY FOR THE DARK ORC...!!
WHAT...? NO...!
THAT'S NOT...
ALL RIGHT. FINE. IN THAT CASE...

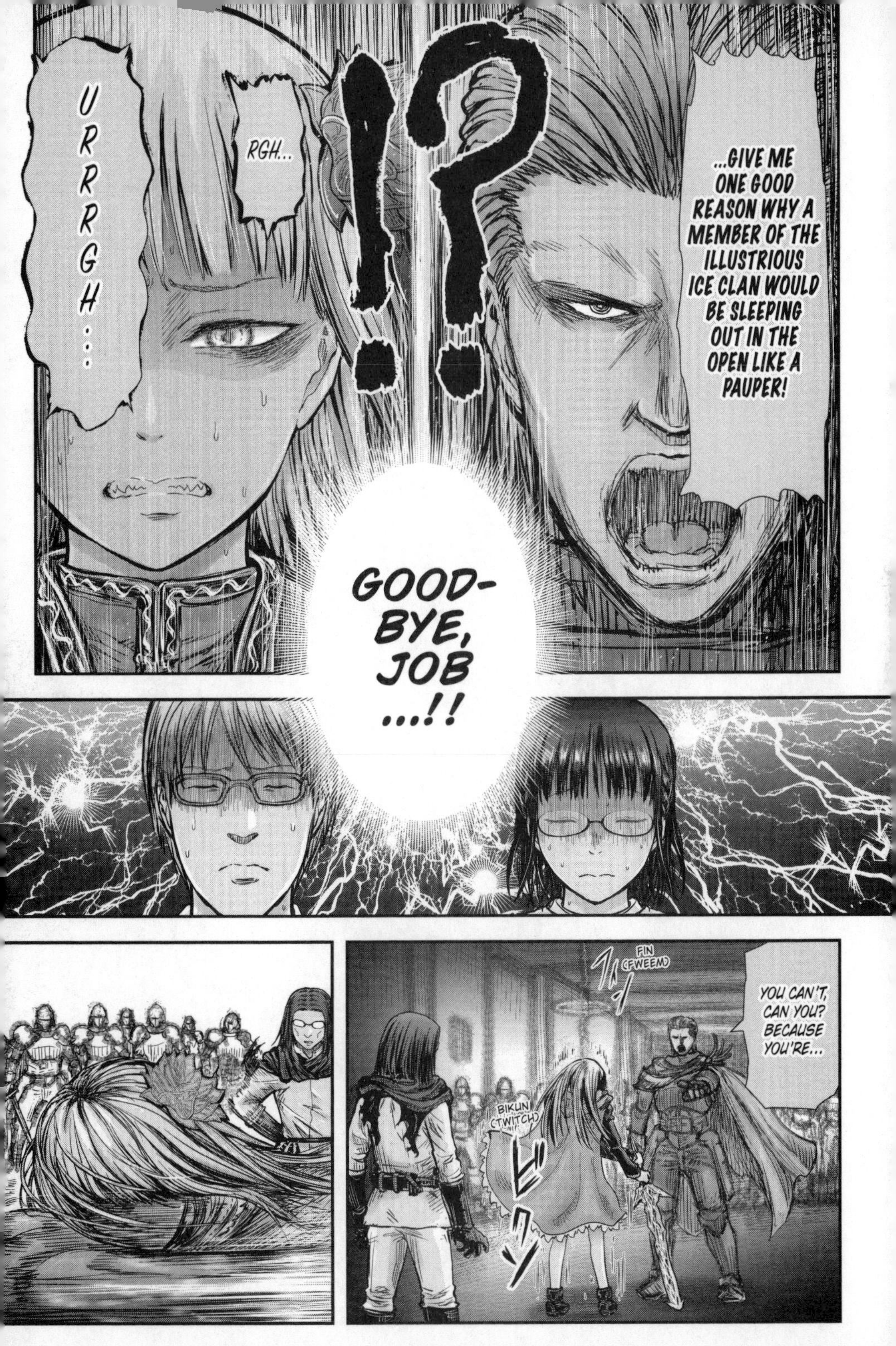

...GIVE ME ONE GOOD REASON WHY A MEMBER OF THE ILLUSTRIOUS ICE CLAN WOULD BE SLEEPING OUT IN THE OPEN LIKE A PAUPER!
!?
RGH...
URRRGH...
GOOD-BYE, JOB...!!
YOU CAN'T, CAN YOU? BECAUSE YOU'RE...
FIN (FWEEM)
BIKUN (TWITCH)

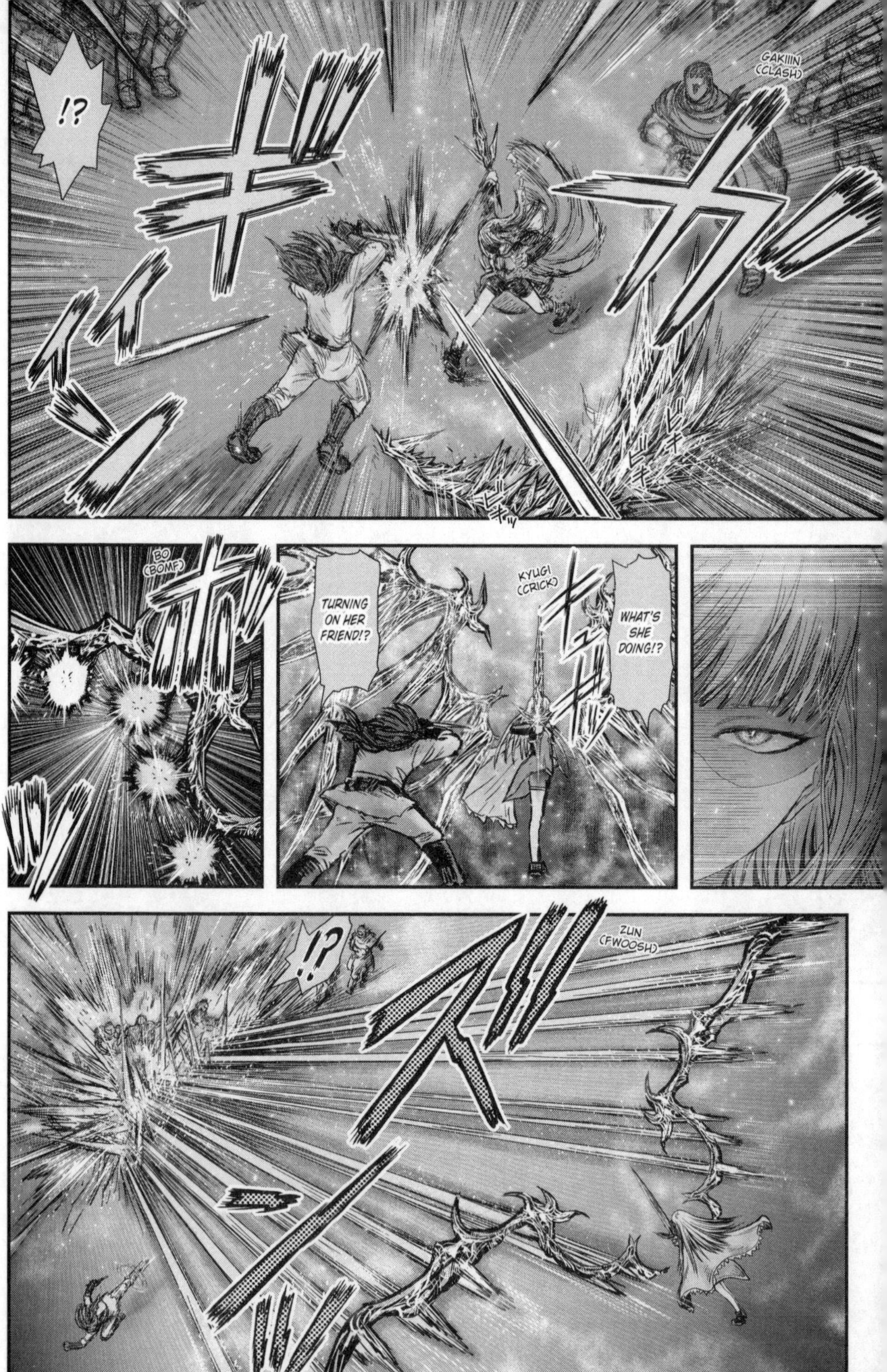
GAKIIIN (CLASH)
!?
WHAT'S SHE DOING!?
KYUGI (CRICK)
TURNING ON HER FRIEND!?
BO (BOMF)
ZUN (FWOOSH)
!?

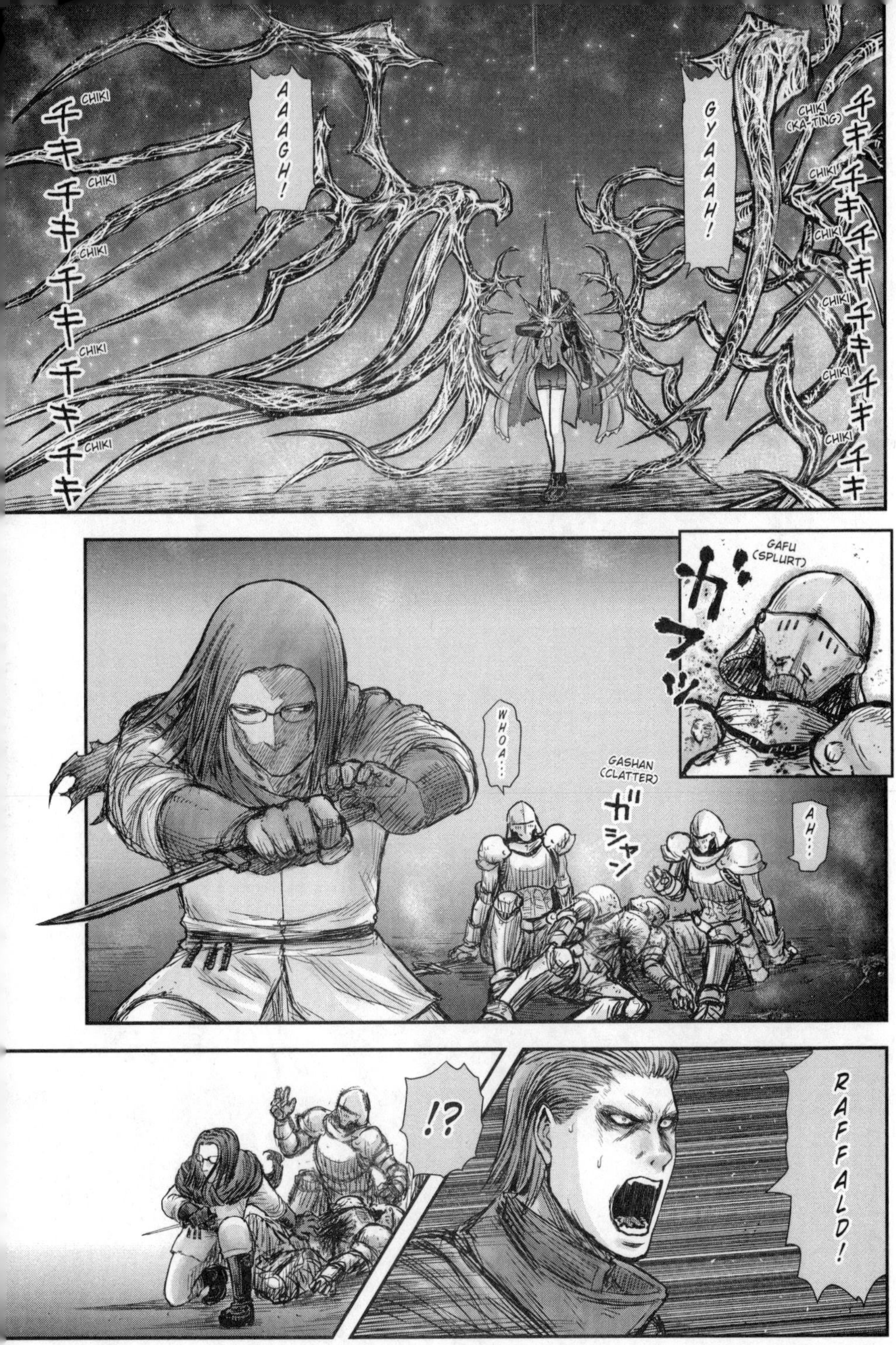
GYAAAAH!
CHIKI (KA-TING)
チキチキチキチキチキ
CHIKI
CHIKI
CHIKI
CHIKI
CHIKI
AAAGH!
CHIKI
チキチキチキチキチキ
CHIKI
CHIKI
CHIKI
CHIKI
GAFU (SPLURT)
ガフッ
AH...
GASHAN (CLATTER)
ガシャン
WHOA...
RAFFALD!
!?

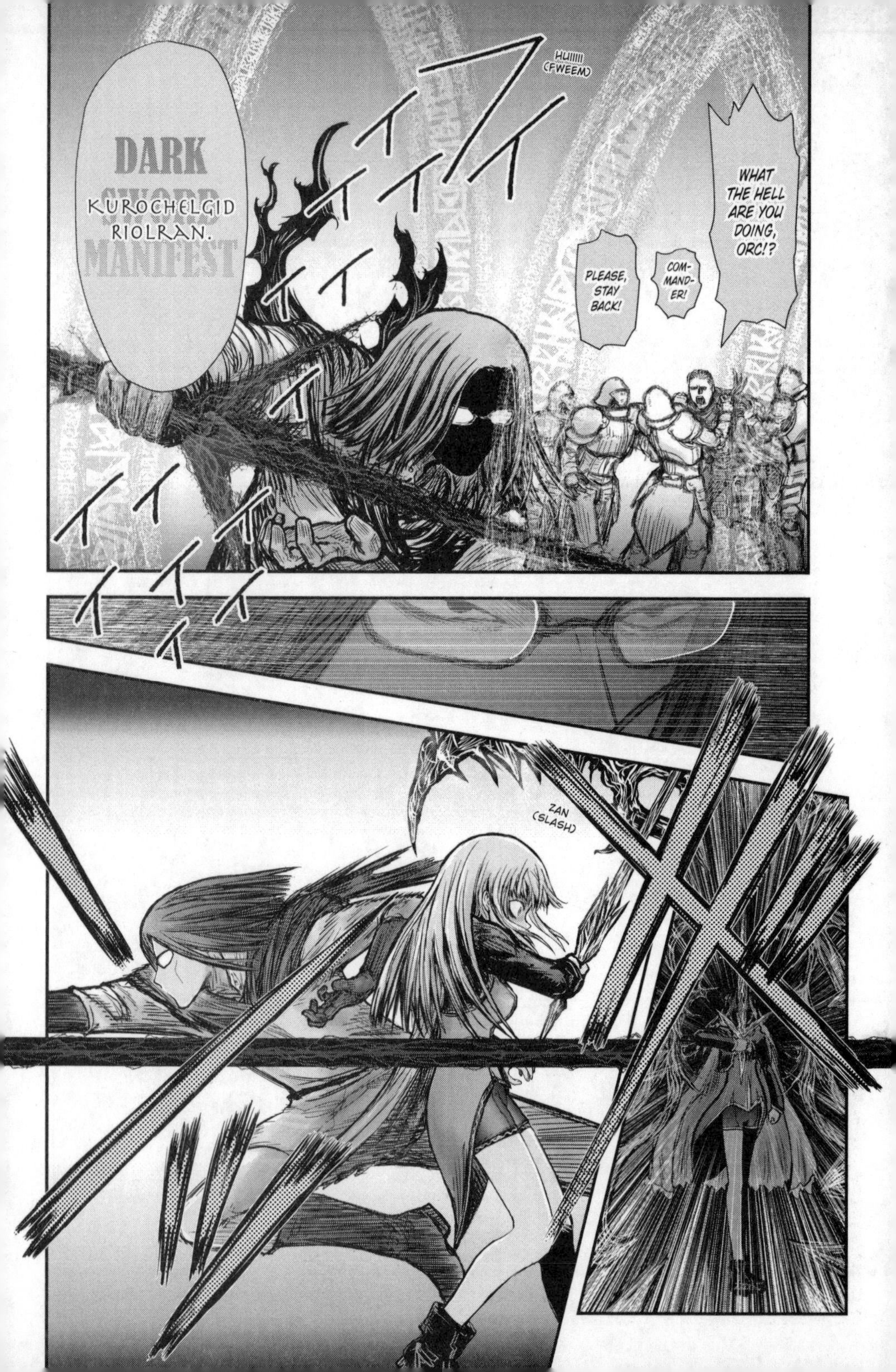
WHAT THE HELL ARE YOU DOING, ORC!?
COM-MAND-ER!
PLEASE, STAY BACK!
HUIIIII (FWEEM)
DARK SWORD MANIFEST
KUROCHELGID RIOLRAN.
ZAN (SLASH)

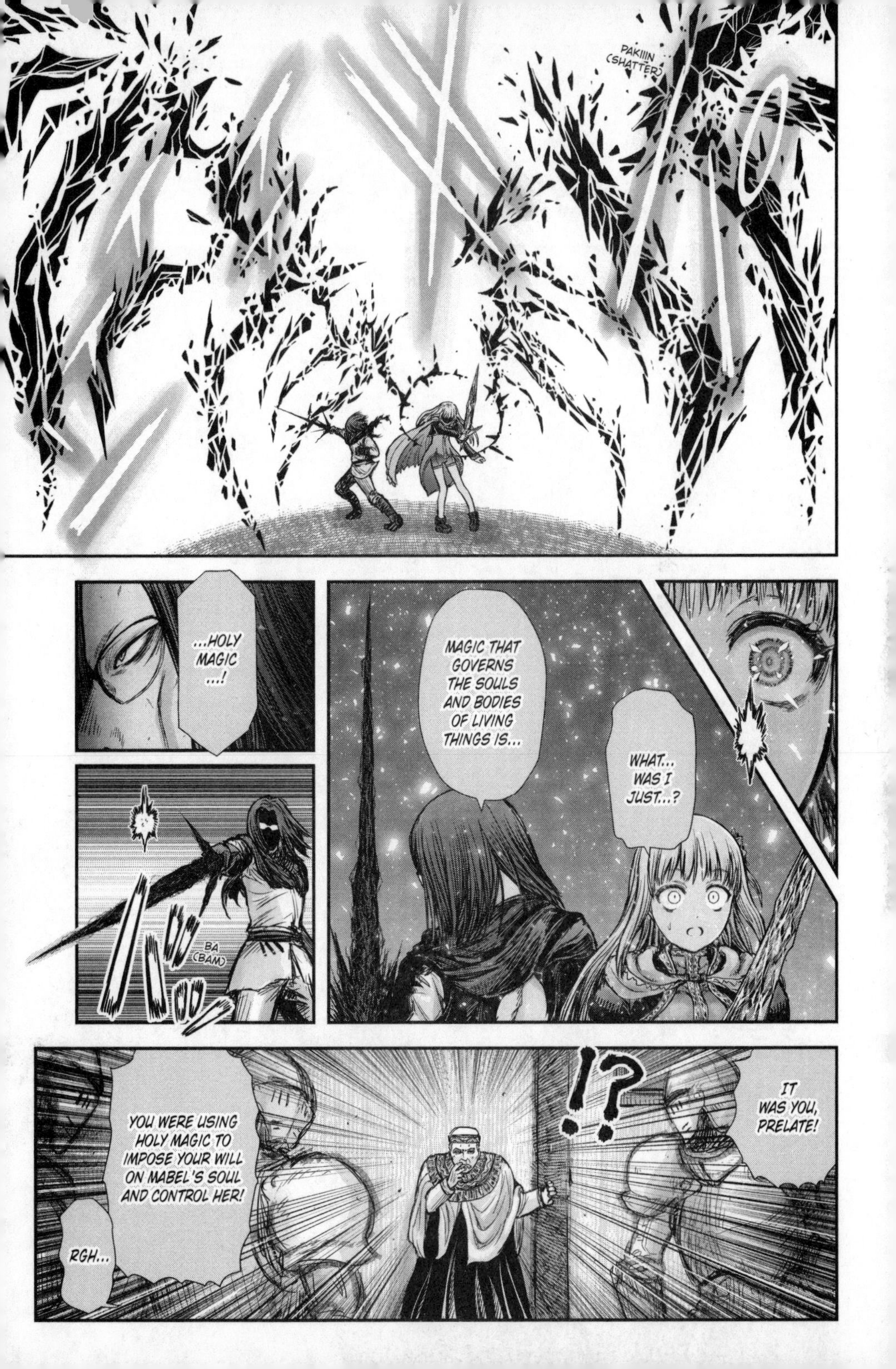
PAKIIIN (SHATTER)
WHAT... WAS I JUST...?
MAGIC THAT GOVERNS THE SOULS AND BODIES OF LIVING THINGS IS...
...HOLY MAGIC ...!
BA (BAM)
IT WAS YOU, PRELATE!
!?
YOU WERE USING HOLY MAGIC TO IMPOSE YOUR WILL ON MABEL'S SOUL AND CONTROL HER!
RGH...

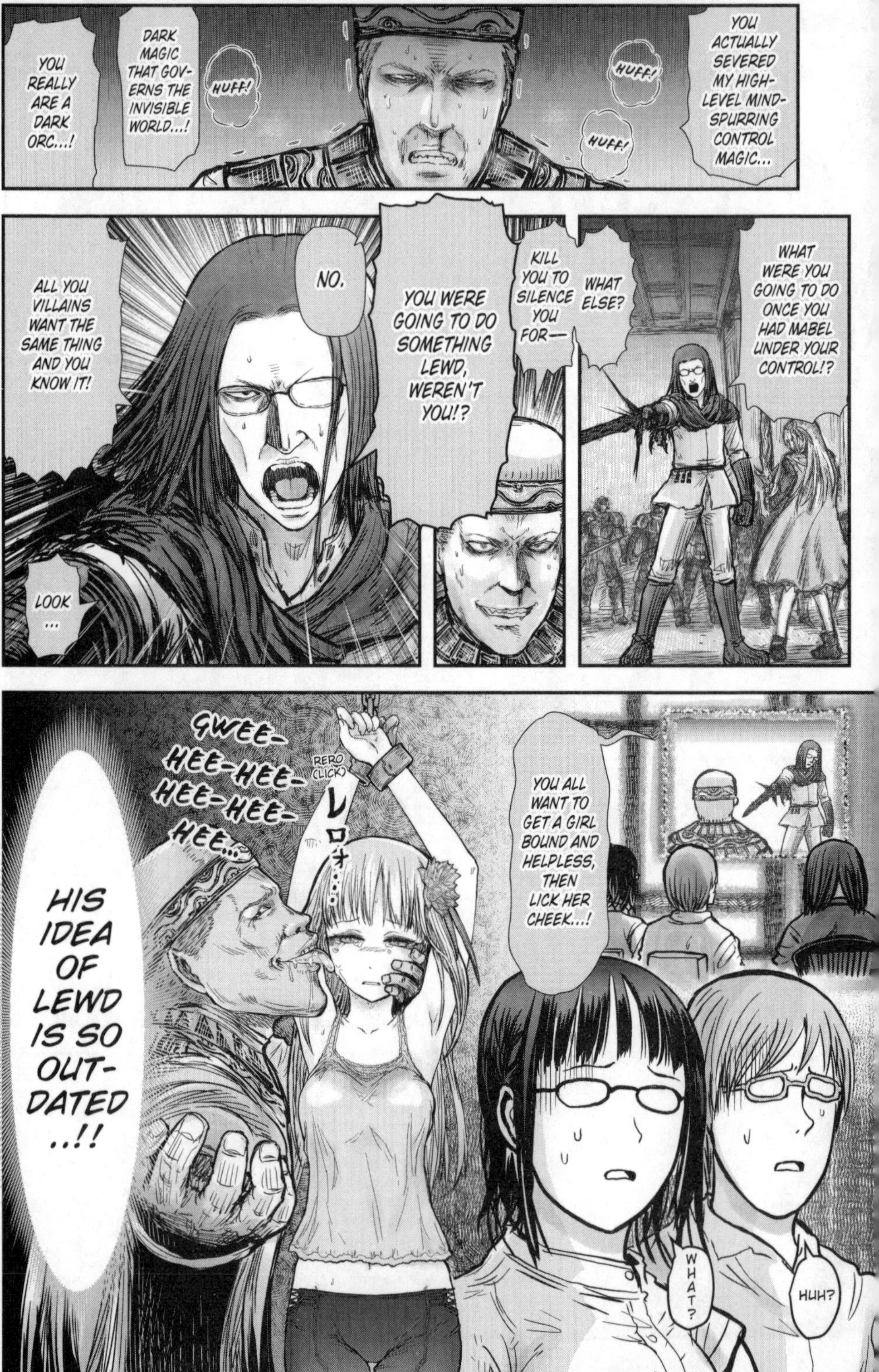
YOU ACTUALLY SEVERED MY HIGH-LEVEL MIND-SPURRING CONTROL MAGIC...
HUFF!
HUFF!
DARK MAGIC THAT GOVERNS THE INVISIBLE WORLD...!
HUFF!
YOU REALLY ARE A DARK ORC...!
WHAT WERE YOU GOING TO DO ONCE YOU HAD MABEL UNDER YOUR CONTROL!?
WHAT ELSE?
KILL YOU TO SILENCE YOU FOR—
NO.
YOU WERE GOING TO DO SOMETHING LEWD, WEREN'T YOU!?
ALL YOU VILLAINS WANT THE SAME THING AND YOU KNOW IT!
LOOK...
YOU ALL WANT TO GET A GIRL BOUND AND HELPLESS, THEN LICK HER CHEEK...!
GWEE-HEE-HEE-HEE-HEE-HEE...
RERO (LICK)
レロォ...
HIS IDEA OF LEWD IS SO OUT-DATED..!!
HUH?
WHAT?

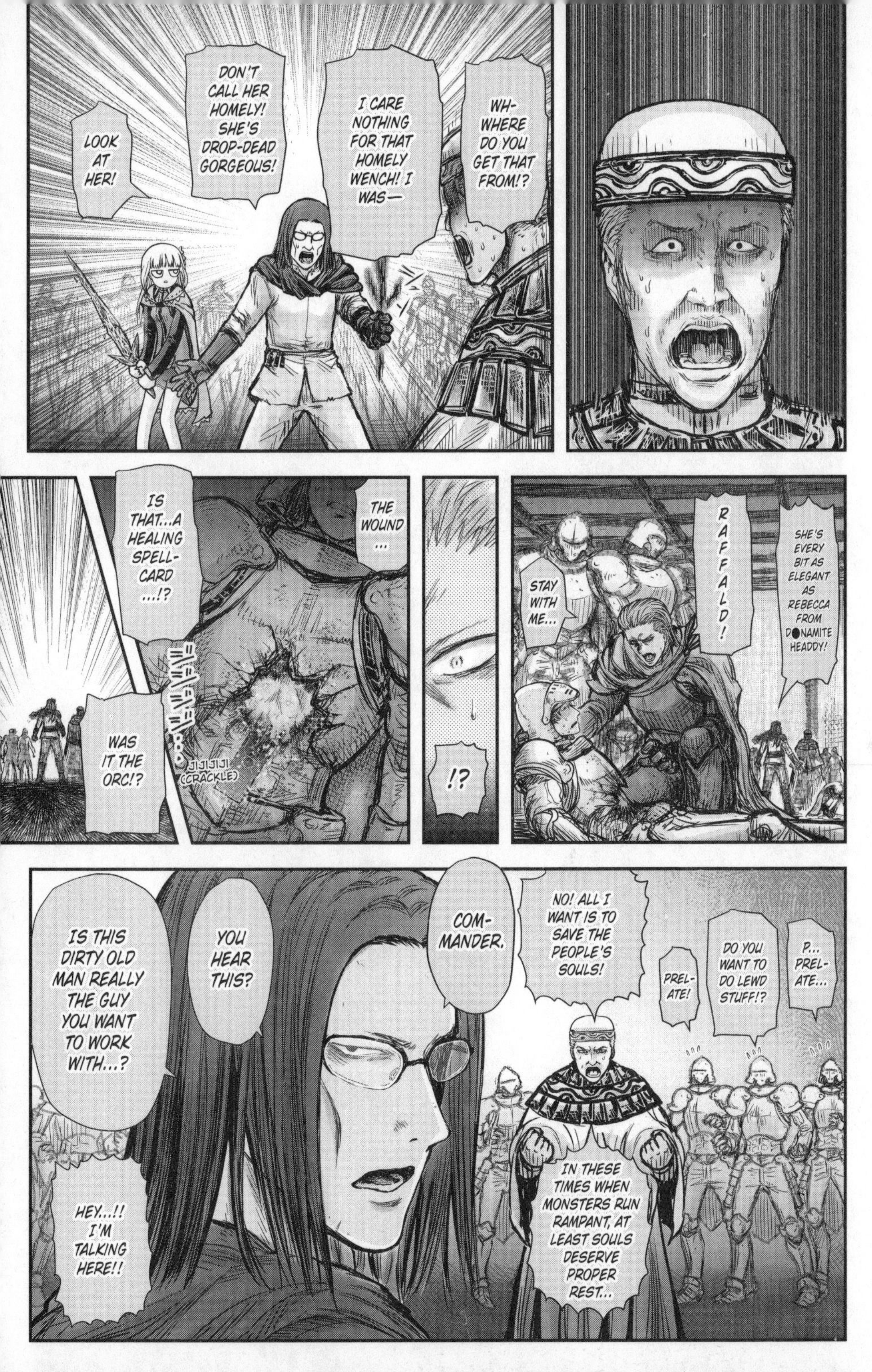
WH- WHERE DO YOU GET THAT FROM!?
I CARE NOTHING FOR THAT HOMELY WENCH! I WAS—
DON'T CALL HER HOMELY! SHE'S DROP-DEAD GORGEOUS!
LOOK AT HER!
SHE'S EVERY BIT AS ELEGANT AS REBECCA FROM D●NAMITE HEADDY!
RAFFALD!
STAY WITH ME...
!?
THE WOUND...
IS THAT...A HEALING SPELL-CARD...!?
JIJIJIJI (CRACKLE)
WAS IT THE ORC!?
P... PRELATE...
DO YOU WANT TO DO LEWD STUFF!?
PRELATE!
NO! ALL I WANT IS TO SAVE THE PEOPLE'S SOULS!
IN THESE TIMES WHEN MONSTERS RUN RAMPANT, AT LEAST SOULS DESERVE PROPER REST...
COM-MANDER.
YOU HEAR THIS?
IS THIS DIRTY OLD MAN REALLY THE GUY YOU WANT TO WORK WITH...?
HEY...!! I'M TALKING HERE!!

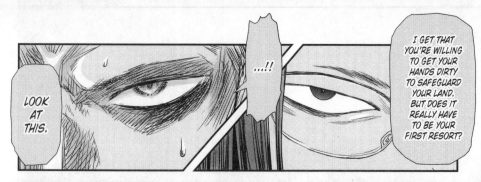

...!!

LOOK AT THIS.

I GET THAT YOU'RE WILLING TO GET YOUR HANDS DIRTY TO SAFEGUARD YOUR LAND. BUT DOES IT REALLY HAVE TO BE YOUR FIRST RESORT?

ZAN (SLASH)

YOU'RE BLESSED WITH ALL THESE PEOPLE WHO LOOK UP TO YOU. DON'T YOU TRUST IN THEIR ABILITIES?

L-LET'S JUST CALL IT OFF!

BA (FWIP)

COM-MANDER!

!

GH...

....

.......!!

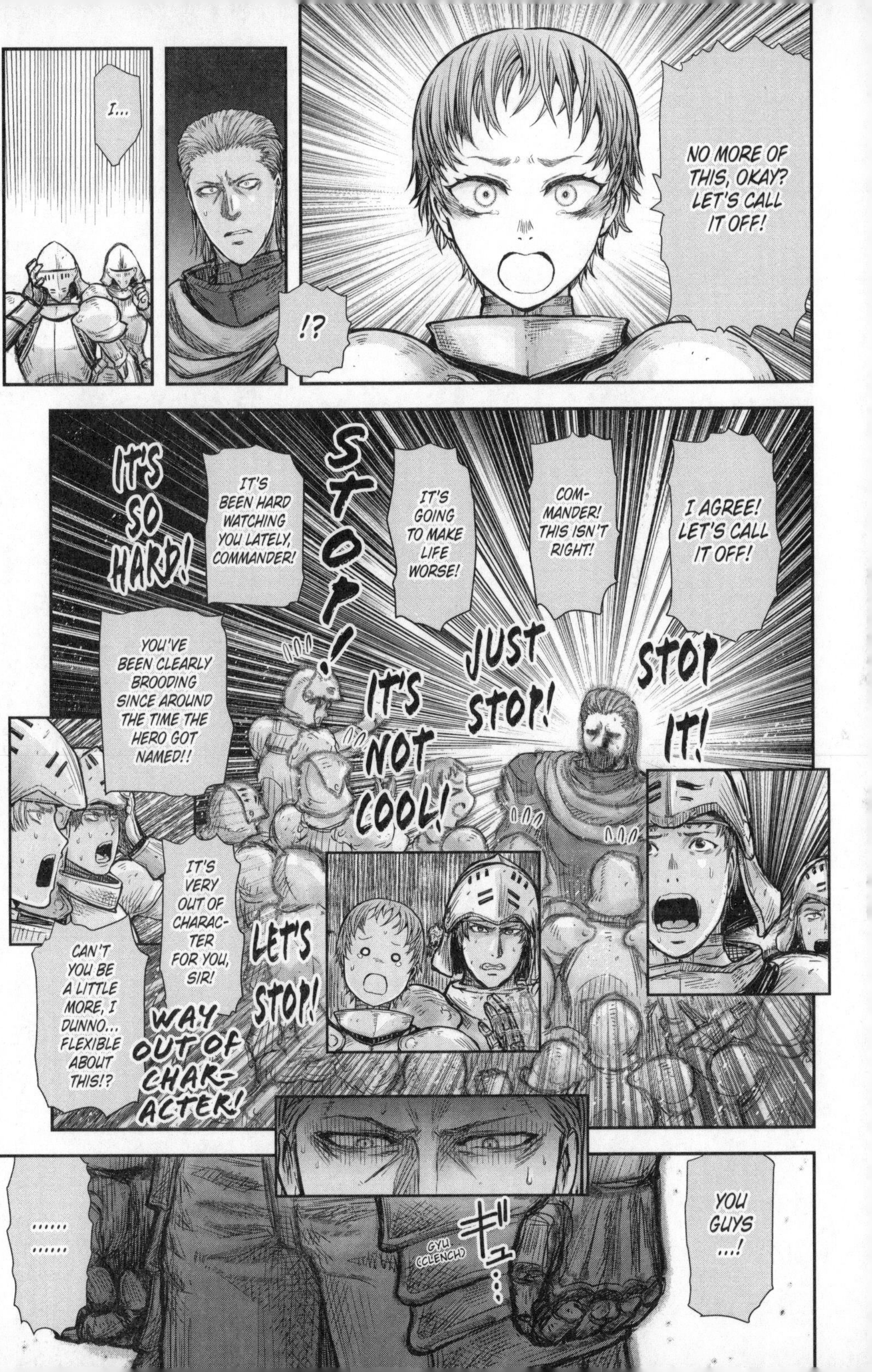
NO MORE OF THIS, OKAY? LET'S CALL IT OFF!
!?
I...
I AGREE! LET'S CALL IT OFF!
COM-MANDER! THIS ISN'T RIGHT!
STOP IT!
IT'S GOING TO MAKE LIFE WORSE!
JUST STOP!
IT'S BEEN HARD WATCHING YOU LATELY, COMMANDER!
STOP!
IT'S SO HARD!
IT'S NOT COOL!
YOU'VE BEEN CLEARLY BROODING SINCE AROUND THE TIME THE HERO GOT NAMED!!
IT'S VERY OUT OF CHARACTER FOR YOU, SIR!
LET'S STOP!
CAN'T YOU BE A LITTLE MORE, I DUNNO... FLEXIBLE ABOUT THIS!?
WAY OUT OF CHAR-ACTER!
YOU GUYS ...!
GYU (CLENCH)
....

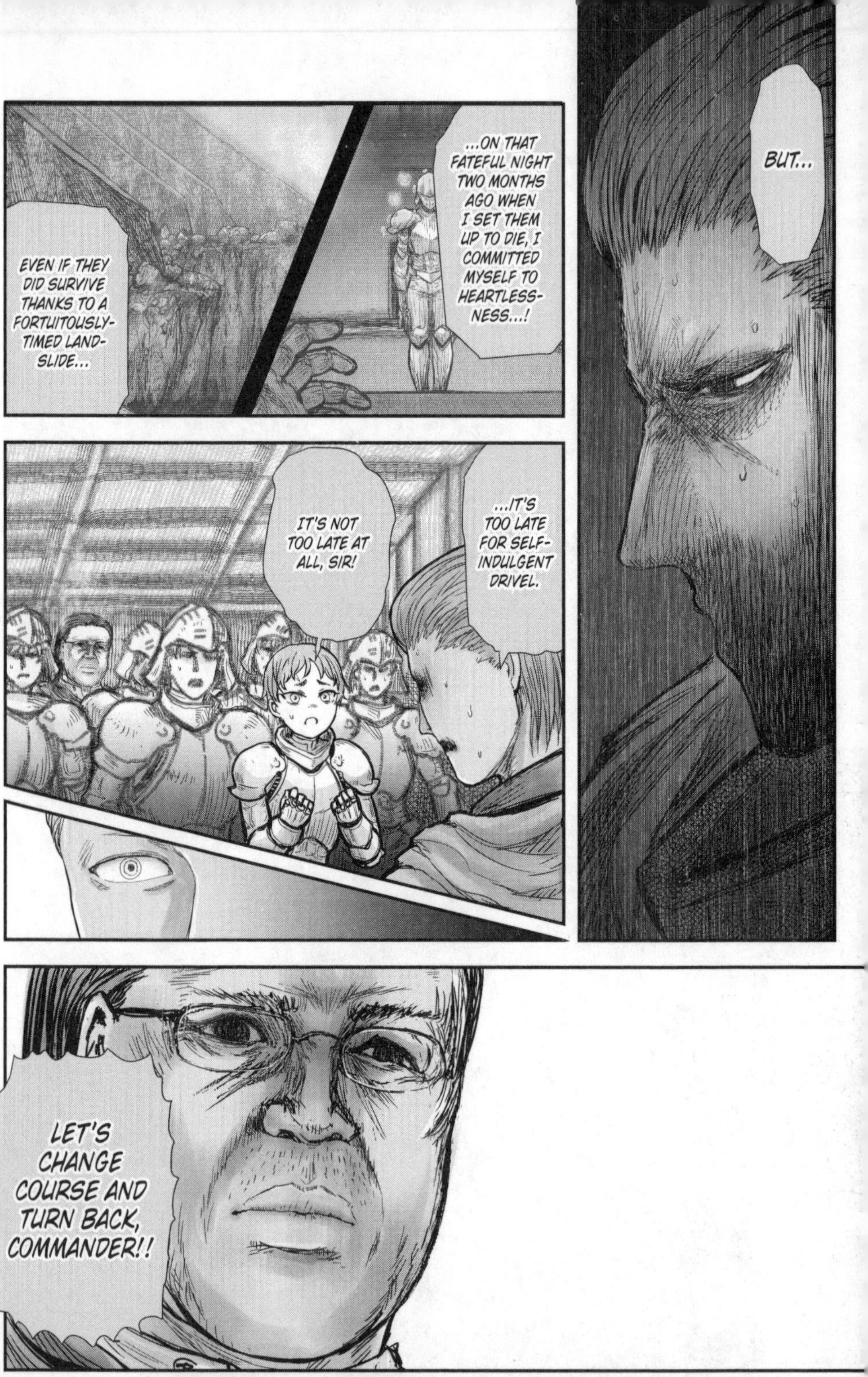
BUT...
...ON THAT FATEFUL NIGHT TWO MONTHS AGO WHEN I SET THEM UP TO DIE, I COMMITTED MYSELF TO HEARTLESSNESS...!
EVEN IF THEY DID SURVIVE THANKS TO A FORTUITOUSLY-TIMED LANDSLIDE...
...IT'S TOO LATE FOR SELF-INDULGENT DRIVEL.
IT'S NOT TOO LATE AT ALL, SIR!
LET'S CHANGE COURSE AND TURN BACK, COMMANDER!!

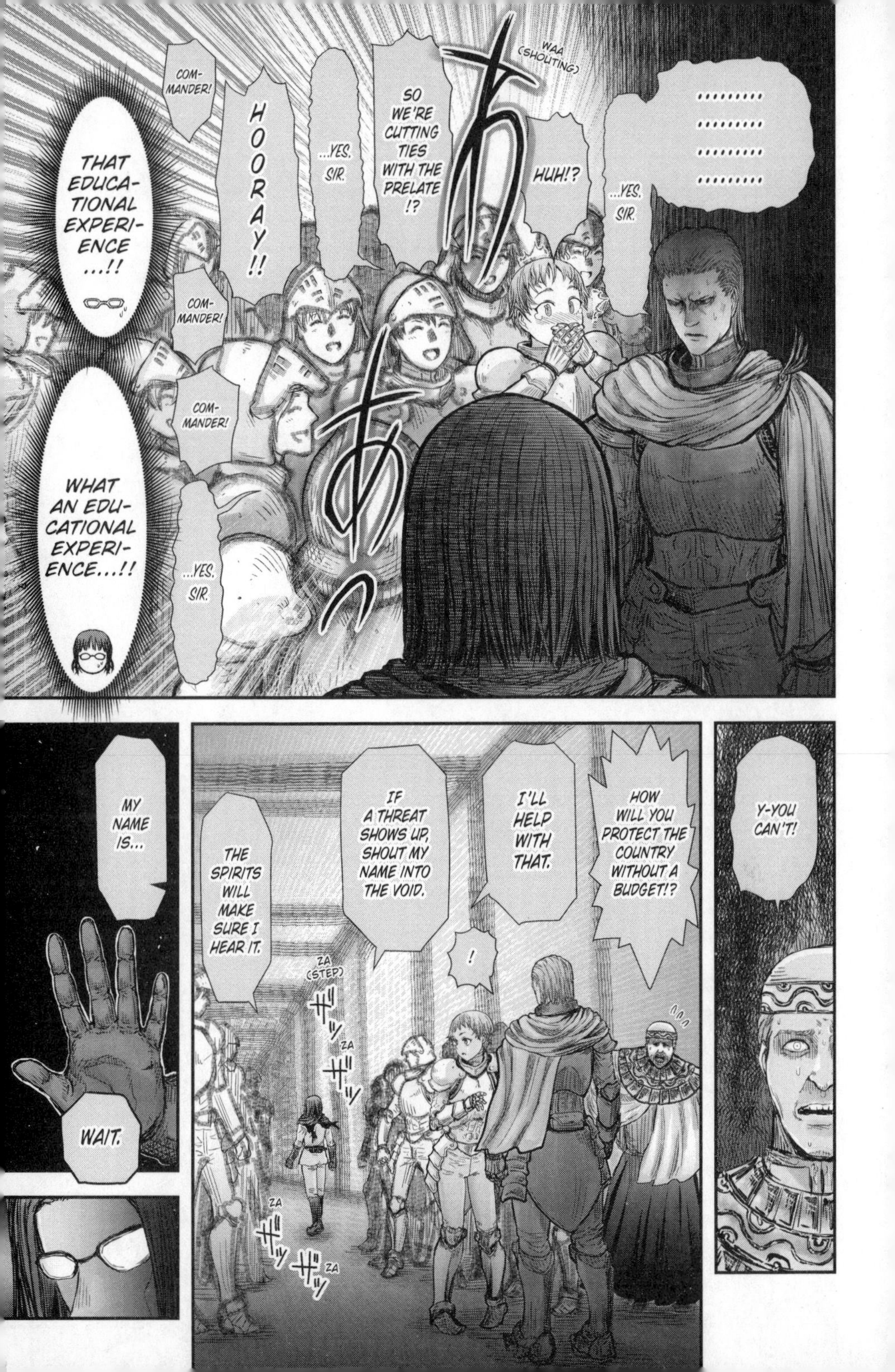
....
....
....
....
...YES. SIR.
HUH!?
WAA (SHOUTING)
SO WE'RE CUTTING TIES WITH THE PRELATE!?
...YES. SIR.
HOORAY!!
COM-MANDER!
THAT EDUCA-TIONAL EXPERI-ENCE...!!
COM-MANDER!
COM-MANDER!
...YES. SIR.
WHAT AN EDU-CATIONAL EXPERI-ENCE...!!
Y-YOU CAN'T!
HOW WILL YOU PROTECT THE COUNTRY WITHOUT A BUDGET!?
I'LL HELP WITH THAT.
!
IF A THREAT SHOWS UP, SHOUT MY NAME INTO THE VOID.
THE SPIRITS WILL MAKE SURE I HEAR IT.
ZA (STEP)
ZA
ZA
ZA
MY NAME IS...
WAIT.

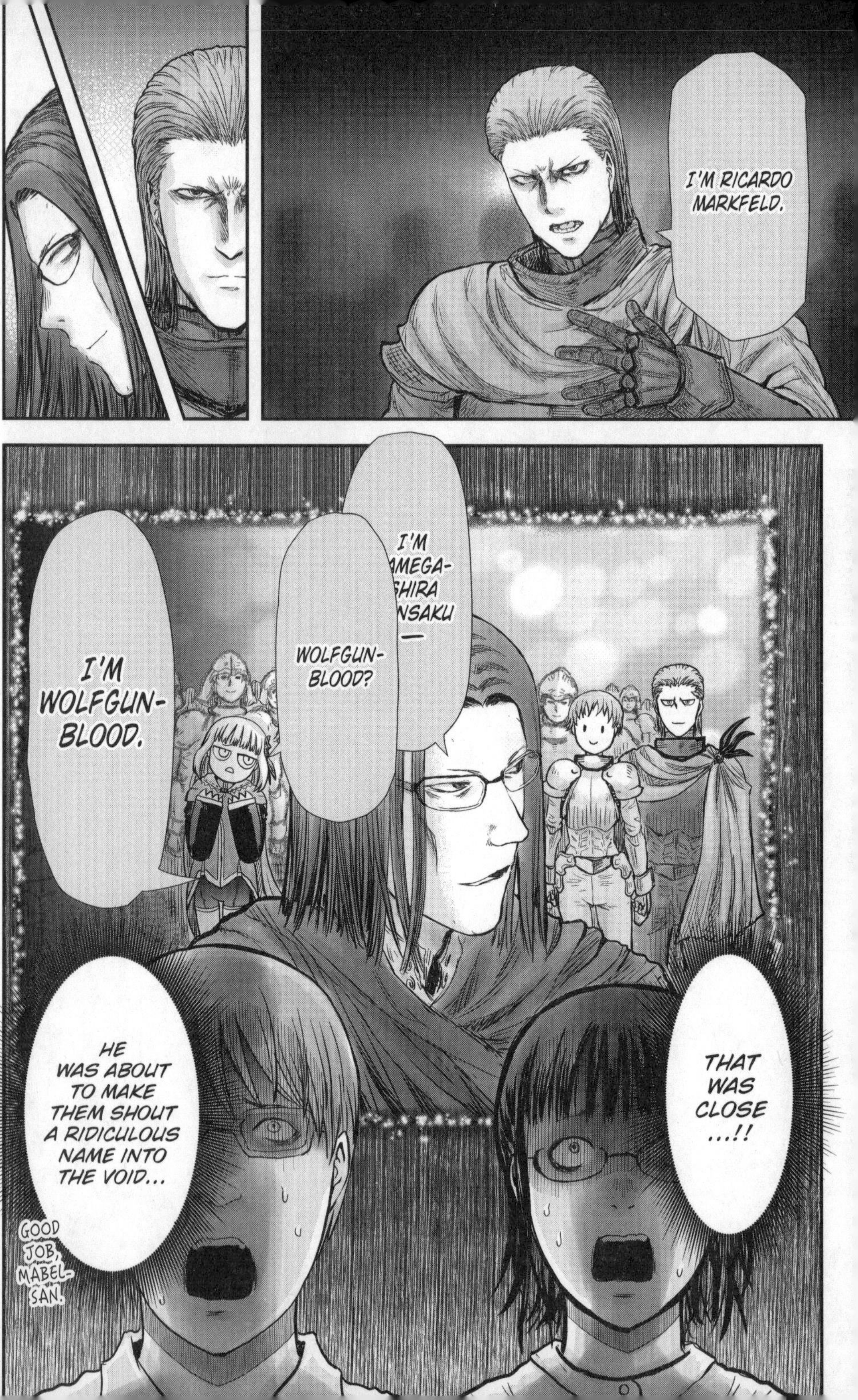
I'M RICARDO MARKFELD.
I'M AMEGA-SHIRA NSAKU —
WOLFGUN-BLOOD?
I'M WOLFGUN-BLOOD.
THAT WAS CLOSE ...!!
HE WAS ABOUT TO MAKE THEM SHOUT A RIDICULOUS NAME INTO THE VOID...
GOOD JOB, MABEL-SAN.

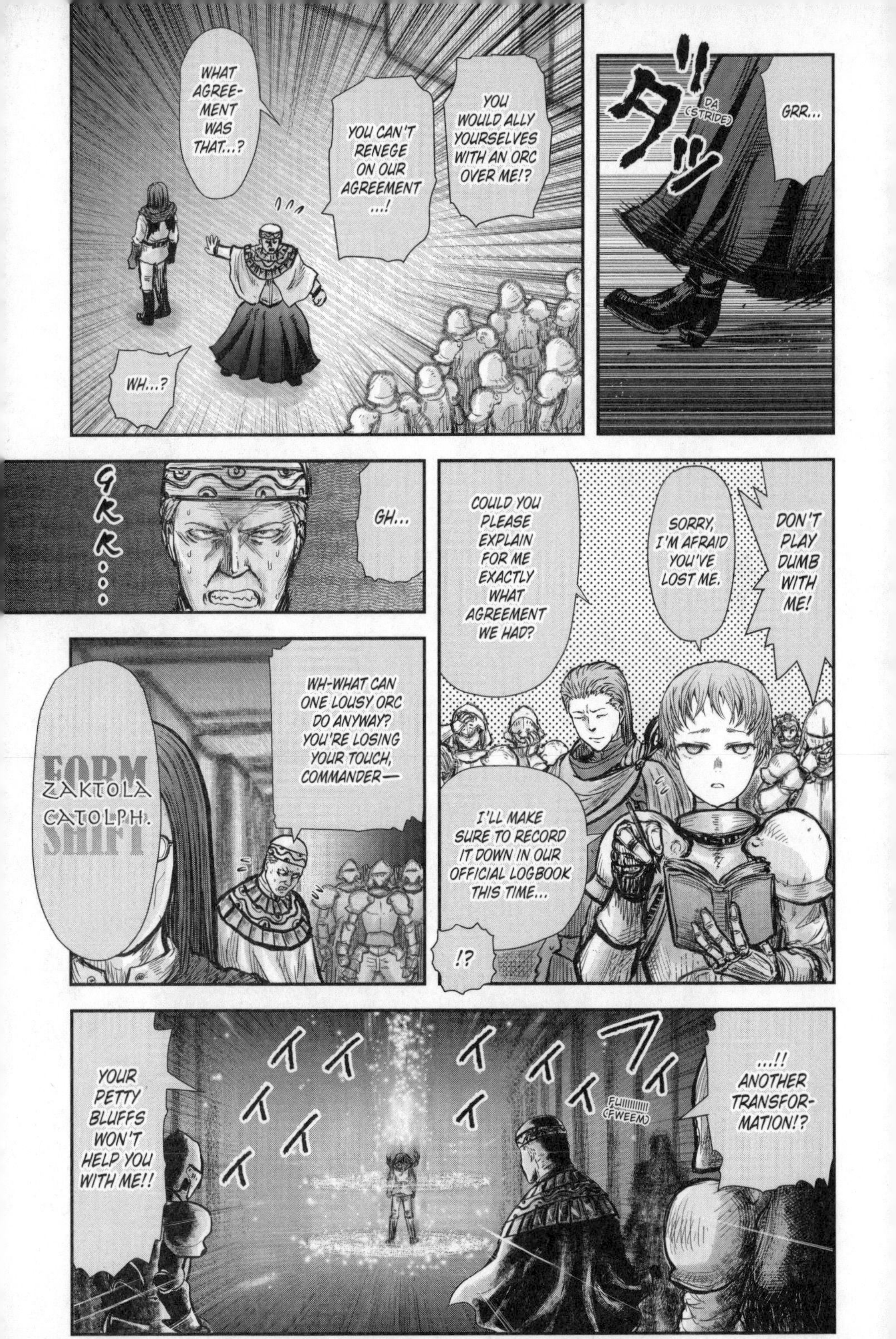
DA (STRIDE)
GRR...
YOU WOULD ALLY YOURSELVES WITH AN ORC OVER ME!?
YOU CAN'T RENEGE ON OUR AGREEMENT...!
WHAT AGREEMENT WAS THAT...?
WH...?
DON'T PLAY DUMB WITH ME!
SORRY, I'M AFRAID YOU'VE LOST ME.
COULD YOU PLEASE EXPLAIN FOR ME EXACTLY WHAT AGREEMENT WE HAD?
I'LL MAKE SURE TO RECORD IT DOWN IN OUR OFFICIAL LOGBOOK THIS TIME...
!?
GH...
GRR...
WH-WHAT CAN ONE LOUSY ORC DO ANYWAY? YOU'RE LOSING YOUR TOUCH, COMMANDER—
FORM SHIFT
ZAKTOLA CATOLPH.
...!! ANOTHER TRANSFORMATION!?
FU (FWEEM)
YOUR PETTY BLUFFS WON'T HELP YOU WITH ME!!

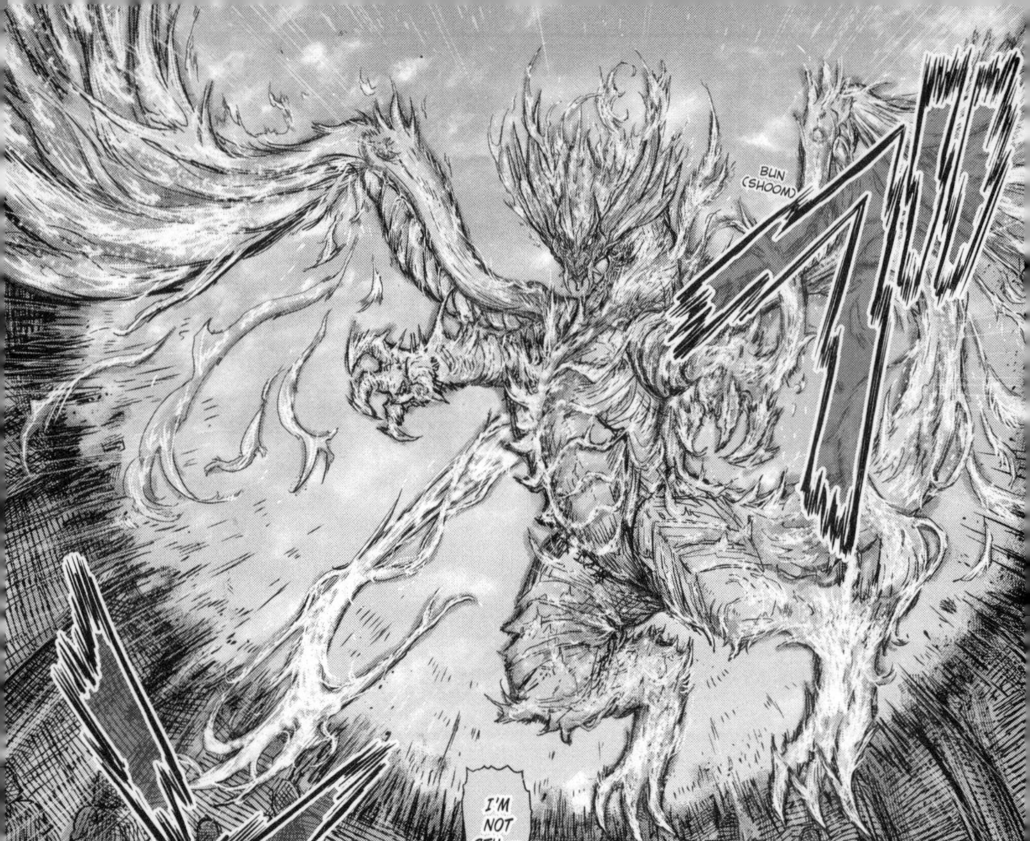
BUN
(SHOOM)
I'M NOT STU—
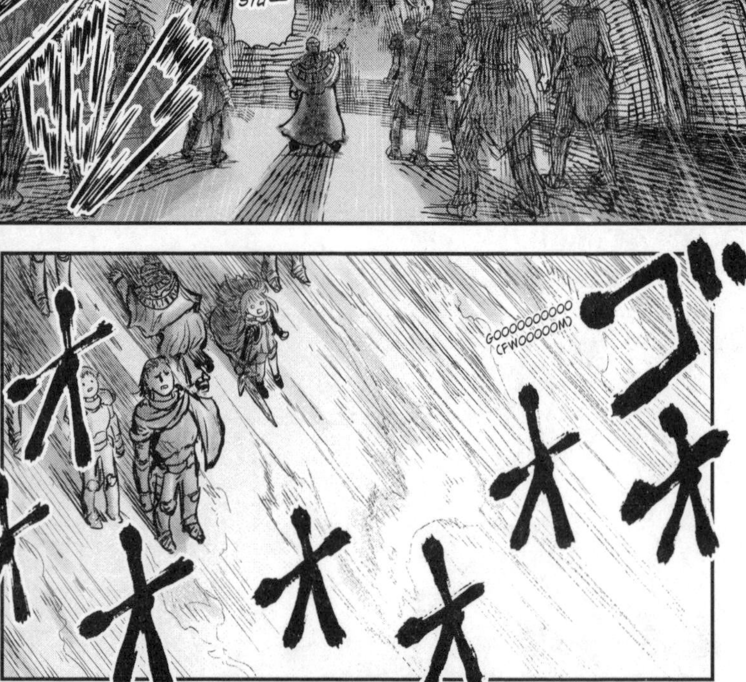
GOOOOOOOOOO
(FWOOOOOM)
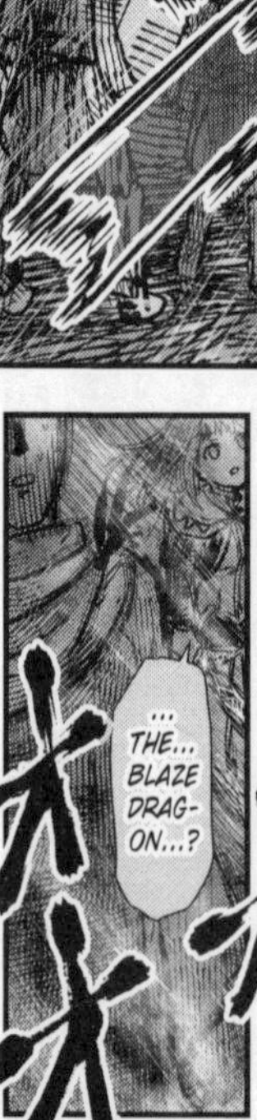
... THE... BLAZE DRAGON...?

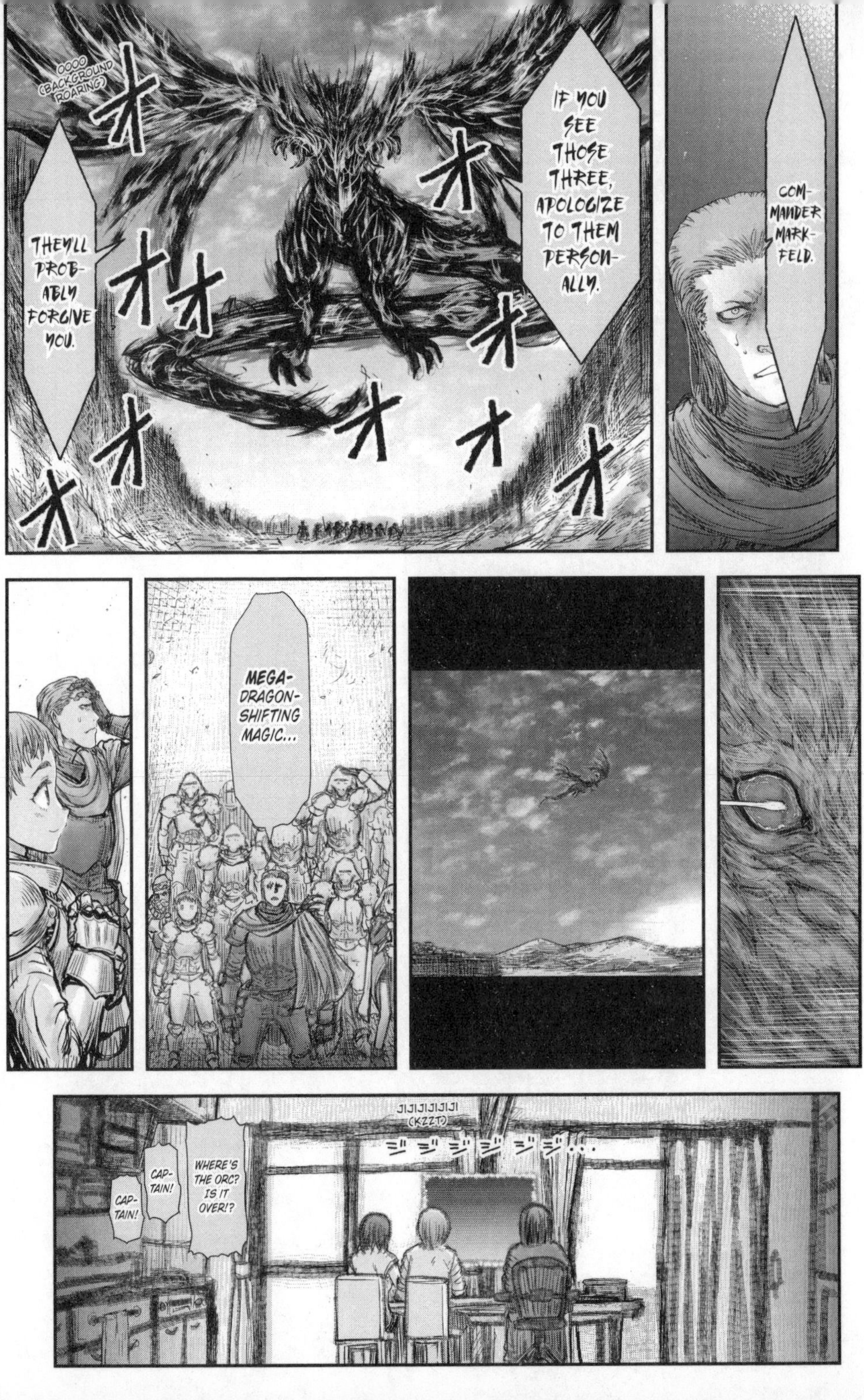
COM-MANDER MARK-FELD.
IF YOU SEE THOSE THREE, APOLOGIZE TO THEM PERSON-ALLY.
OOOO (BACKGROUND ROARING)
THEY'LL PROB-ABLY FORGIVE YOU.
MEGA-DRAGON-SHIFTING MAGIC...
JIJIJIJIJIJI (KZZT)
ジジジジジジ…
WHERE'S THE ORC? IS IT OVER!?
CAP-TAIN!
CAP-TAIN!

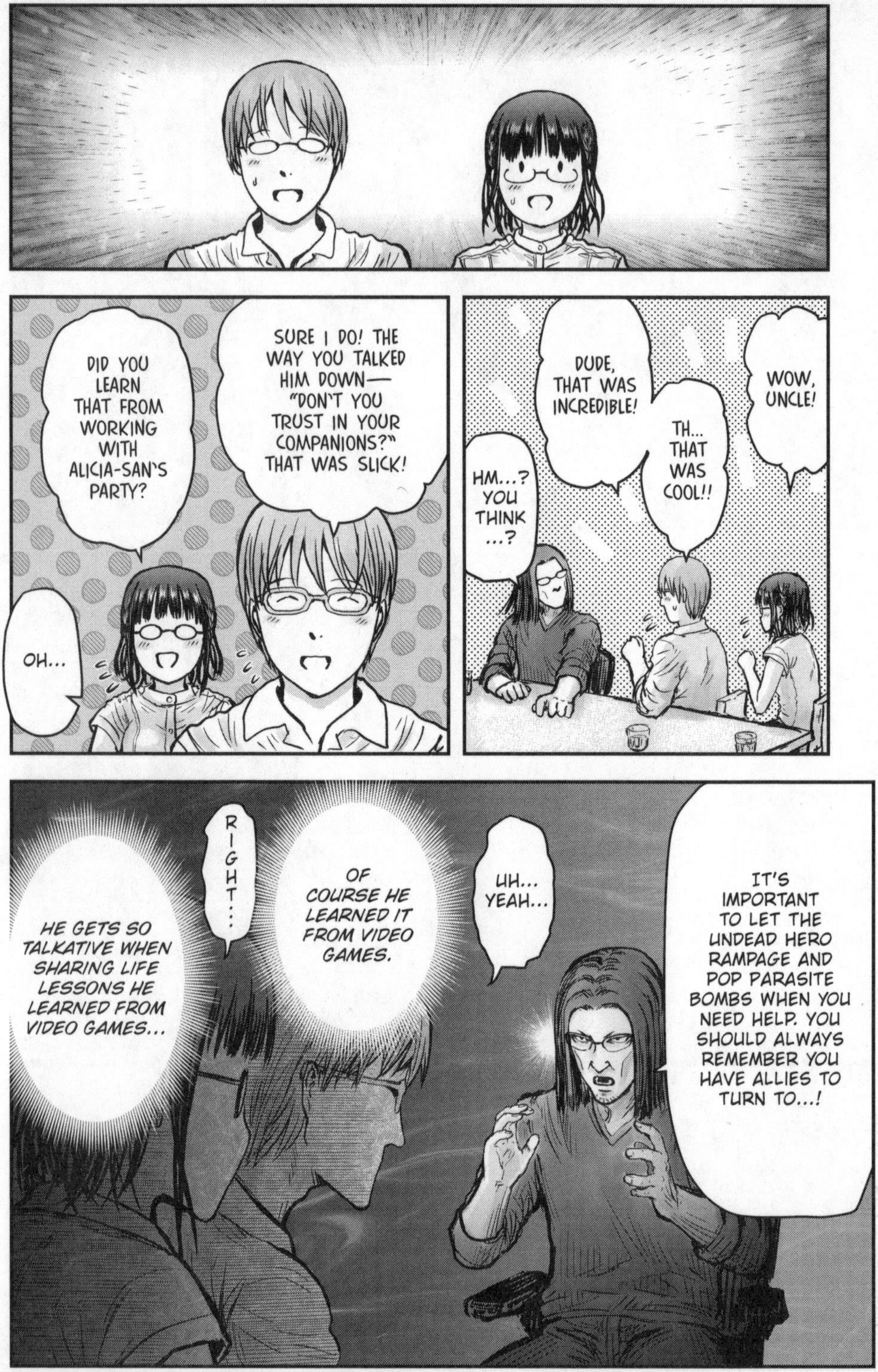
WOW, UNCLE!
DUDE, THAT WAS INCREDIBLE!
TH... THAT WAS COOL!!
HM...? YOU THINK ...?
SURE I DO! THE WAY YOU TALKED HIM DOWN— "DON'T YOU TRUST IN YOUR COMPANIONS?" THAT WAS SLICK!
DID YOU LEARN THAT FROM WORKING WITH ALICIA-SAN'S PARTY?
OH...
IT'S IMPORTANT TO LET THE UNDEAD HERO RAMPAGE AND POP PARASITE BOMBS WHEN YOU NEED HELP. YOU SHOULD ALWAYS REMEMBER YOU HAVE ALLIES TO TURN TO...!
UH... YEAH...
OF COURSE HE LEARNED IT FROM VIDEO GAMES.
RIGHT...
HE GETS SO TALKATIVE WHEN SHARING LIFE LESSONS HE LEARNED FROM VIDEO GAMES...

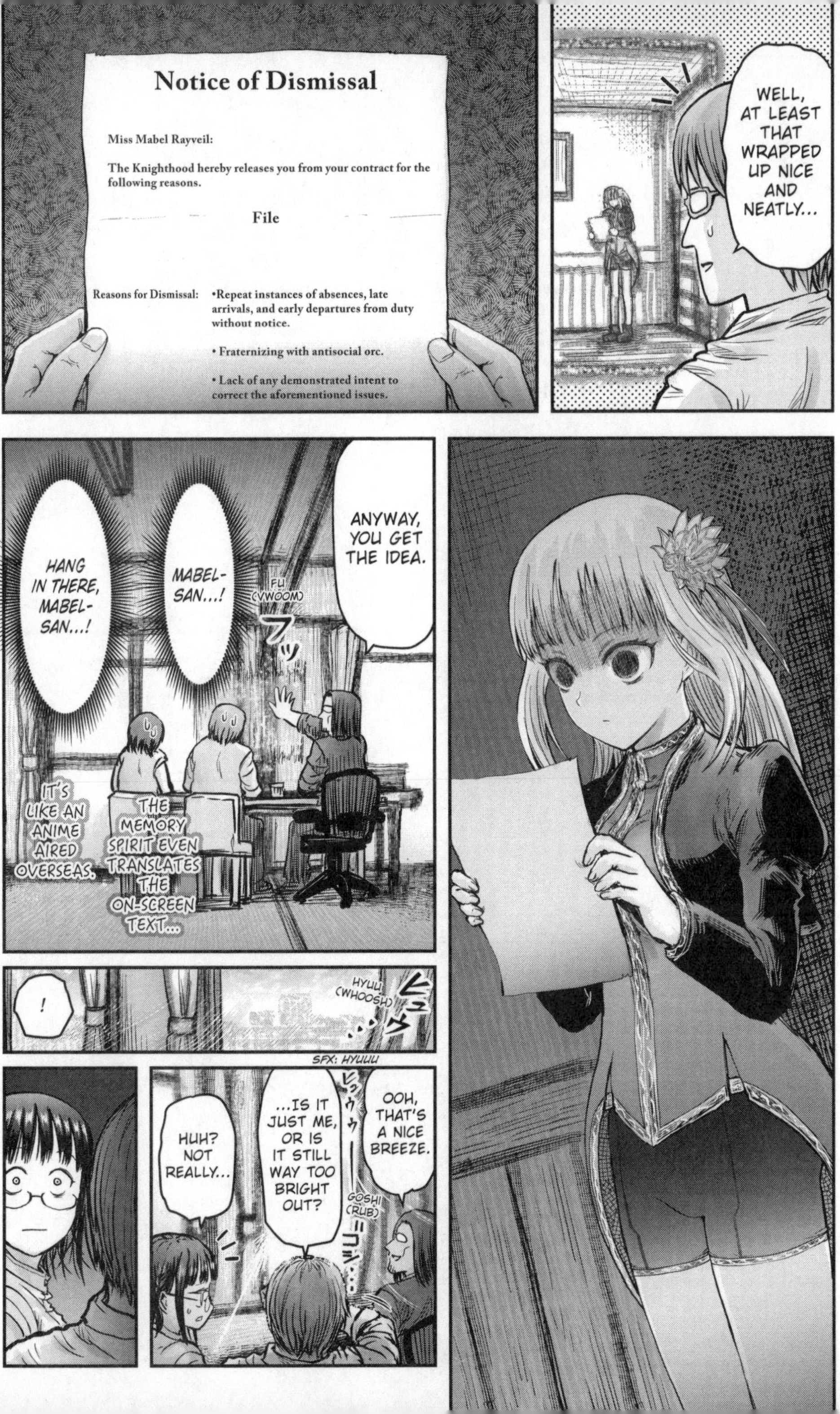
WELL, AT LEAST THAT WRAPPED UP NICE AND NEATLY...
Notice of Dismissal
Miss Mabel Rayveil:
The Knighthood hereby releases you from your contract for the following reasons.
File
Reasons for Dismissal:
•Repeat instances of absences, late arrivals, and early departures from duty without notice.
• Fraternizing with antisocial orc.
• Lack of any demonstrated intent to correct the aforementioned issues.
ANYWAY, YOU GET THE IDEA.
FU (VWOOM)
MABEL-SAN...!
HANG IN THERE, MABEL-SAN...!
THE MEMORY SPIRIT EVEN TRANSLATES THE ON-SCREEN TEXT...
IT'S LIKE AN ANIME AIRED OVERSEAS.
HYUU (WHOOSH)
!
SFX: HYUUU
OOH, THAT'S A NICE BREEZE.
GOSHI (RUB)
...IS IT JUST ME, OR IS IT STILL WAY TOO BRIGHT OUT?
HUH? NOT REALLY...

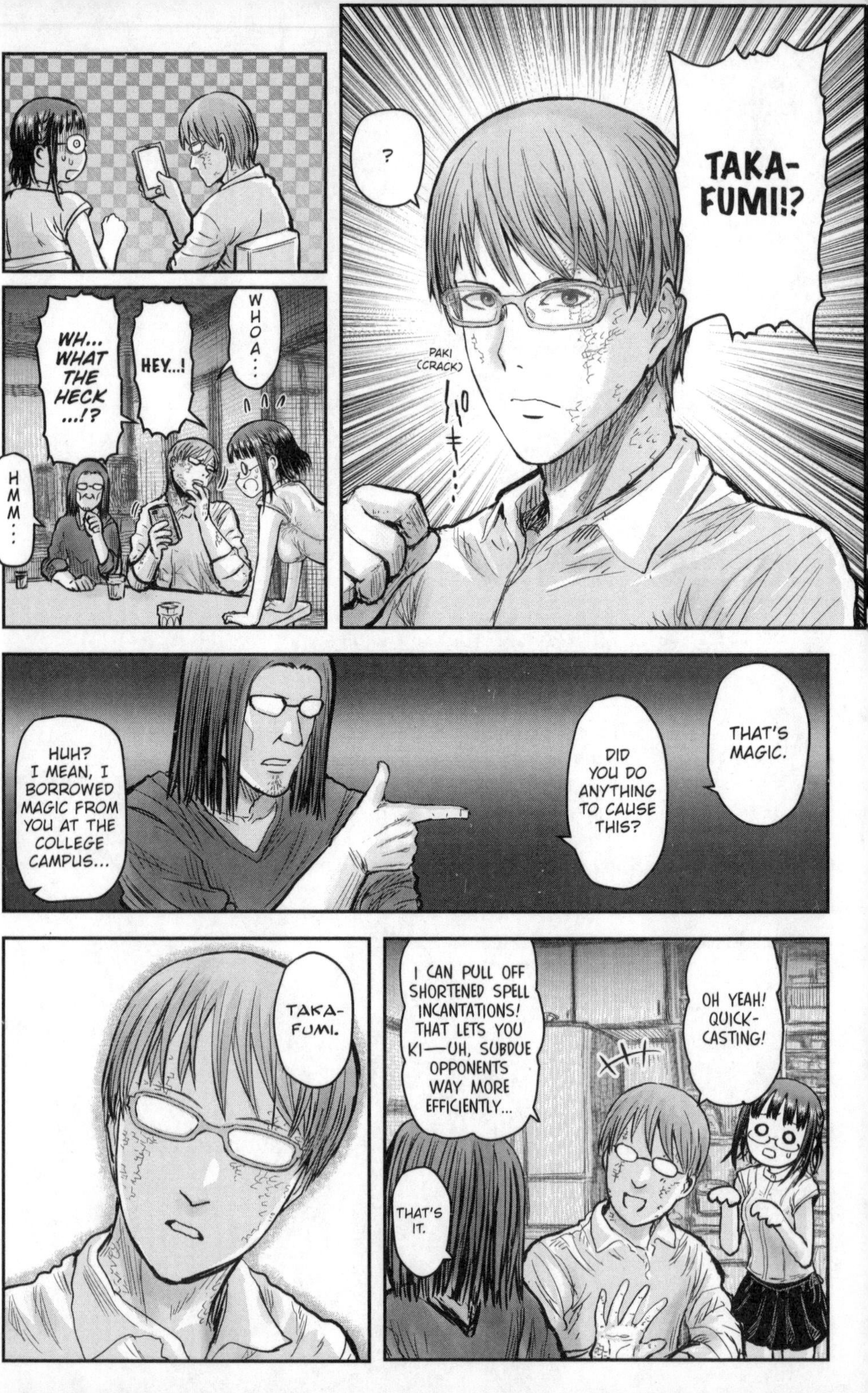
TAKA-FUMI!?
?
PAKI (CRACK)
WHOA...
HEY...!
WH... WHAT THE HECK ...!?
HMM...
THAT'S MAGIC.
DID YOU DO ANYTHING TO CAUSE THIS?
HUH? I MEAN, I BORROWED MAGIC FROM YOU AT THE COLLEGE CAMPUS...
OH YEAH! QUICK-CASTING!
I CAN PULL OFF SHORTENED SPELL INCANTATIONS! THAT LETS YOU KI—UH, SUBDUE OPPONENTS WAY MORE EFFICIENTLY...
THAT'S IT.
TAKA-FUMI.

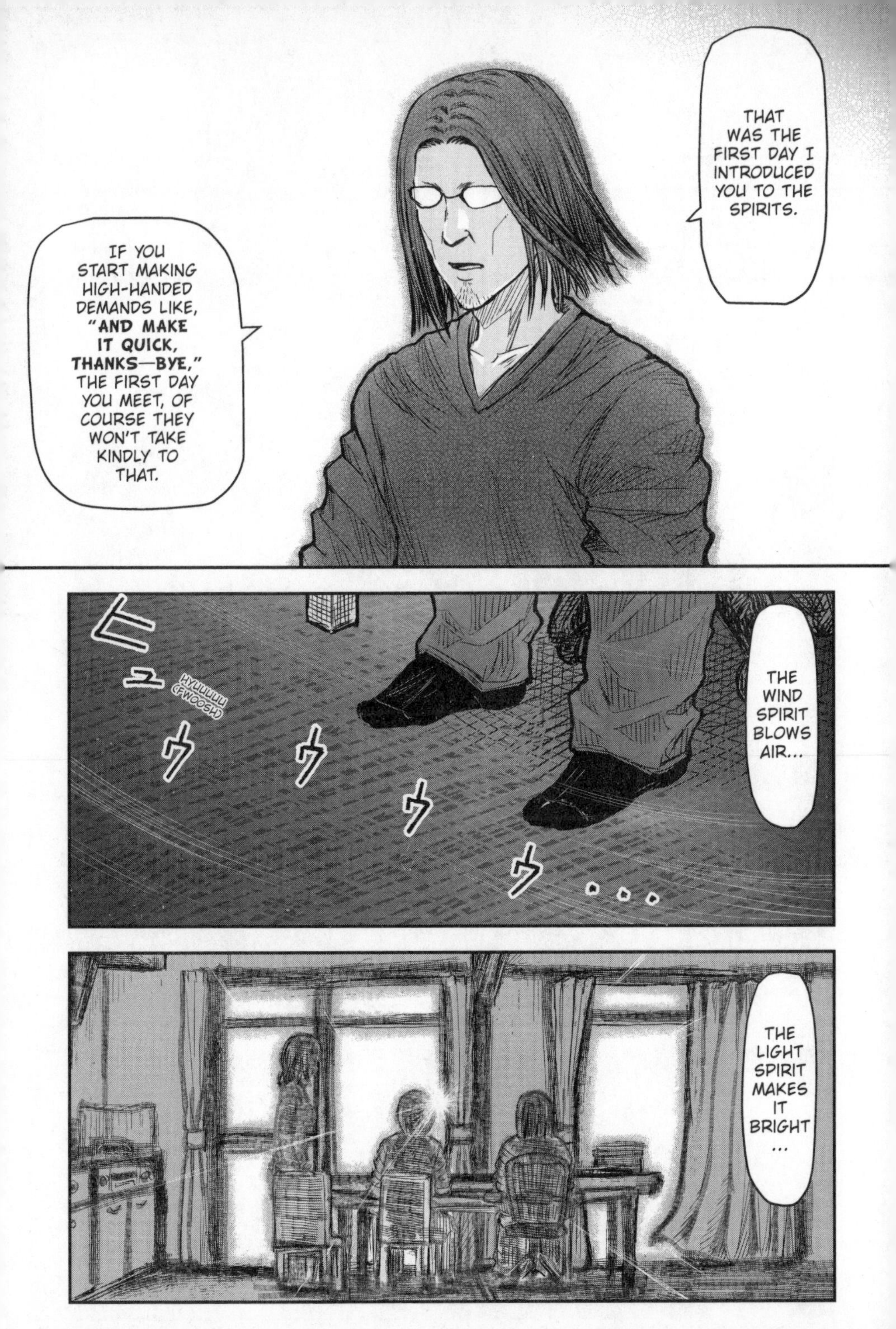
THAT WAS THE FIRST DAY I INTRODUCED YOU TO THE SPIRITS.
IF YOU START MAKING HIGH-HANDED DEMANDS LIKE, **"AND MAKE IT QUICK, THANKS—BYE,"** THE FIRST DAY YOU MEET, OF COURSE THEY WON'T TAKE KINDLY TO THAT.
THE WIND SPIRIT BLOWS AIR...
HYUUUUU (FWOOSH)
THE LIGHT SPIRIT MAKES IT BRIGHT...

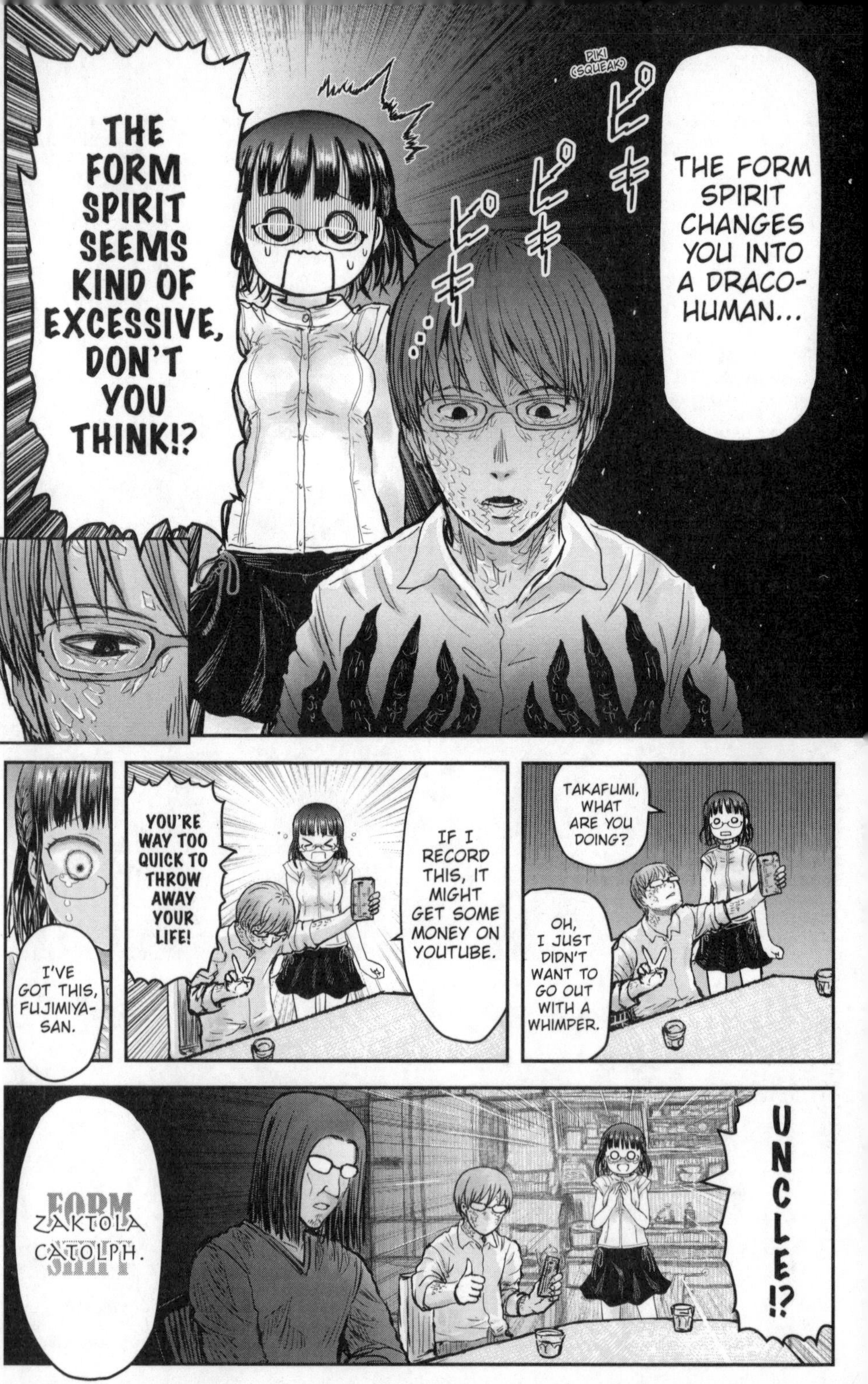
THE FORM SPIRIT CHANGES YOU INTO A DRACO-HUMAN...
PIKI (SQUEAK)
THE FORM SPIRIT SEEMS KIND OF EXCESSIVE, DON'T YOU THINK!?
TAKAFUMI, WHAT ARE YOU DOING?
OH, I JUST DIDN'T WANT TO GO OUT WITH A WHIMPER.
IF I RECORD THIS, IT MIGHT GET SOME MONEY ON YOUTUBE.
YOU'RE WAY TOO QUICK TO THROW AWAY YOUR LIFE!
I'VE GOT THIS, FUJIMIYA-SAN.
UNCLE!?
FORM SHIFT
ZAKTOLA CATOLPH.

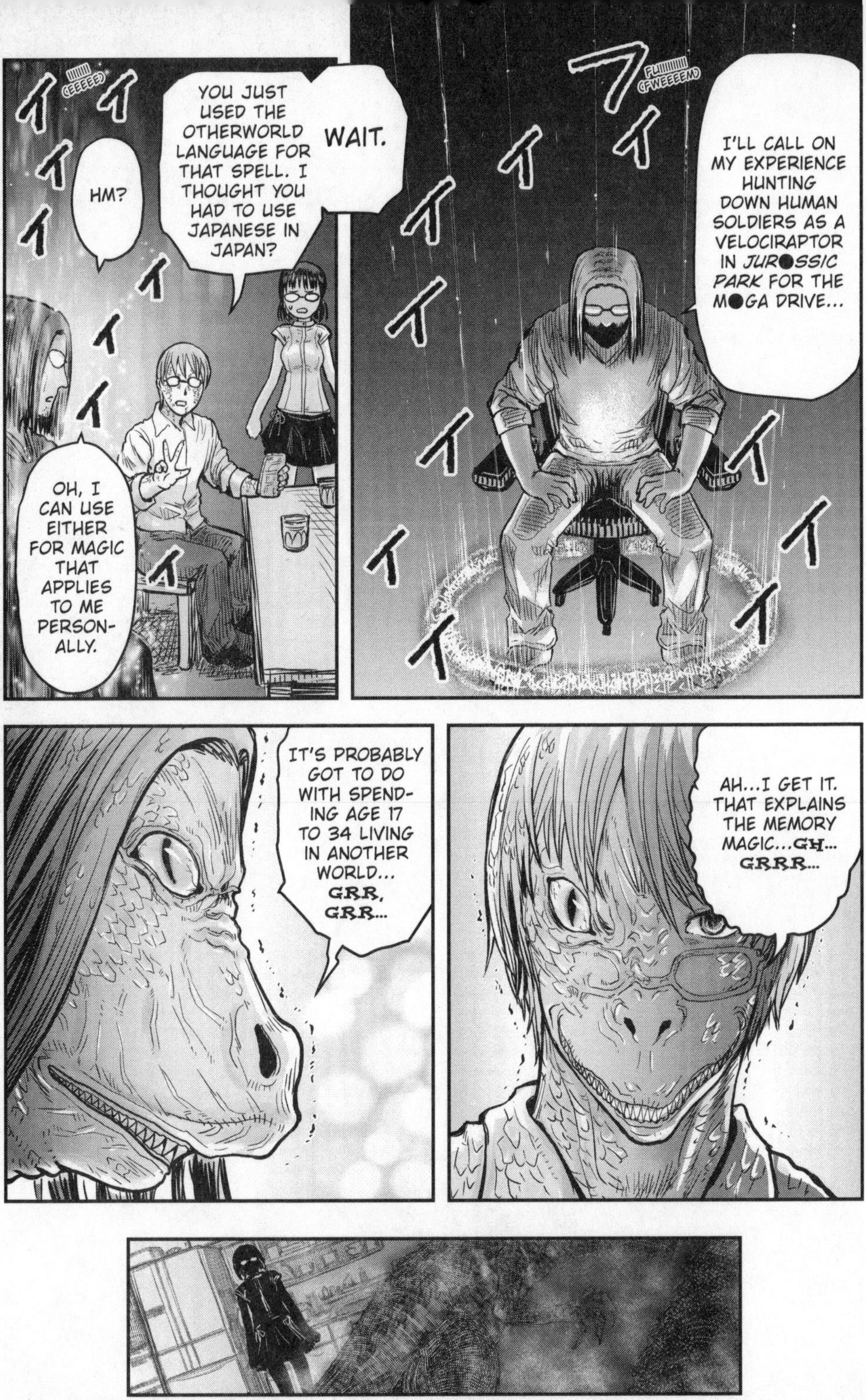
FUIIIIIIII
(FWEEEEM)
I'LL CALL ON MY EXPERIENCE HUNTING DOWN HUMAN SOLDIERS AS A VELOCIRAPTOR IN *JUR●SSIC PARK* FOR THE M●GA DRIVE...
WAIT.
YOU JUST USED THE OTHERWORLD LANGUAGE FOR THAT SPELL. I THOUGHT YOU HAD TO USE JAPANESE IN JAPAN?
IIIIIIII
(EEEEEE)
HM?
OH, I CAN USE EITHER FOR MAGIC THAT APPLIES TO ME PERSON-ALLY.
AH...I GET IT. THAT EXPLAINS THE MEMORY MAGIC...GH... **GRRR...**
IT'S PROBABLY GOT TO DO WITH SPEND-ING AGE 17 TO 34 LIVING IN ANOTHER WORLD... **GRR, GRR...**

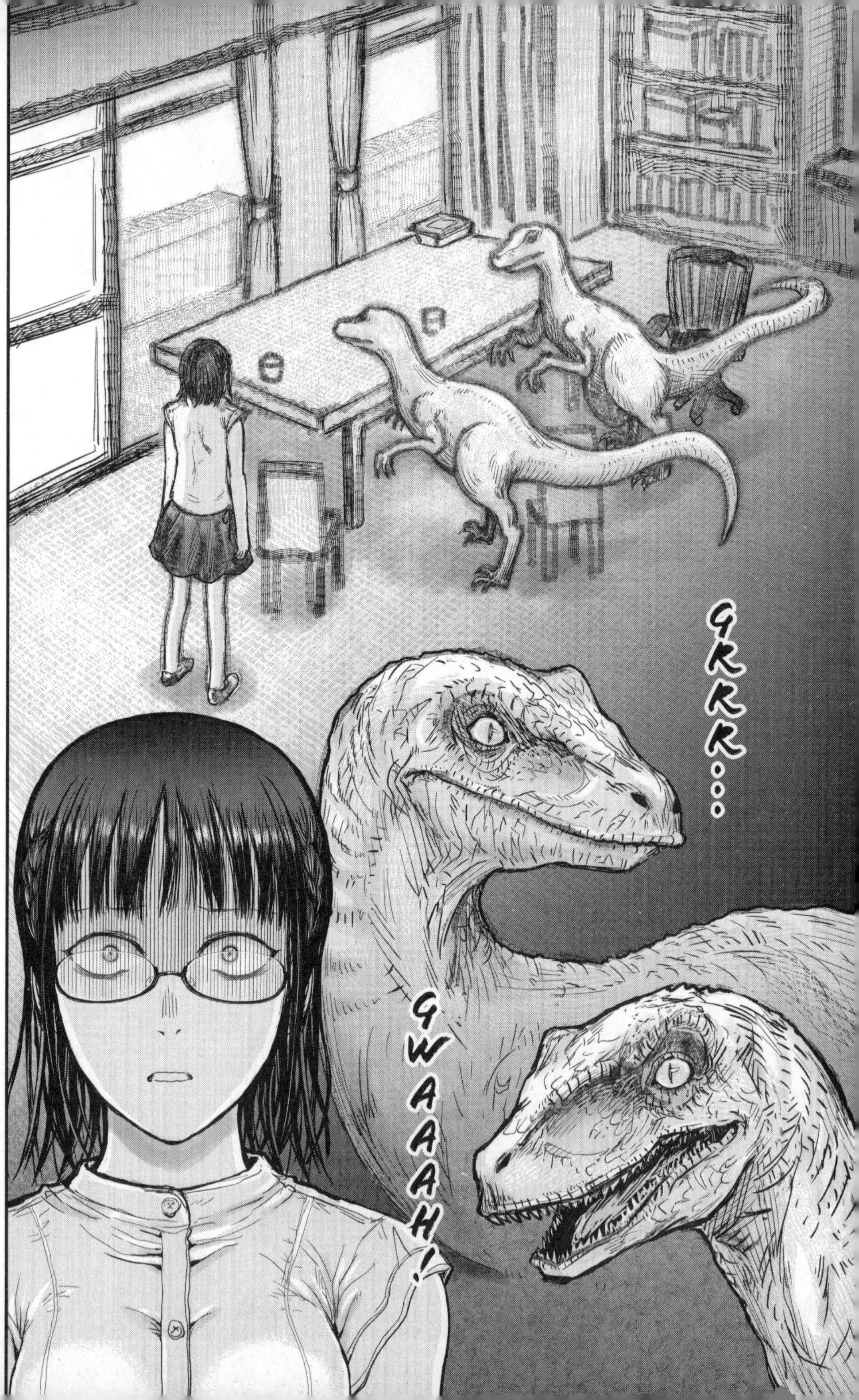
GRRR...
GWAAAAH!

Dragon

A creature that appears in myths and legends.

Dinosaur

A category of large vertebrates that (probably) existed in our world until approximately 66 million years ago.

TIPS

UNCLE from ANOTHER WORLD

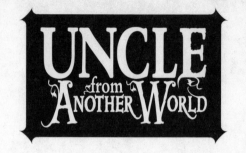

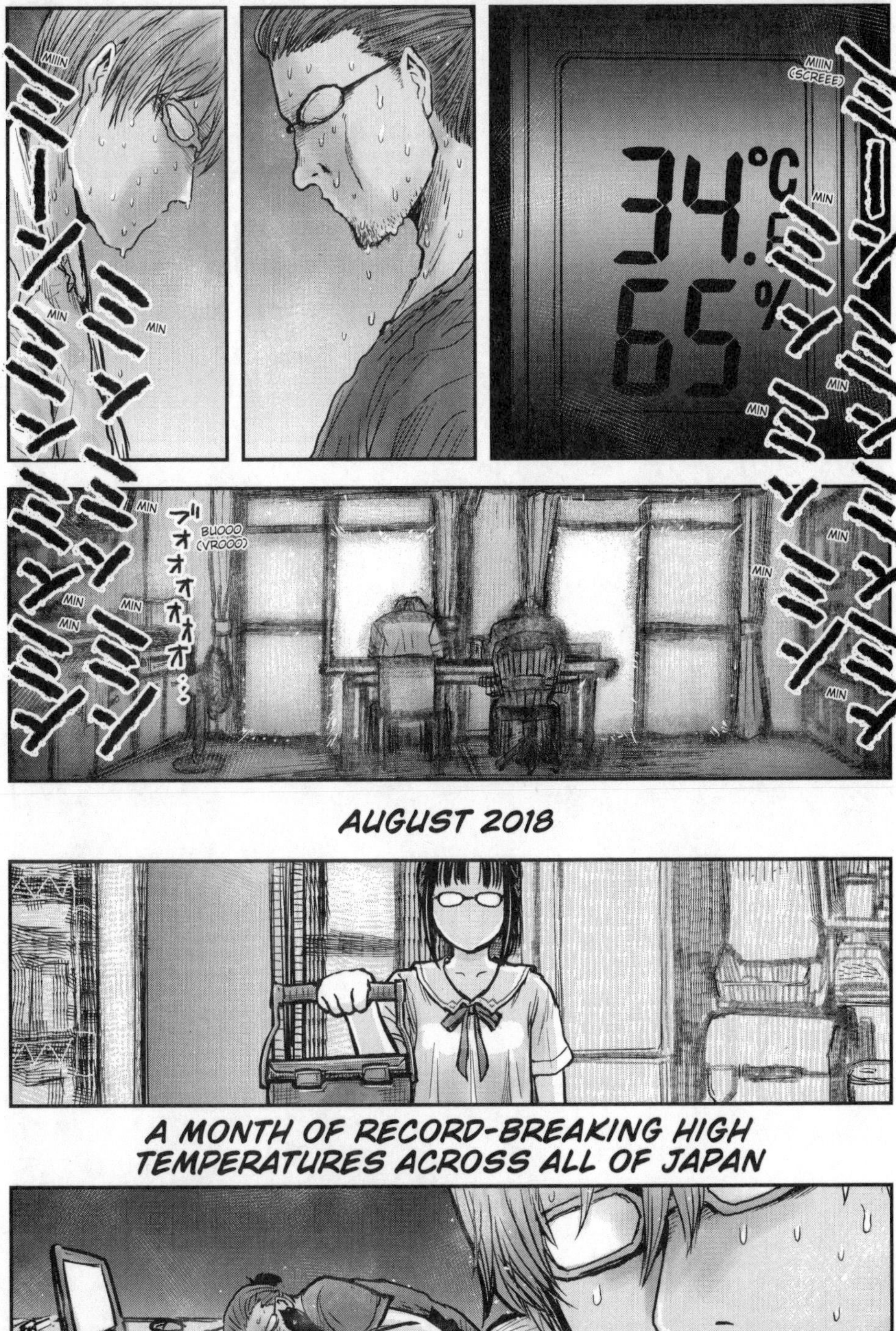
MIIN (SCREEE)
34.5°C
65%
MIN
MIN
MIN
MIIN
MIN
MIN
MIN
MIN
MIN
BUOOO (VROOO)
ブオオオオオオ…
MIN
MIN
MIN
AUGUST 2018
A MONTH OF RECORD-BREAKING HIGH TEMPERATURES ACROSS ALL OF JAPAN

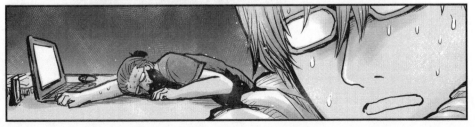

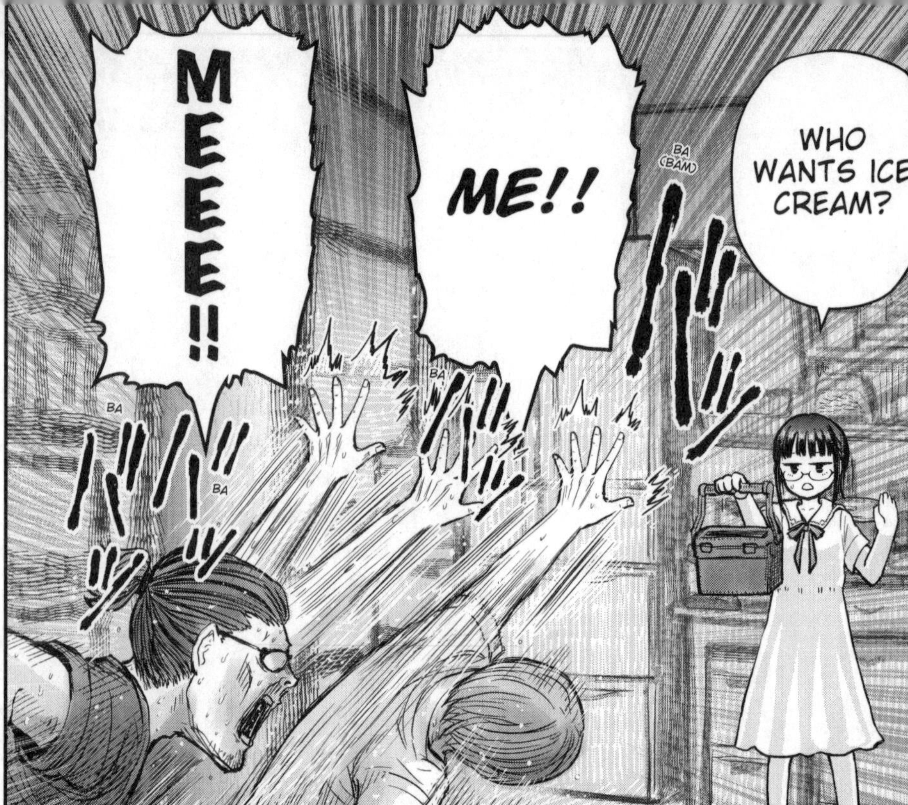
WHO WANTS ICE CREAM?
BA (BAM)
ME!!
MEEEE!!
BA
BA
BA
CHAPTER 22

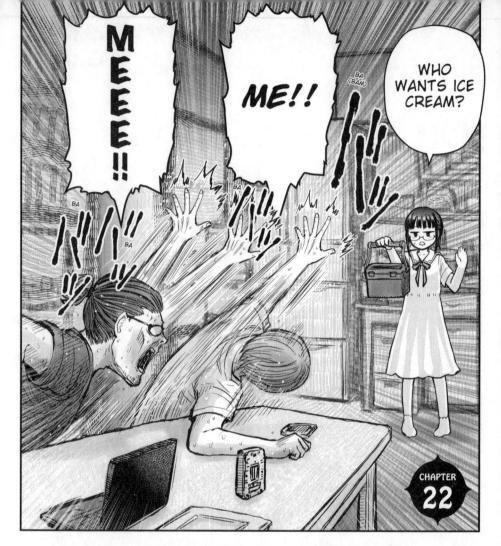

A CATASTROPHIC HEAT WAVE

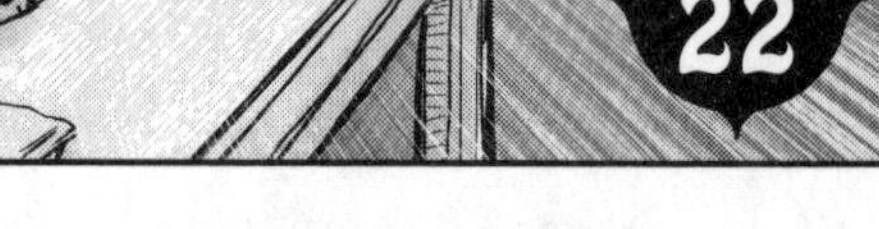
MIIIN (BUZZZZ)
MIN MIN
MIN MIN
MIN MIN
MIN MIN
MIN MIN
MIN MIN
MIIIN

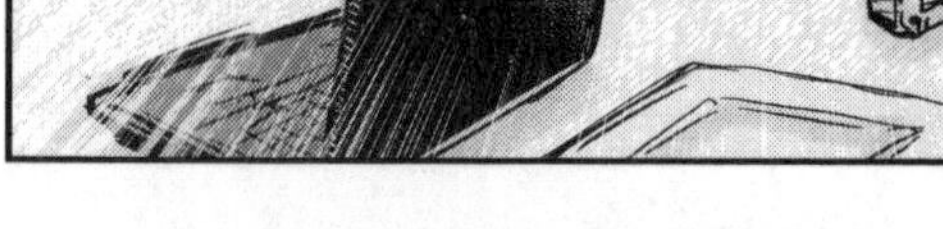
HYAAA (PSHOO)
ヒヤー

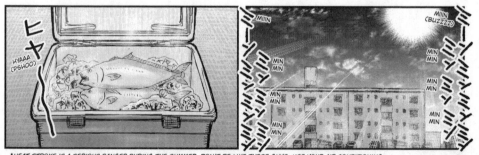

*HEAT STROKE IS A SERIOUS DANGER DURING THE SUMMER. DON'T BE LIKE THESE GUYS. USE YOUR AIR CONDITIONING.

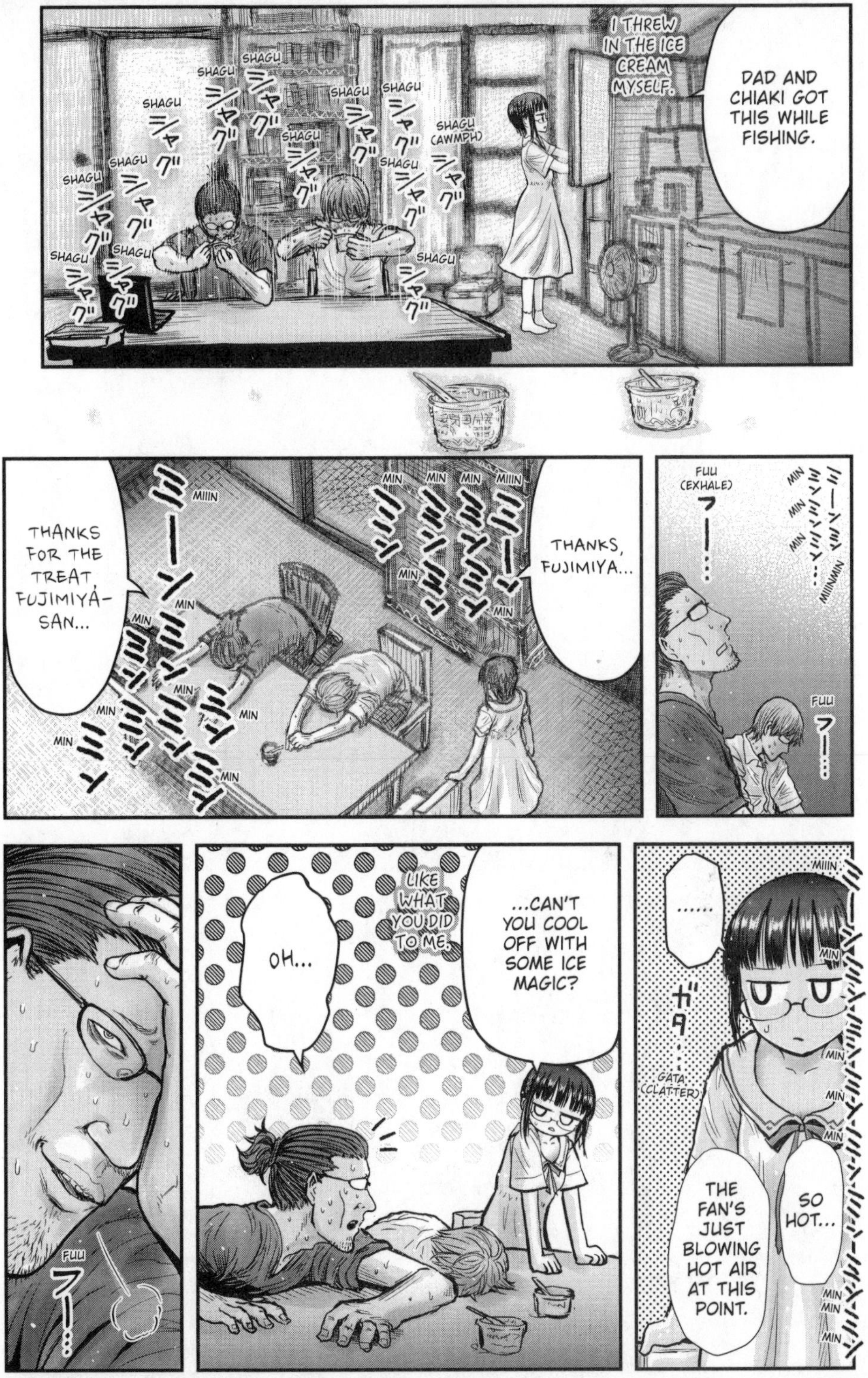
DAD AND CHIAKI GOT THIS WHILE FISHING.
I THREW IN THE ICE CREAM MYSELF.
SHAGU (AWMPH)
SHAGU
SHAGU
SHAGU
SHAGU
SHAGU
SHAGU
SHAGU
SHAGU
SHAGU
SHAGU
FUU (EXHALE)
フー…
MIIIN MIN MIN MIN
ミーンミンミンミン…
FUU
フー…
THANKS, FUJIMIYA...
THANKS FOR THE TREAT, FUJIMIYA-SAN...
MIIIN MIN MIN MIN MIN MIN MIN MIN MIN MIN MIN MIN
......
SO HOT...
THE FAN'S JUST BLOWING HOT AIR AT THIS POINT.
GATA (CLATTER)
ガタ…
MIIIN MIN MIN MIN MIN MIN MIN MIN
...CAN'T YOU COOL OFF WITH SOME ICE MAGIC?
LIKE WHAT YOU DID TO ME.
OH...
FUU
フー…

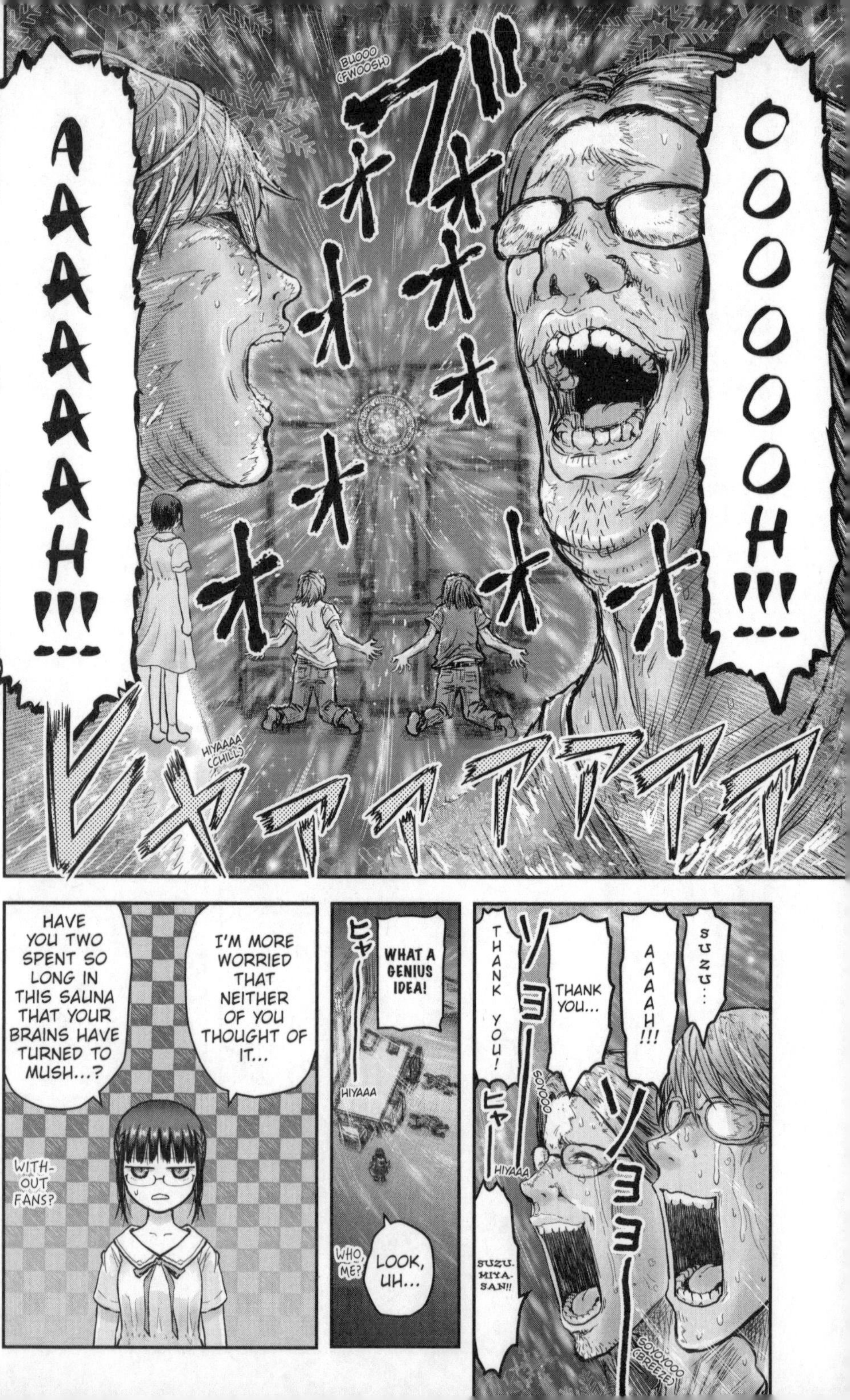
OOOOOOOH!!!...
BUOOO (FWOOSH)
AAAAAAAH!!!...
HIYAAAA (CHILL)
SUZU...
AAAAAH!!!
THANK YOU...
THANK YOU!
SOYOOO
HIYAAA
SUZU-MIYA-SAN!!
SOYOYOOO (BREEZE)
WHAT A GENIUS IDEA!
HIYAAA
LOOK, UH...
WHO, ME?
I'M MORE WORRIED THAT NEITHER OF YOU THOUGHT OF IT...
HAVE YOU TWO SPENT SO LONG IN THIS SAUNA THAT YOUR BRAINS HAVE TURNED TO MUSH...?
WITH-OUT FANS?

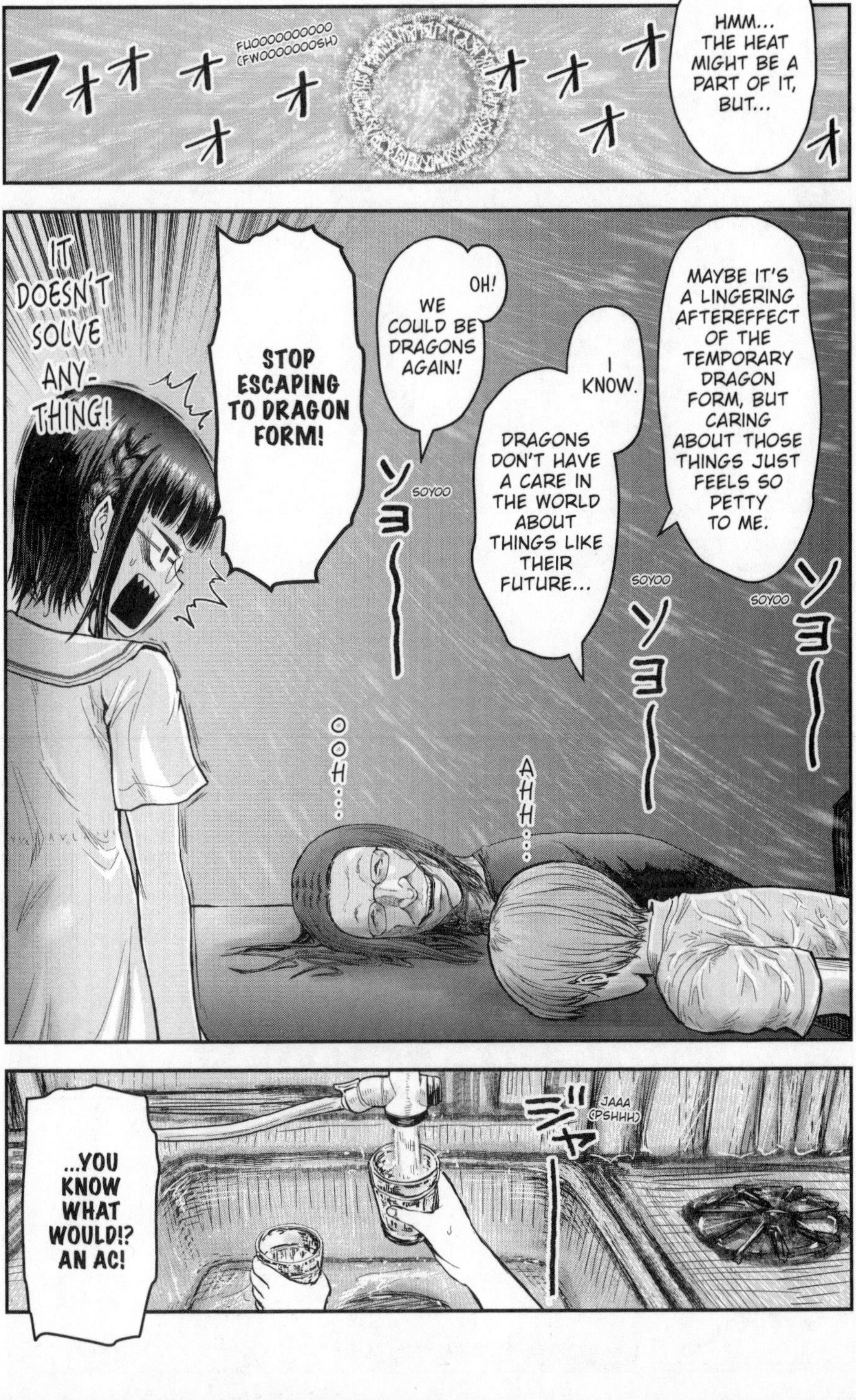

HMM... THE HEAT MIGHT BE A PART OF IT, BUT...
FUOOOOOOOOOO (FWOOOOOOOSH)
MAYBE IT'S A LINGERING AFTEREFFECT OF THE TEMPORARY DRAGON FORM, BUT CARING ABOUT THOSE THINGS JUST FEELS SO PETTY TO ME.
SOYOO
SOYOO
I KNOW.
DRAGONS DON'T HAVE A CARE IN THE WORLD ABOUT THINGS LIKE THEIR FUTURE...
AHH...
OH!
WE COULD BE DRAGONS AGAIN!
SOYOO
OOH...
STOP ESCAPING TO DRAGON FORM!
IT DOESN'T SOLVE ANY-THING!
JAAA (PSHHH)
...YOU KNOW WHAT WOULD!? AN AC!

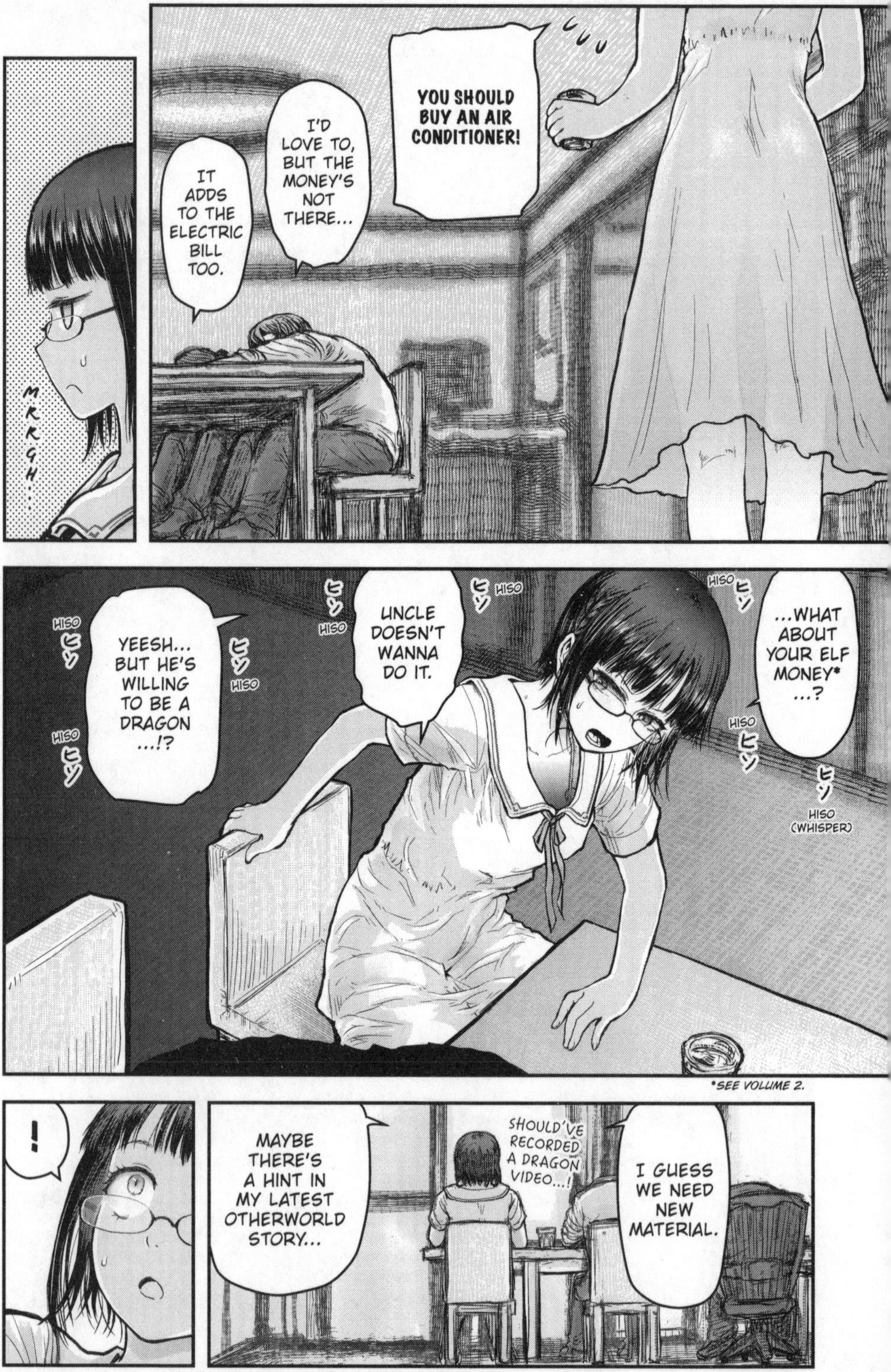
YOU SHOULD BUY AN AIR CONDITIONER!
I'D LOVE TO, BUT THE MONEY'S NOT THERE...
IT ADDS TO THE ELECTRIC BILL TOO.
MRRGH...
...WHAT ABOUT YOUR ELF MONEY*...?
HISO ヒソ
HISO (WHISPER)
UNCLE DOESN'T WANNA DO IT.
HISO ヒソ
YEESH... BUT HE'S WILLING TO BE A DRAGON...!?
HISO ヒソ
I GUESS WE NEED NEW MATERIAL.
SHOULD'VE RECORDED A DRAGON VIDEO...!
MAYBE THERE'S A HINT IN MY LATEST OTHERWORLD STORY...
!

*SEE VOLUME 2.

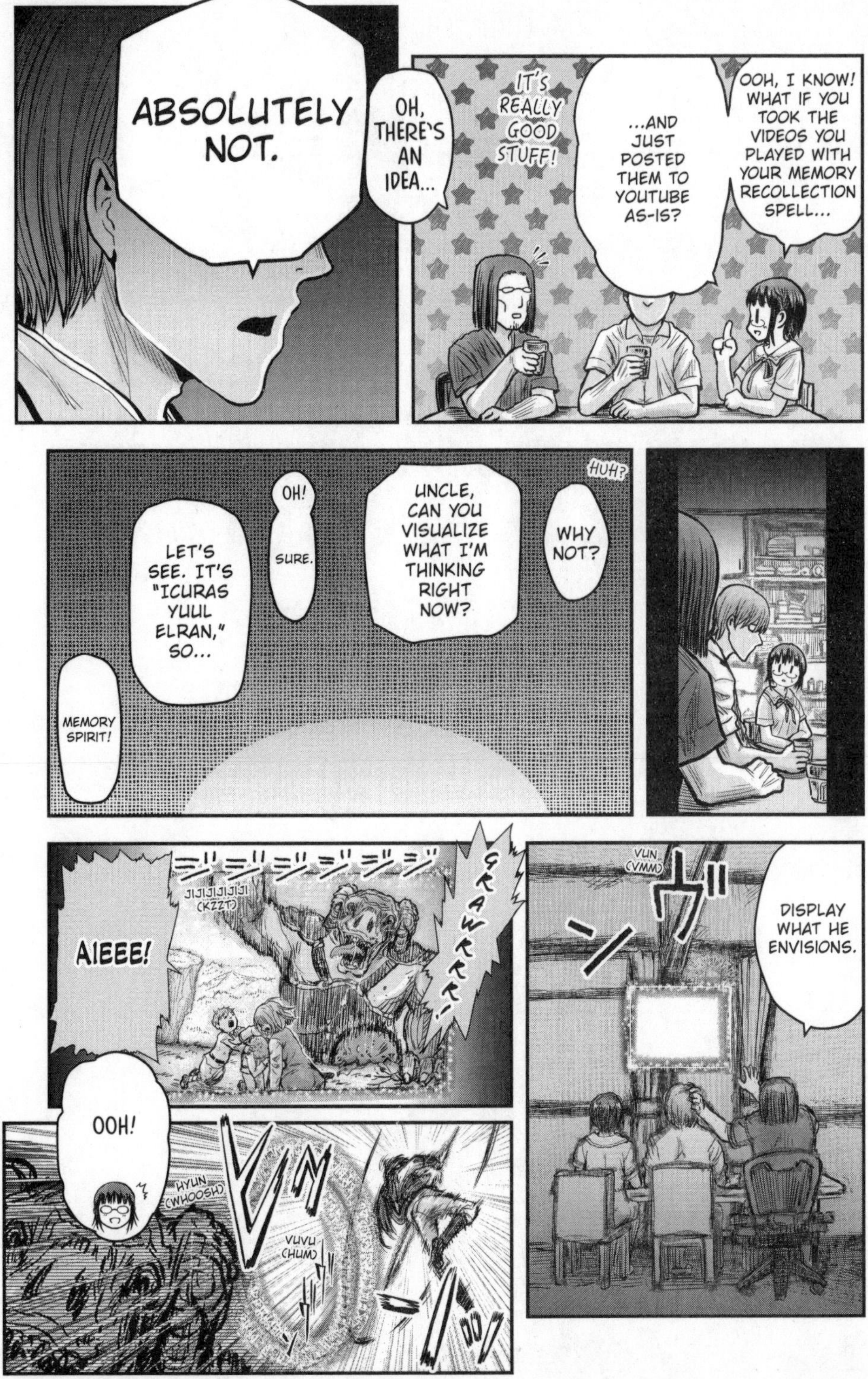
OOH, I KNOW! WHAT IF YOU TOOK THE VIDEOS YOU PLAYED WITH YOUR MEMORY RECOLLECTION SPELL...
...AND JUST POSTED THEM TO YOUTUBE AS-IS?
IT'S REALLY GOOD STUFF!
OH, THERE'S AN IDEA...
ABSOLUTELY NOT.
HUH?
WHY NOT?
UNCLE, CAN YOU VISUALIZE WHAT I'M THINKING RIGHT NOW?
OH!
SURE.
LET'S SEE. IT'S "ICURAS YUUL ELRAN," SO...
MEMORY SPIRIT!
VUN (VMM)
DISPLAY WHAT HE ENVISIONS.
GRAWRRR!
JIJIJIJIJI (KZZT)
AIEEE!
OOH!
HYUN (WHOOSH)
VUVU (HUM)

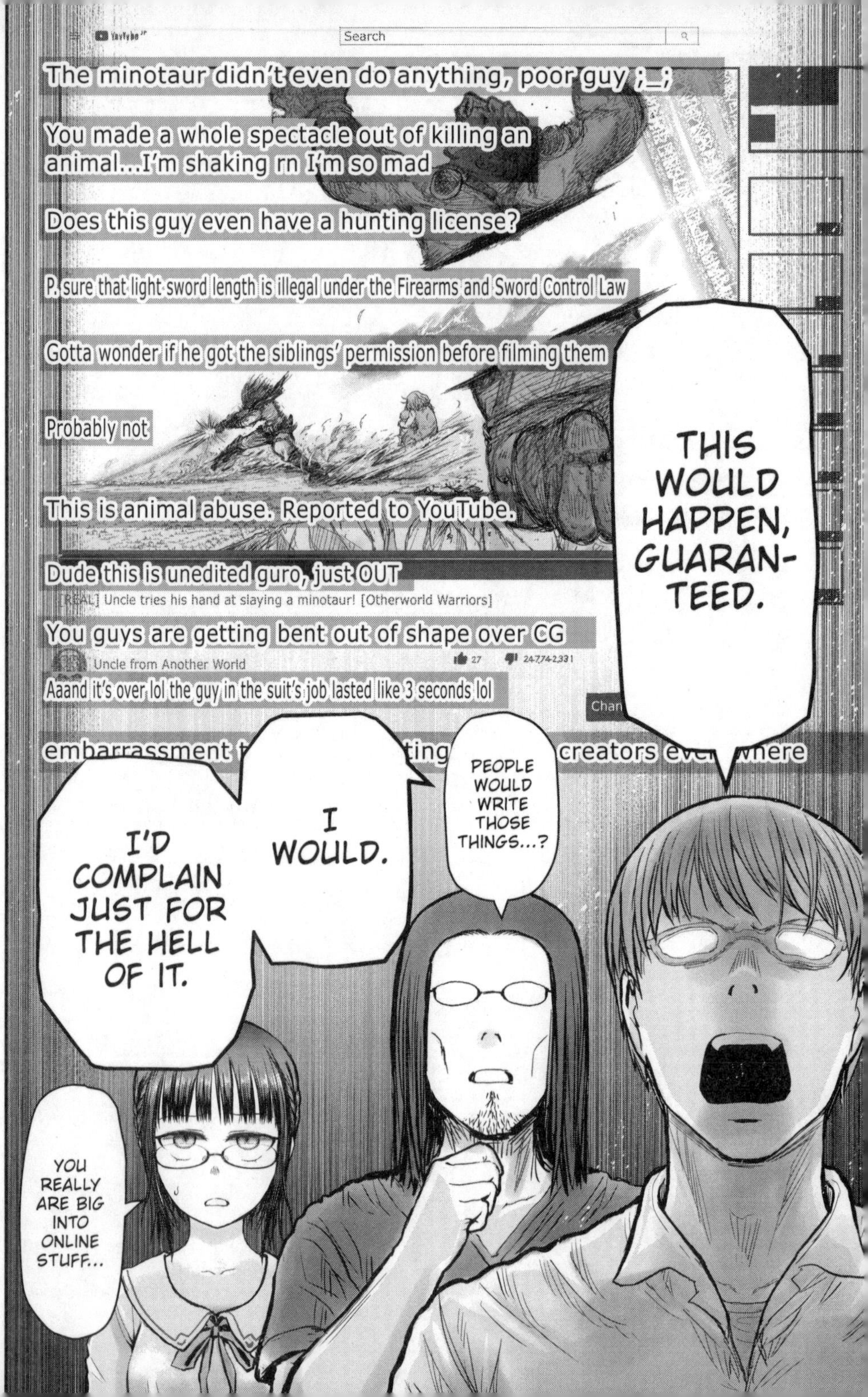
Search
The minotaur didn't even do anything, poor guy ;_;
You made a whole spectacle out of killing an animal...I'm shaking rn I'm so mad
Does this guy even have a hunting license?
P. sure that light sword length is illegal under the Firearms and Sword Control Law
Gotta wonder if he got the siblings' permission before filming them
Probably not
This is animal abuse. Reported to YouTube.
Dude this is unedited guro, just OUT
[REAL] Uncle tries his hand at slaying a minotaur! [Otherworld Warriors]
You guys are getting bent out of shape over CG
Uncle from Another World
27
Aaand it's over lol the guy in the suit's job lasted like 3 seconds lol
THIS WOULD HAPPEN, GUARANTEED.
PEOPLE WOULD WRITE THOSE THINGS...?
I WOULD.
I'D COMPLAIN JUST FOR THE HELL OF IT.
YOU REALLY ARE BIG INTO ONLINE STUFF...

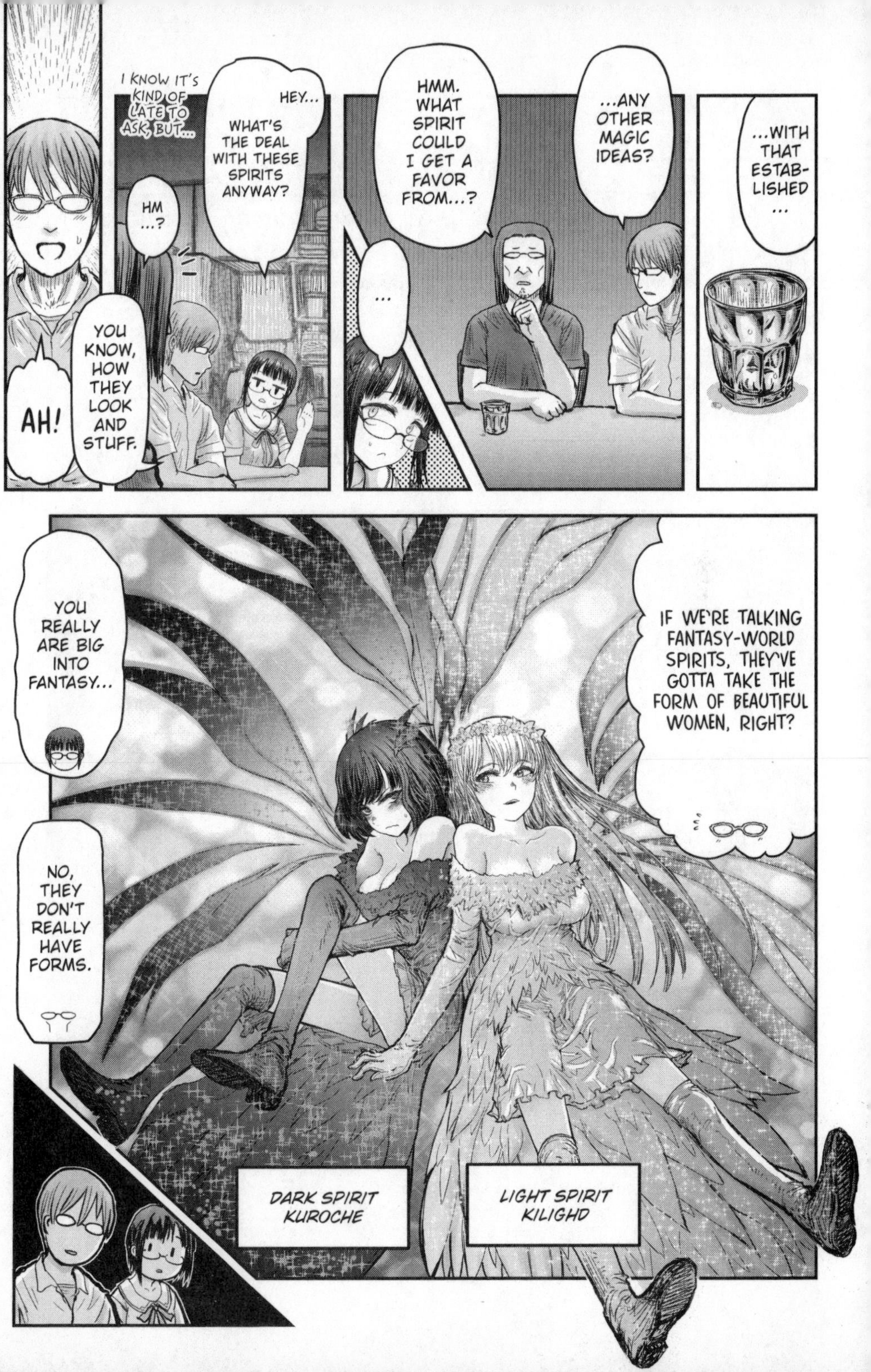
...WITH THAT ESTABLISHED...
...ANY OTHER MAGIC IDEAS?
HMM. WHAT SPIRIT COULD I GET A FAVOR FROM...?
...
HEY... WHAT'S THE DEAL WITH THESE SPIRITS ANYWAY?
I KNOW IT'S KIND OF LATE TO ASK, BUT...
HM ...?
YOU KNOW, HOW THEY LOOK AND STUFF.
AH!
IF WE'RE TALKING FANTASY-WORLD SPIRITS, THEY'VE GOTTA TAKE THE FORM OF BEAUTIFUL WOMEN, RIGHT?
LIGHT SPIRIT KILIGHD
DARK SPIRIT KUROCHE
YOU REALLY ARE BIG INTO FANTASY...
NO, THEY DON'T REALLY HAVE FORMS.

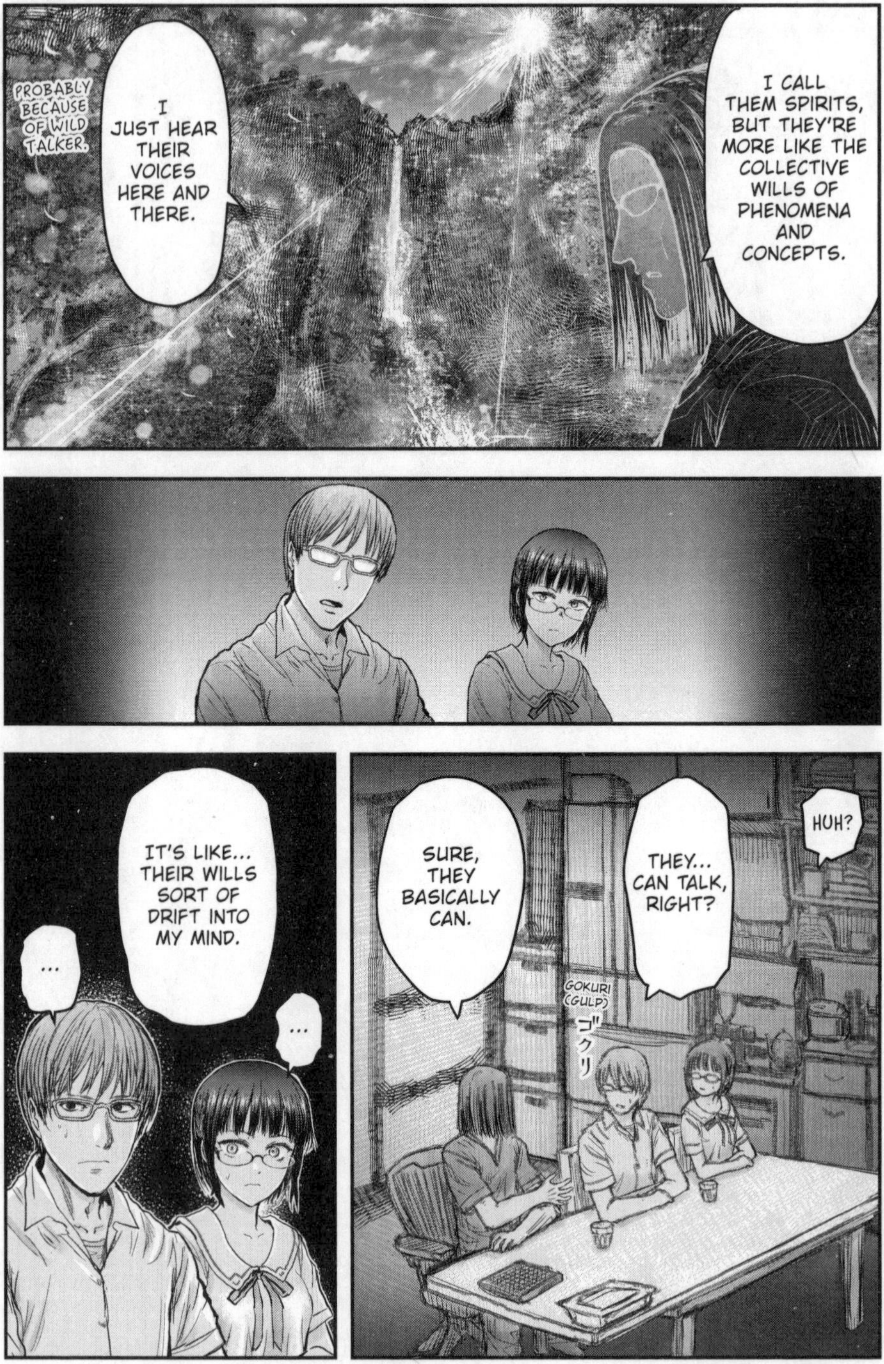
I CALL THEM SPIRITS, BUT THEY'RE MORE LIKE THE COLLECTIVE WILLS OF PHENOMENA AND CONCEPTS.
I JUST HEAR THEIR VOICES HERE AND THERE.
PROBABLY BECAUSE OF WILD TALKER.
HUH?
THEY... CAN TALK, RIGHT?
SURE, THEY BASICALLY CAN.
GOKURI (GULP)
ゴクリ
IT'S LIKE... THEIR WILLS SORT OF DRIFT INTO MY MIND.
...
...

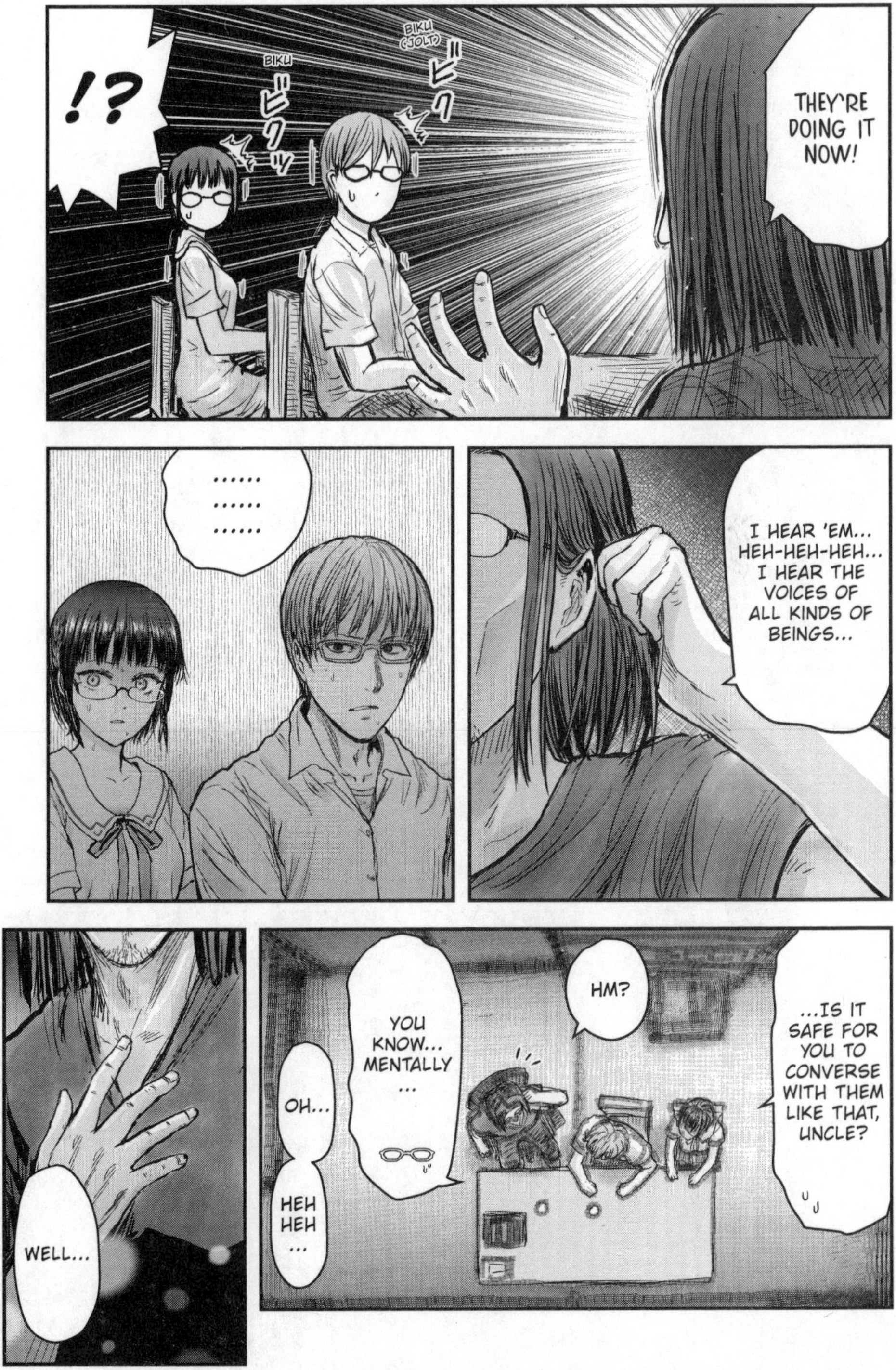
THEY'RE DOING IT NOW!
BIKU (JOLT)
BIKU
!?
I HEAR 'EM... HEH-HEH-HEH... I HEAR THE VOICES OF ALL KINDS OF BEINGS...
......
......
......
...IS IT SAFE FOR YOU TO CONVERSE WITH THEM LIKE THAT, UNCLE?
HM?
YOU KNOW... MENTALLY ...
OH...
HEH HEH ...
WELL...

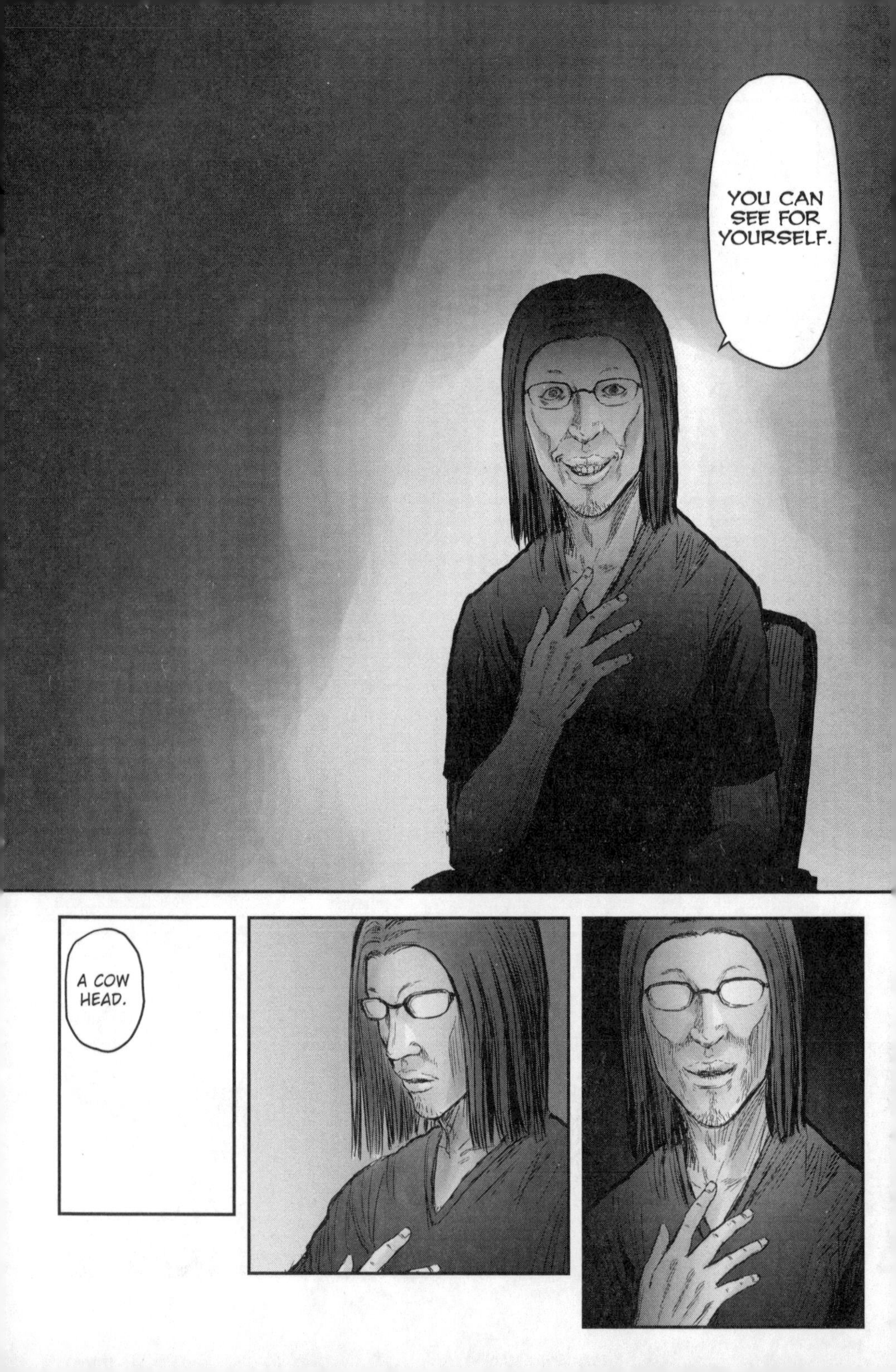
YOU CAN SEE FOR YOURSELF.
A COW HEAD.

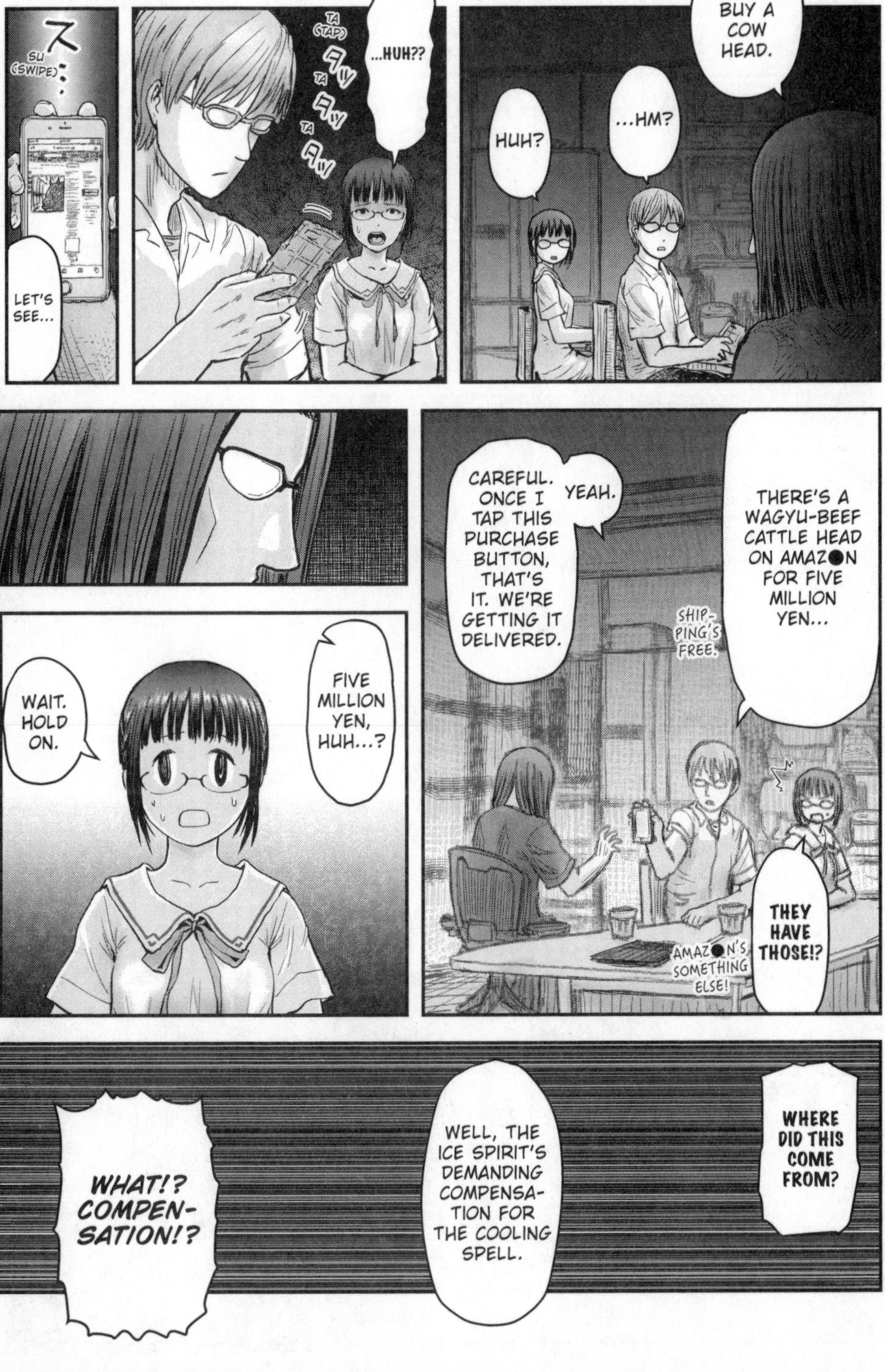
LET'S BUY A COW HEAD.
...HM?
HUH?
...HUH??
TA (TAP) タッ
TA タッ
TA タッ
ス
SU (SWIPE)
LET'S SEE...
THERE'S A WAGYU-BEEF CATTLE HEAD ON AMAZ●N FOR FIVE MILLION YEN...
SHIP-PING'S FREE.
YEAH.
CAREFUL. ONCE I TAP THIS PURCHASE BUTTON, THAT'S IT. WE'RE GETTING IT DELIVERED.
THEY HAVE THOSE!?
AMAZ●N'S SOMETHING ELSE!
FIVE MILLION YEN, HUH...?
WAIT. HOLD ON.
WHERE DID THIS COME FROM?
WELL, THE ICE SPIRIT'S DEMANDING COMPENSATION FOR THE COOLING SPELL.
WHAT!? COMPENSATION!?

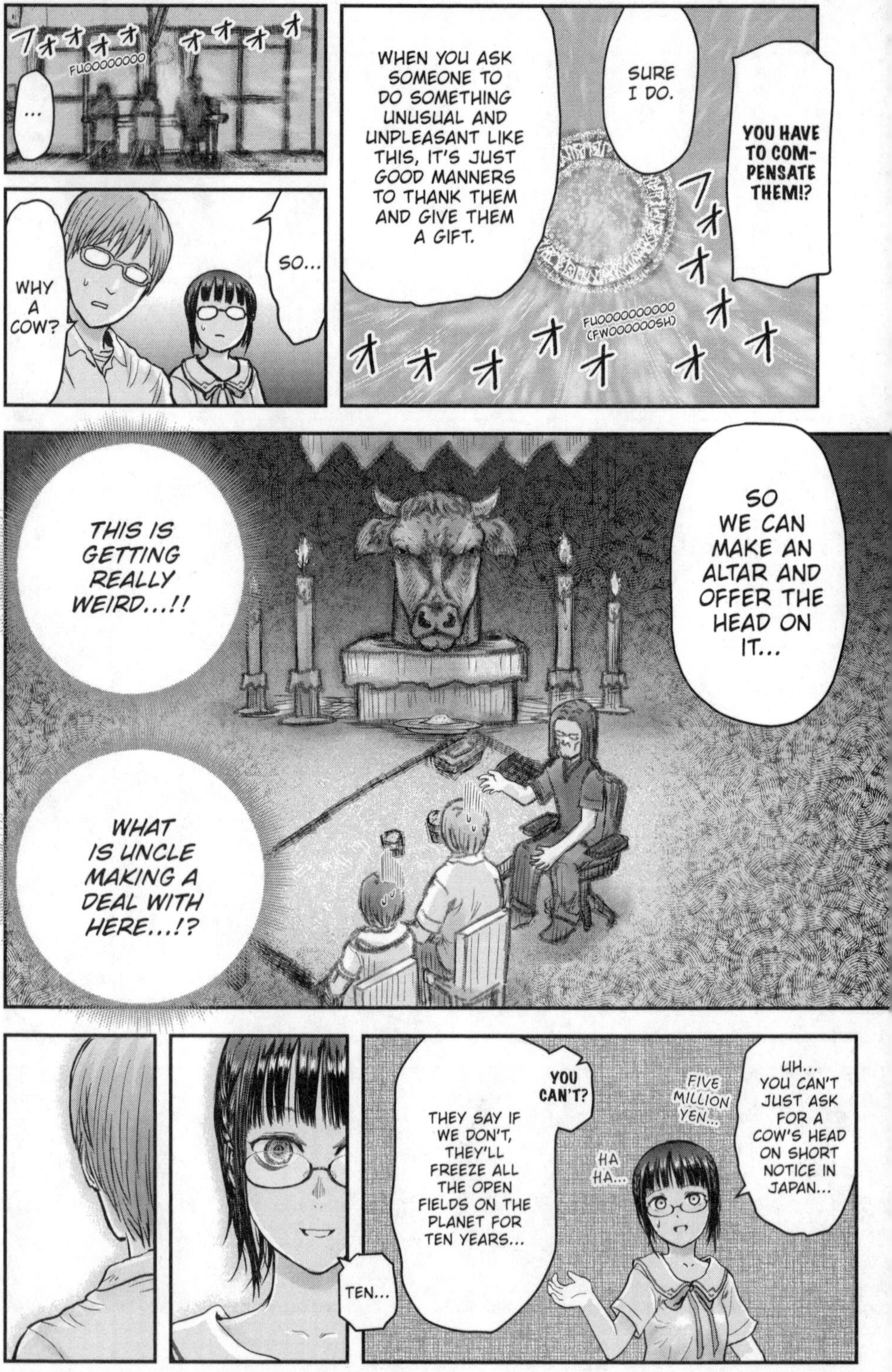
YOU HAVE TO COMPENSATE THEM!?
SURE I DO.
WHEN YOU ASK SOMEONE TO DO SOMETHING UNUSUAL AND UNPLEASANT LIKE THIS, IT'S JUST GOOD MANNERS TO THANK THEM AND GIVE THEM A GIFT.
FUOOOOOOOOOO (FWOOOOOOSH)
フォオオオ オオオオ
FUOOOOOOOO
...
SO...
WHY A COW?
SO WE CAN MAKE AN ALTAR AND OFFER THE HEAD ON IT...
THIS IS GETTING REALLY WEIRD...!!
WHAT IS UNCLE MAKING A DEAL WITH HERE...!?
UH... YOU CAN'T JUST ASK FOR A COW'S HEAD ON SHORT NOTICE IN JAPAN...
HA HA...
FIVE MILLION YEN...
YOU CAN'T?
THEY SAY IF WE DON'T, THEY'LL FREEZE ALL THE OPEN FIELDS ON THE PLANET FOR TEN YEARS...
TEN...

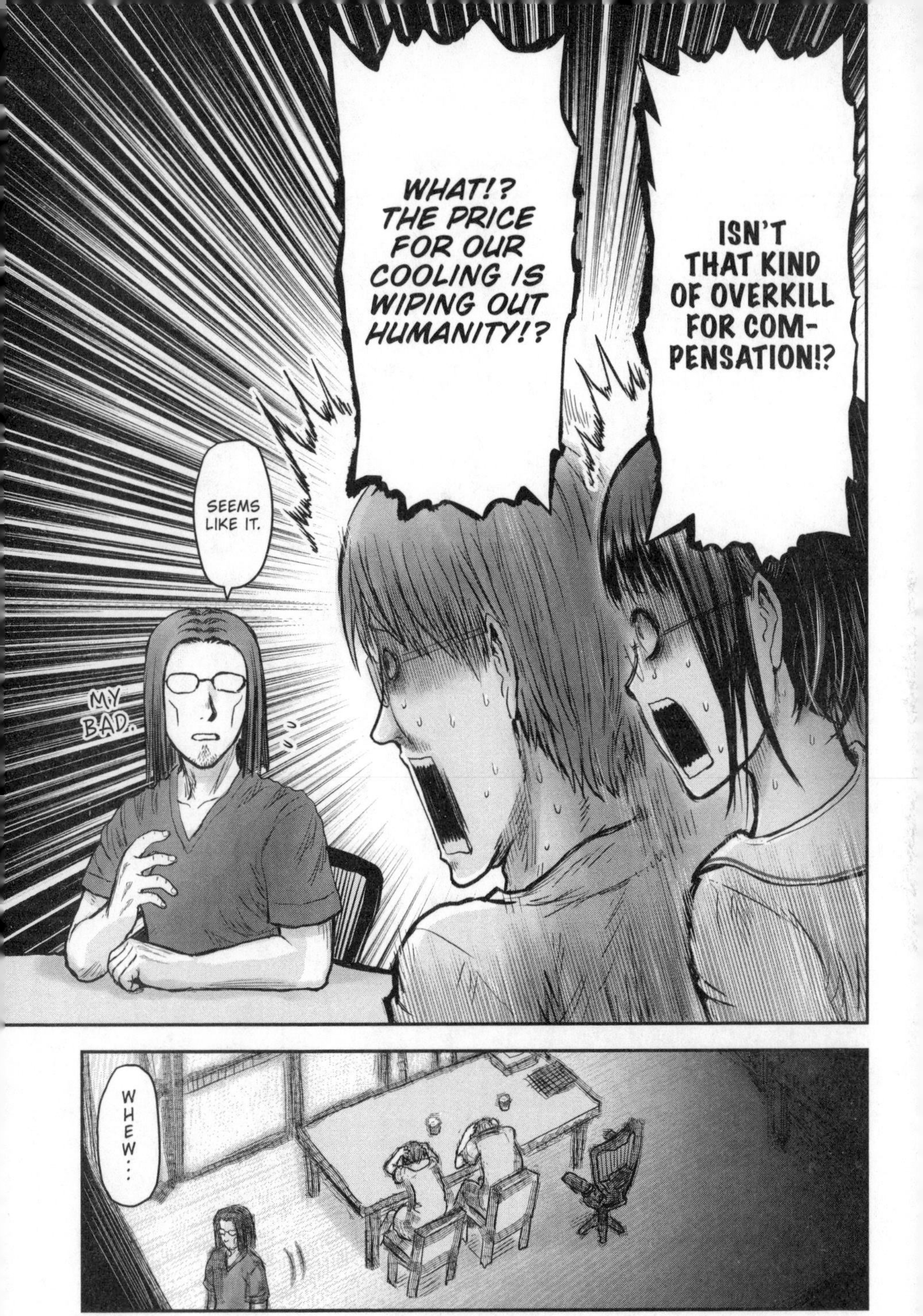
ISN'T THAT KIND OF OVERKILL FOR COM-PENSATION!?
WHAT!? THE PRICE FOR OUR COOLING IS WIPING OUT HUMANITY!?
SEEMS LIKE IT.
MY BAD.
WHEW...

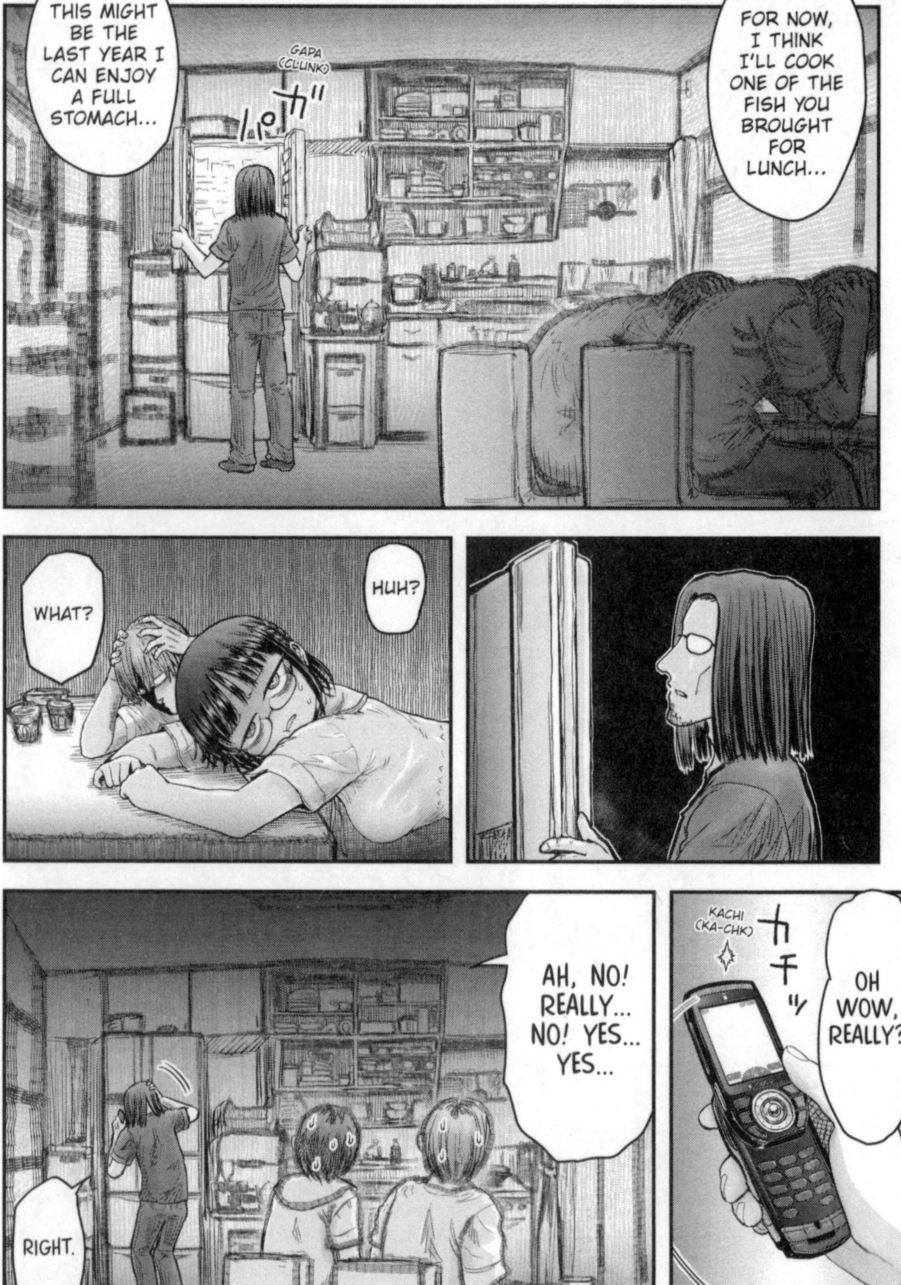
FOR NOW, I THINK I'LL COOK ONE OF THE FISH YOU BROUGHT FOR LUNCH...
GAPA (CLUNK)
ガパ
THIS MIGHT BE THE LAST YEAR I CAN ENJOY A FULL STOMACH...
HUH?
WHAT?
KACHI (KA-CHK)
カチッ
OH WOW, REALLY?
AH, NO! REALLY... NO! YES... YES...
RIGHT.

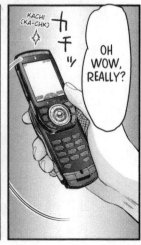

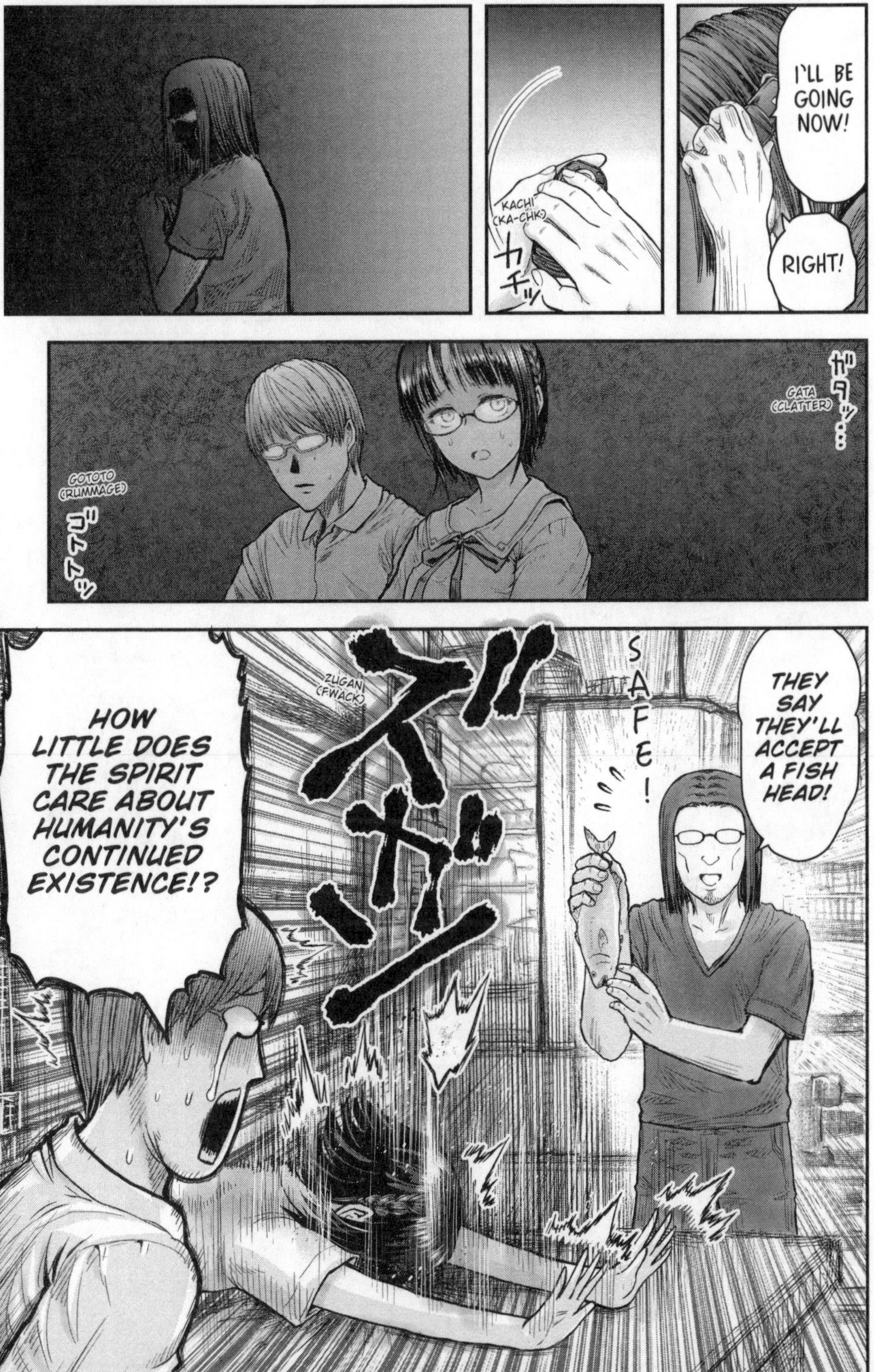
I'LL BE GOING NOW!
RIGHT!
KACHI (KA-CHK)
カチッ
GATA (CLATTER)
ガタッ…
GOTOTO (RUMMAGE)
ゴトトッ
THEY SAY THEY'LL ACCEPT A FISH HEAD!
SAFE!
ZUGAN (FWACK)
ズガン
HOW LITTLE DOES THE SPIRIT CARE ABOUT HUMANITY'S CONTINUED EXISTENCE!?

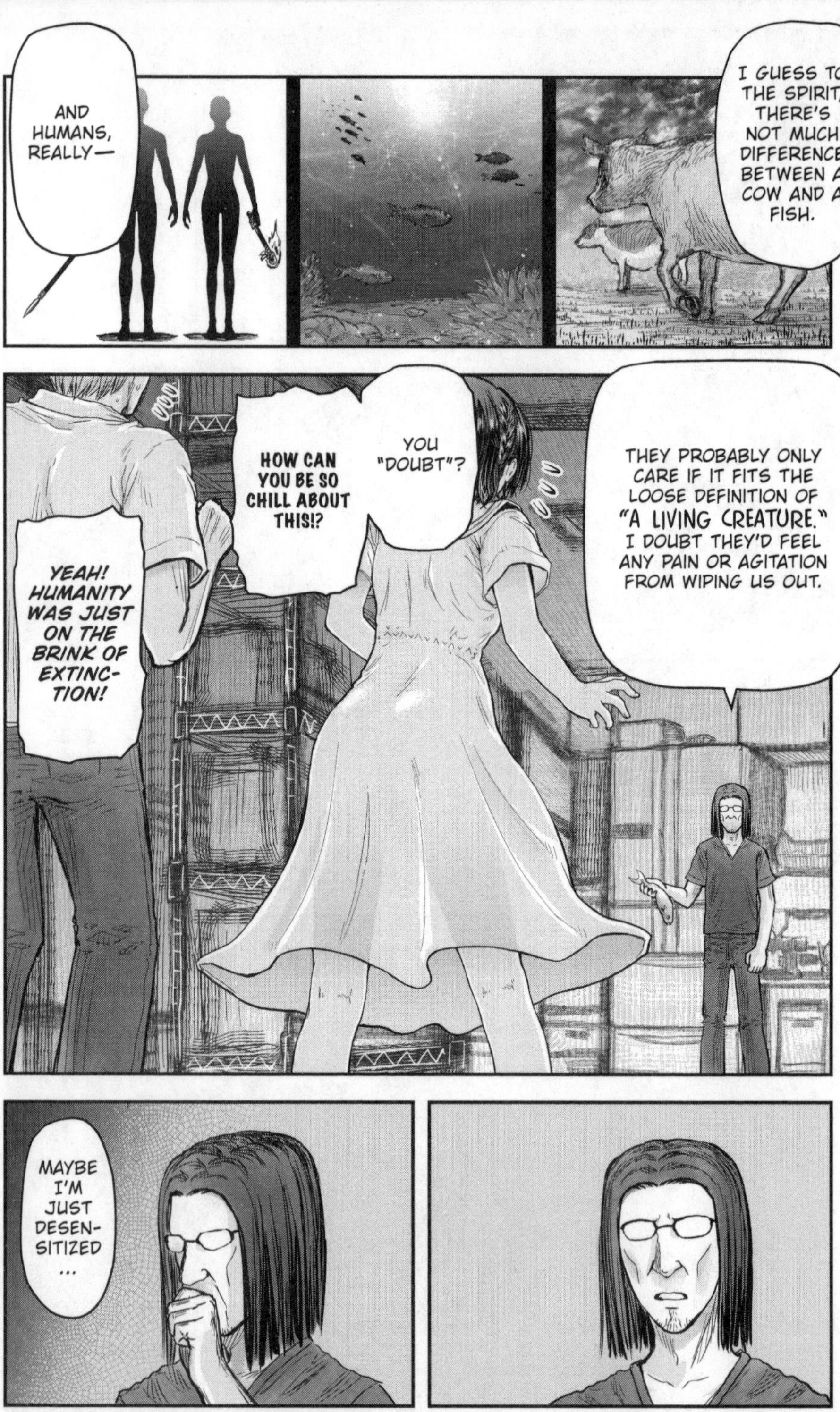
I GUESS TO THE SPIRIT, THERE'S NOT MUCH DIFFERENCE BETWEEN A COW AND A FISH.
AND HUMANS, REALLY—
THEY PROBABLY ONLY CARE IF IT FITS THE LOOSE DEFINITION OF "A LIVING CREATURE." I DOUBT THEY'D FEEL ANY PAIN OR AGITATION FROM WIPING US OUT.
YOU "DOUBT"?
HOW CAN YOU BE SO CHILL ABOUT THIS!?
YEAH! HUMANITY WAS JUST ON THE BRINK OF EXTINCTION!
MAYBE I'M JUST DESENSITIZED ...

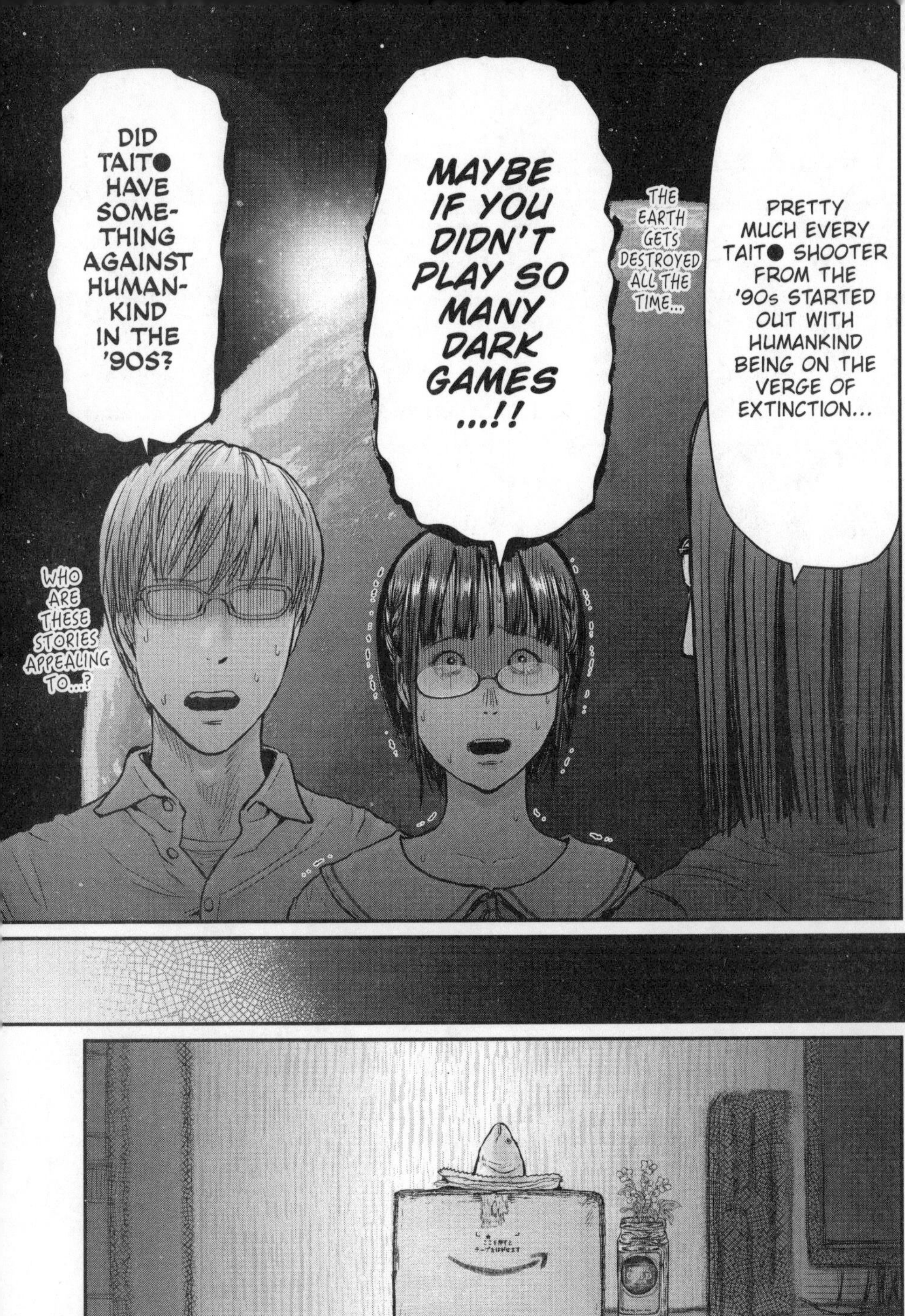
PRETTY MUCH EVERY TAIT● SHOOTER FROM THE '90s STARTED OUT WITH HUMANKIND BEING ON THE VERGE OF EXTINCTION...
THE EARTH GETS DESTROYED ALL THE TIME...
MAYBE IF YOU DIDN'T PLAY SO MANY DARK GAMES ...!!
DID TAIT● HAVE SOMETHING AGAINST HUMANKIND IN THE '90S?
WHO ARE THESE STORIES APPEALING TO...?

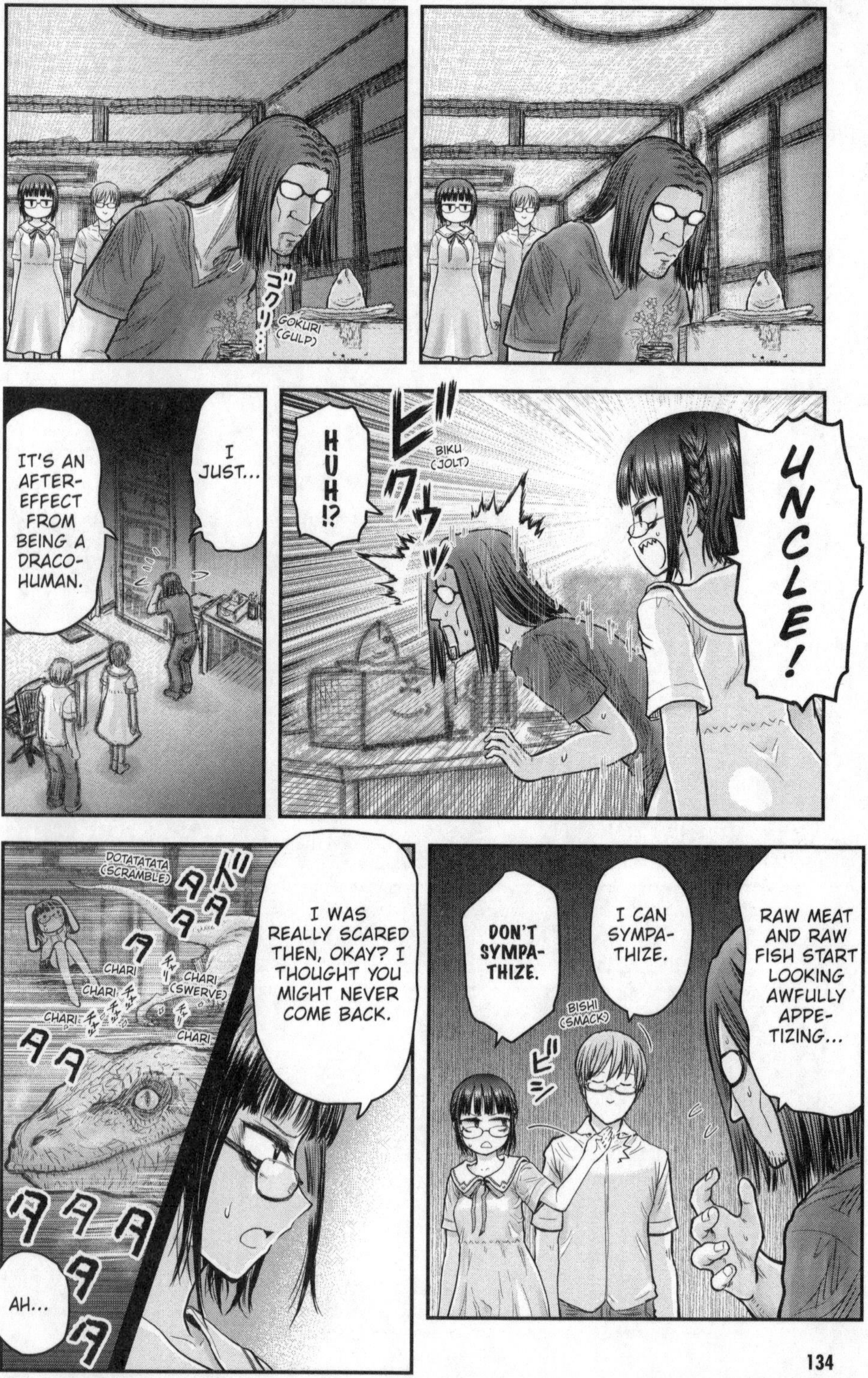
GOKURI (GULP)
UNCLE!
BIKU (JOLT)
HUH!?
I JUST...
IT'S AN AFTER-EFFECT FROM BEING A DRACO-HUMAN.
RAW MEAT AND RAW FISH START LOOKING AWFULLY APPE-TIZING...
I CAN SYMPA-THIZE.
DON'T SYMPA-THIZE.
BISHI (SMACK)
I WAS REALLY SCARED THEN, OKAY? I THOUGHT YOU MIGHT NEVER COME BACK.
DOTATATATA (SCRAMBLE)
CHARI CHARI (SWERVE)
CHARI
CHARI
CHARI
CHARI
AH...

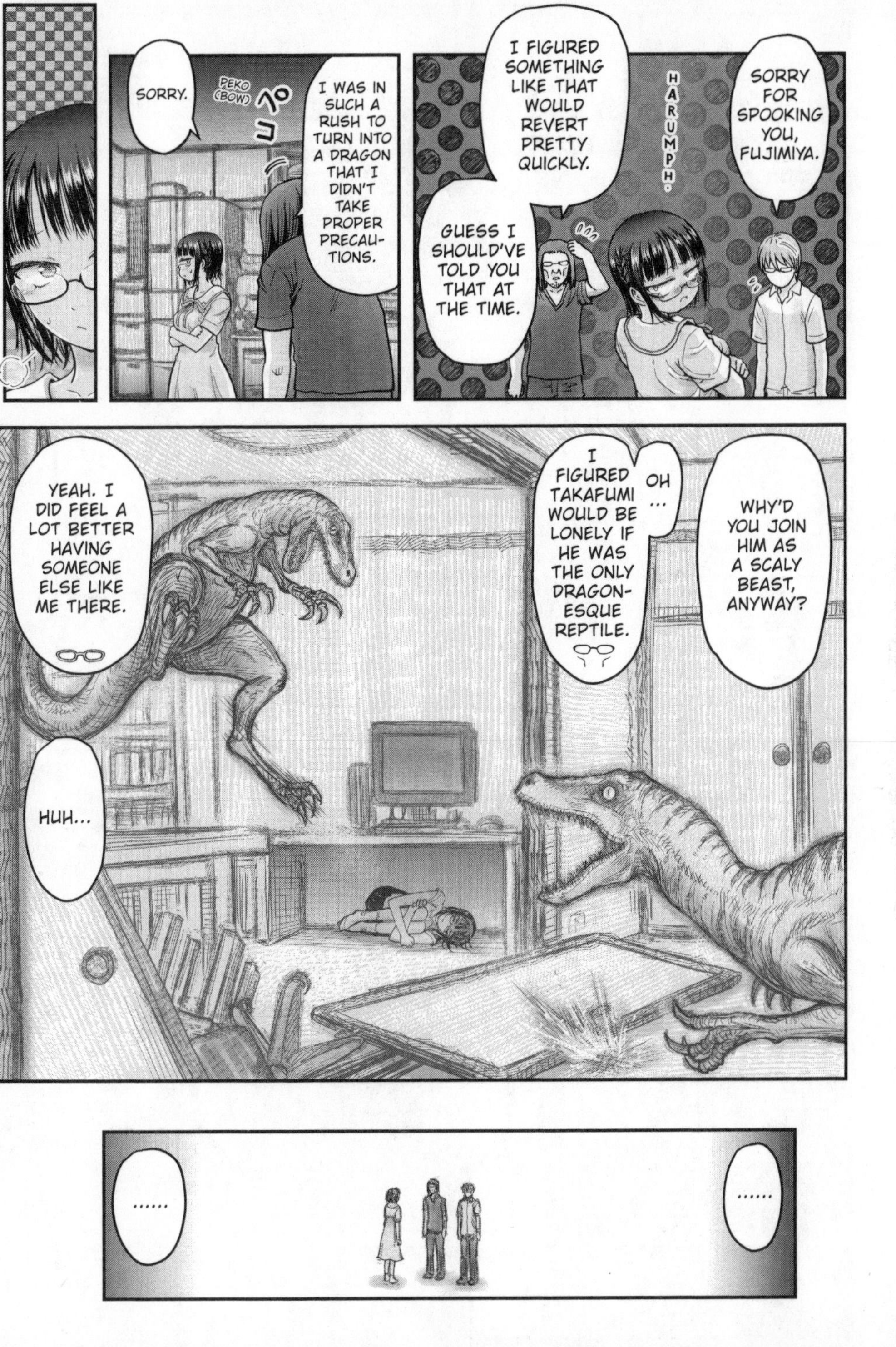

SORRY FOR SPOOKING YOU, FUJIMIYA.
HARUMPH.
I FIGURED SOMETHING LIKE THAT WOULD REVERT PRETTY QUICKLY.
GUESS I SHOULD'VE TOLD YOU THAT AT THE TIME.
I WAS IN SUCH A RUSH TO TURN INTO A DRAGON THAT I DIDN'T TAKE PROPER PRECAU-TIONS.
PEKO (BOW)
SORRY.
WHY'D YOU JOIN HIM AS A SCALY BEAST, ANYWAY?
OH ...
I FIGURED TAKAFUMI WOULD BE LONELY IF HE WAS THE ONLY DRAGON-ESQUE REPTILE.
YEAH. I DID FEEL A LOT BETTER HAVING SOMEONE ELSE LIKE ME THERE.
HUH...
......
......

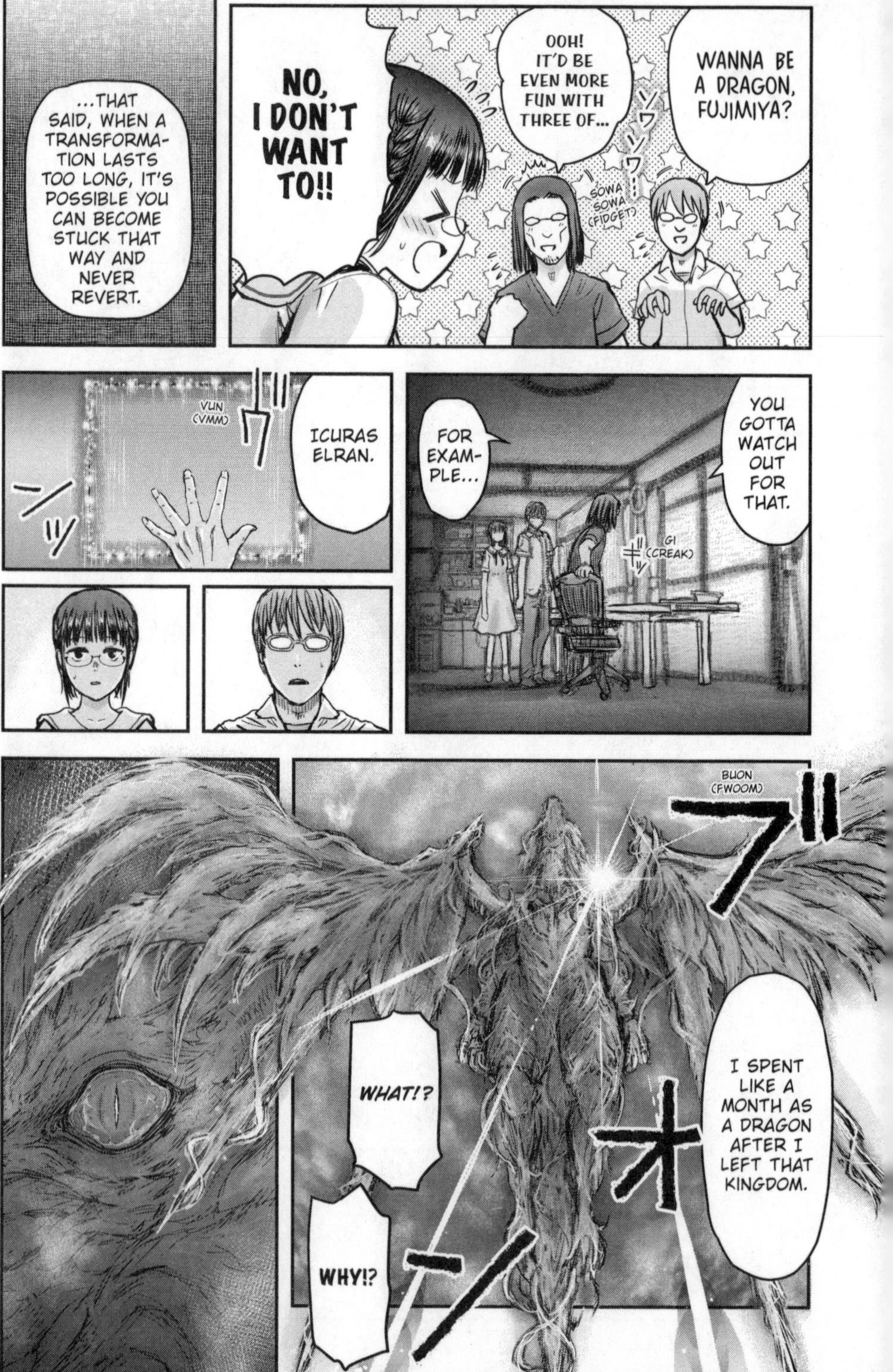
WANNA BE A DRAGON, FUJIMIYA?
OOH! IT'D BE EVEN MORE FUN WITH THREE OF...
SOWA SOWA (FIDGET)
NO, I DON'T WANT TO!!
...THAT SAID, WHEN A TRANSFORMATION LASTS TOO LONG, IT'S POSSIBLE YOU CAN BECOME STUCK THAT WAY AND NEVER REVERT.
YOU GOTTA WATCH OUT FOR THAT.
GI (CREAK)
FOR EXAMPLE...
ICURAS ELRAN.
VUN (VMM)
BUON (FWOOM)
I SPENT LIKE A MONTH AS A DRAGON AFTER I LEFT THAT KINGDOM.
WHAT!?
WHY!?

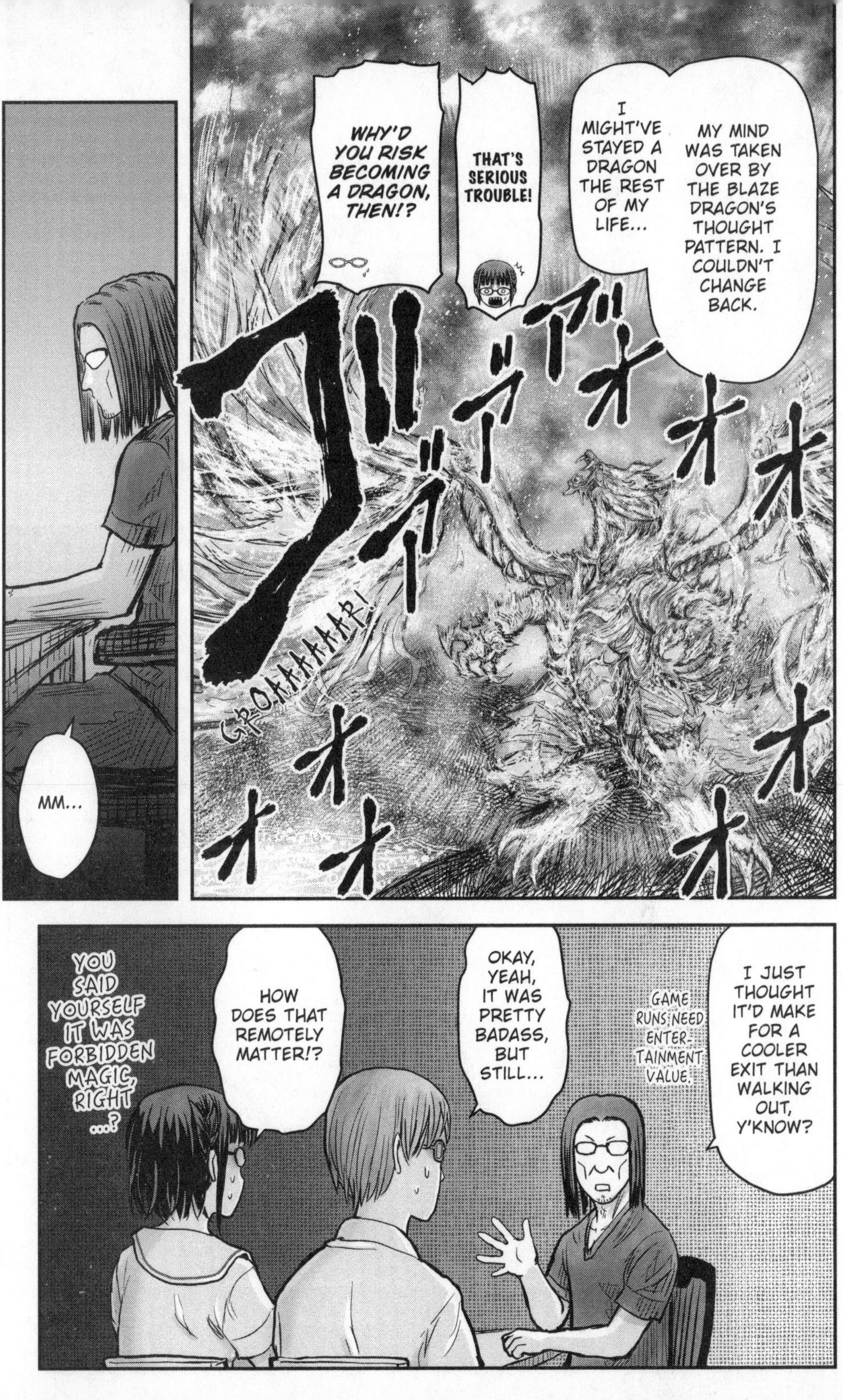
MY MIND WAS TAKEN OVER BY THE BLAZE DRAGON'S THOUGHT PATTERN. I COULDN'T CHANGE BACK.
I MIGHT'VE STAYED A DRAGON THE REST OF MY LIFE...
THAT'S SERIOUS TROUBLE!
WHY'D YOU RISK BECOMING A DRAGON, THEN!?
GROAAAAAAAR!
MM...
I JUST THOUGHT IT'D MAKE FOR A COOLER EXIT THAN WALKING OUT, Y'KNOW?
GAME RUNS NEED ENTER-TAINMENT VALUE.
OKAY, YEAH, IT WAS PRETTY BADASS, BUT STILL...
HOW DOES THAT REMOTELY MATTER!?
YOU SAID YOURSELF IT WAS FORBIDDEN MAGIC, RIGHT...?

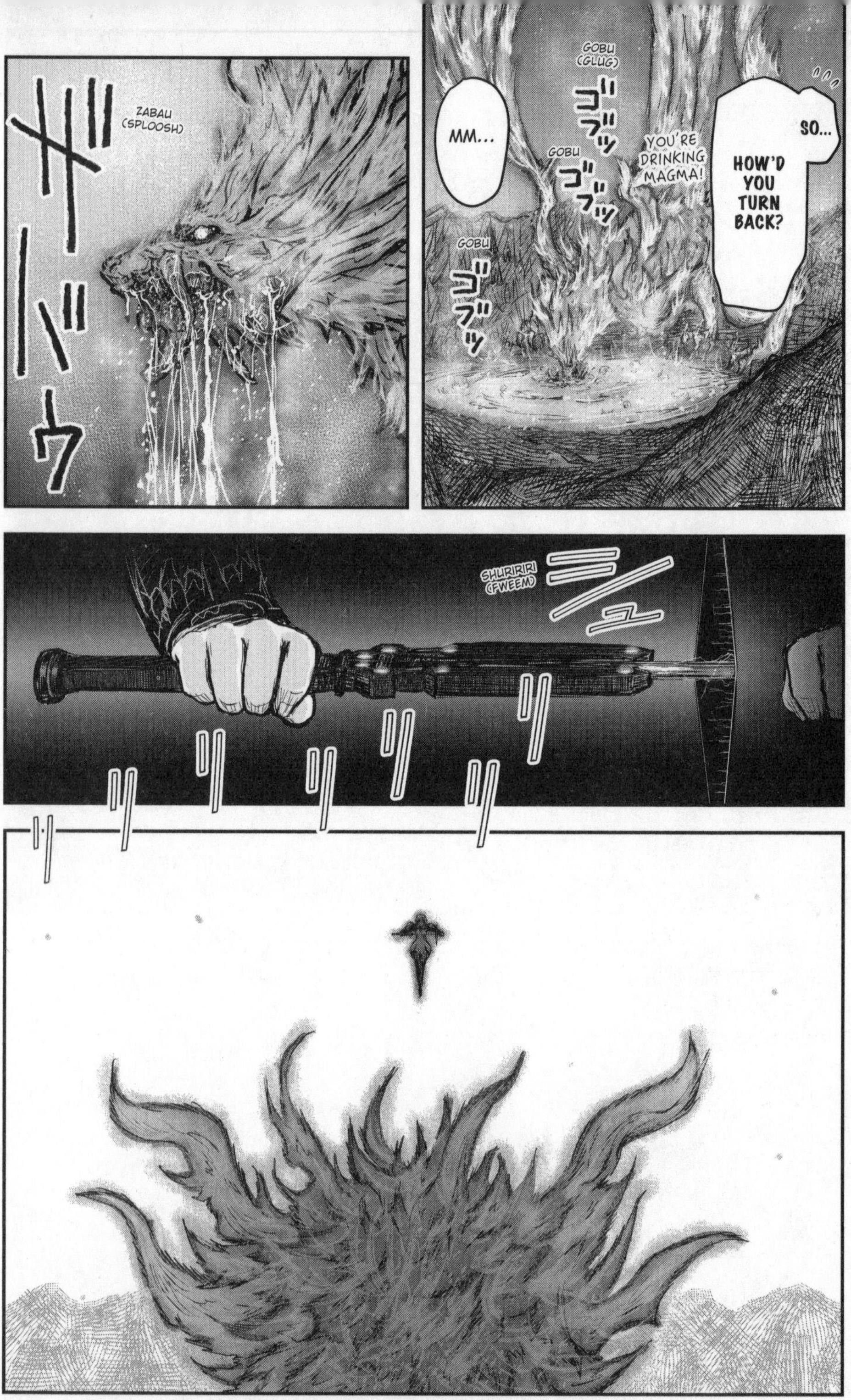
SO...
HOW'D YOU TURN BACK?
YOU'RE DRINKING MAGMA!
GOBU (GLUG)
ゴブッ
GOBU
ゴブッ
MM...
GOBU
ゴブッ
ZABAU (SPLOOSH)
SHURIRIRI (FWEEM)
シュリリリリリリ

RIN
(TING)

I FINALLY FOUND YOU.

GROAAAAAR!

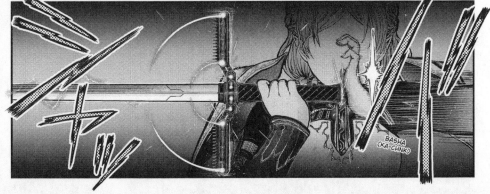

BASHA
(KA-CHNK)

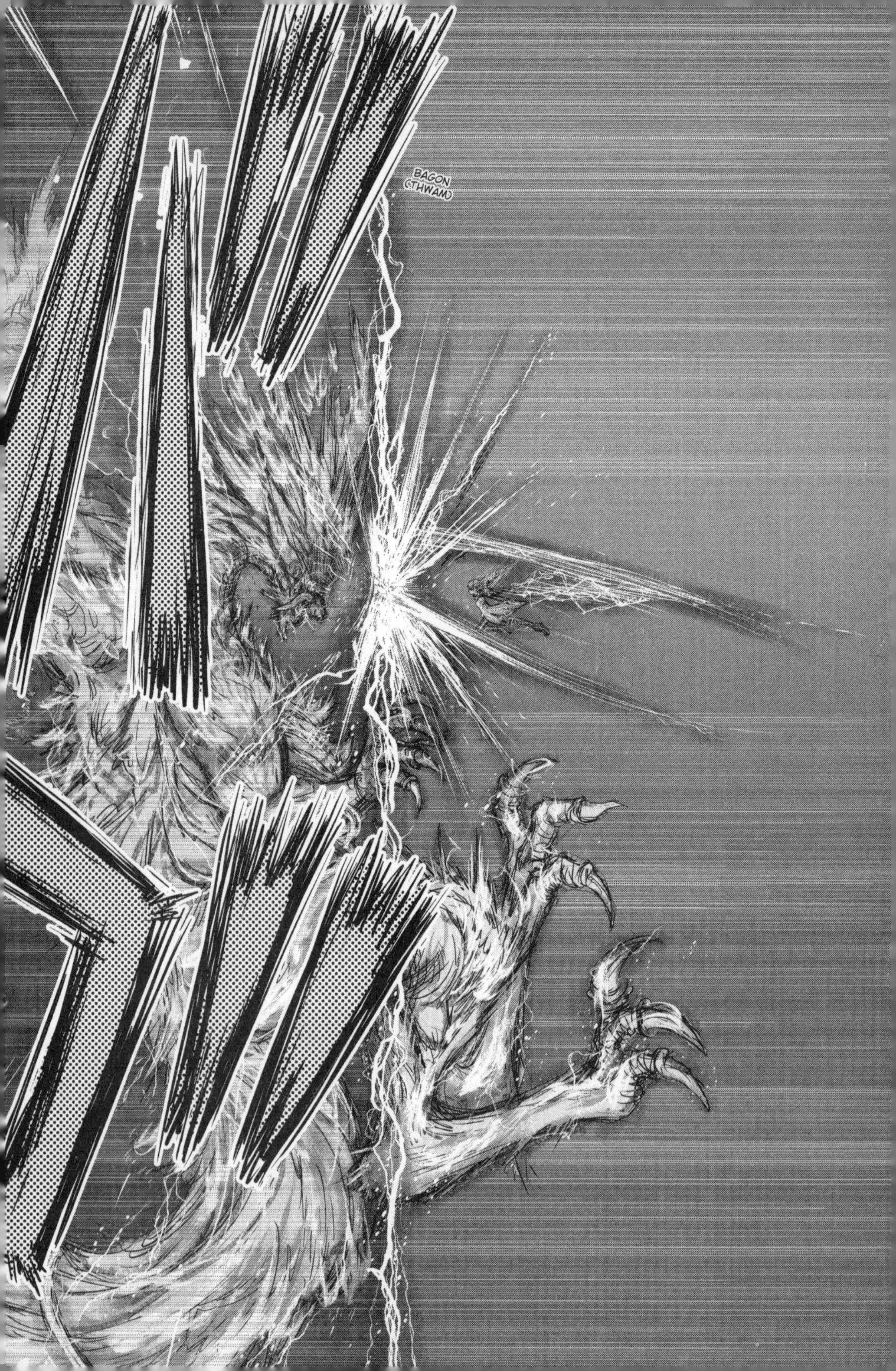
BAGON
(THWAM)

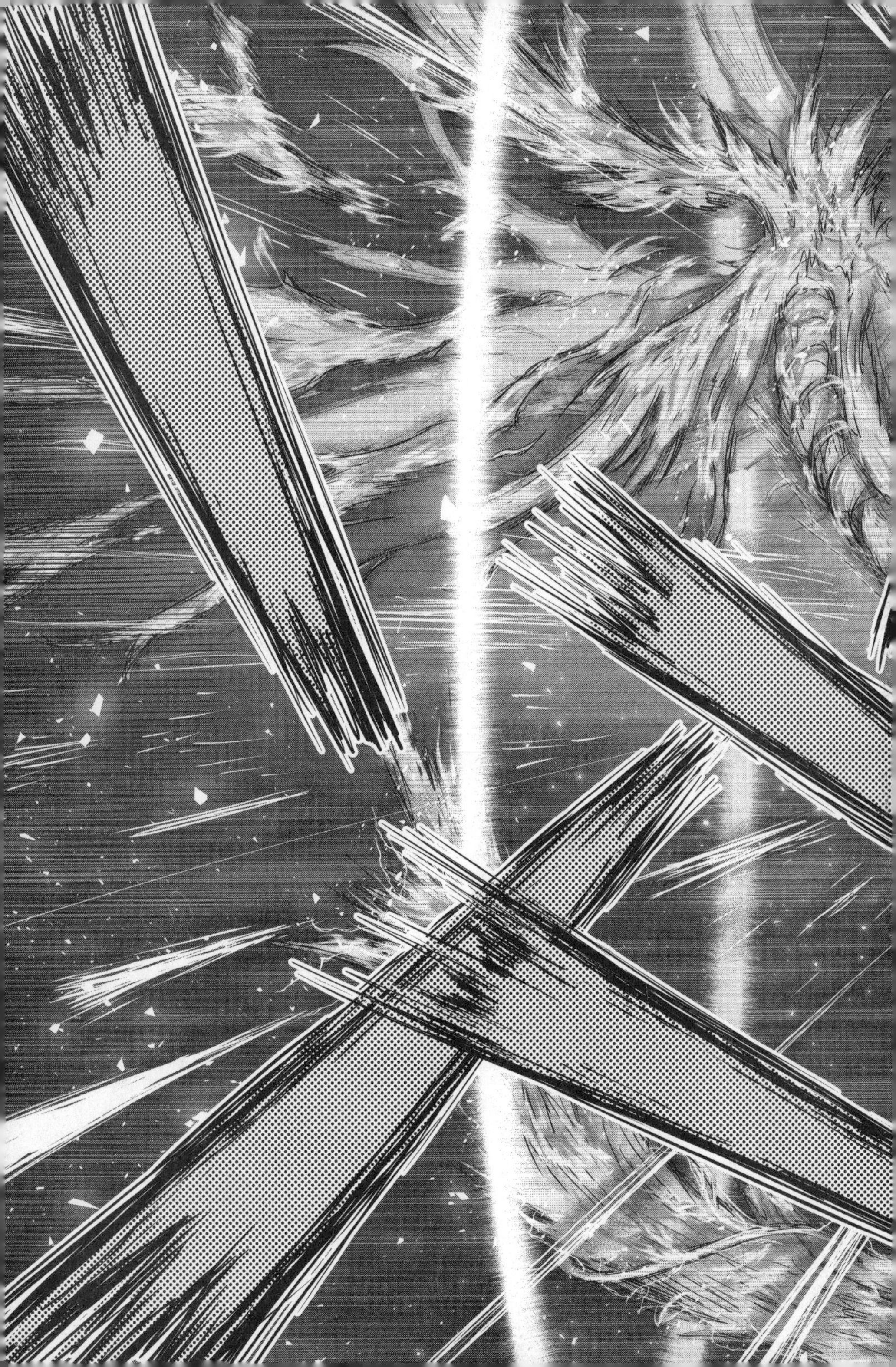

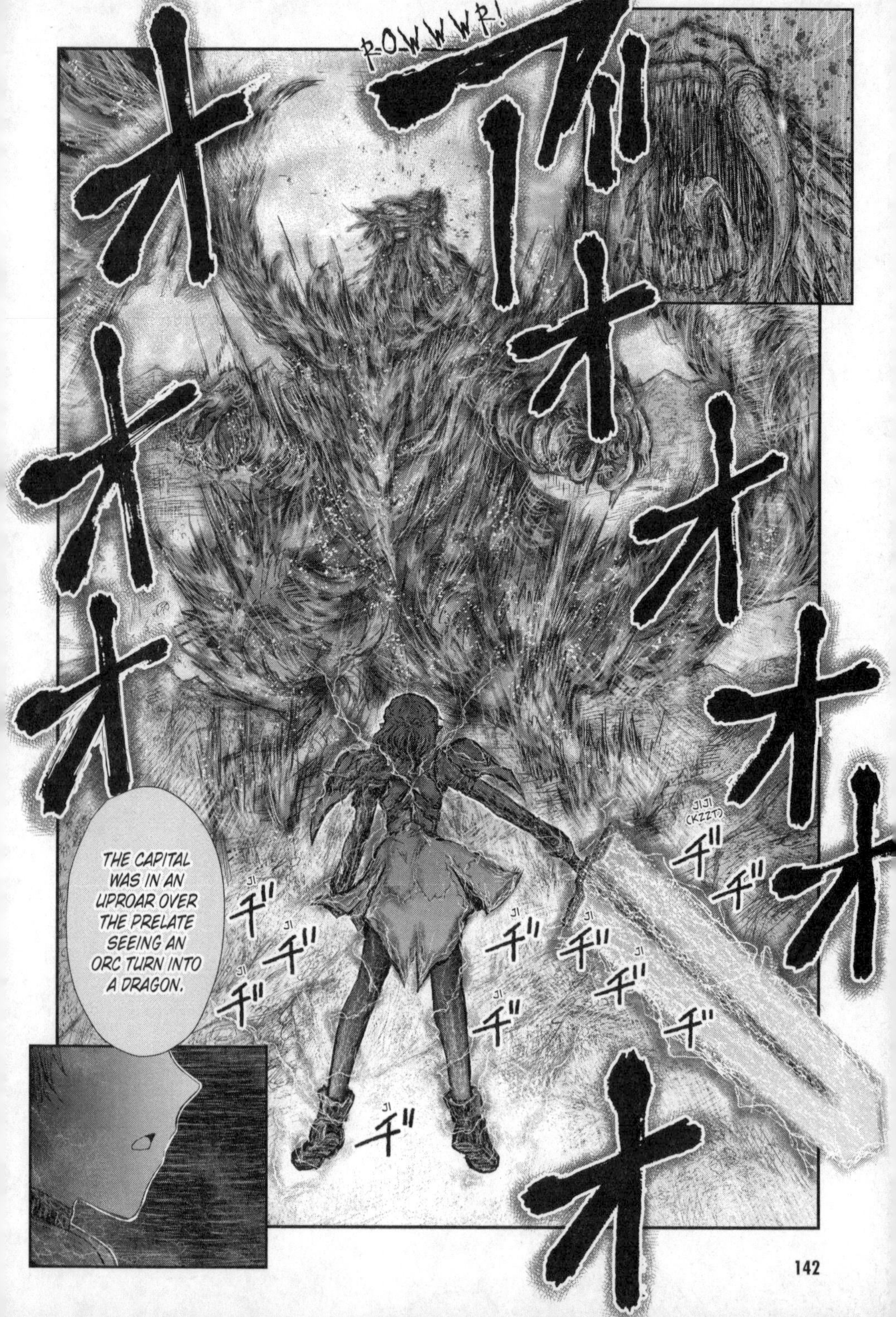
R-O-W-W-W-R!
JIJI (KZZT)
THE CAPITAL WAS IN AN UPROAR OVER THE PRELATE SEEING AN ORC TURN INTO A DRAGON.
JI
JI
JI
JI
JI
JI
JI
JI

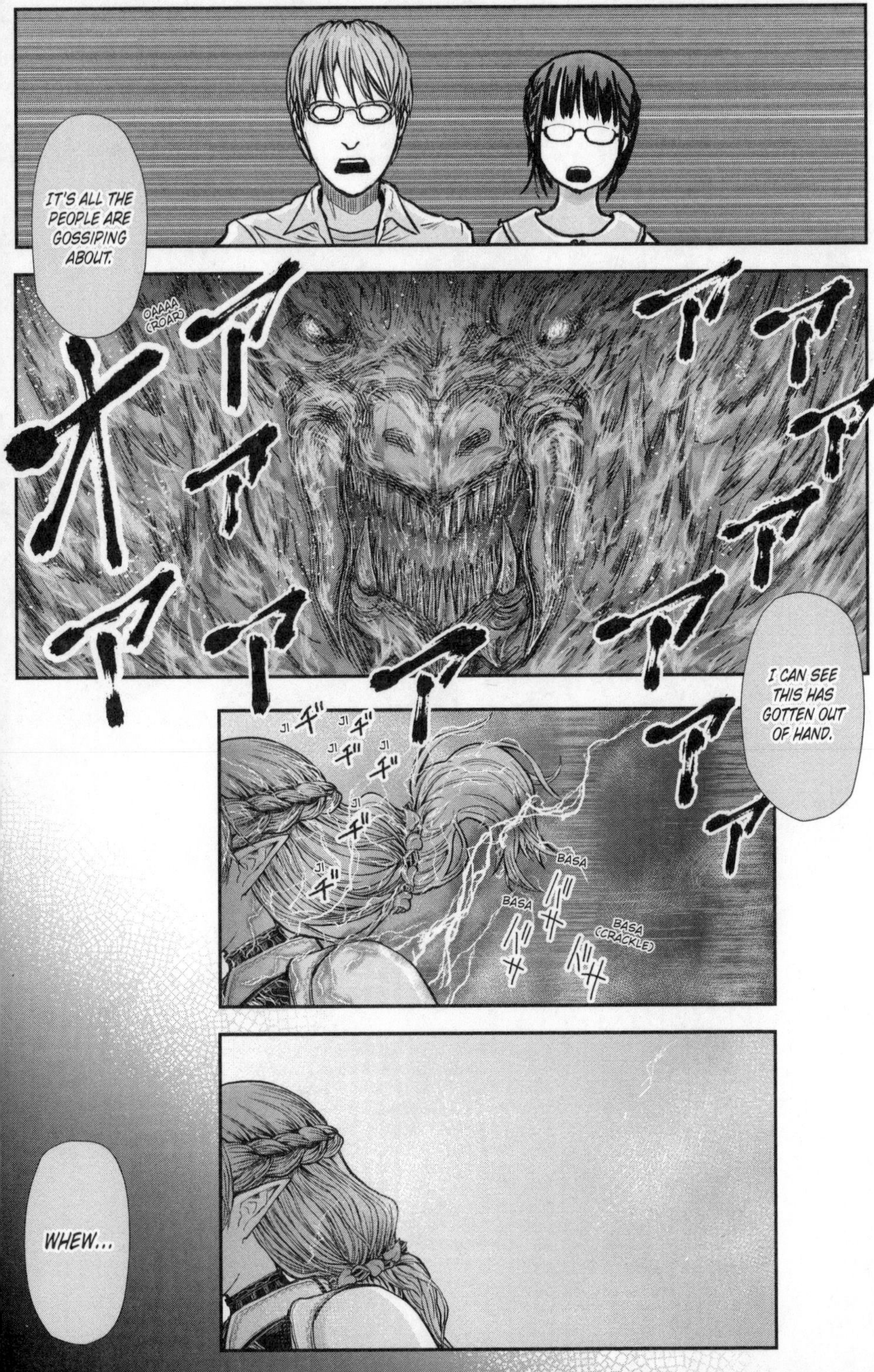
IT'S ALL THE PEOPLE ARE GOSSIPING ABOUT.
OAAAA (ROAR)
I CAN SEE THIS HAS GOTTEN OUT OF HAND.
JI
JI
JI
JI
JI
JI
BASA
BASA
BASA (CRACKLE)
WHEW...

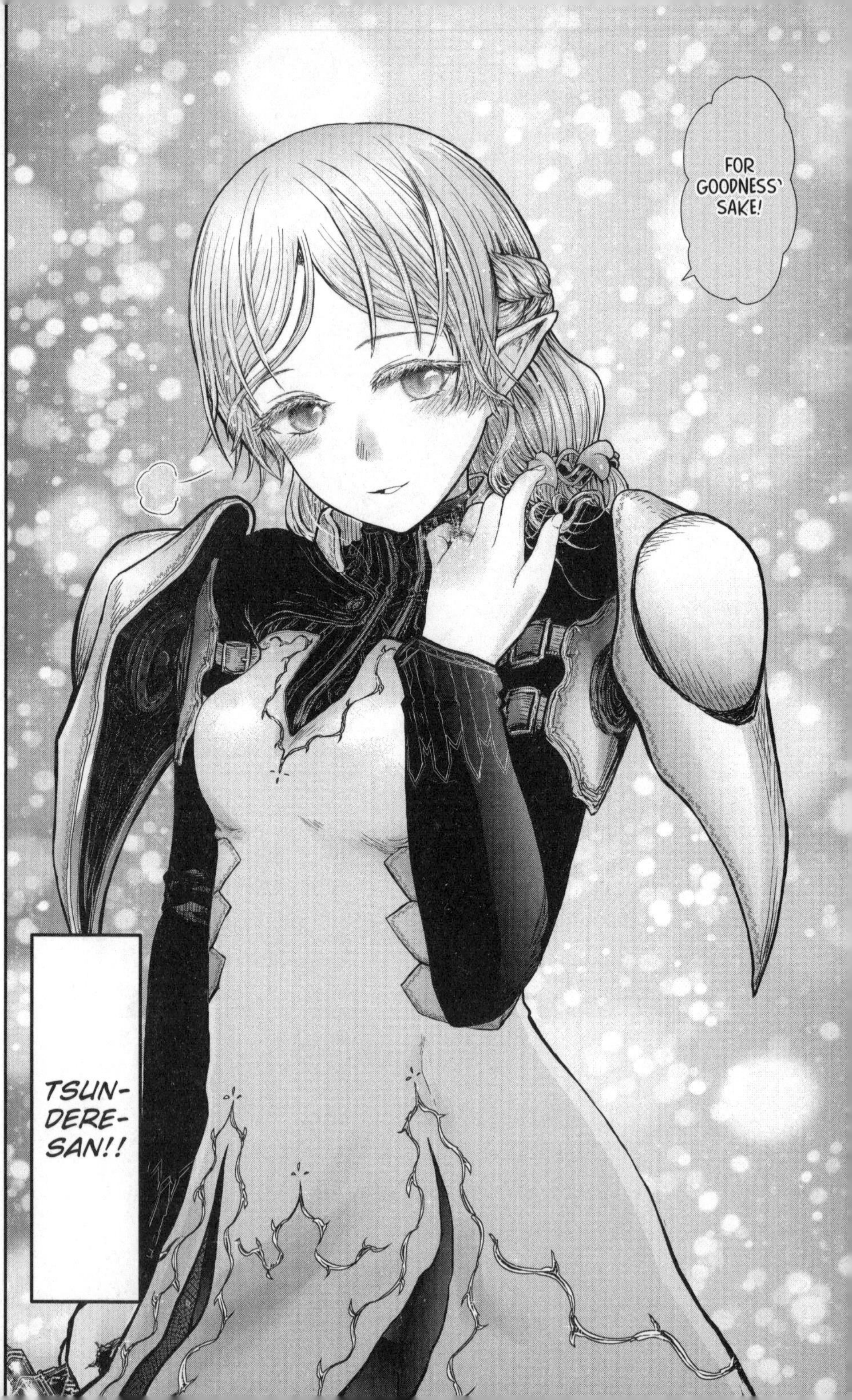
FOR GOODNESS' SAKE!
TSUN-DERE-SAN!!

Summer 2018

This was a summer of record-breaking high temperatures. In Eastern Japan, temperatures reached 1.7°C above average—the highest in recorded history. In Western Japan, they reached 1.1°C above average—the second-highest in recorded history. Kumagaya, Saitama, reached 41.1°C (105.98°F), the highest temperature in Japanese history.
Following this event, the phrase "catastrophic heat" was nominated for 2018's New Word/Trending Word Prize.

TIPS

UNCLE from ANOTHER WORLD

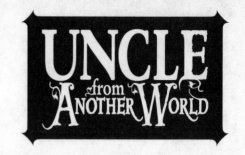

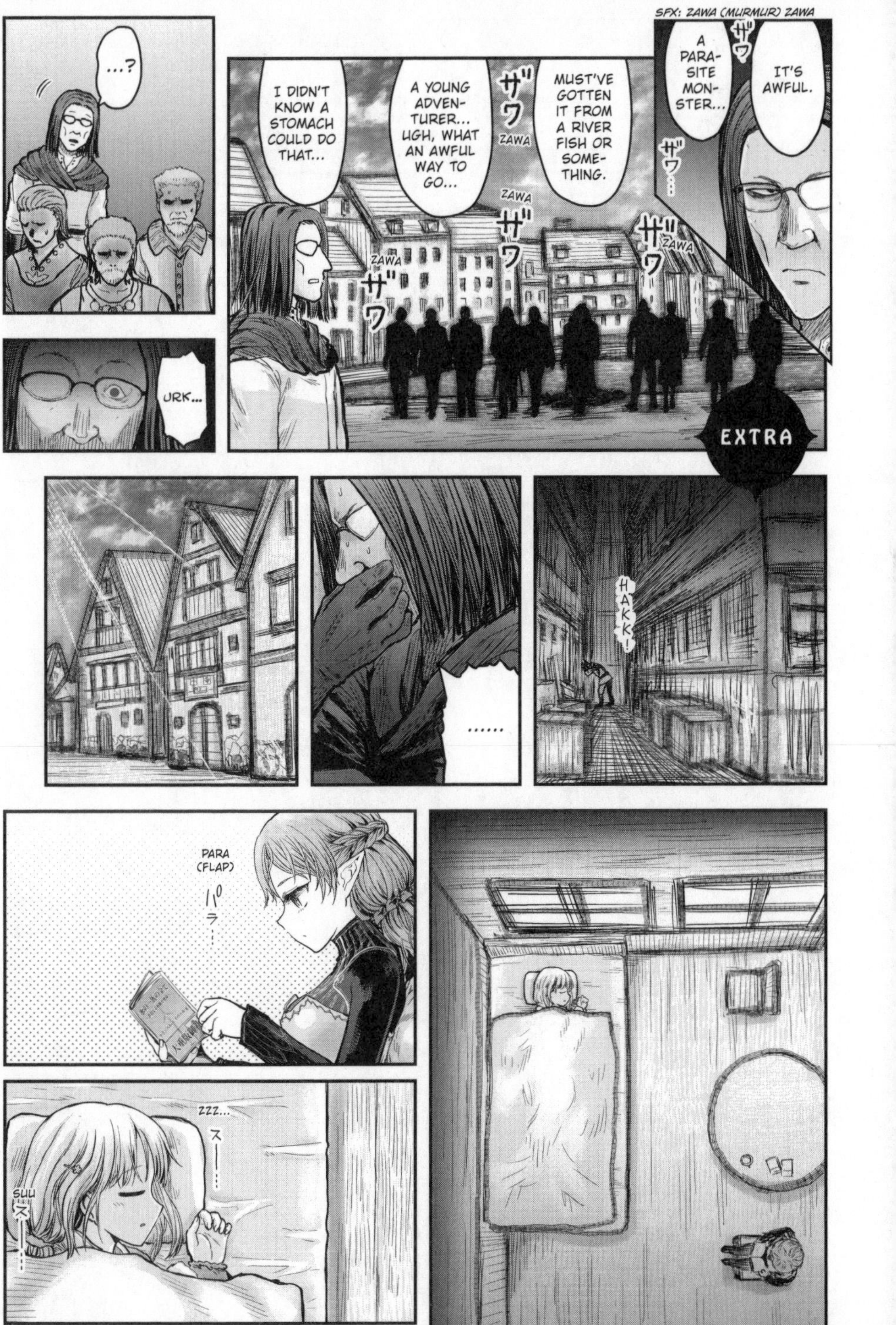
SFX: ZAWA (MURMUR) ZAWA
ザワ
IT'S AWFUL.
A PARASITE MONSTER...
ザワ…
MUST'VE GOTTEN IT FROM A RIVER FISH OR SOMETHING.
ザワ ZAWA
A YOUNG ADVENTURER... UGH, WHAT AN AWFUL WAY TO GO...
I DIDN'T KNOW A STOMACH COULD DO THAT...
ザワ ZAWA
ZAWA ザワ
ZAWA ザワ
...?
URK...
EXTRA
HAKK!
......
PARA (FLAP)
パラ…
ZZZ...
スー…
SUU
スー…

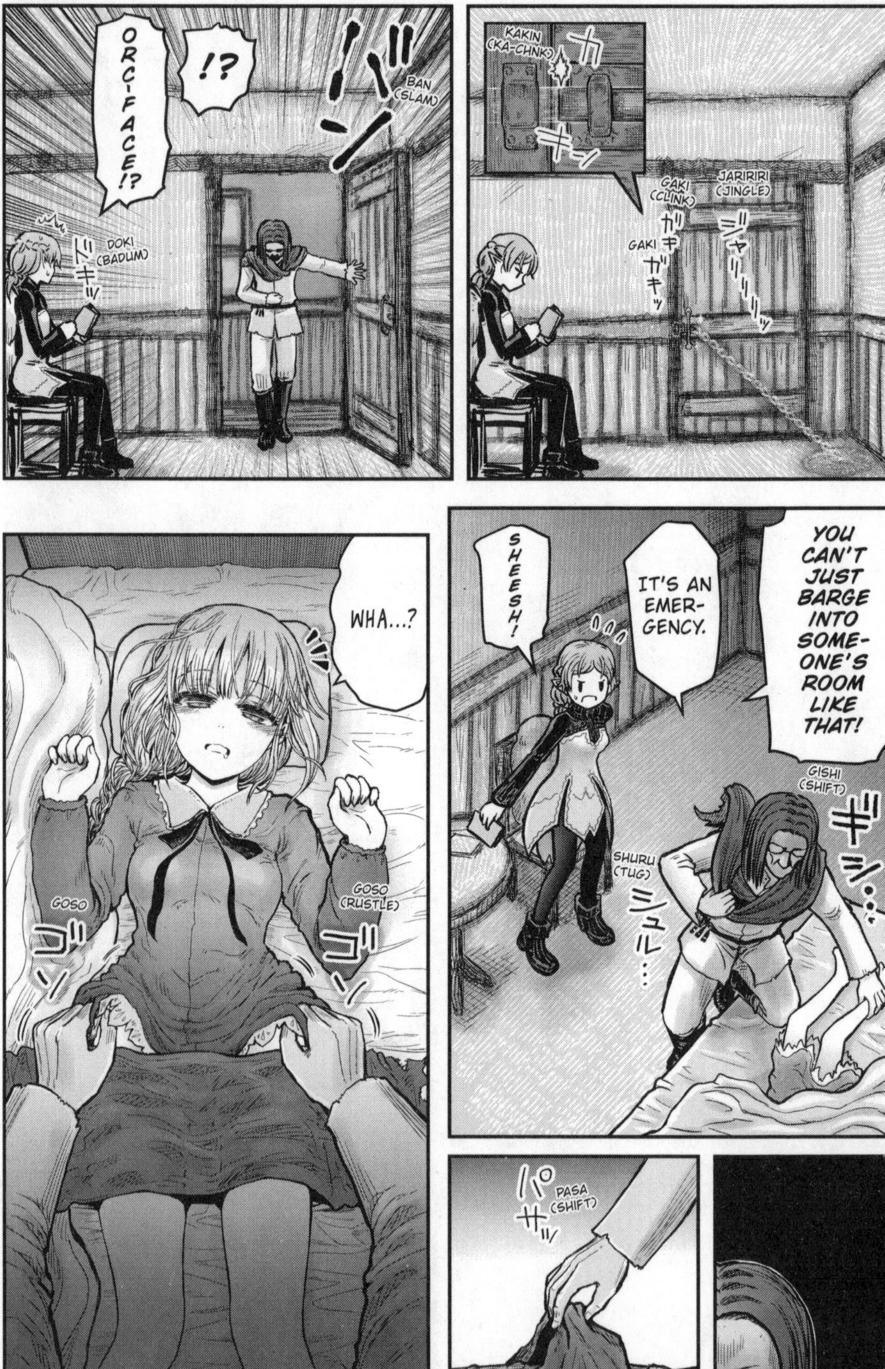
KAKIN (KA-CHNK)
GAKI (CLINK)
GAKI
JARIRIRI (JINGLE)
ORC-FACE!?
!?
BAN (SLAM)
DOKI (BADUM)
YOU CAN'T JUST BARGE INTO SOMEONE'S ROOM LIKE THAT!
IT'S AN EMERGENCY.
SHEESH!
GISHI (SHIFT)
SHURU (TUG)
PASA (SHIFT)
WHA...?
GOSO (RUSTLE)
GOSO

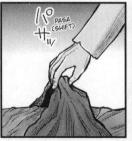

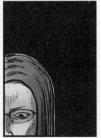

......

!?

DOKI
(TH-THUMP)

BA
(BAM)

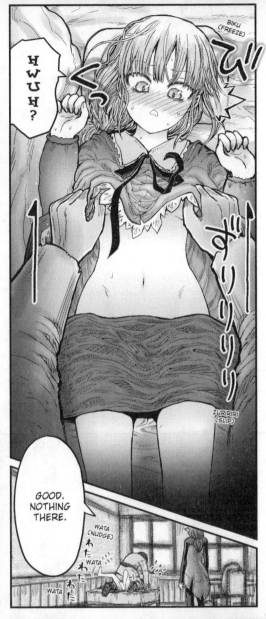

BIKU
(FREEZE)

HWUH?

く？

ずりりりり

ZURIRIRI
(SLIP)

GOOD.
NOTHING
THERE.

WATA
(NUDGE)

WATA

WATA

WATA

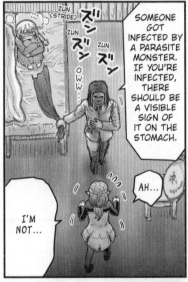

ズン
ZUN
(STRIDE)

ZUN

ZUN

OWW...

AH...

I'M
NOT...

SOMEONE
GOT
INFECTED BY
A PARASITE
MONSTER.
IF YOU'RE
INFECTED,
THERE
SHOULD BE
A VISIBLE
SIGN OF
IT ON THE
STOMACH.

NO,
HOLD
ON...

KYUUUN
(TWINGE)

KACHICHI
(KSHHT)

I'M FINE,
REALLY!

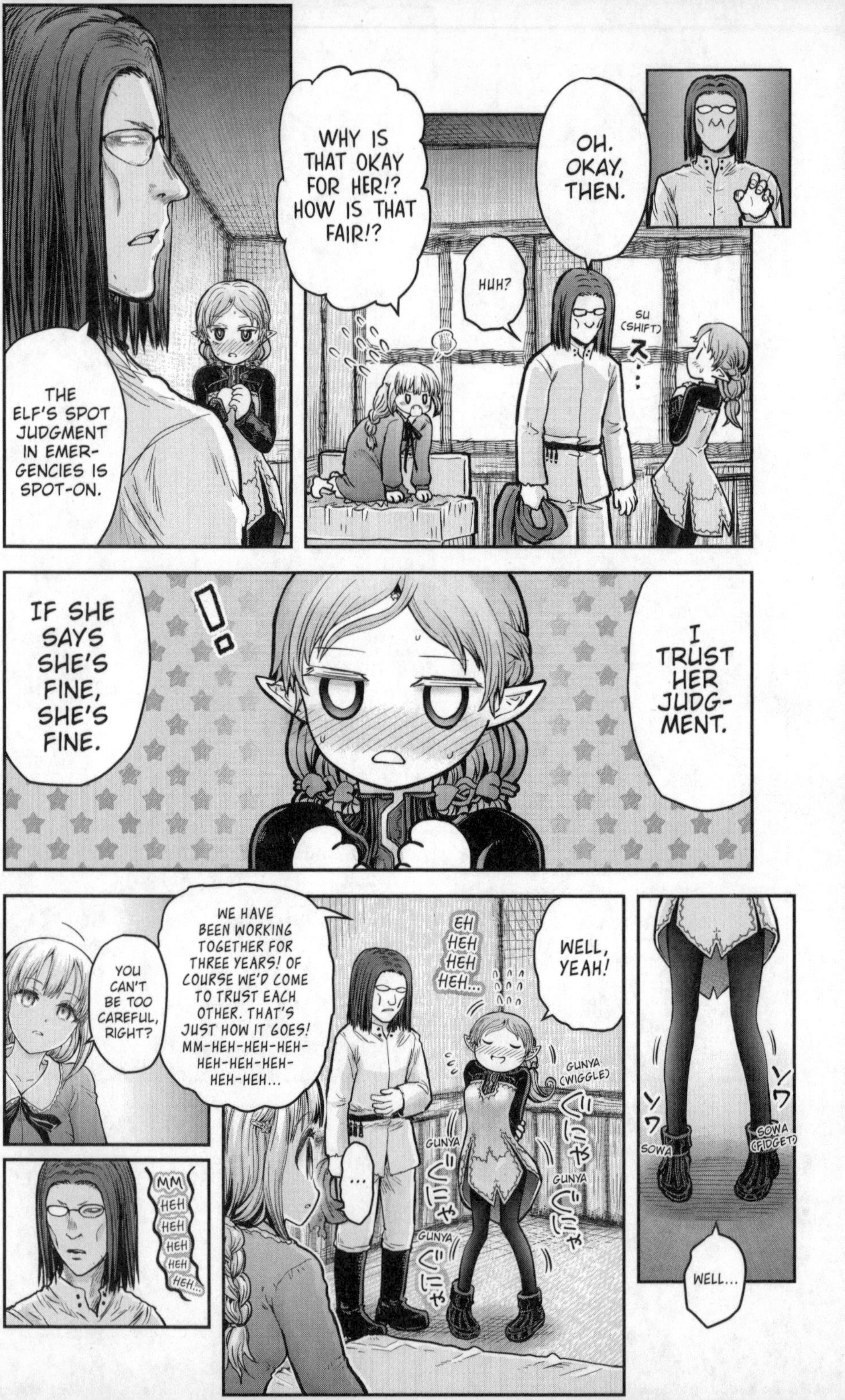
OH. OKAY, THEN.
WHY IS THAT OKAY FOR HER!? HOW IS THAT FAIR!?
HUH?
SU (SHIFT)
THE ELF'S SPOT JUDGMENT IN EMERGENCIES IS SPOT-ON.
I TRUST HER JUDGMENT.
IF SHE SAYS SHE'S FINE, SHE'S FINE.
SOWA (FIDGET)
SOWA
WELL...
WELL, YEAH!
EH HEH HEH HEH...
WE HAVE BEEN WORKING TOGETHER FOR THREE YEARS! OF COURSE WE'D COME TO TRUST EACH OTHER. THAT'S JUST HOW IT GOES! MM-HEH-HEH-HEH-HEH-HEH-HEH-HEH-HEH...
GUNYA (WIGGLE)
GUNYA
GUNYA
GUNYA
...
YOU CAN'T BE TOO CAREFUL, RIGHT?
MM HEH HEH HEH HEH HEH...

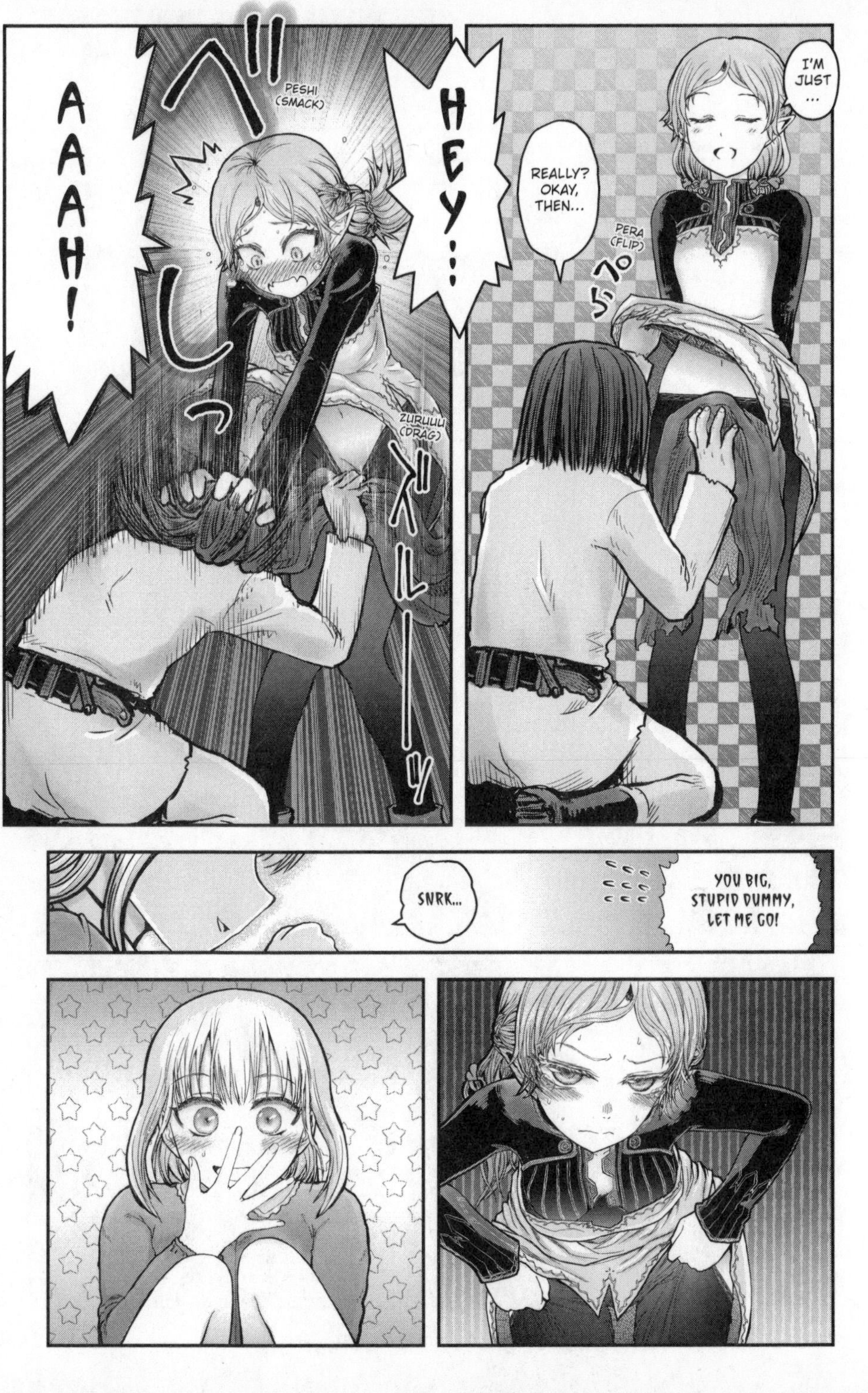
I'M JUST ...
REALLY? OKAY, THEN...
PERA (FLIP)
HEY...!
PESHI (SMACK)
AAAAH!
ZURUUU (DRAG)
YOU BIG, STUPID DUMMY, LET ME GO!
SNRK...

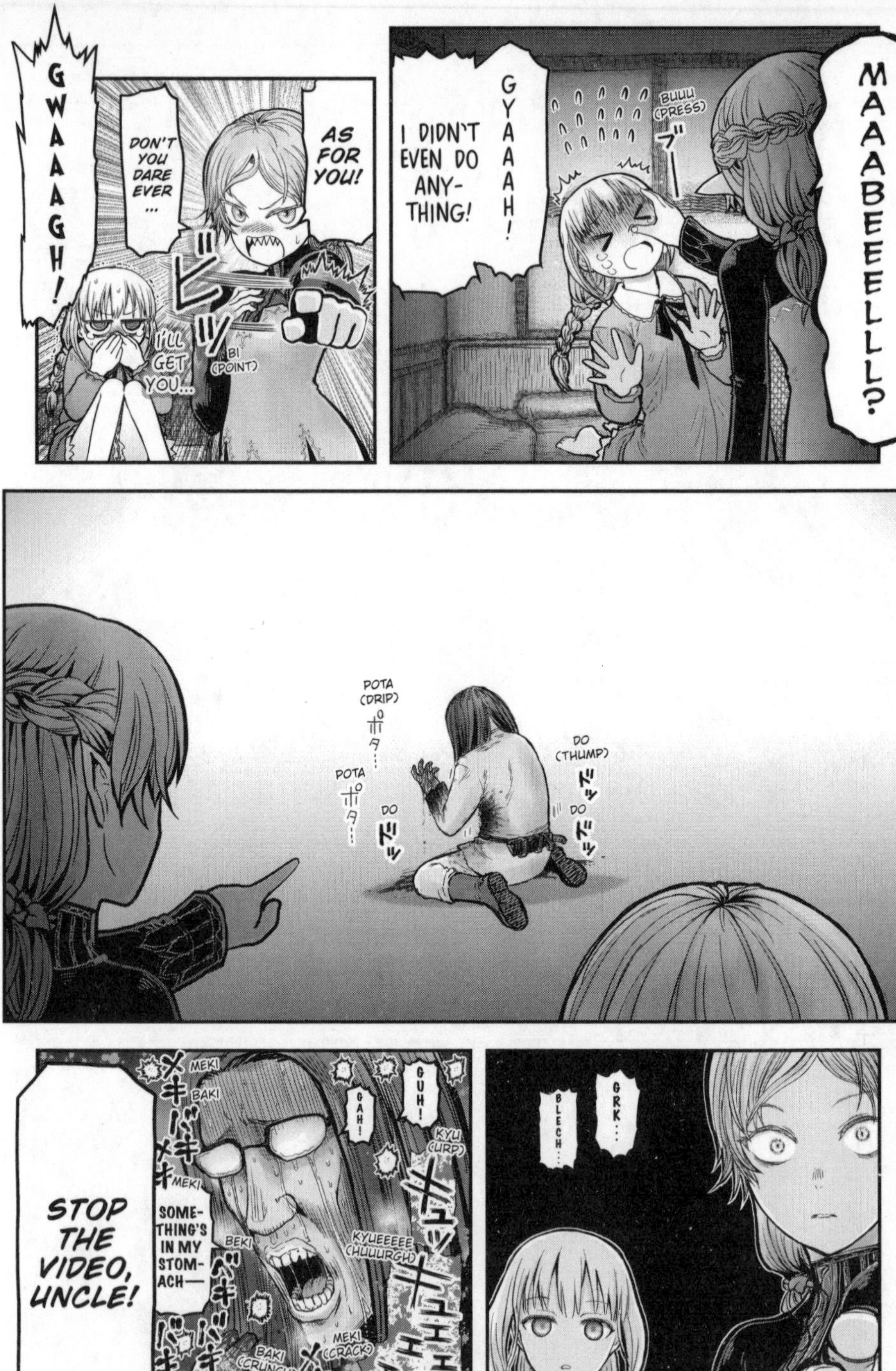
MAAABEEEELLLL?
BUUU (PRESS)
GYAAAH!
I DIDN'T EVEN DO ANYTHING!
AS FOR YOU!
DON'T YOU DARE EVER ...
GWAAAGH!
BI (POINT)
I'LL GET YOU...
POTA (DRIP)
POTA
DO
DO (THUMP)
DO
GRK...
BLECH...
GUH!
GAH!
KYU (URP)
MEKI
BAKI
MEKI
SOMETHING'S IN MY STOMACH—
BEKI
KYUEEEEE (HUUURGH)
MEKI (CRACK)
BAKI (CRUNCH)
BAKI
BAKI
STOP THE VIDEO, UNCLE!

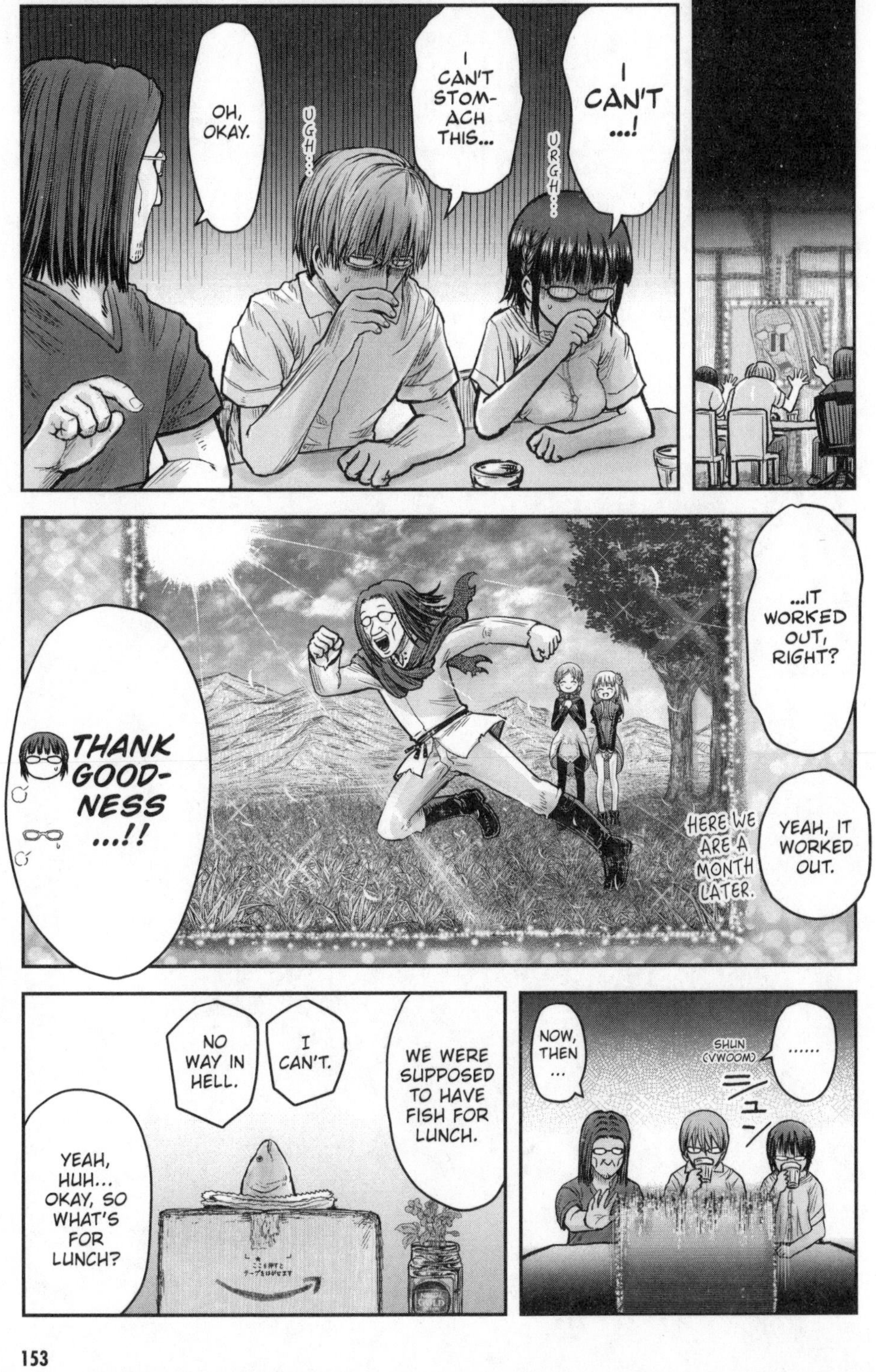
I CAN'T ...!
URGH...
I CAN'T STOMACH THIS...
UGH...
OH, OKAY.
...IT WORKED OUT, RIGHT?
YEAH, IT WORKED OUT.
HERE WE ARE A MONTH LATER.
THANK GOODNESS ...!!
......
SHUN (VWOOM)
NOW, THEN ...
WE WERE SUPPOSED TO HAVE FISH FOR LUNCH.
I CAN'T.
NO WAY IN HELL.
YEAH, HUH... OKAY, SO WHAT'S FOR LUNCH?

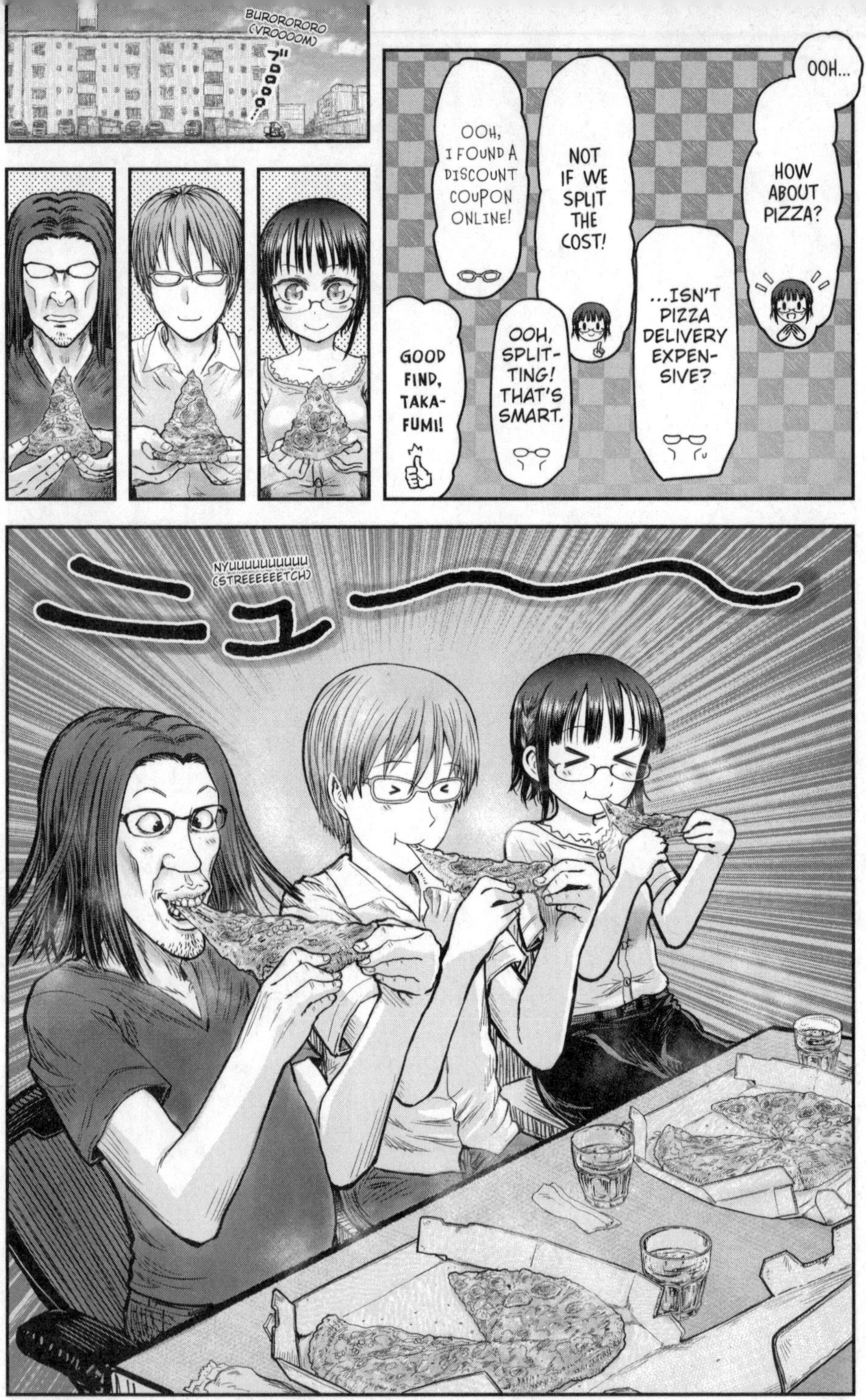

OOH...
HOW ABOUT PIZZA?
...ISN'T PIZZA DELIVERY EXPEN-SIVE?
NOT IF WE SPLIT THE COST!
OOH, SPLIT-TING! THAT'S SMART.
OOH, I FOUND A DISCOUNT COUPON ONLINE!
GOOD FIND, TAKA-FUMI!
BURORORORO (VROOOOM)
NYUUUUUUUUUUU (STREEEEEETCH)

Translation Notes

COMMON HONORIFICS

no honorific: Indicates familiarity or closeness; if used without permission or reason, addressing someone in this manner would constitute an insult.

-san: The Japanese equivalent of Mr./Mrs./Miss. If a situation calls for politeness, this is the fail-safe honorific.

-sama: Conveys great respect; may also indicate that the social status of the speaker is lower than that of the addressee.

-dono: Roughly equivalent to "master" or "milord."

-kun: Used most often when referring to boys, this indicates affection or familiarity. Occasionally used by older men among their peers, but it may also be used by anyone referring to a person of lower standing.

-chan: An affectionate honorific indicating familiarity used mostly in reference to girls; also used in reference to cute persons or animals regardless of gender.

-senpai: An honorific for one's senior classmate, colleague, etc., although not as senior or respected as a *sensei* (teacher).

¥100 is approximately $1 USD.

A●ien Soldier, Uncle's favorite game, is an action title from 1995 known for its extreme emphasis on elaborate boss fights and for being impossibly ambitious in scope.

PAGE 11

"Let's together!" is the catchphrase of the Japanese comedian Lou Ohshiba, who was popular in the 1990s.

PAGE 26

So●ic and its sequels are video games starring the flagship mascot of Se●a.

D●namite Headdy is a 1994 platformer from the creators of *A●ien Soldier*.

PAGE 33

Kuroki Tenma is a character from *A●ien Soldier*. In him resides the evil Epsilon-1, the counterpart to the heroic player character, Epsilon-2.

PAGE 36

Shinrei Jusatsushi● Taroumaru is a 1997 Saturn side-scrolling action game in which players control psychic ninjas. Due to a very small print run, it is one of the console's rarest games.

PAGE 44

The **M●ga Drive** was a 1988 16-bit home video game console released by Se●a touted for its "blast processing," and was released in North America under a different name. At the time, the console and its rivals emphasized the fact that they were **16-bit** systems and therefore superior to the previous generation's hardware—though what exactly "bits" were was unexplained in advertisements.

The **Se●a Saturn** was a 1994 home console. While capable of 3D graphics, its original emphasis on 2D sprite graphics put it at a disadvantage against its competitors.

PAGE 82

Wolfgunblood (one word) is a boss character from *A●ien Soldier.*

PAGE 90

Uncle's illusion of his "fight" with Mabel greatly resembles the battle against Shell Shogun in *A●ien Soldier.*

PAGE 102

Kamegashira Gansaku is another character from *A●ien Soldier*, in whom resides the boss character Shell Shogun.

PAGE 106

The **Undead Hero** is from a 1997 game where players can attack using either silhouettes or mirages.

PAGE 111

Jur●ssic Park is a 1993 action game based on a popular film that was, in turn, based on a book about a theme park filled with artificially-created dinosaurs.

PAGE 118

Suzumiya, while a perfectly common Japanese surname, is a play on words here—combining Fujimiya's name with the Japanese word for "cool" (*suzushii*).

PAGE 122

The **Swords and Firearms Possession Control Law**, originally passed in Japan in 1958, places severe restrictions on sword and gun ownership in Japan—limiting civilian registration of such weapons to ones that are deemed works of art.

PAGE 133

Tait● is a video game, arcade, and toy publisher known not only for their shoot-'em-ups, but also for their adorable dinosaur mascots.

PAGE 144

Tsundere is an archetype common to anime and manga where a character either grows from hating someone to loving someone, or acts especially prickly toward a character they have feelings for.

PAGE 154

Compared with the United States, delivery pizza is very expensive in Japan, often costing two to four times the typical price in the US.

PAGE 173

"Ground Upper" in Japanese sounds very similar to "Grand Upper," so it makes sense that Uncle would mistakenly remember it as "Great Upper." In fact, until the game's composer revealed the actual name of the attack, it was mistranslated as "Grand Upper" for many years.

INSIDE COVER (FRONT)

YuYu H●kusho: Makyou Touitsusen is a 1994 fighting game based on a popular 1990s battle manga about a high school delinquent who becomes a spirit detective.

Tet●is is a puzzle game where players stack and rotate blocks, scoring by completing and clearing lines of blocks. Originally created in the Soviet Union in 1984, it has since become one of the most successful video game series of all time.

UNCLE from ANOTHER WORLD

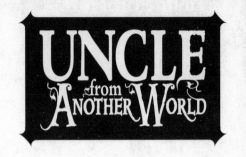

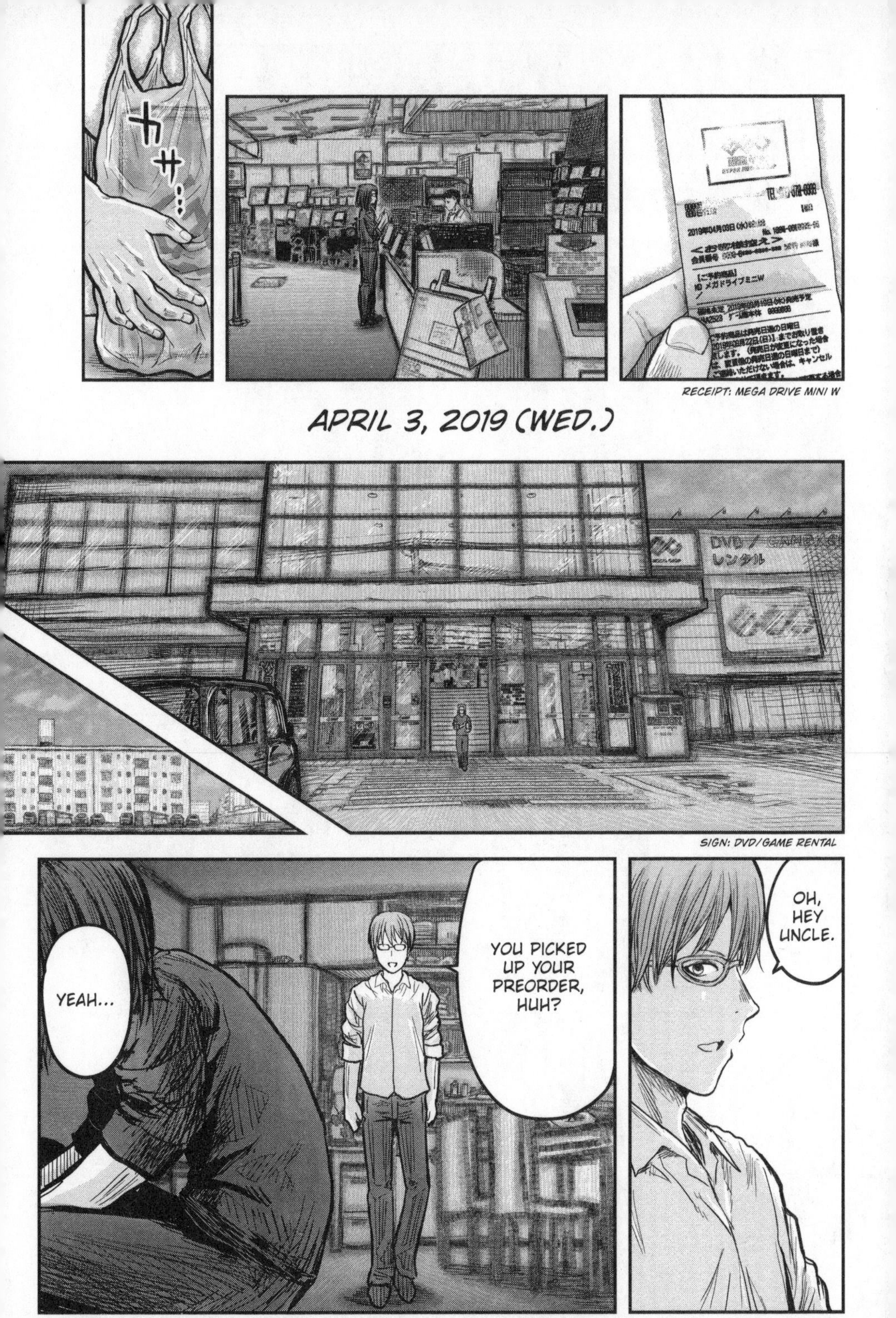
RECEIPT: MEGA DRIVE MINI W
カサ…
APRIL 3, 2019 (WED.)
DVD / GAME レンタル
SIGN: DVD/GAME RENTAL
OH, HEY UNCLE.
YOU PICKED UP YOUR PREORDER, HUH?
YEAH…

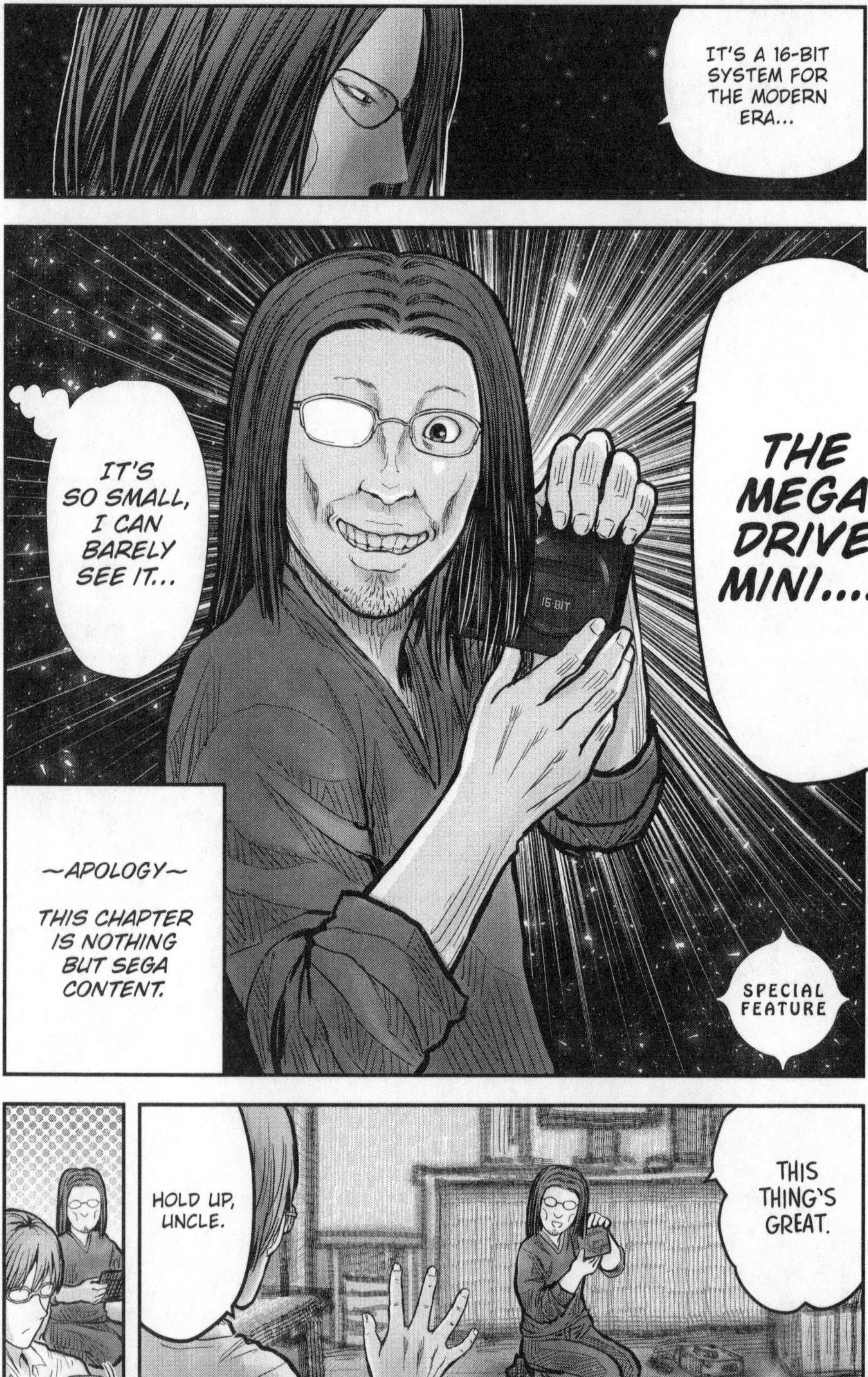
IT'S A 16-BIT SYSTEM FOR THE MODERN ERA...
THE MEGA DRIVE MINI...!
16-BIT
IT'S SO SMALL, I CAN BARELY SEE IT...
SPECIAL FEATURE
~APOLOGY~ THIS CHAPTER IS NOTHING BUT SEGA CONTENT.
THIS THING'S GREAT.
HOLD UP, UNCLE.

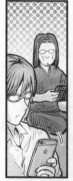

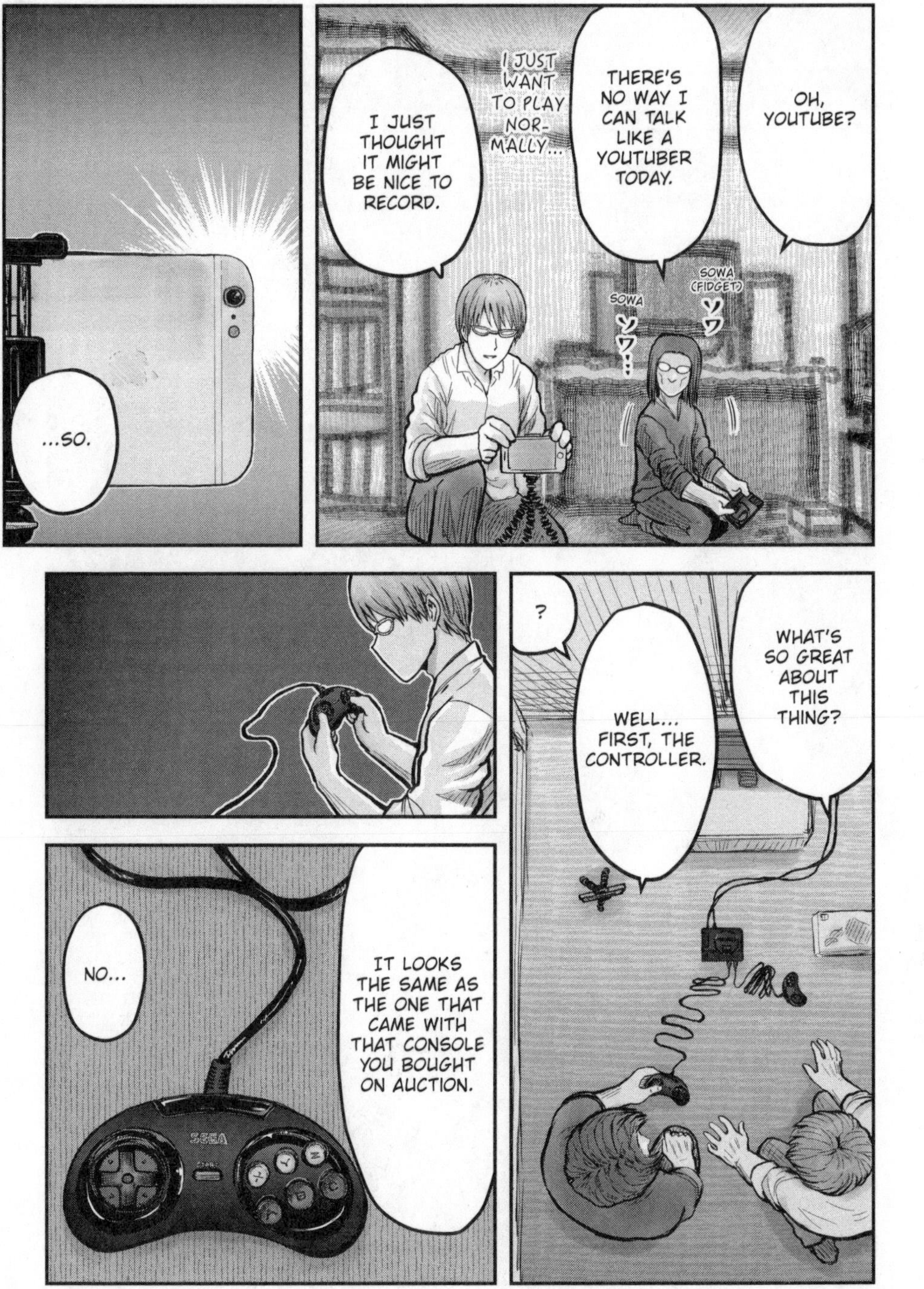
OH, YOUTUBE?
THERE'S NO WAY I CAN TALK LIKE A YOUTUBER TODAY.
I JUST WANT TO PLAY NOR-MALLY...
I JUST THOUGHT IT MIGHT BE NICE TO RECORD.
SOWA (FIDGET) ソワ
SOWA ソワ…
...SO.
WHAT'S SO GREAT ABOUT THIS THING?
?
WELL... FIRST, THE CONTROLLER.
IT LOOKS THE SAME AS THE ONE THAT CAME WITH THAT CONSOLE YOU BOUGHT ON AUCTION.
NO...
SEGA

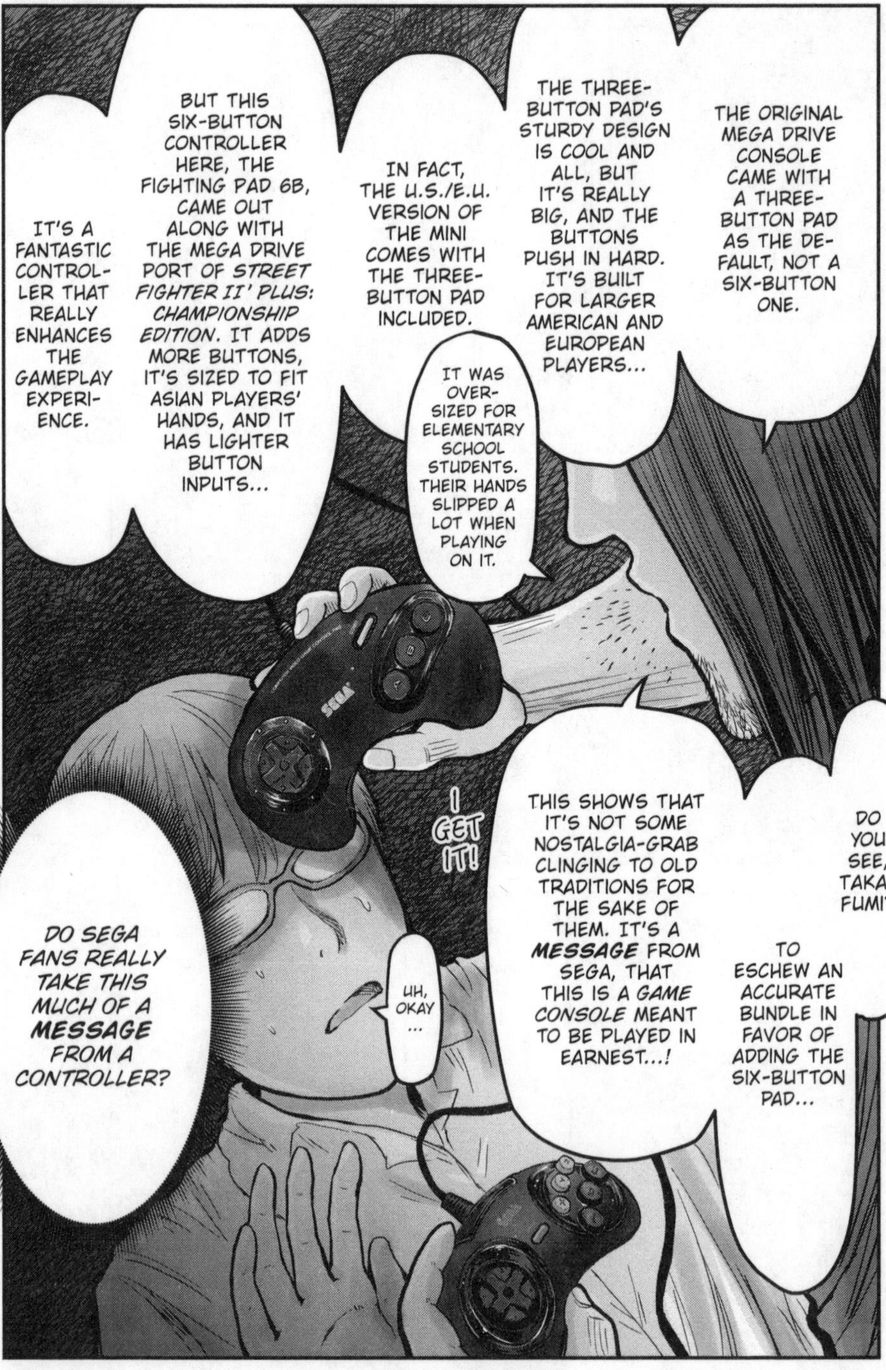
THE ORIGINAL MEGA DRIVE CONSOLE CAME WITH A THREE-BUTTON PAD AS THE DE-FAULT, NOT A SIX-BUTTON ONE.
THE THREE-BUTTON PAD'S STURDY DESIGN IS COOL AND ALL, BUT IT'S REALLY BIG, AND THE BUTTONS PUSH IN HARD. IT'S BUILT FOR LARGER AMERICAN AND EUROPEAN PLAYERS...
IT WAS OVER-SIZED FOR ELEMENTARY SCHOOL STUDENTS. THEIR HANDS SLIPPED A LOT WHEN PLAYING ON IT.
IN FACT, THE U.S./E.U. VERSION OF THE MINI COMES WITH THE THREE-BUTTON PAD INCLUDED.
BUT THIS SIX-BUTTON CONTROLLER HERE, THE FIGHTING PAD 6B, CAME OUT ALONG WITH THE MEGA DRIVE PORT OF *STREET FIGHTER II' PLUS: CHAMPIONSHIP EDITION*. IT ADDS MORE BUTTONS, IT'S SIZED TO FIT ASIAN PLAYERS' HANDS, AND IT HAS LIGHTER BUTTON INPUTS...
IT'S A FANTASTIC CONTROL-LER THAT REALLY ENHANCES THE GAMEPLAY EXPERI-ENCE.
DO YOU SEE, TAKA-FUMI?
TO ESCHEW AN ACCURATE BUNDLE IN FAVOR OF ADDING THE SIX-BUTTON PAD...
THIS SHOWS THAT IT'S NOT SOME NOSTALGIA-GRAB CLINGING TO OLD TRADITIONS FOR THE SAKE OF THEM. IT'S A **MESSAGE** FROM SEGA, THAT THIS IS A *GAME CONSOLE* MEANT TO BE PLAYED IN EARNEST...!
I GET IT!
UH, OKAY...
DO SEGA FANS REALLY TAKE THIS MUCH OF A ***MESSAGE*** *FROM A CONTROLLER?*

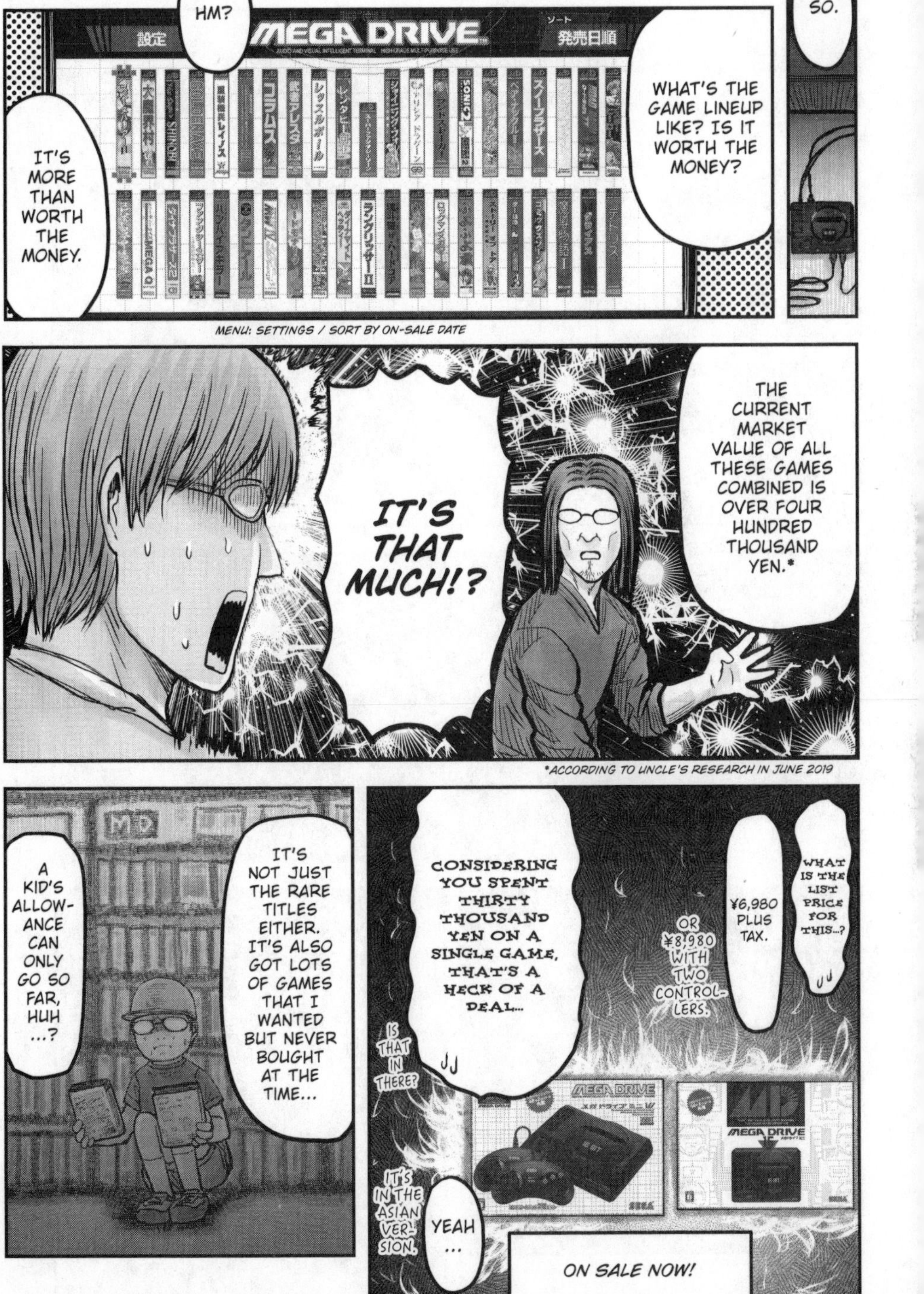
SO.
WHAT'S THE GAME LINEUP LIKE? IS IT WORTH THE MONEY?
HM?
設定
MEGA DRIVE
ソート
発売日順
IT'S MORE THAN WORTH THE MONEY.
MENU: SETTINGS / SORT BY ON-SALE DATE
THE CURRENT MARKET VALUE OF ALL THESE GAMES COMBINED IS OVER FOUR HUNDRED THOUSAND YEN.*
IT'S THAT MUCH!?
*ACCORDING TO UNCLE'S RESEARCH IN JUNE 2019
WHAT IS THE LIST PRICE FOR THIS...?
¥6,980 PLUS TAX.
OR ¥8,980 WITH TWO CONTROLLERS.
CONSIDERING YOU SPENT THIRTY THOUSAND YEN ON A SINGLE GAME, THAT'S A HECK OF A DEAL...
IS THAT IN THERE?
IT'S IN THE ASIAN VERSION.
YEAH...
ON SALE NOW!
MEGA DRIVE
IT'S NOT JUST THE RARE TITLES EITHER. IT'S ALSO GOT LOTS OF GAMES THAT I WANTED BUT NEVER BOUGHT AT THE TIME...
A KID'S ALLOWANCE CAN ONLY GO SO FAR, HUH...?

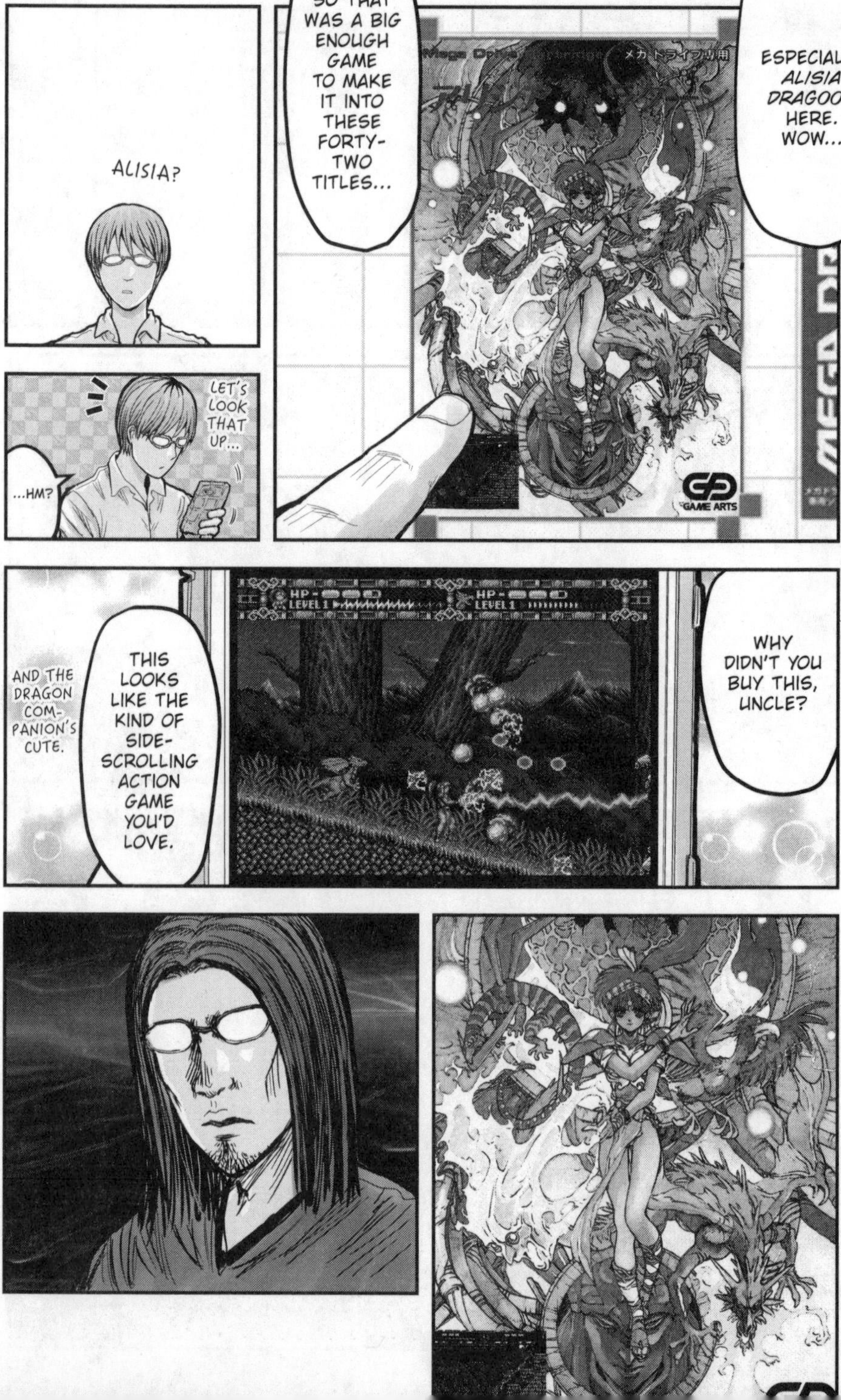

ESPECIALLY *ALISIA DRAGOON* HERE. WOW...
SO THAT WAS A BIG ENOUGH GAME TO MAKE IT INTO THESE FORTY-TWO TITLES...
メガドライブ専用
GAME ARTS
MEGA DR
ALISIA?
LET'S LOOK THAT UP...
...HM?
WHY DIDN'T YOU BUY THIS, UNCLE?
HP-
LEVEL 1
HP-
LEVEL 1
THIS LOOKS LIKE THE KIND OF SIDE-SCROLLING ACTION GAME YOU'D LOVE.
AND THE DRAGON COMPANION'S CUTE.

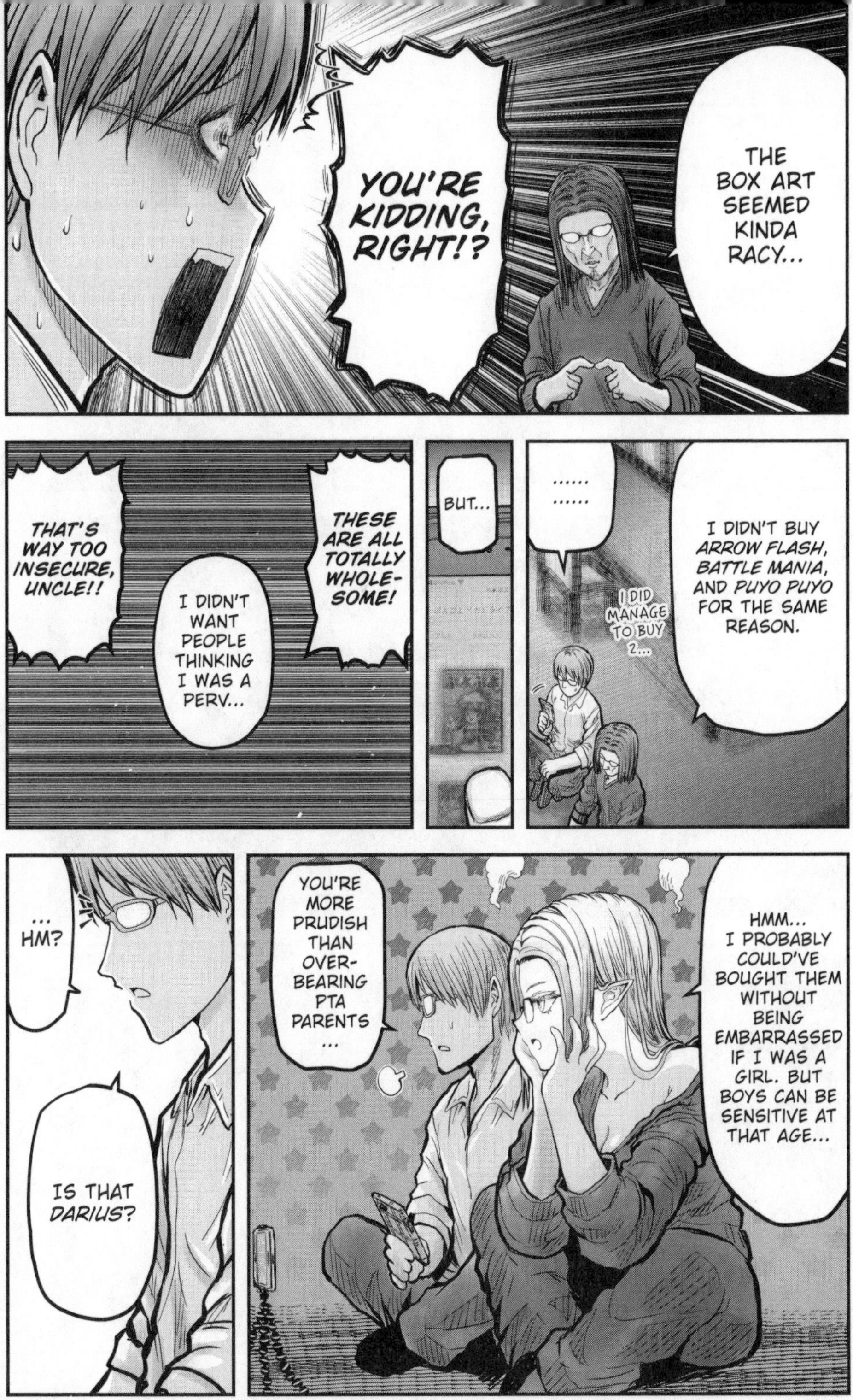
THE BOX ART SEEMED KINDA RACY...
YOU'RE KIDDING, RIGHT!?
I DIDN'T BUY ARROW FLASH, BATTLE MANIA, AND PUYO PUYO FOR THE SAME REASON.
I DID MANAGE TO BUY 2...
....
BUT...
THESE ARE ALL TOTALLY WHOLE-SOME!
THAT'S WAY TOO INSECURE, UNCLE!!
I DIDN'T WANT PEOPLE THINKING I WAS A PERV...
HMM... I PROBABLY COULD'VE BOUGHT THEM WITHOUT BEING EMBARRASSED IF I WAS A GIRL. BUT BOYS CAN BE SENSITIVE AT THAT AGE...
YOU'RE MORE PRUDISH THAN OVER-BEARING PTA PARENTS ...
... HM?
IS THAT DARIUS?

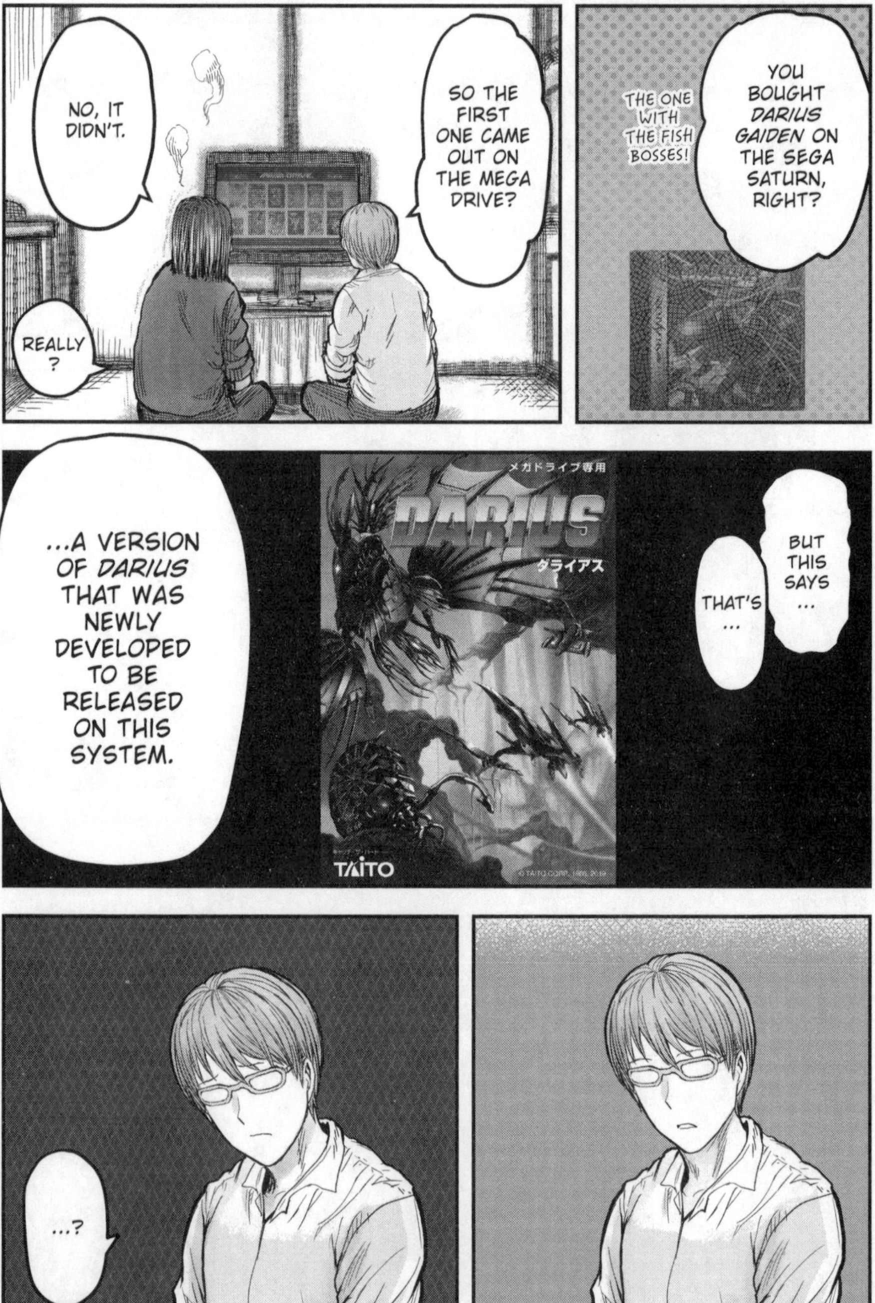
YOU BOUGHT *DARIUS GAIDEN* ON THE SEGA SATURN, RIGHT?
THE ONE WITH THE FISH BOSSES!
SO THE FIRST ONE CAME OUT ON THE MEGA DRIVE?
NO, IT DIDN'T.
REALLY?
BUT THIS SAYS...
THAT'S...
メガドライブ専用
DARIUS
ダライアス
TAITO
...A VERSION OF *DARIUS* THAT WAS NEWLY DEVELOPED TO BE RELEASED ON THIS SYSTEM.
...?

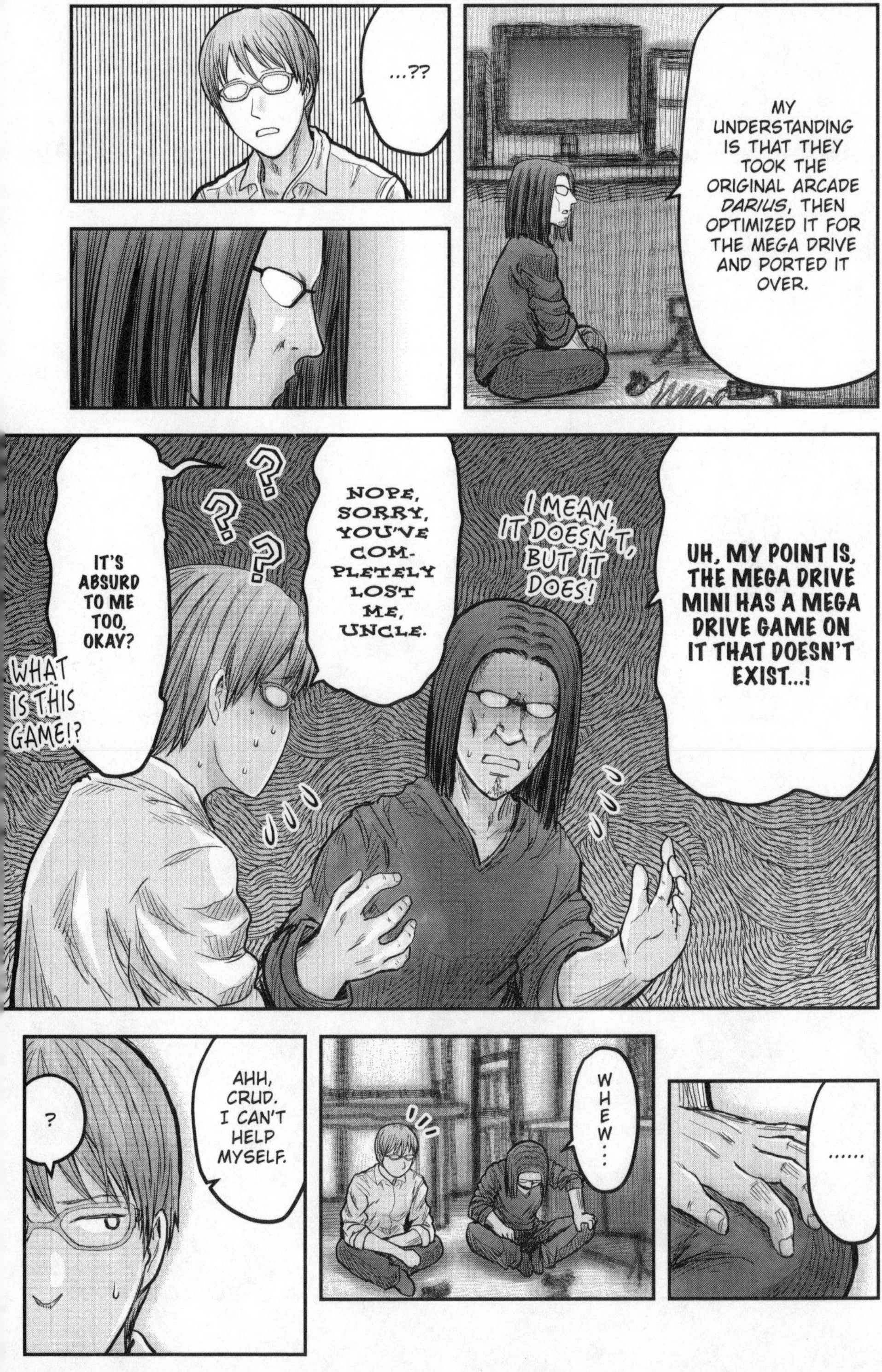
MY UNDERSTANDING IS THAT THEY TOOK THE ORIGINAL ARCADE *DARIUS*, THEN OPTIMIZED IT FOR THE MEGA DRIVE AND PORTED IT OVER.
...??
UH, MY POINT IS, THE MEGA DRIVE MINI HAS A MEGA DRIVE GAME ON IT THAT DOESN'T EXIST...!
I MEAN, IT DOESN'T, BUT IT DOES!
NOPE, SORRY, YOU'VE COM-PLETELY LOST ME, UNCLE.
IT'S ABSURD TO ME TOO, OKAY?
WHAT IS THIS GAME!?
......
WHEW...
AHH, CRUD. I CAN'T HELP MYSELF.
?

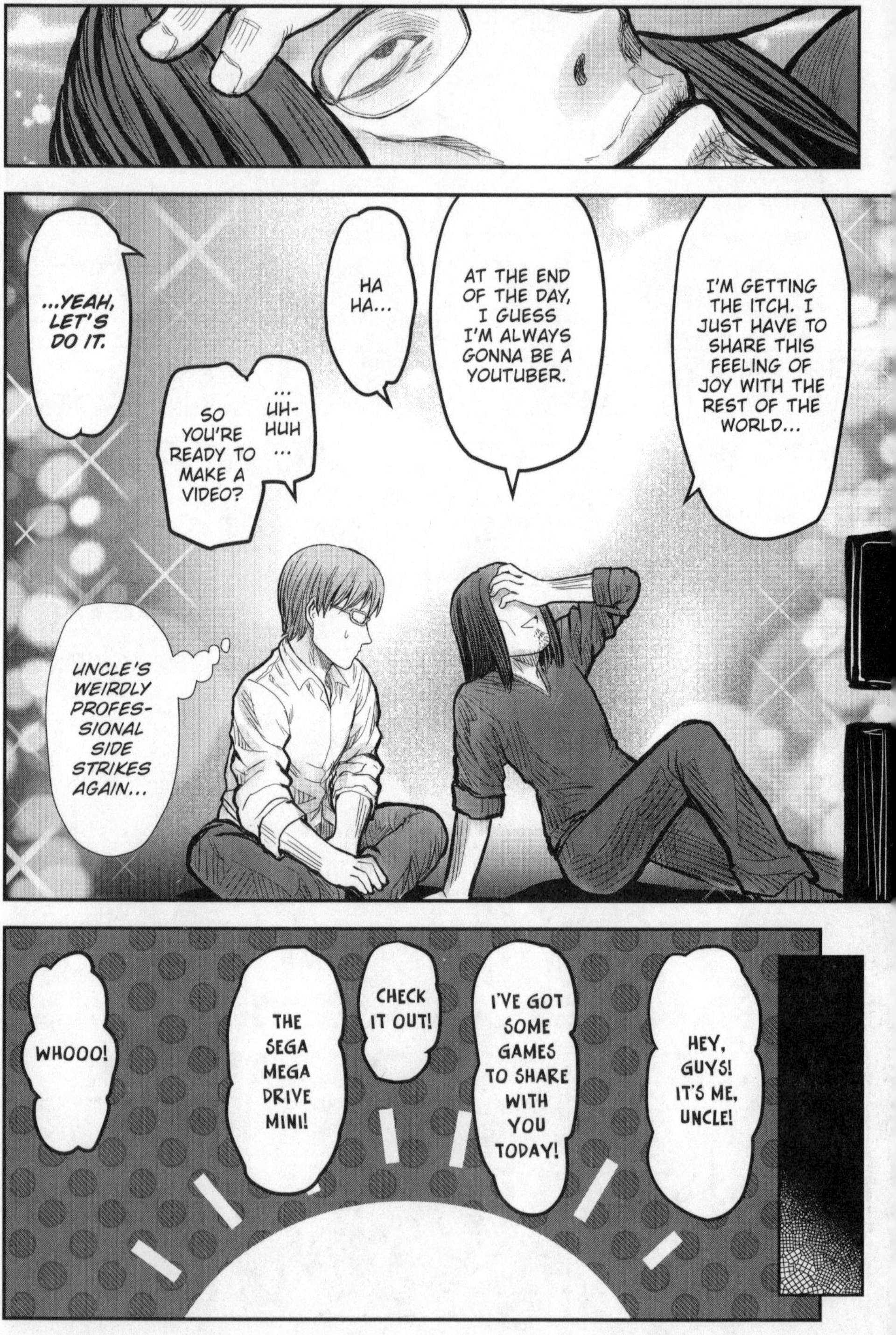
I'M GETTING THE ITCH. I JUST HAVE TO SHARE THIS FEELING OF JOY WITH THE REST OF THE WORLD...
AT THE END OF THE DAY, I GUESS I'M ALWAYS GONNA BE A YOUTUBER.
HA HA...
...UH-HUH...
SO YOU'RE READY TO MAKE A VIDEO?
...YEAH, LET'S DO IT.
UNCLE'S WEIRDLY PROFES-SIONAL SIDE STRIKES AGAIN...
HEY, GUYS! IT'S ME, UNCLE!
I'VE GOT SOME GAMES TO SHARE WITH YOU TODAY!
CHECK IT OUT!
THE SEGA MEGA DRIVE MINI!
WHOOO!

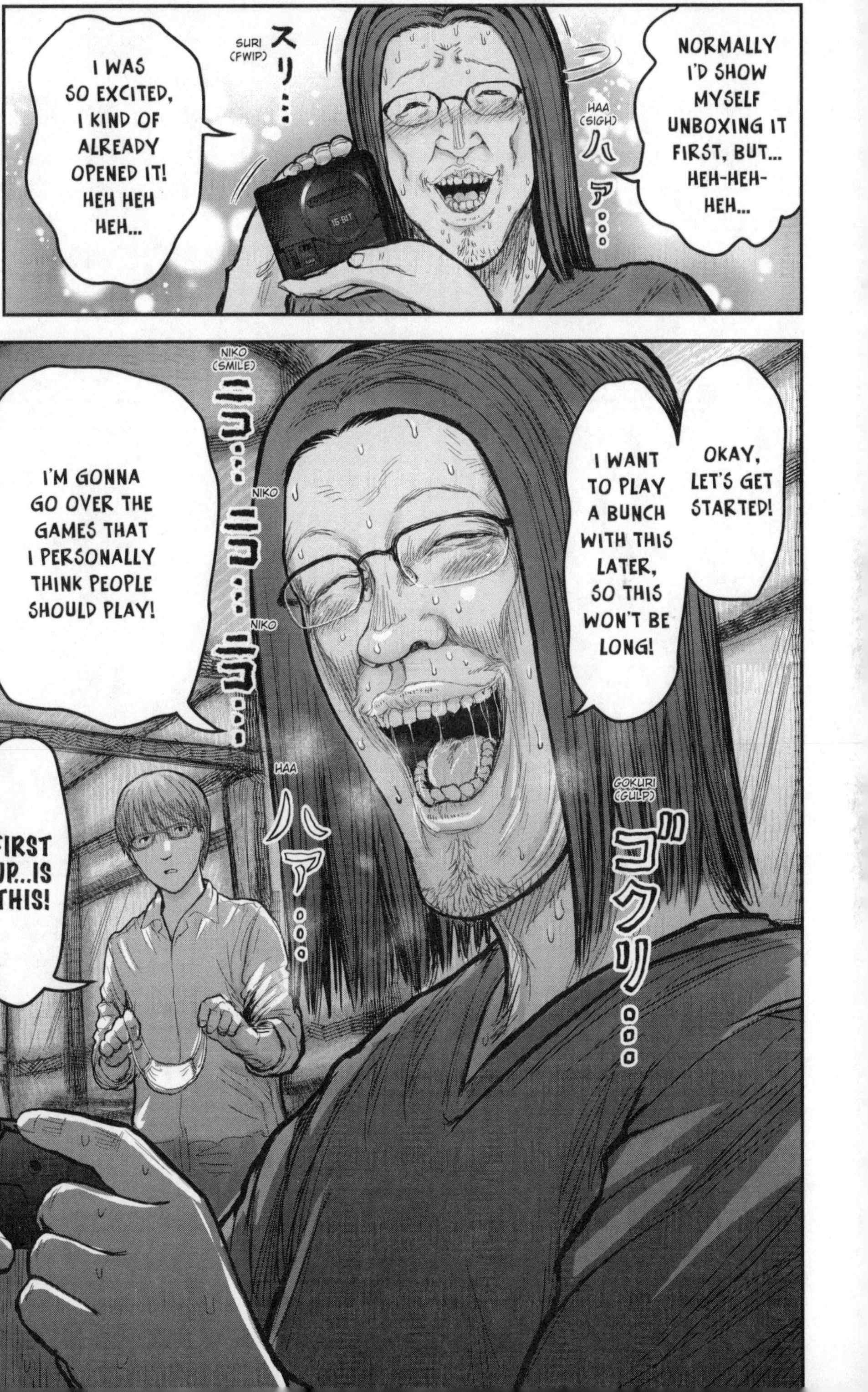
NORMALLY I'D SHOW MYSELF UNBOXING IT FIRST, BUT... HEH-HEH-HEH...
HAA (SIGH)
ハァ…
SURI (FWIP)
スリ…
I WAS SO EXCITED, I KIND OF ALREADY OPENED IT! HEH HEH HEH...
16 BIT
OKAY, LET'S GET STARTED!
I WANT TO PLAY A BUNCH WITH THIS LATER, SO THIS WON'T BE LONG!
GOKURI (GULP)
ゴクリ…
HAA
ハァ…
NIKO (SMILE)
ニコ…
NIKO
ニコ…
NIKO
ニコ…
I'M GONNA GO OVER THE GAMES THAT I PERSONALLY THINK PEOPLE SHOULD PLAY!
FIRST UP...IS THIS!

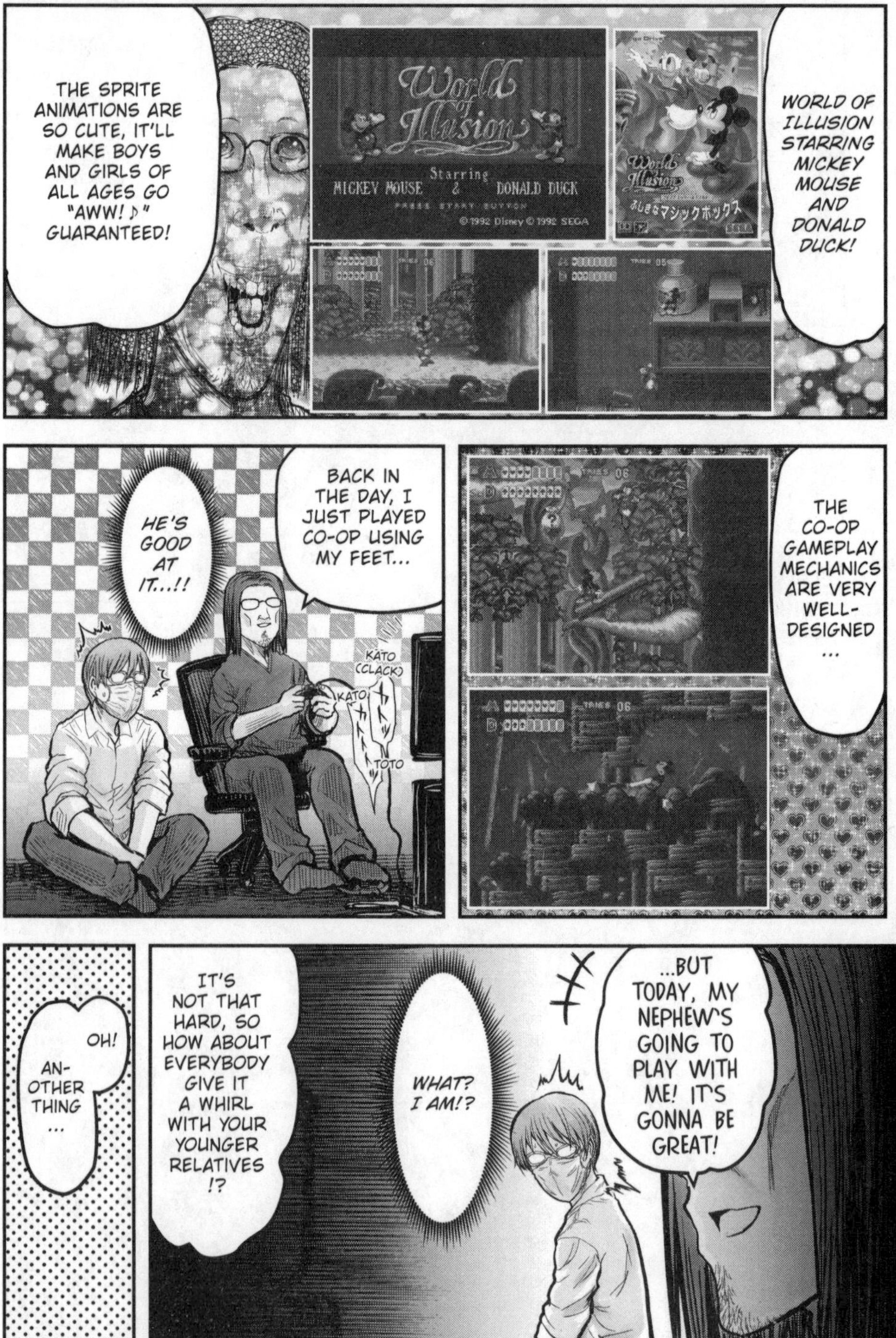
WORLD OF ILLUSION STARRING MICKEY MOUSE AND DONALD DUCK!
ふしぎなマジックボックス
World of Illusion
Starring
MICKEV MOUSE & DONALD DUCK
PRESS START BUTTON
© 1992 Disney © 1992 SEGA
THE SPRITE ANIMATIONS ARE SO CUTE, IT'LL MAKE BOYS AND GIRLS OF ALL AGES GO "AWW! ♪" GUARANTEED!
THE CO-OP GAMEPLAY MECHANICS ARE VERY WELL-DESIGNED ...
BACK IN THE DAY, I JUST PLAYED CO-OP USING MY FEET...
HE'S GOOD AT IT...!!
KATO (CLACK)
KATO
TOTO
...BUT TODAY, MY NEPHEW'S GOING TO PLAY WITH ME! IT'S GONNA BE GREAT!
WHAT? I AM!?
IT'S NOT THAT HARD, SO HOW ABOUT EVERYBODY GIVE IT A WHIRL WITH YOUR YOUNGER RELATIVES !?
OH!
AN-OTHER THING ...

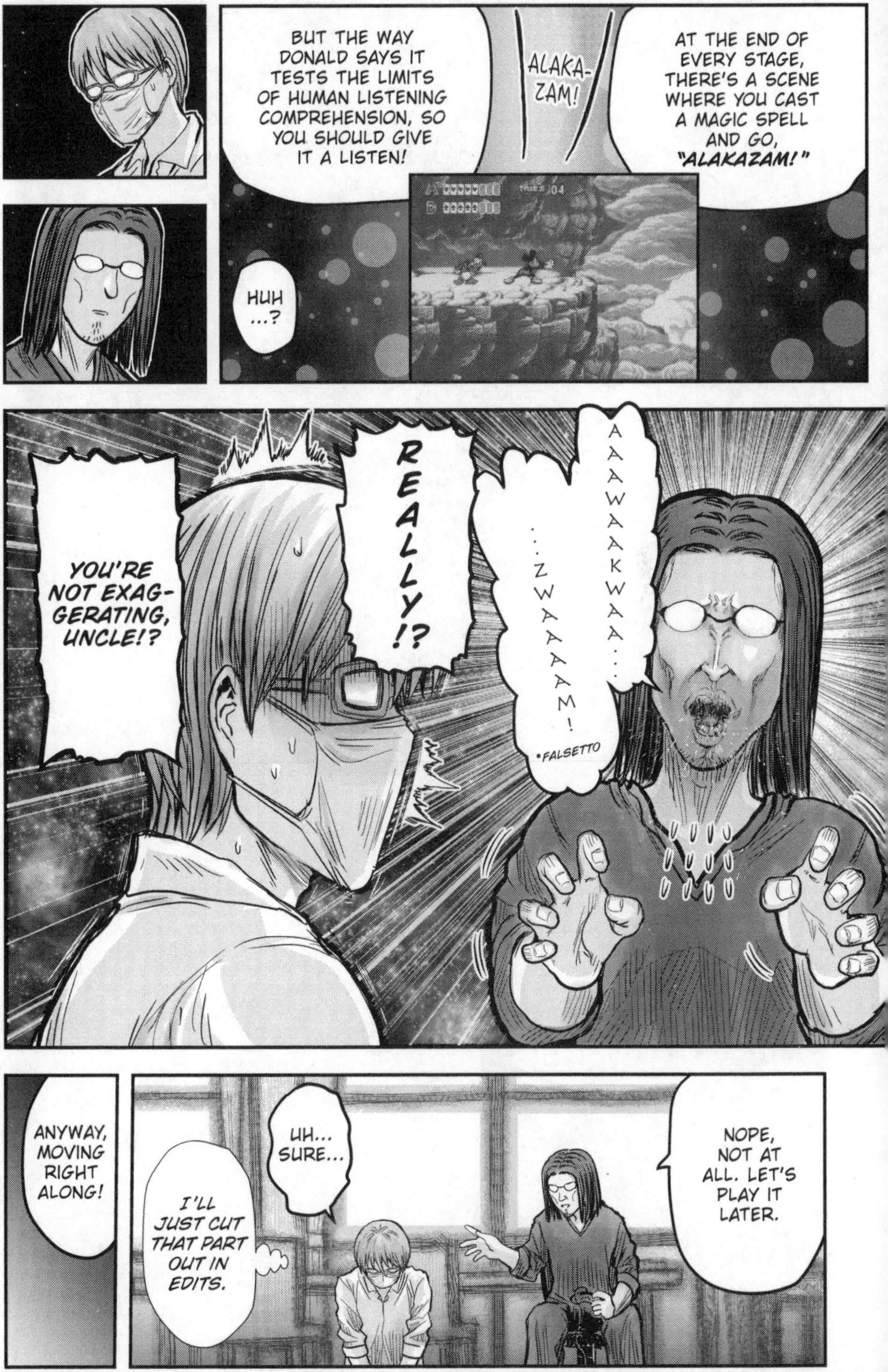
AT THE END OF EVERY STAGE, THERE'S A SCENE WHERE YOU CAST A MAGIC SPELL AND GO, "ALAKAZAM!"
ALAKA-ZAM!
BUT THE WAY DONALD SAYS IT TESTS THE LIMITS OF HUMAN LISTENING COMPREHENSION, SO YOU SHOULD GIVE IT A LISTEN!
HUH ...?
AAAWAAAKWAA... ...ZWAAAAAM!
*FALSETTO
REALLY!?
YOU'RE NOT EXAG-GERATING, UNCLE!?
NOPE, NOT AT ALL. LET'S PLAY IT LATER.
UH... SURE...
I'LL JUST CUT THAT PART OUT IN EDITS.
ANYWAY, MOVING RIGHT ALONG!

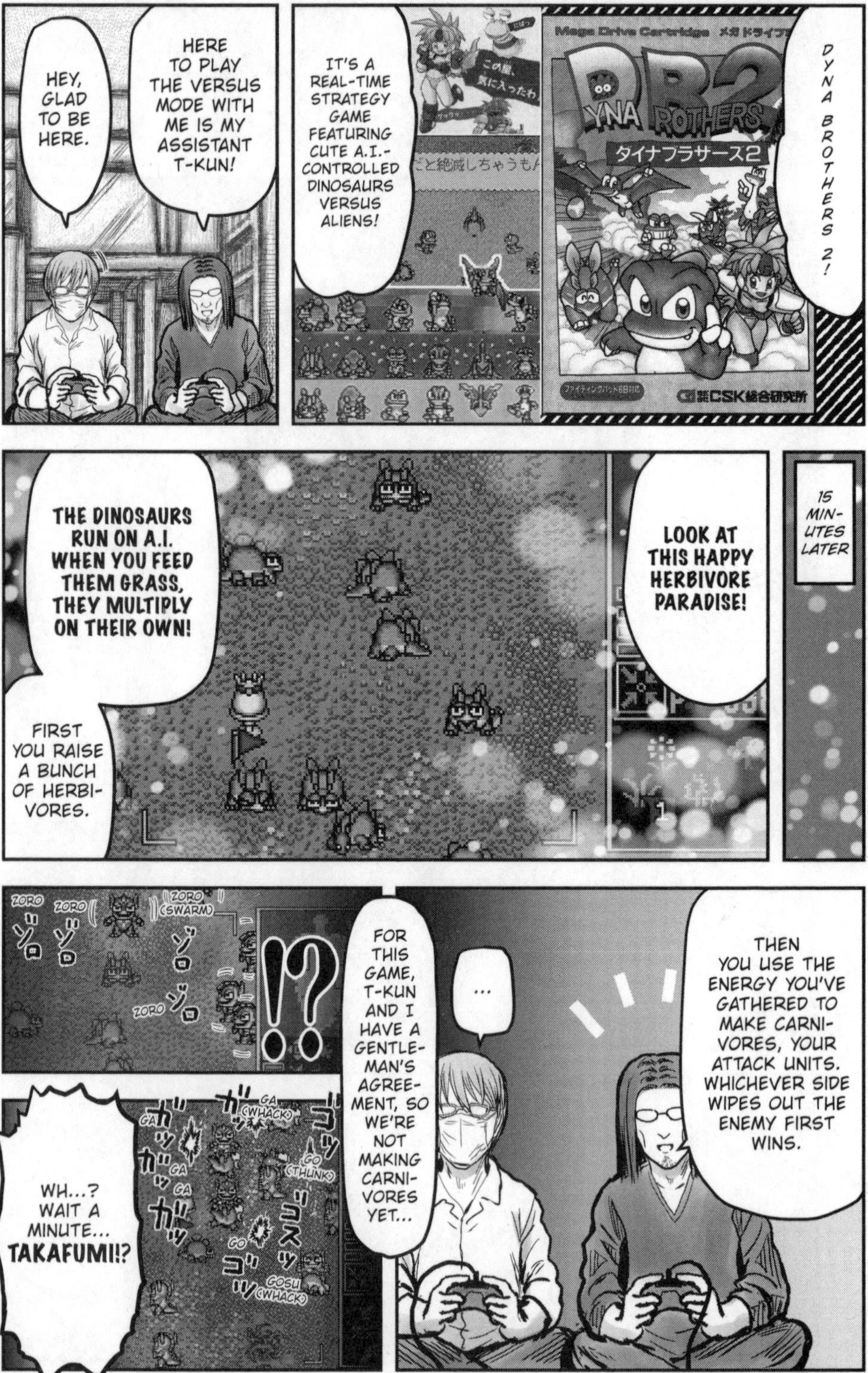
DYNA BROTHERS 2!
Mega Drive Cartridge
DYNA BROTHERS
ダイナブラザース2
CSK総合研究所
IT'S A REAL-TIME STRATEGY GAME FEATURING CUTE A.I.-CONTROLLED DINOSAURS VERSUS ALIENS!
HERE TO PLAY THE VERSUS MODE WITH ME IS MY ASSISTANT T-KUN!
HEY, GLAD TO BE HERE.
15 MINUTES LATER
LOOK AT THIS HAPPY HERBIVORE PARADISE!
THE DINOSAURS RUN ON A.I. WHEN YOU FEED THEM GRASS, THEY MULTIPLY ON THEIR OWN!
FIRST YOU RAISE A BUNCH OF HERBIVORES.
THEN YOU USE THE ENERGY YOU'VE GATHERED TO MAKE CARNIVORES, YOUR ATTACK UNITS. WHICHEVER SIDE WIPES OUT THE ENEMY FIRST WINS.
...
FOR THIS GAME, T-KUN AND I HAVE A GENTLEMAN'S AGREEMENT, SO WE'RE NOT MAKING CARNIVORES YET...
ZORO (SWARM)
ZORO
ZORO
ZORO
!?
GA (WHACK)
GA
GA
GA
GO (THUNK)
GO
GOSU (WHACK)
WH...? WAIT A MINUTE... TAKAFUMI!?

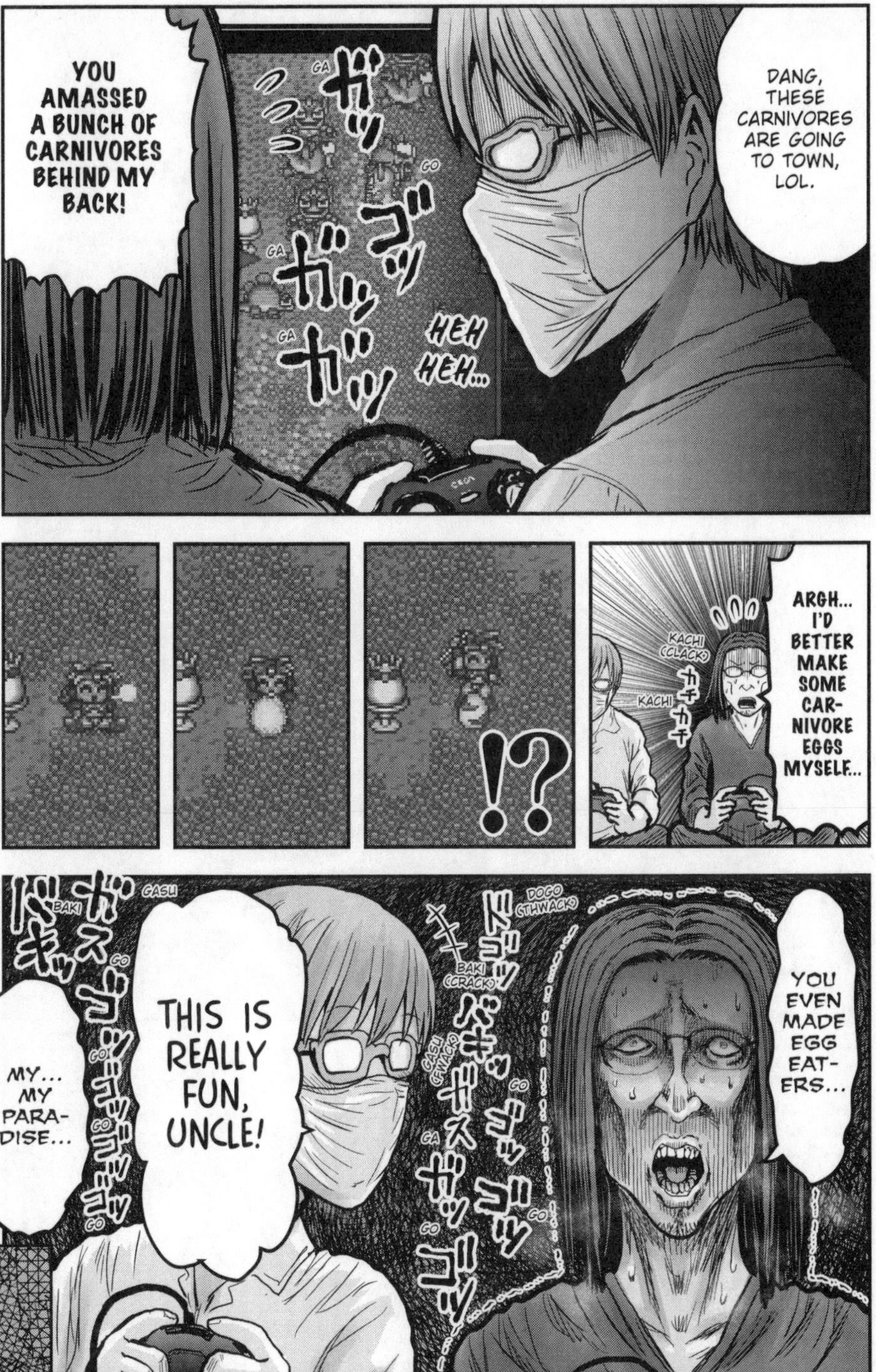
DANG, THESE CARNIVORES ARE GOING TO TOWN, LOL.
HEH HEH...
GA GO GA GA
YOU AMASSED A BUNCH OF CARNIVORES BEHIND MY BACK!
ARGH... I'D BETTER MAKE SOME CARNIVORE EGGS MYSELF...
KACHI (CLACK) KACHI
!?
YOU EVEN MADE EGG EATERS...
DOGO (THWACK) BAKI (CRACK) GASU (GWACK) GO GA GO GO
THIS IS REALLY FUN, UNCLE!
GASU BAKI GO GO GO GO
MY... MY PARADISE...

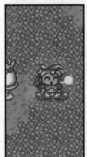

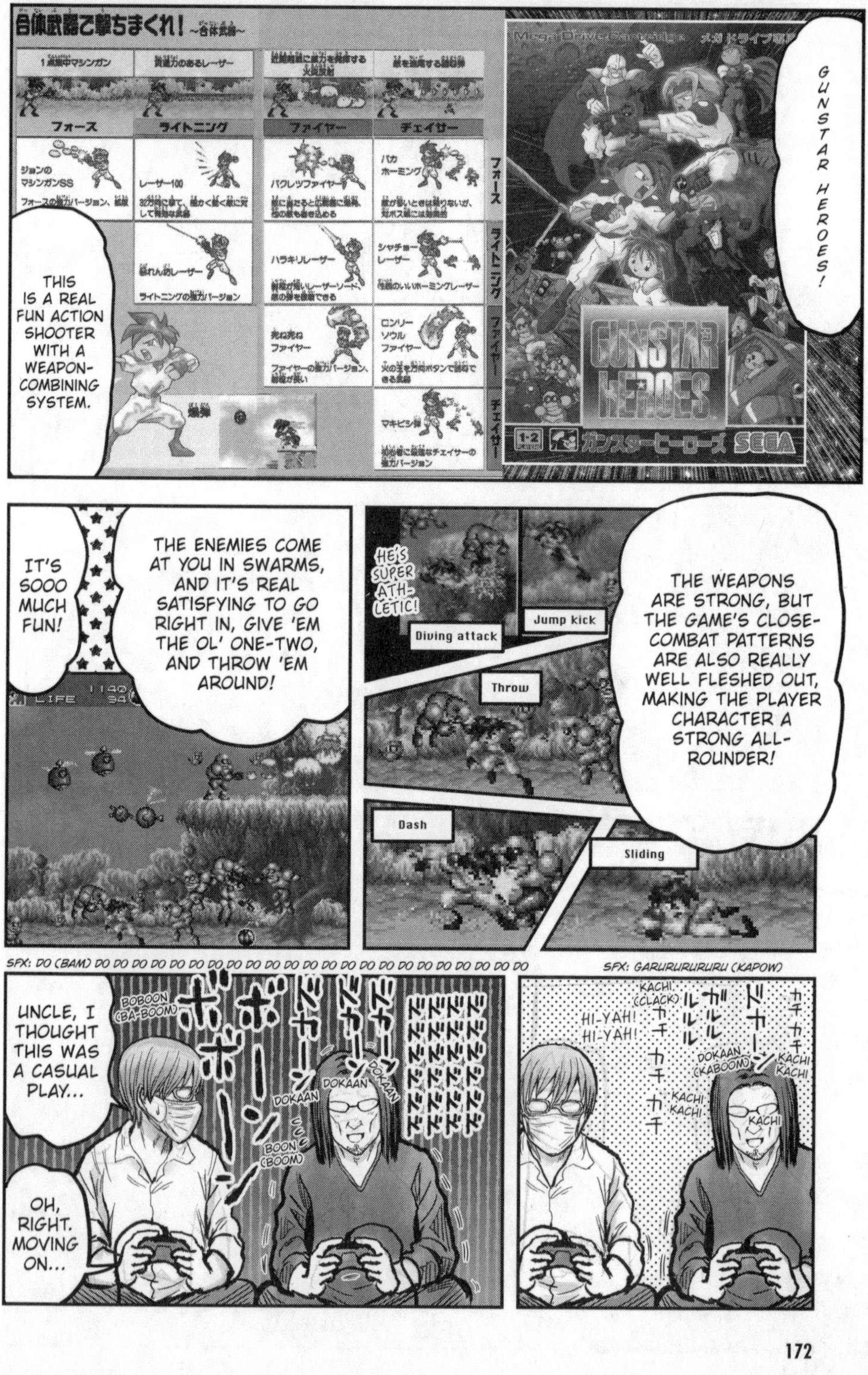
GUNSTAR HEROES!
GUNSTAR HEROES
ガンスターヒーローズ
SEGA
合体武器で撃ちまくれ！～合体武器～
フォース
ライトニング
ファイヤー
チェイサー
THIS IS A REAL FUN ACTION SHOOTER WITH A WEAPON-COMBINING SYSTEM.
THE WEAPONS ARE STRONG, BUT THE GAME'S CLOSE-COMBAT PATTERNS ARE ALSO REALLY WELL FLESHED OUT, MAKING THE PLAYER CHARACTER A STRONG ALL-ROUNDER!
Jump kick
HE'S SUPER ATHLETIC!
Diving attack
Throw
Sliding
Dash
THE ENEMIES COME AT YOU IN SWARMS, AND IT'S REAL SATISFYING TO GO RIGHT IN, GIVE 'EM THE OL' ONE-TWO, AND THROW 'EM AROUND!
IT'S SOOO MUCH FUN!
LIFE
SFX: GARURURURURU (KAPOW)
KACHI KACHI
DOKAAN (KABOOM)
KACHI (CLACK)
HI-YAH! HI-YAH!
KACHI KACHI
KACHI
SFX: DO (BAM) DO DO DO DO DO DO DO DO DO DO DO DO DO DO DO DO DO DO DO DO DO DO DO DO DO DO
DOKAAN
DOKAAN
DOKAAN
BOON (BOOM)
BOBOON (BA-BOOM)
UNCLE, I THOUGHT THIS WAS A CASUAL PLAY...
OH, RIGHT. MOVING ON...

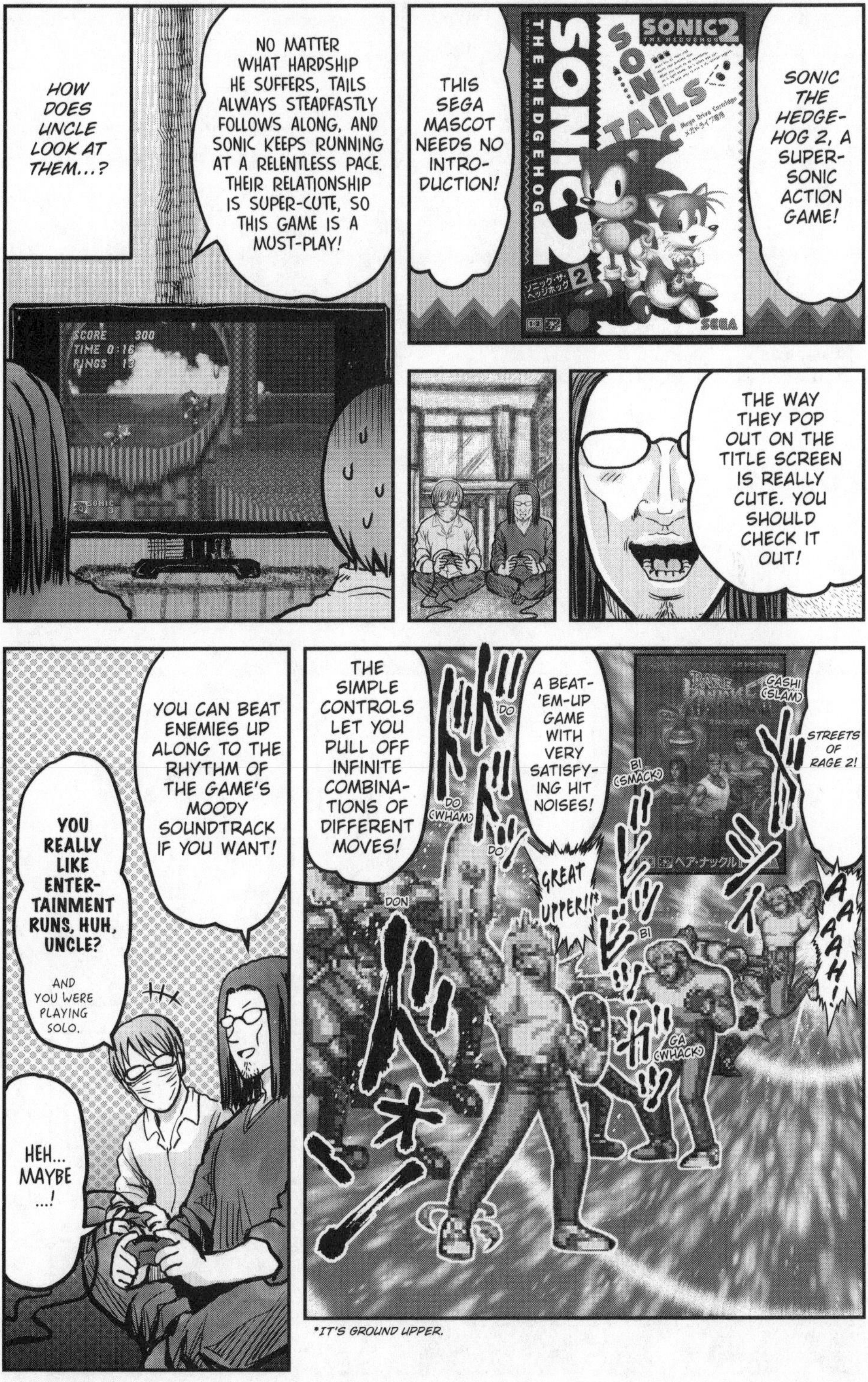
SONIC THE HEDGEHOG 2, A SUPER-SONIC ACTION GAME!
THIS SEGA MASCOT NEEDS NO INTRODUCTION!
SONIC THE HEDGEHOG 2
SONIC & TAILS
SEGA
THE WAY THEY POP OUT ON THE TITLE SCREEN IS REALLY CUTE. YOU SHOULD CHECK IT OUT!
NO MATTER WHAT HARDSHIP HE SUFFERS, TAILS ALWAYS STEADFASTLY FOLLOWS ALONG, AND SONIC KEEPS RUNNING AT A RELENTLESS PACE. THEIR RELATIONSHIP IS SUPER-CUTE, SO THIS GAME IS A MUST-PLAY!
HOW DOES UNCLE LOOK AT THEM...?
SCORE 300
TIME 0:16
RINGS 13
STREETS OF RAGE 2!
GASHI (SLAM)
A BEAT-'EM-UP GAME WITH VERY SATISFYING HIT NOISES!
THE SIMPLE CONTROLS LET YOU PULL OFF INFINITE COMBINATIONS OF DIFFERENT MOVES!
DO
DO (WHAM)
DO
BI (SMACK)
GREAT UPPER!!*
AAAAH!
BI
DON
GA (WHACK)
YOU CAN BEAT ENEMIES UP ALONG TO THE RHYTHM OF THE GAME'S MOODY SOUNDTRACK IF YOU WANT!
YOU REALLY LIKE ENTERTAINMENT RUNS, HUH, UNCLE?
AND YOU WERE PLAYING SOLO.
HEH... MAYBE ...!

*IT'S GROUND UPPER.

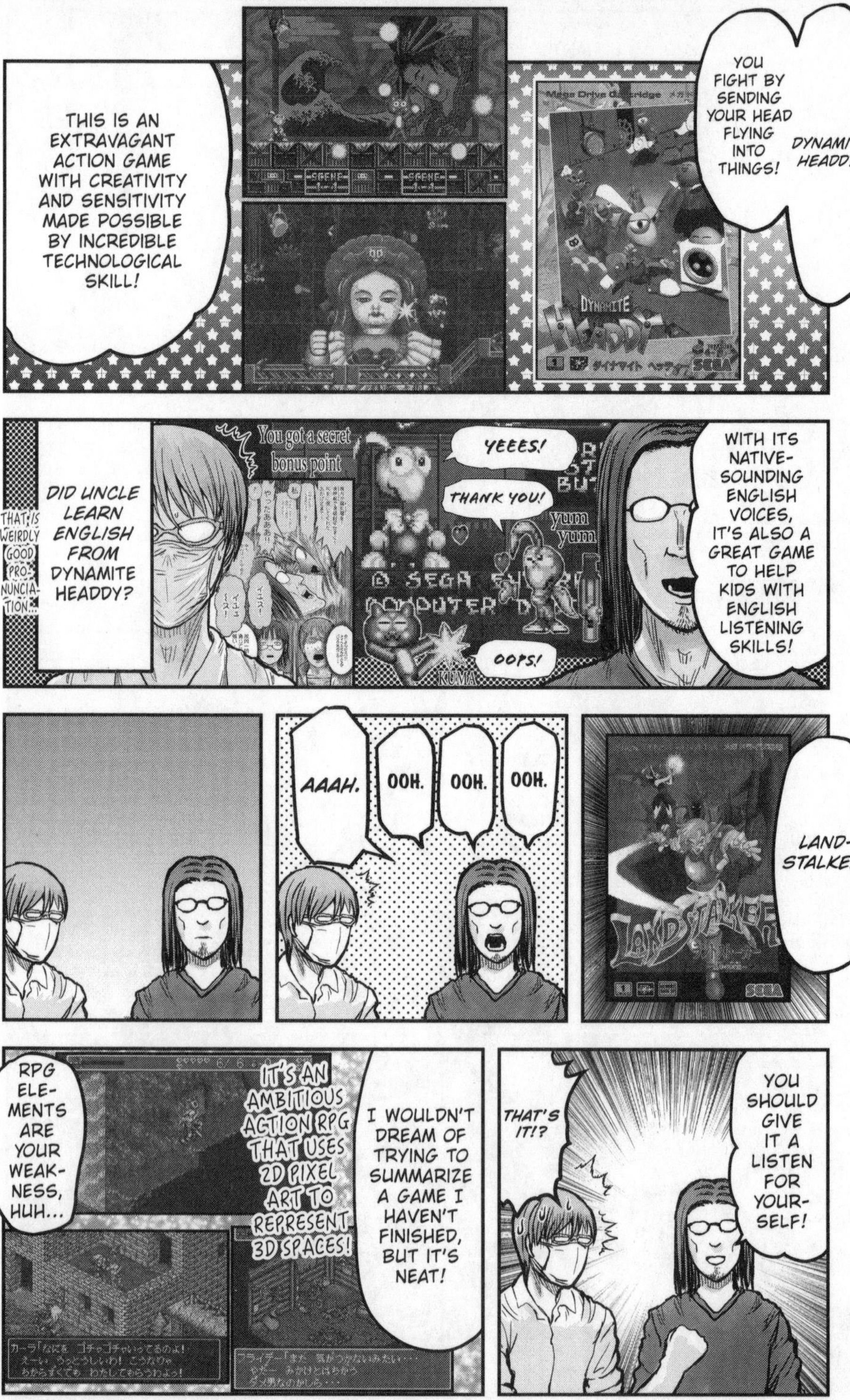

DYNAMITE HEADDY!
YOU FIGHT BY SENDING YOUR HEAD FLYING INTO THINGS!
DYNAMITE HEADDY
SEGA
THIS IS AN EXTRAVAGANT ACTION GAME WITH CREATIVITY AND SENSITIVITY MADE POSSIBLE BY INCREDIBLE TECHNOLOGICAL SKILL!
WITH ITS NATIVE-SOUNDING ENGLISH VOICES, IT'S ALSO A GREAT GAME TO HELP KIDS WITH ENGLISH LISTENING SKILLS!
YEEES!
THANK YOU!
yum yum
You got a secret bonus point
OOPS!
KUMA
DID UNCLE LEARN ENGLISH FROM DYNAMITE HEADDY?
THAT IS WEIRDLY GOOD PRO-NUNCIA-TION...
LAND-STALKER!
SEGA
OOH.
OOH.
OOH.
AAAH.
YOU SHOULD GIVE IT A LISTEN FOR YOURSELF!
THAT'S IT!?
I WOULDN'T DREAM OF TRYING TO SUMMARIZE A GAME I HAVEN'T FINISHED, BUT IT'S NEAT!
IT'S AN AMBITIOUS ACTION RPG THAT USES 2D PIXEL ART TO REPRESENT 3D SPACES!
RPG ELE-MENTS ARE YOUR WEAK-NESS, HUH...

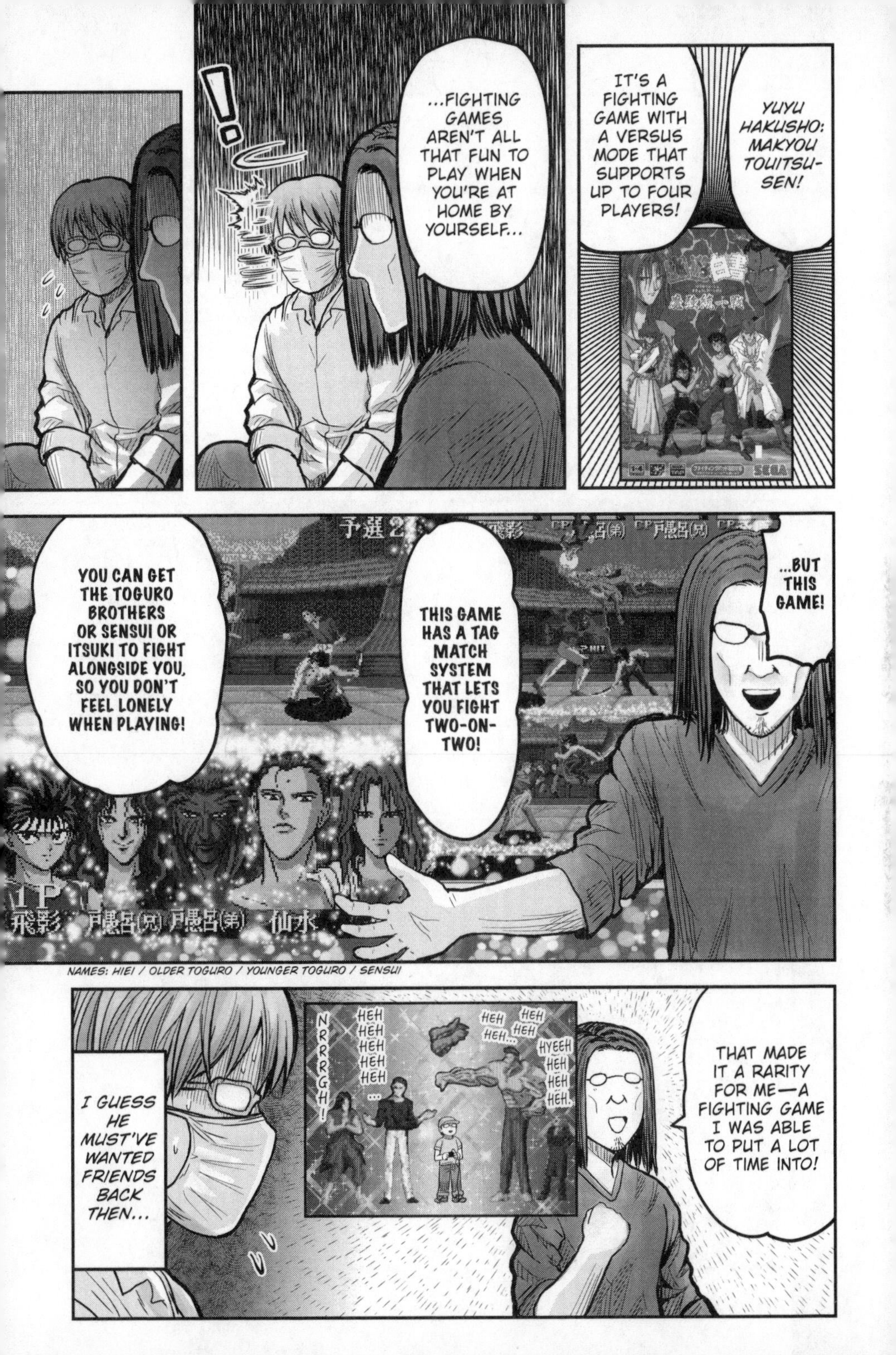
YUYU HAKUSHO: MAKYOU TOUITSU-SEN!
IT'S A FIGHTING GAME WITH A VERSUS MODE THAT SUPPORTS UP TO FOUR PLAYERS!
SEGA
...FIGHTING GAMES AREN'T ALL THAT FUN TO PLAY WHEN YOU'RE AT HOME BY YOURSELF...
!
...BUT THIS GAME!
THIS GAME HAS A TAG MATCH SYSTEM THAT LETS YOU FIGHT TWO-ON-TWO!
YOU CAN GET THE TOGURO BROTHERS OR SENSUI OR ITSUKI TO FIGHT ALONGSIDE YOU, SO YOU DON'T FEEL LONELY WHEN PLAYING!
予選2
飛影
戸愚呂(弟)
戸愚呂(兄)
1P
飛影 戸愚呂(兄) 戸愚呂(弟) 仙水
NAMES: HIEI / OLDER TOGURO / YOUNGER TOGURO / SENSUI
THAT MADE IT A RARITY FOR ME—A FIGHTING GAME I WAS ABLE TO PUT A LOT OF TIME INTO!
HEH HEH HEH...
HEH HEH
HYEEH HEH HEH HEH.
HEH HEH HEH HEH HEH
...
NRRRGH!
I GUESS HE MUST'VE WANTED FRIENDS BACK THEN...

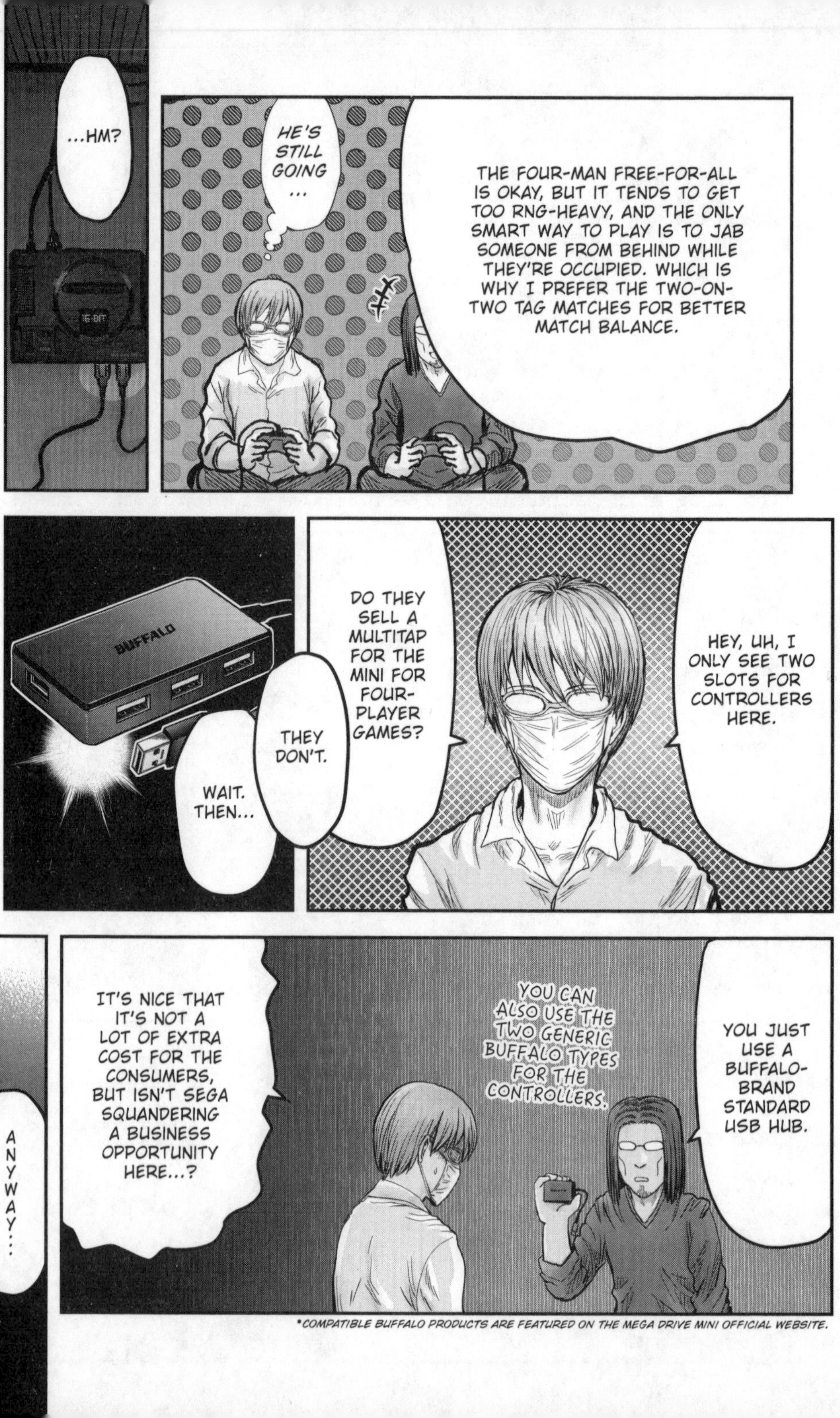
THE FOUR-MAN FREE-FOR-ALL IS OKAY, BUT IT TENDS TO GET TOO RNG-HEAVY, AND THE ONLY SMART WAY TO PLAY IS TO JAB SOMEONE FROM BEHIND WHILE THEY'RE OCCUPIED. WHICH IS WHY I PREFER THE TWO-ON-TWO TAG MATCHES FOR BETTER MATCH BALANCE.
HE'S STILL GOING ...
...HM?
HEY, UH, I ONLY SEE TWO SLOTS FOR CONTROLLERS HERE.
DO THEY SELL A MULTITAP FOR THE MINI FOR FOUR-PLAYER GAMES?
THEY DON'T.
WAIT. THEN...
BUFFALO
YOU JUST USE A BUFFALO-BRAND STANDARD USB HUB.
YOU CAN ALSO USE THE TWO GENERIC BUFFALO TYPES FOR THE CONTROLLERS.
IT'S NICE THAT IT'S NOT A LOT OF EXTRA COST FOR THE CONSUMERS, BUT ISN'T SEGA SQUANDERING A BUSINESS OPPORTUNITY HERE...?
ANYWAY...

*COMPATIBLE BUFFALO PRODUCTS ARE FEATURED ON THE MEGA DRIVE MINI OFFICIAL WEBSITE.

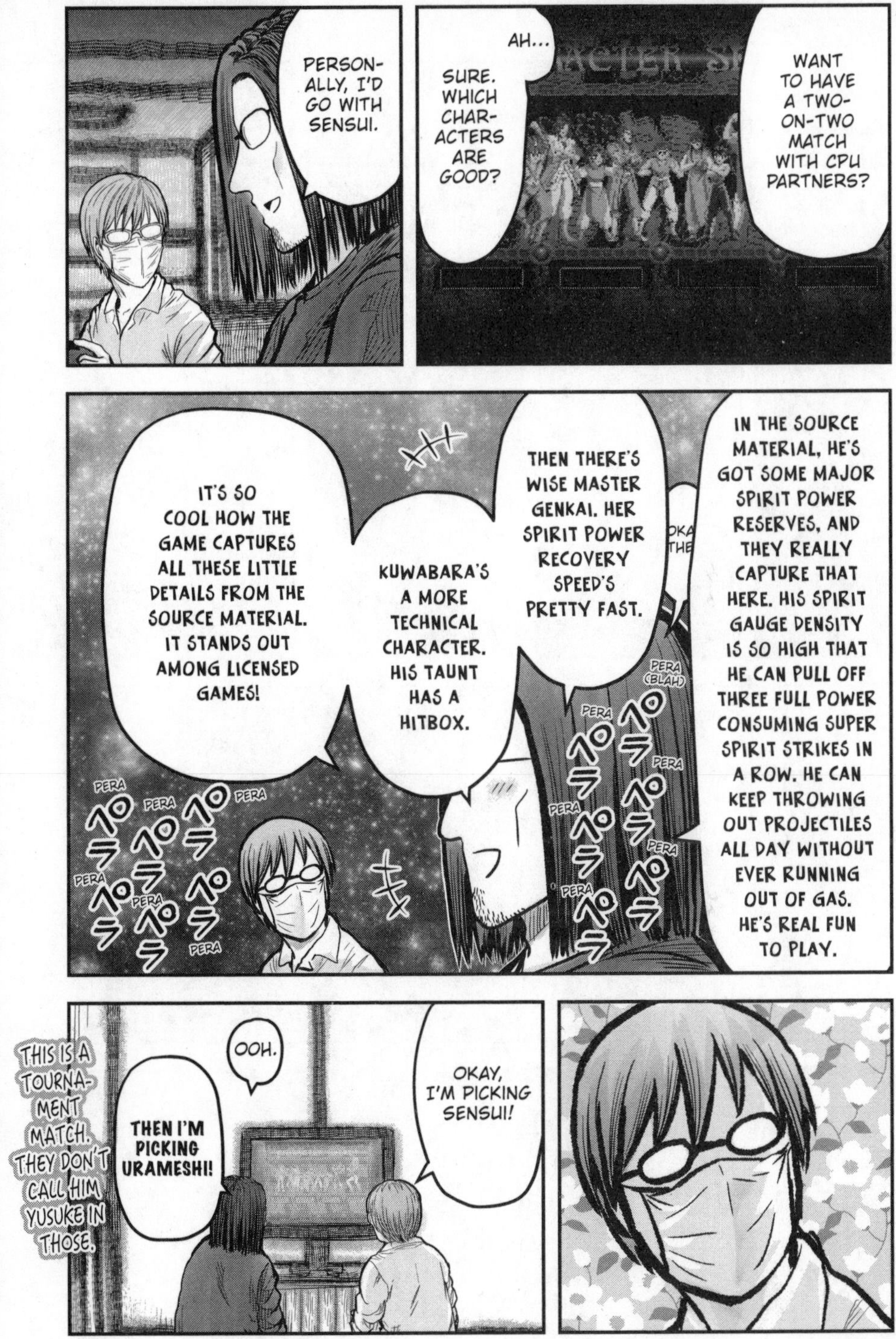
WANT TO HAVE A TWO-ON-TWO MATCH WITH CPU PARTNERS?
AH...
SURE. WHICH CHARACTERS ARE GOOD?
PERSONALLY, I'D GO WITH SENSUI.
IN THE SOURCE MATERIAL, HE'S GOT SOME MAJOR SPIRIT POWER RESERVES, AND THEY REALLY CAPTURE THAT HERE. HIS SPIRIT GAUGE DENSITY IS SO HIGH THAT HE CAN PULL OFF THREE FULL POWER CONSUMING SUPER SPIRIT STRIKES IN A ROW. HE CAN KEEP THROWING OUT PROJECTILES ALL DAY WITHOUT EVER RUNNING OUT OF GAS. HE'S REAL FUN TO PLAY.
THEN THERE'S WISE MASTER GENKAI. HER SPIRIT POWER RECOVERY SPEED'S PRETTY FAST.
KUWABARA'S A MORE TECHNICAL CHARACTER. HIS TAUNT HAS A HITBOX.
IT'S SO COOL HOW THE GAME CAPTURES ALL THESE LITTLE DETAILS FROM THE SOURCE MATERIAL. IT STANDS OUT AMONG LICENSED GAMES!
ペラ PERA (BLAH)
ペラ PERA
ペラ PERA
ペラ PERA
OKAY, I'M PICKING SENSUI!
OOH.
THEN I'M PICKING URAMESHI!
THIS IS A TOURNAMENT MATCH. THEY DON'T CALL HIM YUSUKE IN THOSE.

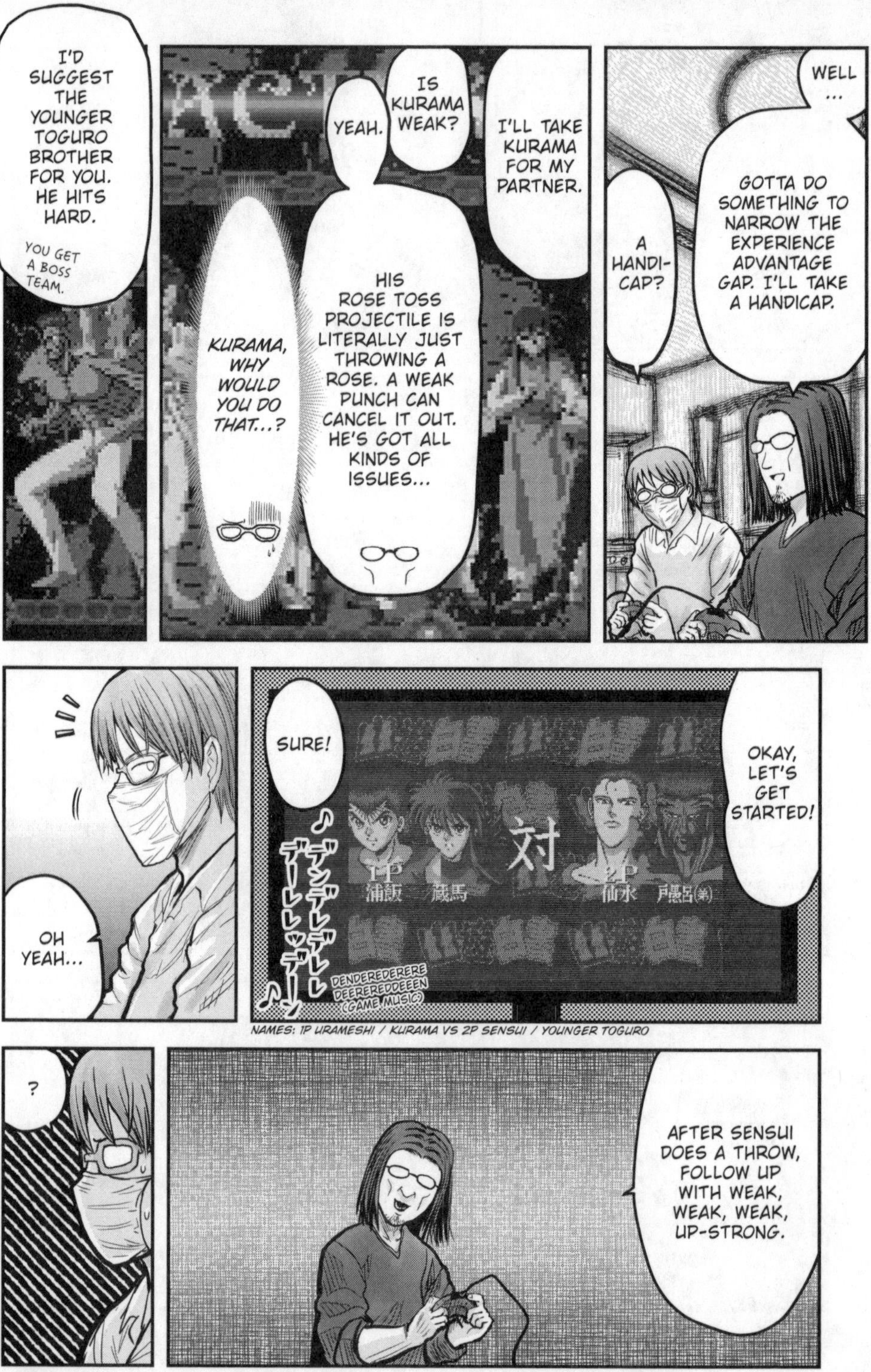
WELL ...
GOTTA DO SOMETHING TO NARROW THE EXPERIENCE ADVANTAGE GAP. I'LL TAKE A HANDICAP.
A HANDI-CAP?
I'LL TAKE KURAMA FOR MY PARTNER.
IS KURAMA WEAK?
YEAH.
HIS ROSE TOSS PROJECTILE IS LITERALLY JUST THROWING A ROSE. A WEAK PUNCH CAN CANCEL IT OUT. HE'S GOT ALL KINDS OF ISSUES...
KURAMA, WHY WOULD YOU DO THAT...?
I'D SUGGEST THE YOUNGER TOGURO BROTHER FOR YOU. HE HITS HARD.
YOU GET A BOSS TEAM.
OKAY, LET'S GET STARTED!
SURE!
1P 浦飯 蔵馬 対 2P 仙水 戸愚呂(弟)
♪デンデレデレレデーレレッデーン♪
DENDEREDERERE DEEREREDDEEEN (GAME MUSIC)
NAMES: 1P URAMESHI / KURAMA VS 2P SENSUI / YOUNGER TOGURO
OH YEAH...
AFTER SENSUI DOES A THROW, FOLLOW UP WITH WEAK, WEAK, WEAK, UP-STRONG.
?

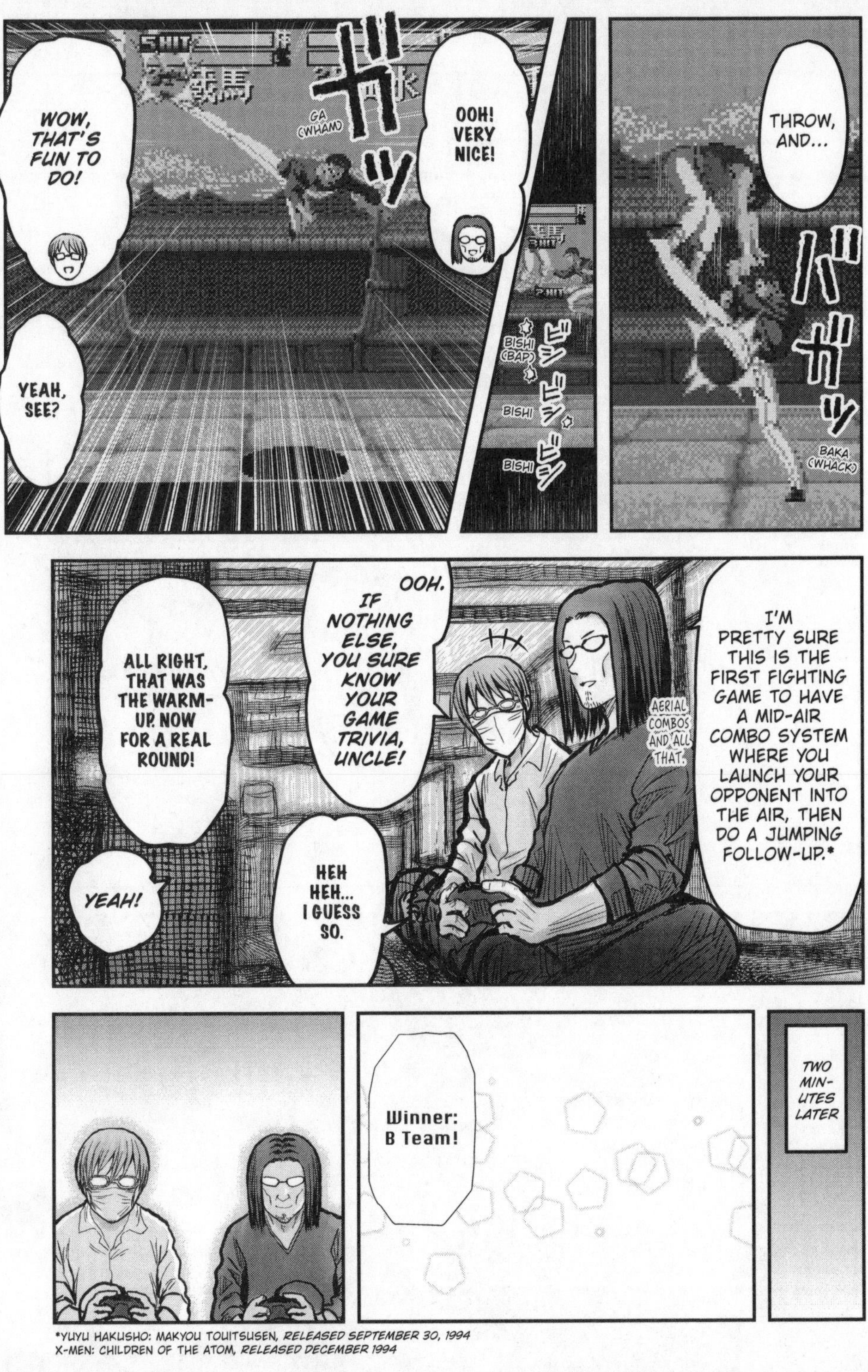
THROW, AND...
BAKA (WHACK)
BISHI (BAP)
BISHI
BISHI
OOH! VERY NICE!
GA (WHAM)
WOW, THAT'S FUN TO DO!
YEAH, SEE?
I'M PRETTY SURE THIS IS THE FIRST FIGHTING GAME TO HAVE A MID-AIR COMBO SYSTEM WHERE YOU LAUNCH YOUR OPPONENT INTO THE AIR, THEN DO A JUMPING FOLLOW-UP.*
AERIAL COMBOS AND ALL THAT.
OOH. IF NOTHING ELSE, YOU SURE KNOW YOUR GAME TRIVIA, UNCLE!
HEH HEH... I GUESS SO.
ALL RIGHT, THAT WAS THE WARM-UP. NOW FOR A REAL ROUND!
YEAH!
TWO MIN-UTES LATER
Winner: B Team!

*YUYU HAKUSHO: MAKYOU TOUITSUSEN, *RELEASED SEPTEMBER 30, 1994*
X-MEN: CHILDREN OF THE ATOM, *RELEASED DECEMBER 1994*

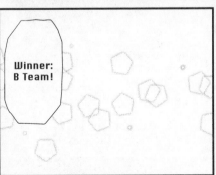

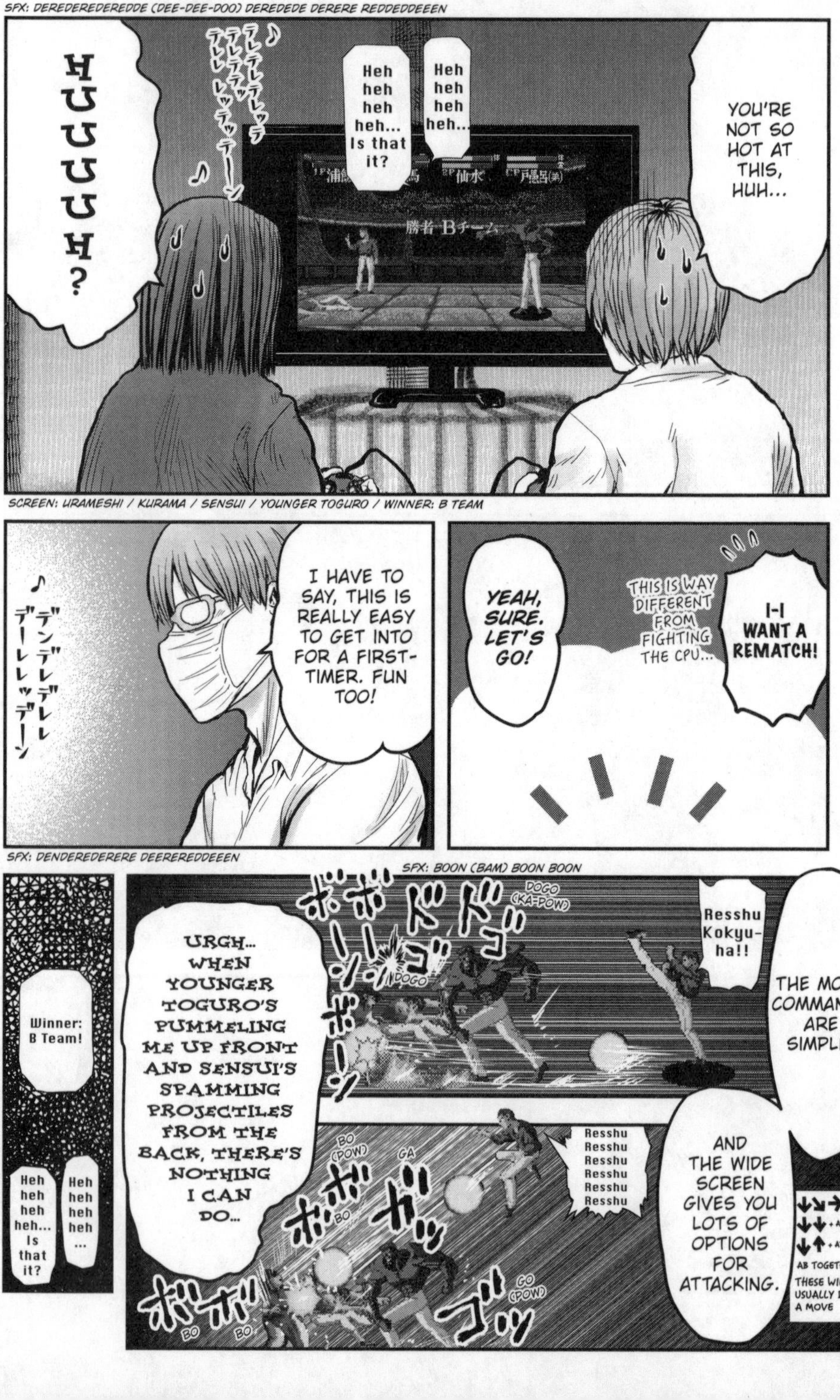
SFX: DEREDEREDEREDDE (DEE-DEE-DOO) DEREDEDE DERERE REDDEDDEEEN
YOU'RE NOT SO HOT AT THIS, HUH...
Heh heh heh heh...
Heh heh heh heh... Is that it?
HUUUUUH?
SCREEN: URAMESHI / KURAMA / SENSUI / YOUNGER TOGURO / WINNER: B TEAM
I-I WANT A REMATCH!
THIS IS WAY DIFFERENT FROM FIGHTING THE CPU...
YEAH, SURE. LET'S GO!
I HAVE TO SAY, THIS IS REALLY EASY TO GET INTO FOR A FIRST-TIMER. FUN TOO!
デンデレデレレ デーレレッデーン
SFX: DENDEREDERERE DEEREREDDEEEN
SFX: BOON (BAM) BOON BOON
THE MOVE COMMANDS ARE SIMPLE.
Resshu Kokyu-ha!!
DOGO (KA-POW)
DOGO
URGH... WHEN YOUNGER TOGURO'S PUMMELING ME UP FRONT AND SENSUI'S SPAMMING PROJECTILES FROM THE BACK, THERE'S NOTHING I CAN DO...
AND THE WIDE SCREEN GIVES YOU LOTS OF OPTIONS FOR ATTACKING.
↓↘→ + ATTACK
↓↓ + ATTACK
↓↑ + ATTACK
AB TOGETHER
THESE WILL USUALLY DO A MOVE
Resshu Resshu Resshu Resshu Resshu Resshu
GA
BO (POW)
BO
GO (POW)
BO
BO
Winner: B Team!
Heh heh heh heh...
Heh heh heh heh... Is that it?

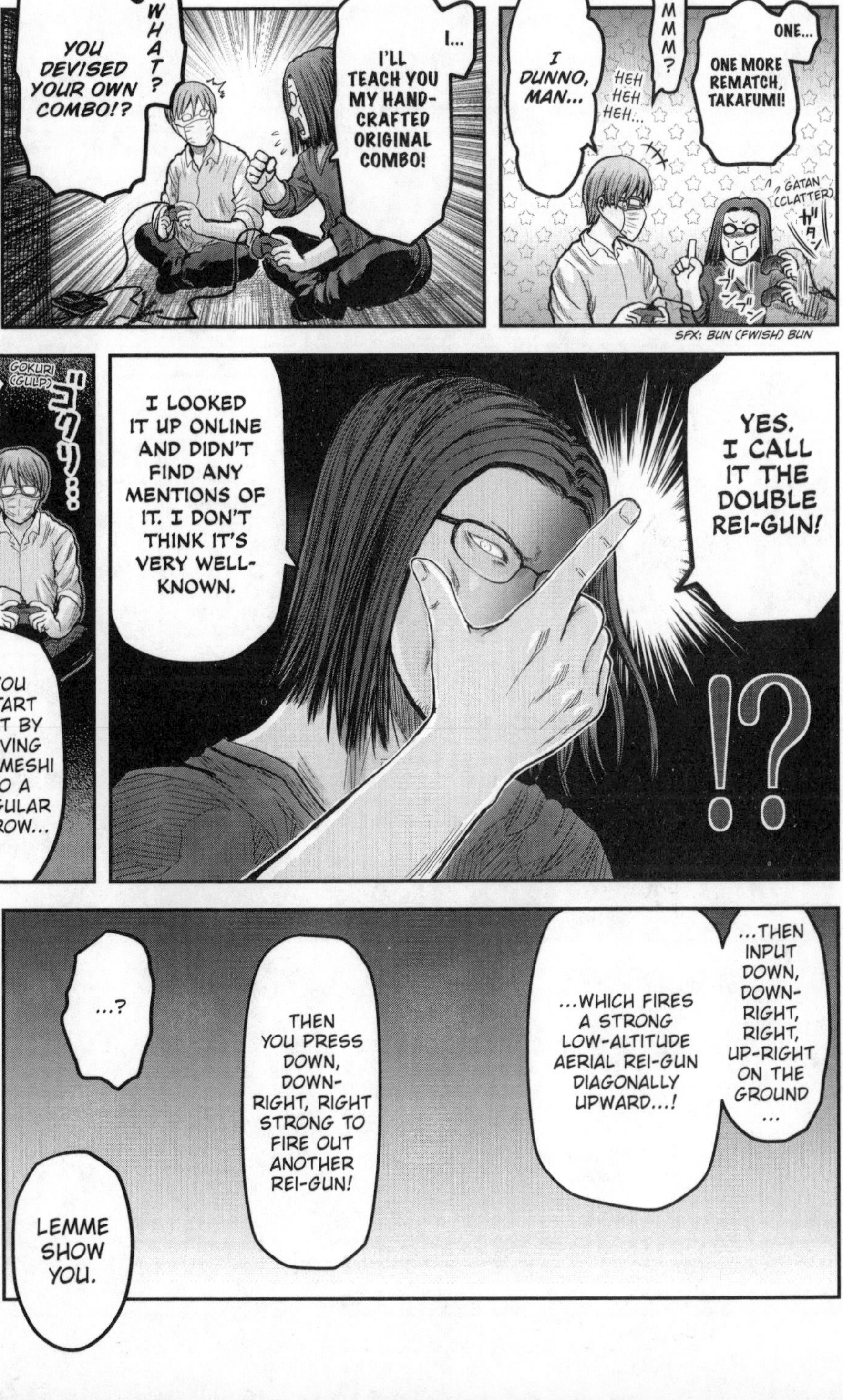
ONE...
ONE MORE REMATCH, TAKAFUMI!
HMMM?
HEH HEH HEH...
I DUNNO, MAN...
GATAN (CLATTER)
SFX: BUN (FWISH) BUN
I...
I'LL TEACH YOU MY HAND-CRAFTED ORIGINAL COMBO!
WHAT?
YOU DEVISED YOUR OWN COMBO!?
YES. I CALL IT THE DOUBLE REI-GUN!
I LOOKED IT UP ONLINE AND DIDN'T FIND ANY MENTIONS OF IT. I DON'T THINK IT'S VERY WELL-KNOWN.
!?
GOKURI (GULP)
...!
YOU START OUT BY HAVING URAMESHI DO A REGULAR THROW...
...THEN INPUT DOWN, DOWN-RIGHT, RIGHT, UP-RIGHT ON THE GROUND...
...WHICH FIRES A STRONG LOW-ALTITUDE AERIAL REI-GUN DIAGONALLY UPWARD...!
THEN YOU PRESS DOWN, DOWN-RIGHT, RIGHT STRONG TO FIRE OUT ANOTHER REI-GUN!
...?
LEMME SHOW YOU.

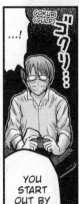

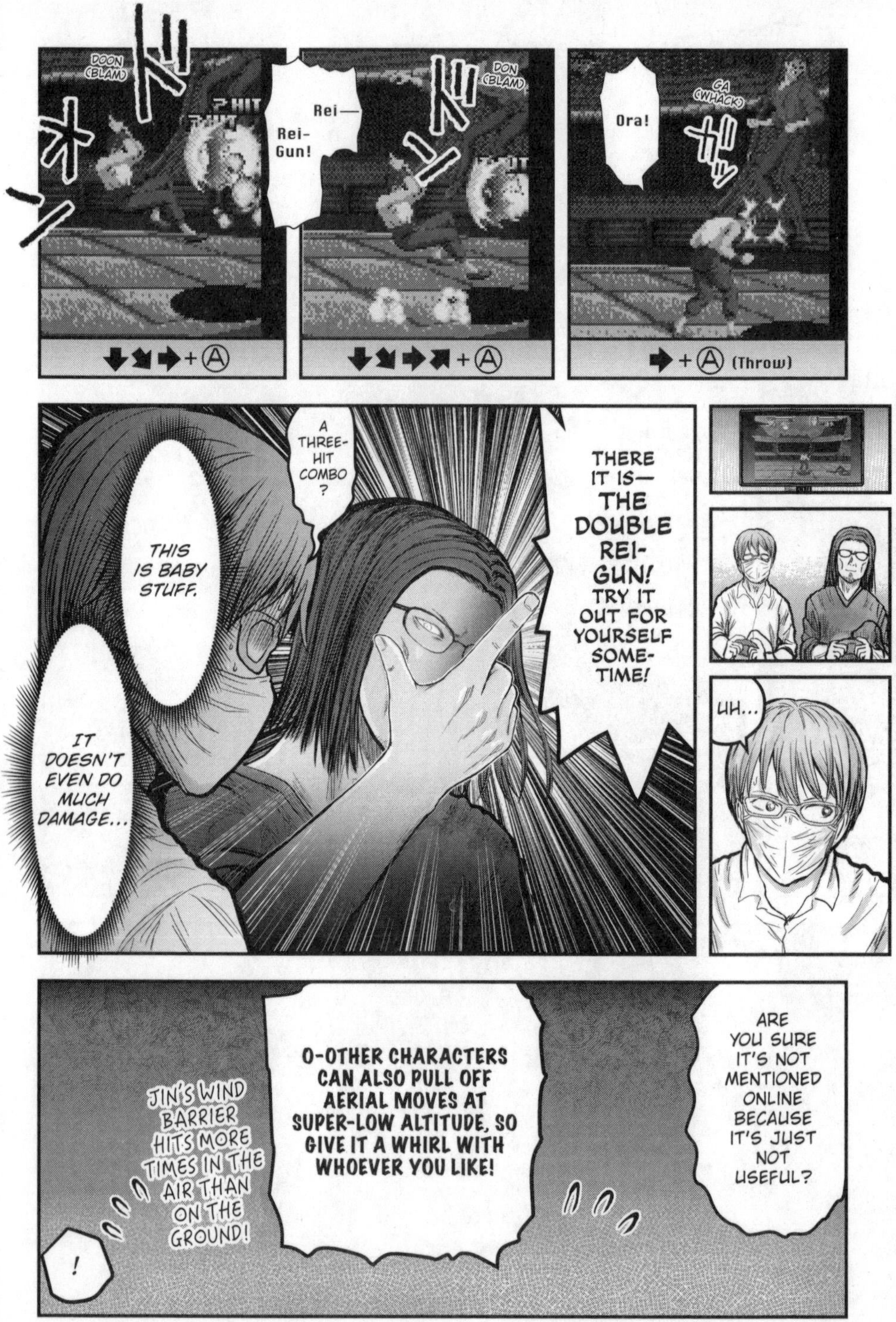
GA (WHACK)
Ora!
➡+Ⓐ (Throw)
DON (BLAM)
Rei— Rei-Gun!
⬇↘➡↗+Ⓐ
DOON (BLAM)
⬇↘➡+Ⓐ
UH...
THERE IT IS— THE DOUBLE REI-GUN! TRY IT OUT FOR YOURSELF SOMETIME!
A THREE-HIT COMBO?
THIS IS BABY STUFF.
IT DOESN'T EVEN DO MUCH DAMAGE...
ARE YOU SURE IT'S NOT MENTIONED ONLINE BECAUSE IT'S JUST NOT USEFUL?
O-OTHER CHARACTERS CAN ALSO PULL OFF AERIAL MOVES AT SUPER-LOW ALTITUDE, SO GIVE IT A WHIRL WITH WHOEVER YOU LIKE!
JIN'S WIND BARRIER HITS MORE TIMES IN THE AIR THAN ON THE GROUND!
!

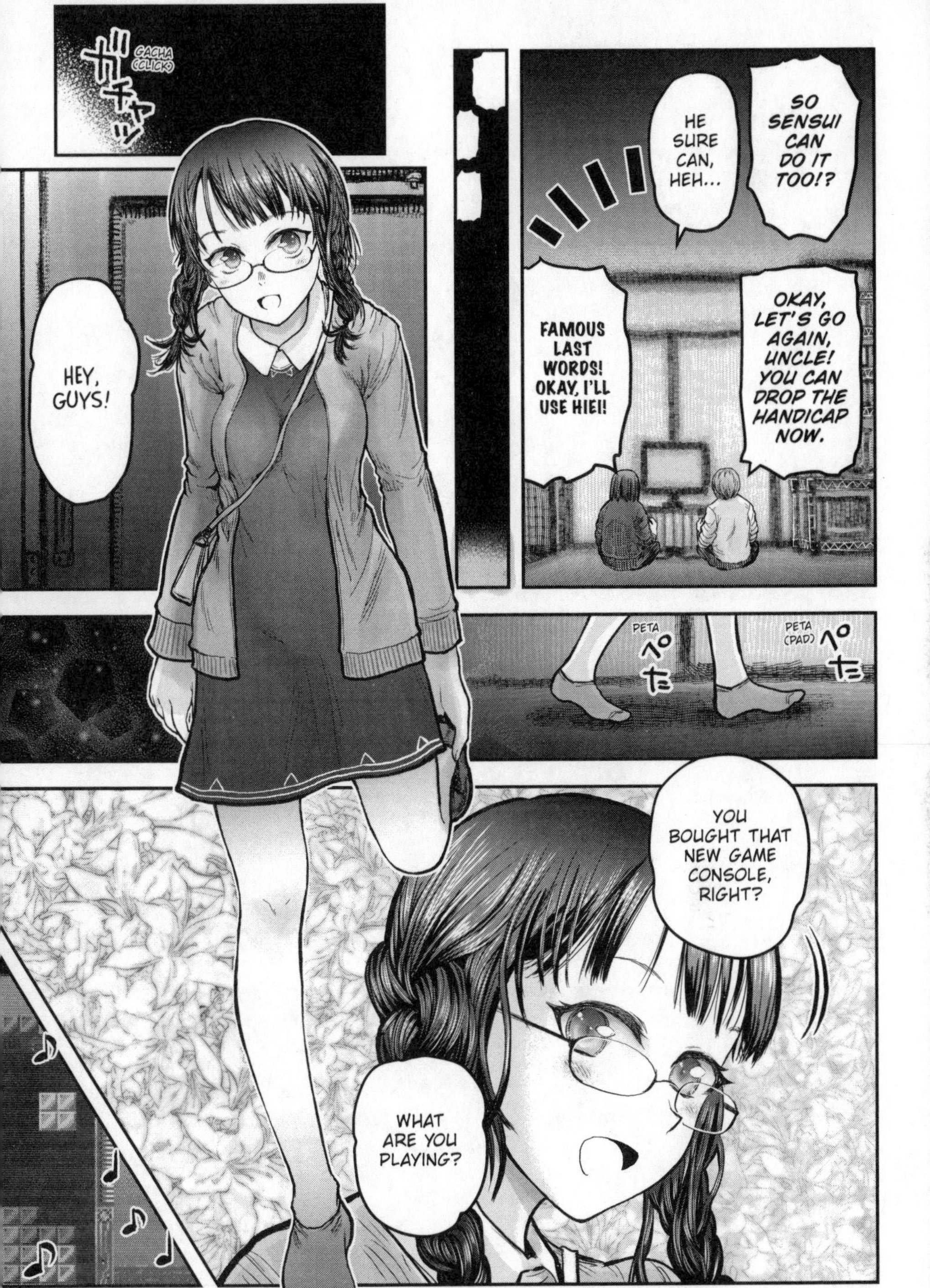
SO SENSUI CAN DO IT TOO!?
HE SURE CAN, HEH...
OKAY, LET'S GO AGAIN, UNCLE! YOU CAN DROP THE HANDICAP NOW.
FAMOUS LAST WORDS! OKAY, I'LL USE HIEI!
GACHA (CLICK)
HEY, GUYS!
PETA (PAD)
PETA
YOU BOUGHT THAT NEW GAME CONSOLE, RIGHT?
WHAT ARE YOU PLAYING?

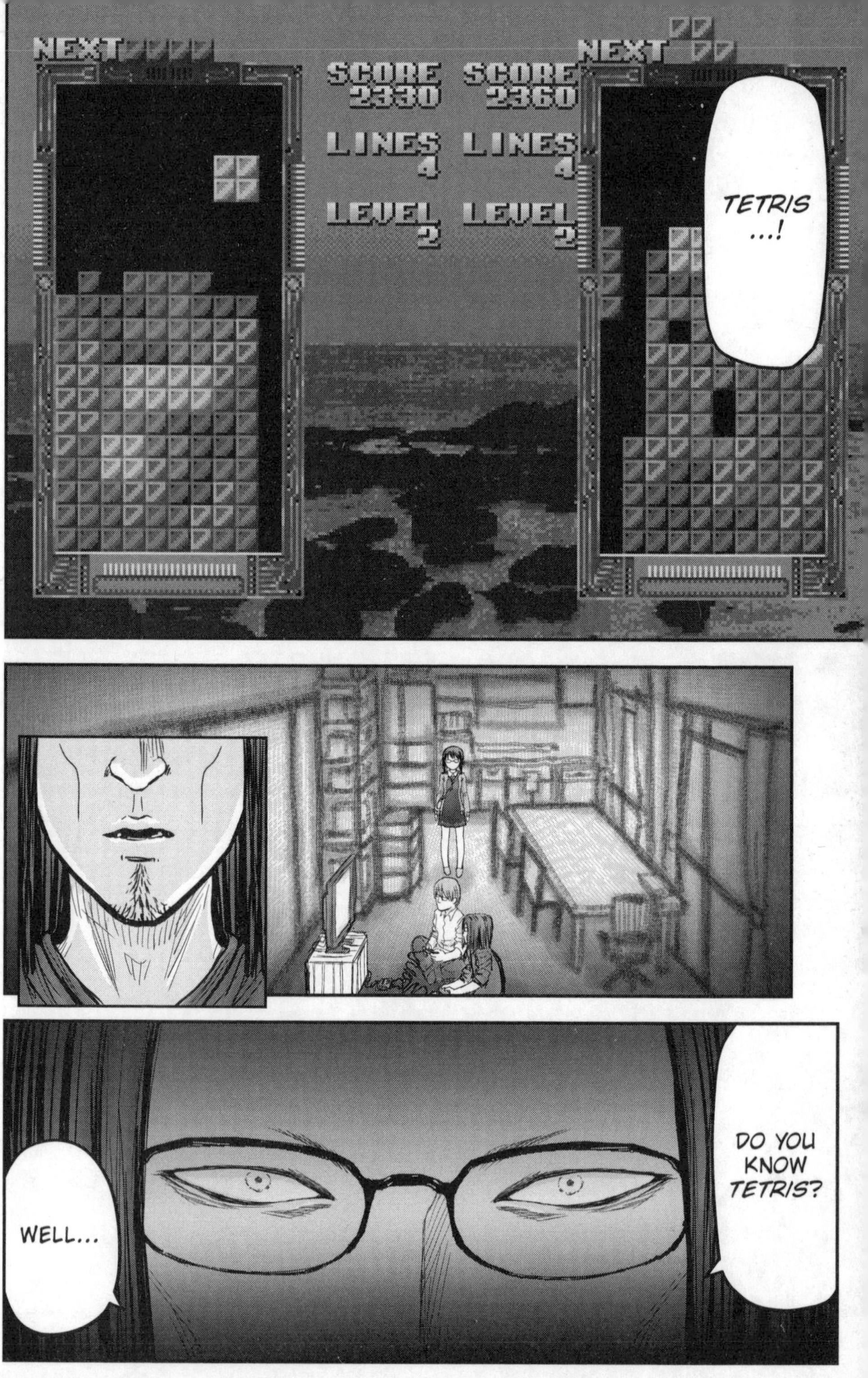
NEXT
SCORE 2360
LINES 4
LEVEL 2
TETRIS ...!
NEXT
SCORE 2330
LINES 4
LEVEL 2
DO YOU KNOW TETRIS?
WELL...

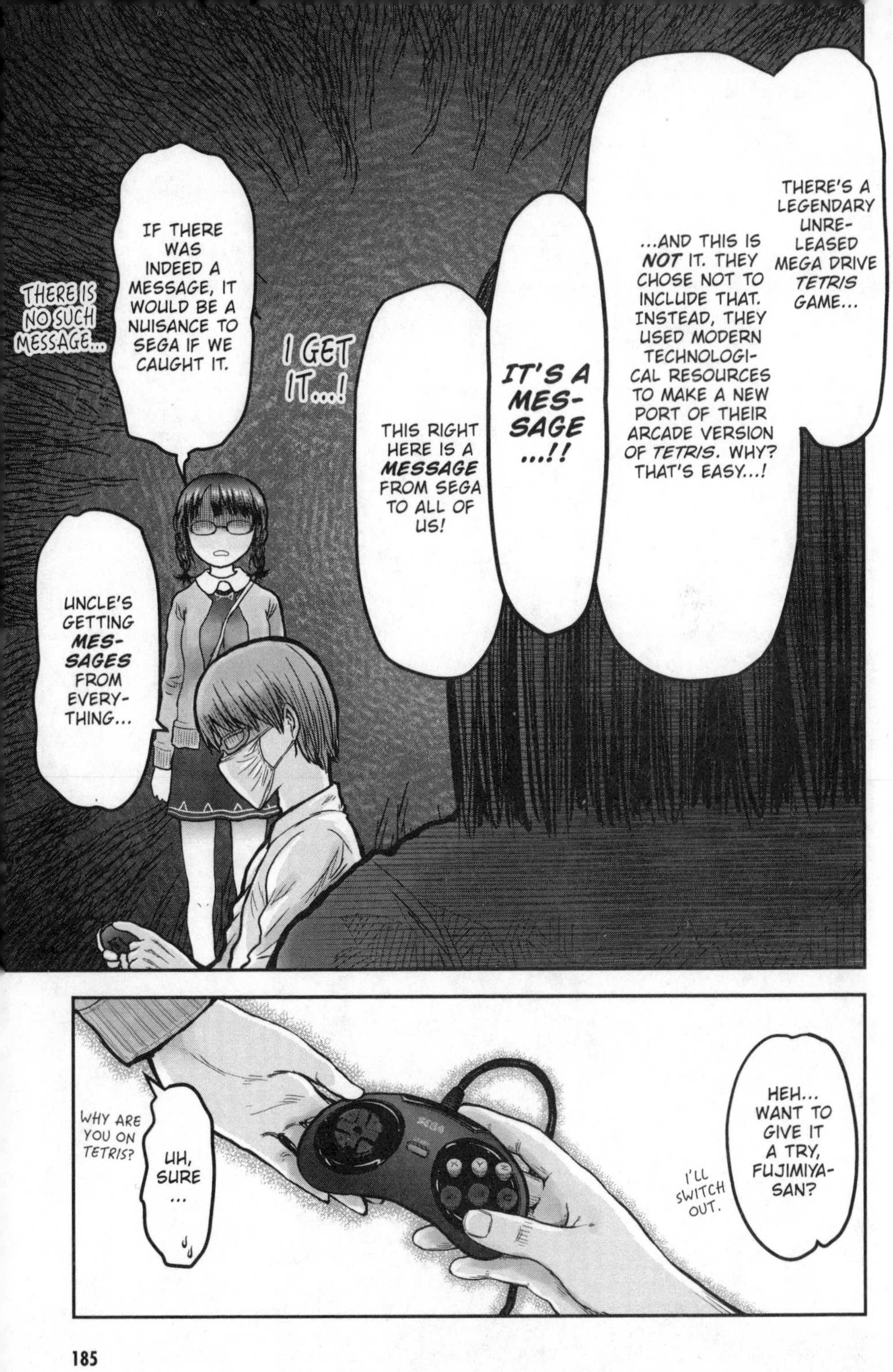
THERE'S A LEGENDARY UNRE-LEASED MEGA DRIVE *TETRIS* GAME...
...AND THIS IS **NOT** IT. THEY CHOSE NOT TO INCLUDE THAT. INSTEAD, THEY USED MODERN TECHNOLOGI-CAL RESOURCES TO MAKE A NEW PORT OF THEIR ARCADE VERSION OF *TETRIS*. WHY? THAT'S EASY...!
IT'S A MES-SAGE ...!!
THIS RIGHT HERE IS A ***MESSAGE*** FROM SEGA TO ALL OF US!
I GET IT...!
IF THERE WAS INDEED A MESSAGE, IT WOULD BE A NUISANCE TO SEGA IF WE CAUGHT IT.
THERE IS NO SUCH MESSAGE...
UNCLE'S GETTING ***MES-SAGES*** FROM EVERY-THING...
SEGA
HEH... WANT TO GIVE IT A TRY, FUJIMIYA-SAN?
I'LL SWITCH OUT.
UH, SURE ...
WHY ARE YOU ON TETRIS?

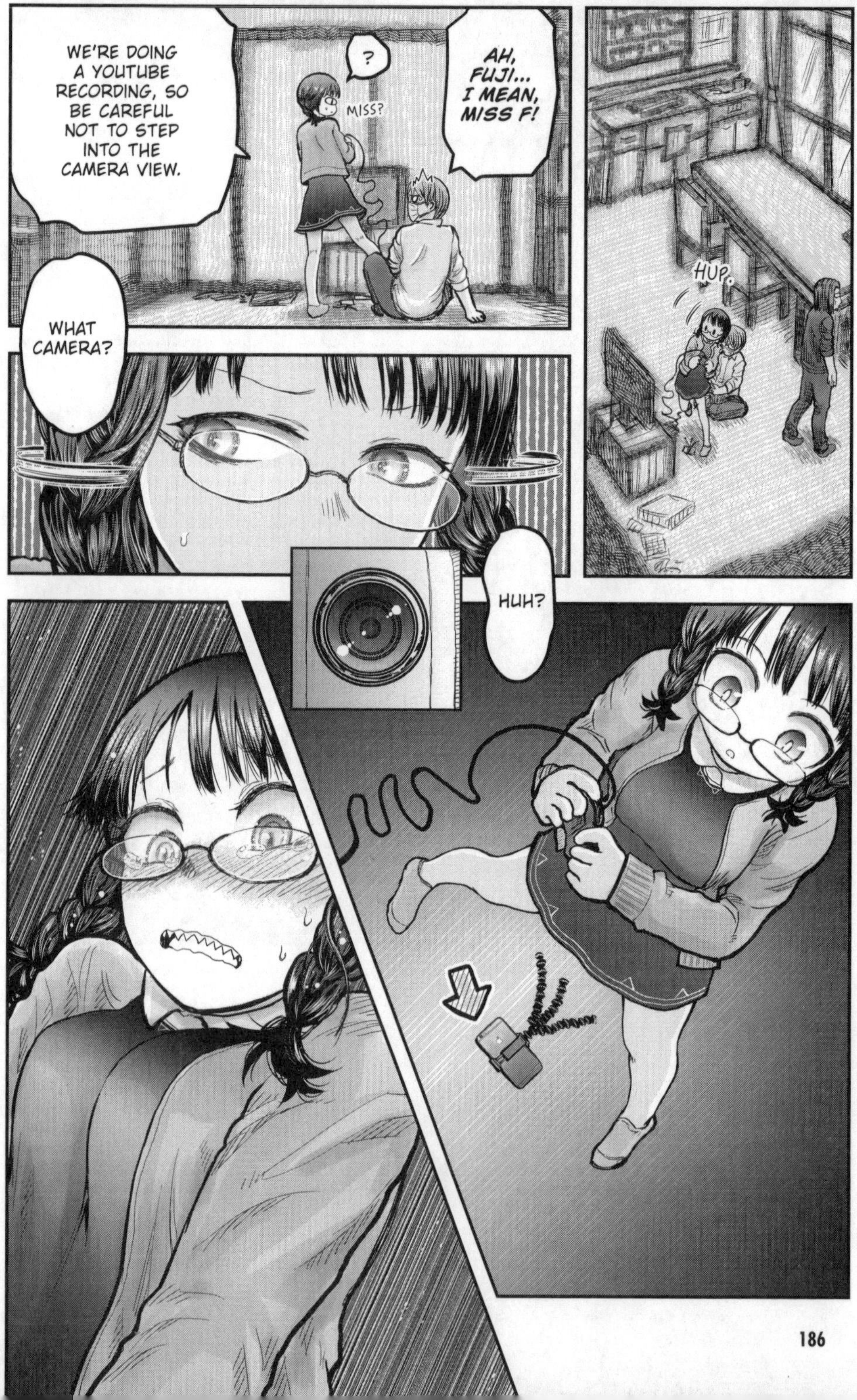
HUP.
AH, FUJI... I MEAN, MISS F!
?
MISS?
WE'RE DOING A YOUTUBE RECORDING, SO BE CAREFUL NOT TO STEP INTO THE CAMERA VIEW.
WHAT CAMERA?
HUH?

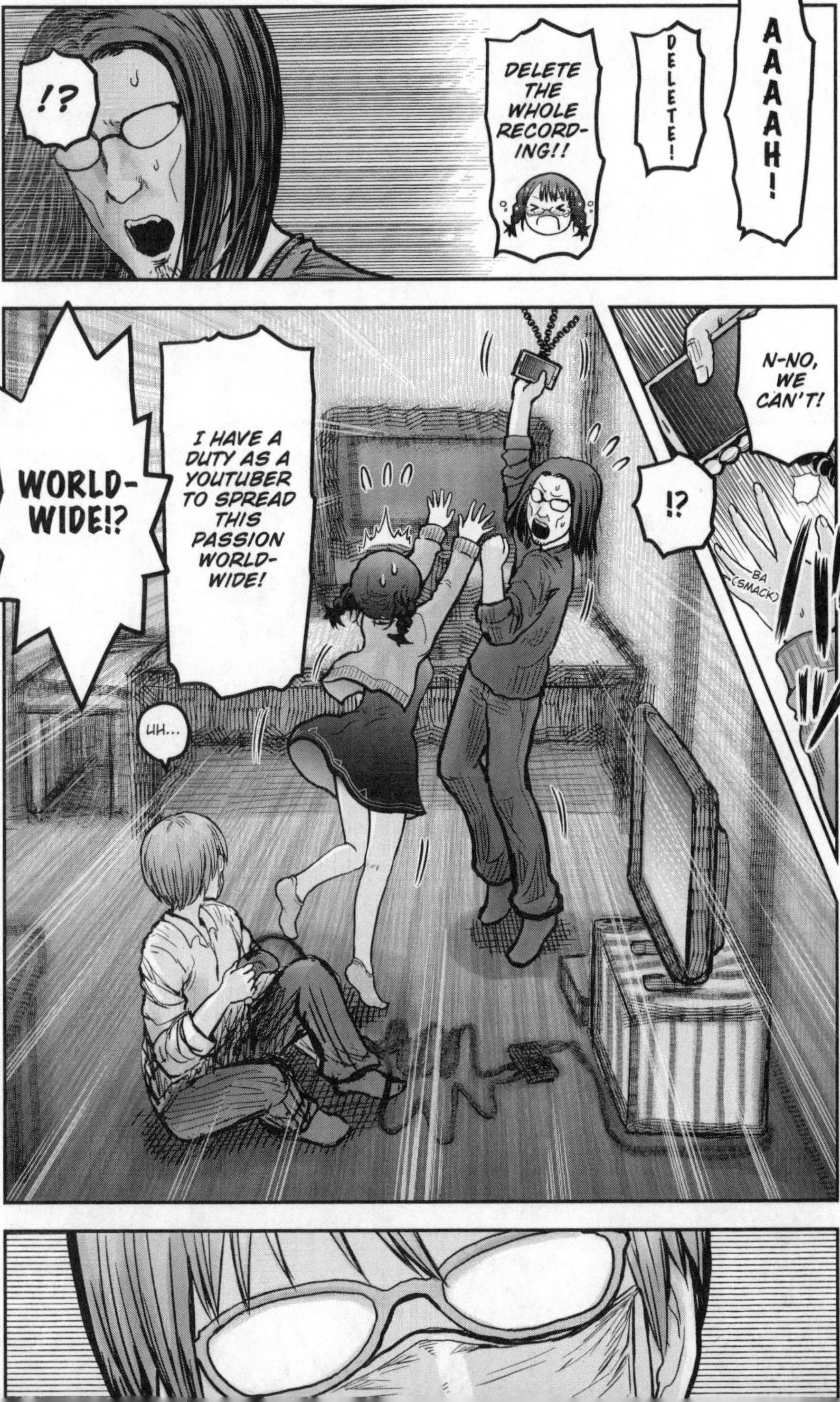
AAAAH!
DELETE!
DELETE THE WHOLE RECORD-ING!!
!?
N-NO, WE CAN'T!
!?
BA (SMACK)
I HAVE A DUTY AS A YOUTUBER TO SPREAD THIS PASSION WORLD-WIDE!
WORLD-WIDE!?
UH...

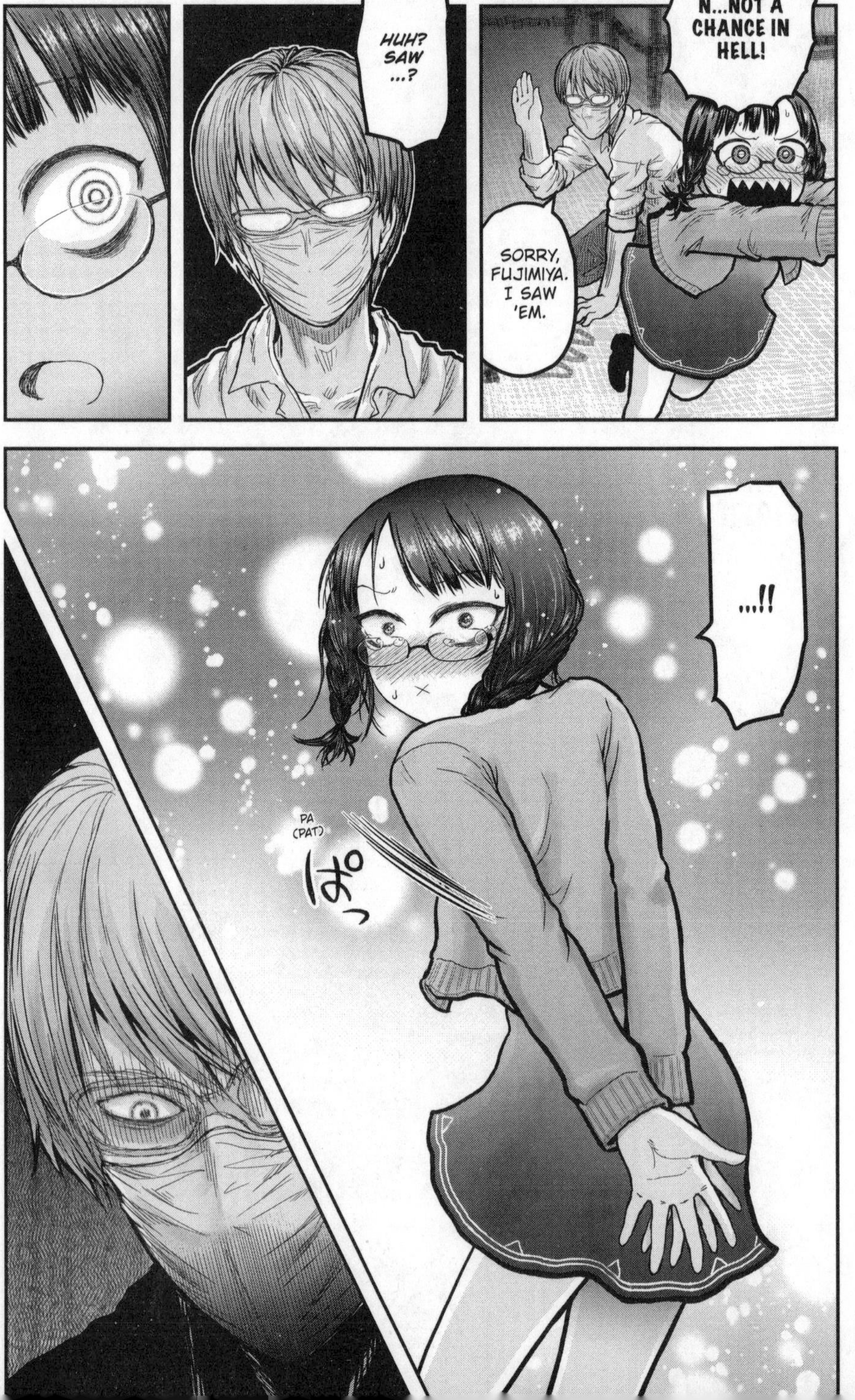
N...NOT A CHANCE IN HELL!
SORRY, FUJIMIYA. I SAW 'EM.
HUH? SAW ...?
...!!
PA (PAT)
ぱっ

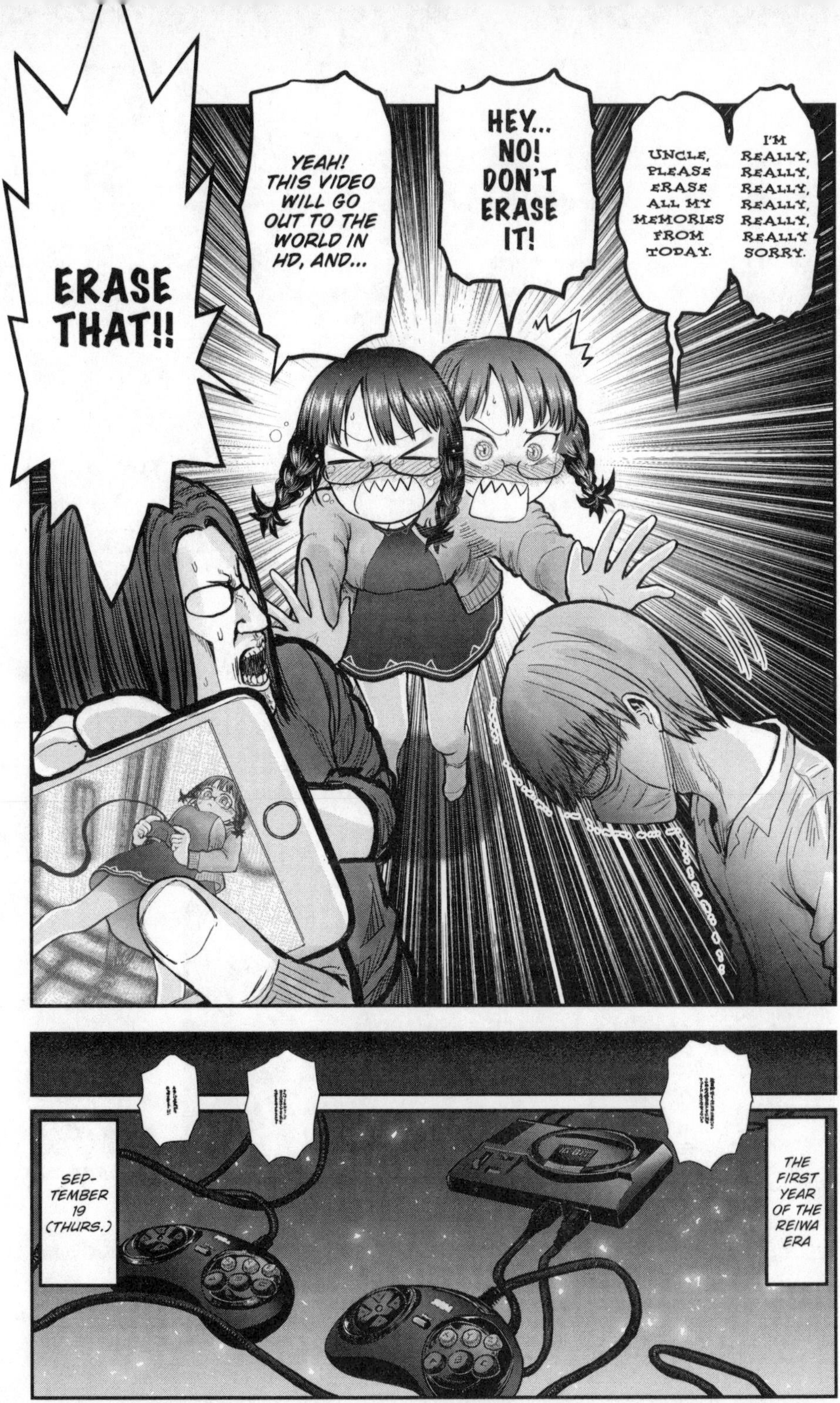
I'M REALLY, REALLY, REALLY, REALLY, REALLY, REALLY SORRY.
UNCLE, PLEASE ERASE ALL MY MEMORIES FROM TODAY.
HEY... NO! DON'T ERASE IT!
YEAH! THIS VIDEO WILL GO OUT TO THE WORLD IN HD, AND...
ERASE THAT!!
THE FIRST YEAR OF THE REIWA ERA
SEP-TEMBER 19 (THURS.)

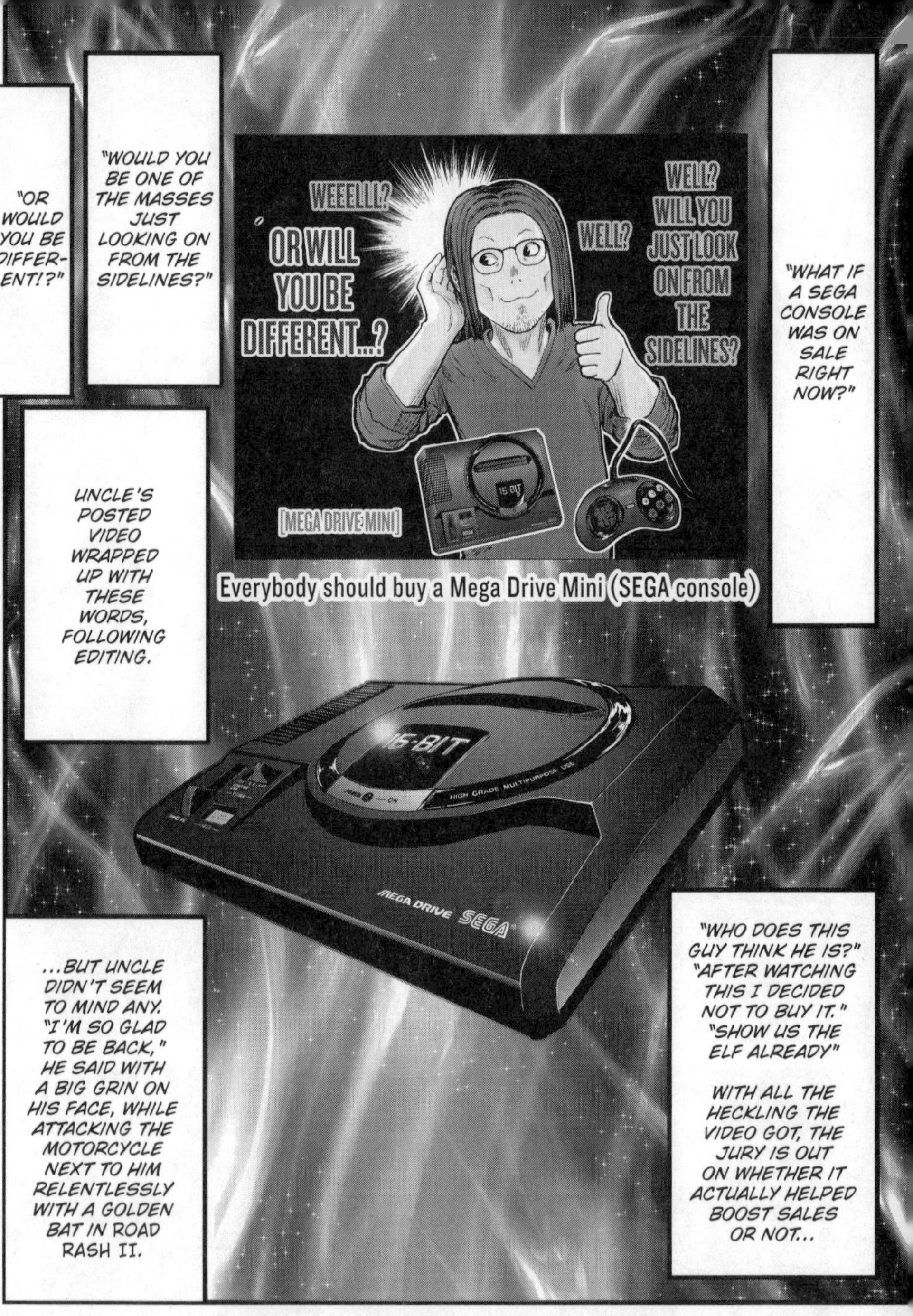
"WHAT IF A SEGA CONSOLE WAS ON SALE RIGHT NOW?"
WELL? WILL YOU JUST LOOK ON FROM THE SIDELINES?
WELL?
WEEELLL?
OR WILL YOU BE DIFFERENT...?
16-BIT
[MEGA DRIVE MINI]
Everybody should buy a Mega Drive Mini (SEGA console)
"WOULD YOU BE ONE OF THE MASSES JUST LOOKING ON FROM THE SIDELINES?"
"OR WOULD YOU BE DIFFER-ENT!?"
UNCLE'S POSTED VIDEO WRAPPED UP WITH THESE WORDS, FOLLOWING EDITING.
16-BIT
HIGH GRADE MULTIPURPOSE USE
MEGA DRIVE SEGA
"WHO DOES THIS GUY THINK HE IS?" "AFTER WATCHING THIS I DECIDED NOT TO BUY IT." "SHOW US THE ELF ALREADY"
WITH ALL THE HECKLING THE VIDEO GOT, THE JURY IS OUT ON WHETHER IT ACTUALLY HELPED BOOST SALES OR NOT...
...BUT UNCLE DIDN'T SEEM TO MIND ANY. "I'M SO GLAD TO BE BACK," HE SAID WITH A BIG GRIN ON HIS FACE, WHILE ATTACKING THE MOTORCYCLE NEXT TO HIM RELENTLESSLY WITH A GOLDEN BAT IN ROAD RASH II.

Mega Drive Mini

Release Date:	September 19, 2019 (Thurs)	
MSRP:	Mega Drive Mini (1 PAD)	¥6,980 (plus tax)
	Mega Drive Mini W (2 PAD)	¥8,980 (plus tax)
Console Size:	Width: 154 mm x Height: 39 mm x Length: 116 mm	

TIPS

IV

Hotondoshindeiru

TRANSLATOR: **Christina Rose**
LETTERER: **Phil Christie**

ISEKAI OJISAN Vol. 4
©Hotondoshindeiru 2020
©SEGA

First published in Japan in 2020 by KADOKAWA CORPORATION, Tokyo.
English translation rights arranged with KADOKAWA CORPORATION, Tokyo through
TUTTLE-MORI AGENCY, Inc.

English translation © 2022 by Yen Press, LLC

Yen Press
150 West 30th Street, 19th Floor
New York, NY 10001

Visit us at yenpress.com + facebook.com/yenpress
twitter.com/yenpress + yenpress.tumblr.com + instagram.com/yenpress

First Yen Press Edition: March 2022

Yen Press is an imprint of Yen Press, LLC.
The Yen Press name and logo are trademarks of Yen Press, LLC.

The publisher is not responsible for websites (or their content) that are not owned by the publisher.

Library of Congress Control Number: 2021932161

ISBNs: 978-1-9753-4059-9 (paperback)
       978-1-9753-4060-5 (ebook)

10 9 8 7 6 5 4 3 2 1

WOR

Printed in the United States of America